Syntax

Introducing Linguistics

This outstanding series is an indispensable resource for students and teachers – a concise and engaging introduction to the central subjects of contemporary linguistics. Presupposing no prior knowledge on the part of the reader, each volume sets out the fundamental skills and knowledge of the field, and so provides the ideal educational platform for further study in linguistics.

Syntax
A Generative Introduction
Third Edition

Andrew Carnie

WILEY-BLACKWELL

A John Wiley & Sons, Ltd., Publication

This third edition first published 2013
© 2013 Andrew Carnie

Edition History: Blackwell Publishing, Ltd (1e, 2002 and 2e, 2007)

Wiley-Blackwell is an imprint of John Wiley & Sons, formed by the merger of Wiley's global Scientific, Technical and Medical business with Blackwell Publishing.

Registered Office
John Wiley & Sons Ltd, The Atrium, Southern Gate, Chichester, West Sussex, PO19 8SQ, UK

Editorial Offices
350 Main Street, Malden, MA 02148-5020, USA

9600 Garsington Road, Oxford, OX4 2DQ, UK

The Atrium, Southern Gate, Chichester, West Sussex, PO19 8SQ, UK

For details of our global editorial offices, for customer services, and for information about how to apply for permission to reuse the copyright material in this book please see our website at www.wiley.com/wiley-blackwell.

The right of Andrew Carnie to be identified as the author of this work has been asserted in accordance with the UK Copyright, Designs and Patents Act 1988.

Library of Congress Cataloging-in-Publication Data

Carnie, Andrew, 1969-
  Syntax : a generative introduction / Andrew Carnie. -- Third Edition.
    pages cm. -- (Introducing linguistics ; 16)
  Includes bibliographical references and index.
  ISBN 978-0-470-65531-3 (pbk.)
1. Grammar, Comparative and general--Syntax. 2. Generative grammar. I. Title.
  P295.C37 2012
  415--dc23
                          2012009763

A catalogue record for this book is available from the British Library.

Cover Image: Vassily Kandinsky, Sweet Pink, ink with watercolour, 1929, Roethel 925. Sotheby's, London / Superstock. © ADAGP, Paris and DACS, London 2012.
Cover design by Nicki Averill
Set in 10 point Palatino 10 point Arial by Language Technologies Incorporated
Printed in Singapore by C.O.S. Printers Pte Ltd

5   2015

Dedicated with love to my parents, Robert and Jean
and in memory of my teacher and mentor, Ken Hale

This book is accompanied by a workbook: *The Syntax Workbook: A Companion to Carnie's Syntax*, available for purchase from http://www.wiley.com. The workbook is optional and serves as a supplement for students who want additional practice in syntactic analysis.

Additional online material including bonus chapters can be found on the book's website:
                   http://www.wiley.com/go/carnie

The text formatting in this book has been adapted and modified by ReadSmart®, an algorithm which imposes almost undetectable changes in presentation. This formatting is based on simple psycholinguistic principles, and has been shown in studies to enhance readers' reading speed, comprehension and enjoyment and to make the text more persuasive. The ReadSmart® treatment of the text was provided by Language Technologies Inc., which offers this service for all forms of publication.
                   www.readsmart.com

Contents

Go to

www.wiley.com/go/carnie

for bonus chapters on Lexical-Functional Grammar (LFG) and Head-driven Phrase Structure Grammar (HPSG), as well as a glossary and other supplementary materials.

Preface and Acknowledgments

Almost every preface to every syntax textbook out there starts out by telling the reader how different this book is from every other syntax textbook. On one hand, this is often the truth: each author shows their own particular spin or emphasis. This is certainly true of this textbook. For example, you'll be hard-pressed to find another textbook on Principles and Parameters syntax that uses as many Irish examples as this one does. Nor will you find another P&P textbook with a supplementary discussion of alternative theoretical approaches like LFG or HPSG. On the other hand, let's face facts. The basic material to be covered in an introductory textbook doesn't really vary much. One linguist may prefer a little more on binding theory, and a little less on control, etc. In this text, I've attempted to provide a relatively balanced presentation of most of the major issues and I've tried to do this in a student-friendly way. I've occasionally abstracted away from some of the thornier controversies, when I felt they weren't crucial to a student understanding the basics. This may make the professional syntactician feel that I've cut corners or laid out too rosy a picture. I did this on purpose, however, to give students a chance to absorb the fundamentals before challenging the issues. This was a deliberate pedagogical choice. I'm well aware that sometimes I've glossed over controversies, but I think a student has to learn the basics of how the system works before they can seriously critique and evaluate the model. This is a textbook, not a scholarly tome, so its aim is to reach as many students as possible. The style is deliberately low-key and friendly. This doesn't mean I don't want the students to challenge the material I've presented here. Throughout the book, you'll find grey "textboxes" that contain issues for further discussion or interesting tidbits. Many of the problem sets also invite the student to challenge the black and white presentation I've given in the text. I encourage instructors to assign these, and students to do them, as they form an important part of the textbook. Instructors may note that if a favorite topic is not dealt with in the body of the text, a problem set may very well treat the question.

A quick word on the level of this textbook: This book is intended as an introduction to syntactic theory. It takes the student through most of the major issues in Principles and Parameters, from tree drawing to constraints on movement. While this book is written as an introduction, some students have reported it to be challenging. I use this text in my upper-division undergraduate introduction to syntax course with success, but I can certainly see it being used in more advanced classes. I hope instructors will flesh out the book, and walk their students through some of the thornier issues.

This textbook has grown out of my lecture notes for my own classes. Needless to say, the form and shape of these notes have been influenced in terms of choice of material and presentation by the textbooks my own students have used. While the book you are reading is entirely my fault, it does owe a particular intellectual debt to the following three textbooks, which I have used in teaching at various times:

> Cowper, Elizabeth (1992) *A Concise Introduction to Syntactic Theory: The Government and Binding Approach.* Chicago: Chicago University Press.
>
> Haegeman, Liliane (1994) *Introduction to Government and Binding Theory* (2nd edition). Oxford: Blackwell.
>
> Radford, Andrew (1988) *Transformational Grammar: A First Course.* Cambridge: Cambridge University Press.

I'd like to thank the authors of these books for breaking ground in presenting a complicated and integrated theory to the beginner. Writing this book has given me new appreciation for the difficulty of this task and their presentation of the material has undoubtedly influenced mine.

Sadly, during the final stages of putting the first edition of this text together, my dissertation director, teacher, mentor, and academic hero, Ken Hale, passed away after a long illness. Ken always pushed the idea that theoretical syntax is best informed by cross-linguistic research, while at the same time the accurate documentation of languages requires a sophisticated understanding of grammatical theory. These were important lessons that I learned from Ken and I hope students will glean the significance of both by reading this text. While I was writing this book (and much other work) Ken gave me many comments and his unfettered support. He was a great man and I will miss him terribly.

This, the third edition of this book, is quite different from the first two. A reasonably complete list of changes can be found in the instructor's handbook. These include some important changes to definitions that instructors who have used previous editions will want to look at. The major changes to this volume are:

- A companion workbook, with answers, for students to practice assignments.
- New exercises in almost every chapter.
- New chapters on Auxiliaries, Ellipsis and Non-configurational Languages.
- The chapters on LFG and HPSG are now to be found for free on the book's companion website: www.wiley.com/go/carnie.

I hope that instructors and students will find these revisions helpful. I have attempted where possible to take into account all the many comments and suggestions I received from people using the first and second editions, although of course, in order to maintain consistency, I was unable to implement them all.

Acknowledgments:

I'd like to thank the many people who taught me syntax through the years: Barb Brunson, Noam Chomsky, Elizabeth Cowper, Ken Hale, Alec Marantz, Diane Massam, Jim McCloskey, Shigeru Miyagawa, and David Pesetsky. A number of people have read through this book or the previous editions and have given me helpful comments; others have helped on smaller issues but have had no less of an impact on the work and still others have contributed problem sets or editorial advice. This long list includes: David Adger, William Alexander, Dean Allemang, Diana Archangeli, Ash Asudeh, Brett Baker, Uldis Balodis, Mark Baltin, Luis Barragan, Andy Barss, Dane Bell, Emily Bender, Abbas Benmamoun, Jeff Berry, Tom Bever, Claire Bowern, Michael Bauer, Laura Blumenthal, Joan Bresnan, Aaron Broadwell, Dirk Bury, Roy Chan, Ronald Charles, Danny Chen, Deborah Chen-Pichler, Jaehoon Choi, Barbara Citko, Peter Cole, Chris Collins, Jennifer Columbus, Andrew Comrie, Lorenzo Demery, Sheila Dooley, Yehuda Falk, Muriel Fisher, Sandiway Fong, Leslie Ford, Amy Fountain, Stefan Frisch, Alexandra Galani, Jila Ghomeshi, David Gil, Carrie Gillion, Erin Good-Ament, Andrea Haber, Paul Hagstrom, Ken Hale, John Halle, Mike Hammond, Jack Hardy, Heidi Harley, Josh Harrison, Rachel Hayes-Harb, David Heap, Bernhard Heigl, One-Soon Her, Caroline Heycock, Stephan Hurtubise, John Ivens, Eloise Jelinek, Alana Johns, Mark Johnson, Hyun Kyoung Jung, Arsalan Kahnemuyipour, Dalina Kalluli, Simin Karimi, Andreas Kathol, Chris Kennedy, Greg Key, Amy LaCross, Péter Lazar, Carlos Gelormini Lezama, Jeff Lidz, Anne Lobeck, Leila Lomashivili, Sarah Longstaff, Alicia Lopez, Ahmad Reza Lotfi, Ricardo Mairal, Joan Maling, Jack Martin, Diane Massam, Martha McGinnis, Nathan McWhorter, Dave Medeiros, Mirjana Miskovic-Lukovic, Alan Munn, MaryLou Myers, Chris Nicholas, Janet Nicol, Jon Nissenbaum, Peter Norquest, Diane Ohala, Kazutoshi Ohno, Heidi Orcutt-Gachiri, Hiroyuki Oshita, Panayiotis Pappas, Jaime Parchment, Hyeson Park, Barbara Partee, Matt Pearson, David Pesetsky, Colin Phillips, Carl Pollard, Bill Poser, Kristen Pruett, Jeff Punske, Mike Putnam, Janet Randall, Marlita Reddy-Hjelmfelt, Sylvia Reed, Norvin Richards, Frank Richter, Betsy Ritter, Ed Rubin, Jeff Runner, Ivan Sag, Nathan Sanders, Yosuke Sato and his students, Theresa Satterfield, Leslie Saxon, Kevin Schluter, Carson Schütze, Jim Scobbie, Deborah Shapiro, Leah Shocket, Dan Siddiqi, Echo Ki Sihui, Peter Slomanson, Kyle Smith, Norvel Smith, Nick Sobin, Peggy Speas, Megan Stone, Tania Strahan, Joshua Strauss, Maggie Tallerman, Takashi Tanaka, Chris Tancredi, Deniz Tat, Brian ten Eyck, Lisa deMena Travis, Alex Trueman, Adam Ussishkin, Robert Van Valin, Enwei Wang, Shan Wang, Natasha Warner, Andy Wedel, Jennifer Wees, Mary Ann Willie, Marian Wiseley, Dainon Woudstra, Susi Wurmbrand, Kimberley Young, Kim Youngroung, and several anonymous Blackwell and Wiley reviewers. I'm absolutely convinced I've left someone off this large list. If it's you many apologies – I really did appreciate the help you gave me. The students in my *Introduction to Syntax* classes in Michigan in 1997, and in Arizona in 1998–2012, have used all or parts of this textbook. Glynis Baguley, Ada Brunstein, Sarah Coleman, Danielle Descoteaux, Lisa Eaton, Simon Eckley, Charlotte Frost, Graham Frankland, Tami Kaplan, Becky Kennison, Julia Kirk, Leah Morin, Allison Medoff, Anna Oxbury, Rhonda Pearce, Iain Potter, Beth Remmes, and Steve Smith of Wiley-Blackwell and their subcontractors all deserve many thanks for help getting this and the previous two editions to press. My family (my mother Jean, my late father Bob, Morag, Fiona, Pangur) were all incredible in their support and love. Go raibh maith agaibh agus tapadh leibh!

The artwork in chapters 3 and 6 was created by Dane Bell and is used with permission.

Part 1

Preliminaries

Generative Grammar

Learning Objectives

After reading chapter 1 you should walk away having mastered the following ideas and skills:

1. Explain why Language is a psychological property of humans.
2. Distinguish between prescriptive and descriptive rules.
3. Explain the scientific method as it applies to syntax.
4. Explain the differences between the kinds of data gathering, including corpora and linguistic judgments.
5. Explain the difference between competence and performance.
6. Provide at least three arguments for Universal Grammar.
7. Explain the logical problem of language acquisition.
8. Distinguish between learning and acquisition.
9. Distinguish among observational, descriptive and explanatory adequacy.

0. PRELIMINARIES

Although we use it every day, and although we all have strong opinions about its proper form and appropriate use, we rarely stop to think about the wonder of language. So-called language "experts" like William Safire tell

Syntax: A Generative Introduction, Third Edition. Andrew Carnie.
© 2013 Andrew Carnie. Published 2013 by John Wiley & Sons, Inc.

us about the misuse of *hopefully* or lecture us about the origins of the word *boondoggle*, but surprisingly, they never get at the true wonder of language: how it actually works as a complex machine. Think about it for a minute. You are reading this and understanding it, but you have no conscious knowledge of how you are doing it. The study of this mystery is the science of linguistics. This book is about one aspect of how language works: how sentences are structured, or the study of *syntax*.

Language is a psychological or cognitive property of humans. That is, there is some set of neurons in my head firing madly away that allows me to sit here and produce this set of letters, and there is some other set of neurons in your head firing away that allows you to translate these squiggles into coherent ideas and thoughts. There are several subsystems at work here. If you were listening to me speak, I would be producing sound waves with my vocal cords and articulating particular speech sounds with my tongue, lips, and vocal cords. On the other end of things you'd be hearing those sound waves and translating them into speech sounds using your auditory apparatus. The study of the acoustics and articulation of speech is called *phonetics*. Once you've translated the waves of sound into mental representations of speech sounds, you analyze them into syllables and pattern them appropriately. For example, speakers of English know that the made-up word *bluve* is a possible word of English, but the word *bnuck* is not. This is part of the science called *phonology*. Then you take these groups of sounds and organize them into meaningful units (called morphemes) and words. For example, the word *dancer* is made up of two meaningful bits: *dance* and the suffix *-er*. The study of this level of Language is called *morphology*. Next you organize the words into phrases and sentences. *Syntax* is the cover term for studies at this level of Language. Finally, you take the sentences and phrases you hear and translate them into thoughts and ideas. This last step is what we refer to as the *semantic* level of Language.

Syntax studies the level of Language that lies between words and the meaning of utterances: sentences. It is the level that mediates between sounds that someone produces (organized into words) and what they intend to say.

Perhaps one of the truly amazing aspects of the study of Language is not the origins of the word *demerit*, or how to properly punctuate a quote inside parentheses, or how kids have, like, destroyed the English language, eh? Instead it's the question of how we subconsciously get from sounds and words to meaning. This is the study of syntax.

Language vs. language

When I utter the term *language*, most people immediately think of some particular language such as English, French, or KiSwahili. But this is not the way linguists use the term; when linguists talk about **Language** (also known as i-language), they are generally talking about the *ability* of humans to speak any (particular) language. Noam Chomsky also calls this the **Human Language Capacity**. Language (written with a capital L) is the part of the mind or brain that allows you to speak, whereas *language* (with a lower-case l) (also known as e-language) is an instantiation of this ability (like French or English). In this book we'll be using language as our primary data, but we'll be trying to come up with a model of Language.

1. SYNTAX AS A COGNITIVE SCIENCE

Cognitive science is a cover term for a group of disciplines that all have the same goal: describing and explaining human beings' ability to think (or more particularly, to think about abstract notions like subatomic particles, the possibility of life on other planets or even how many angels can fit on the head of a pin, etc.). One thing that distinguishes us from other animals, even relatively smart ones like chimps and elephants, is our ability to use productive, combinatory Language. Language plays an important role in how we think about abstract notions, or, at the very least, Language appears to be structured in such a way that it allows us to express abstract notions.[1] The discipline of linguistics is thus one of the important subdisciplines of cognitive science.[2] Sentences are how we get at expressing abstract thought processes, so the study of syntax is an important foundation stone for understanding how we communicate and interact with each other as humans.

---

[1] Whether language constrains what abstract things we can think about (this idea is called the Sapir–Whorf hypothesis) is a matter of great debate and one that lies outside the domain of syntax per se.

[2] Along with psychology, neuroscience, communication, philosophy, and computer science.

2. MODELING SYNTAX

The dominant theory of syntax is due to Noam Chomsky and his colleagues, starting in the mid 1950s and continuing to this day. This theory, which has had many different names through its development (Transformational Grammar (TG), Transformational Generative Grammar, Standard Theory, Extended Standard Theory, Government and Binding Theory (GB), Principles and Parameters approach (P&P) and Minimalism (MP)), is often given the blanket name *Generative Grammar*. A number of alternate theories of syntax have also branched off of this research program. These include Lexical-Functional Grammar (LFG) and Head-Driven Phrase Structure Grammar (HPSG). These are also considered part of generative grammar; but we won't cover them extensively in this book. But I have included two additional chapters on these theories in the web resources for this book at www.wiley.com/go/carnie. The particular version of generative grammar that we will mostly look at here is roughly the *Principles and Parameters* approach, although we will occasionally stray from this into the more recent version called *Minimalism*.

The underlying thesis of generative grammar is that sentences are generated by a subconscious set of procedures (like computer programs). These procedures are part of our minds (or of our cognitive abilities if you prefer). The goal of syntactic theory is to model these procedures. In other words, we are trying to figure out what we subconsciously know about the syntax of our language.

In generative grammar, the means for modeling these procedures is through a set of formal grammatical *rules*. Note that these rules are nothing like the rules of grammar you might have learned in school. These rules don't tell you how to properly punctuate a sentence or not to split an infinitive. Instead, they tell you the order in which to put your words. In English, for example, we put the subject of a sentence before its verb. This is the kind of information encoded in generative rules. These rules are thought to generate the sentences of a language, hence the name *generative* grammar. You can think of these rules as being like the command lines in a computer program. They tell you step by step how to put together words into a sentence. We'll look at precise examples of these rules in the next few chapters. But first, let's look at some of the underlying assumptions of generative grammar.

Noam Chomsky

Avram Noam Chomsky was born on 7 December 1928, in Philadelphia. His father was a Hebrew grammarian and his mother a teacher. Chomsky got his Ph.D. from the University of Pennsylvania, where he studied linguistics under Zellig Harris. He took a position in machine translation and language teaching at the Massachusetts Institute of Technology. Eventually his ideas about the structure of language transformed the field of linguistics. Reviled by some and admired by others, Chomsky's ideas have laid the groundwork for the discipline of linguistics, and have been very influential in computer science and philosophy. Outside of linguistics, Chomsky is also one of the leading intellectuals in the anarchist socialist movement. His writings about the media and political injustice are also widely read. Chomsky is among the most quoted authors in the world (among the top ten and the only living person on the list).

3. SYNTAX AS SCIENCE – THE SCIENTIFIC METHOD

For many people, the study of language properly belongs in the humanities. That is, the study of language is all about the beauty of its usage in fine (and not so fine) literature. However, there is no particular reason, other than our biases, that the study of language should be confined to a humanistic approach. It is also possible to approach the study of language from a scientific perspective; this is the domain of linguistics. People who study literature often accuse linguists of abstracting away from the richness of good prose and obscuring the beauty of language. Nothing could be further from the truth. Most linguists, including the present author, enjoy nothing more than reading a finely crafted piece of fiction, and many linguists often study, as a sideline, the more humanistic aspects of language. This doesn't mean, however, that one can't appreciate and study the formal properties (or rules) of language and do it from a scientific perspective. The two approaches to language study are both valid; they complement each other; and neither takes away from the other.

Science is perhaps one of the most poorly defined words of the English language. We regularly talk of scientists as people who study bacteria, particle physics, and the formation of chemical compounds, but ask your average Joe or Jill on the street what science means, and you'll be hard pressed to get a decent definition. But among scientists themselves, *science* refers to a particular methodology for study: the scientific method. The scientific method dates backs to the ancient Greeks, such as Aristotle,

Euclid, and Archimedes. The method involves observing some data, making some generalizations about patterns in the data, developing hypotheses that account for these generalizations, and testing the hypotheses against more data. Finally, the hypotheses are revised to account for any new data and then tested again. A flow chart showing the method is given in (1):

1)

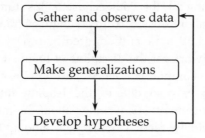

In syntax, we apply this methodology to sentence structure. Syntacticians start[3] by observing data about the language they are studying, then they make generalizations about patterns in the data (e.g., in simple English declarative sentences, the subject precedes the verb). They then generate a hypothesis and test the hypothesis against more syntactic data, and if necessary go back and re-evaluate their hypotheses.

Hypotheses are only useful to the extent that they make **predictions**. A hypothesis that makes no predictions (or worse yet, predicts everything) is useless from a scientific perspective. In particular, the hypothesis must be *falsifiable*. That is, we must in principle be able to look for some data, which, if true, show that the hypothesis is wrong. This means that we are often looking for the cases where our hypotheses predict that a sentence will be grammatical (and it is not), or the cases where they predict that the sentence will be ungrammatical (contra to fact).

In syntax, hypotheses are called **rules**, and the group of hypotheses that describe a language's syntax is called a **grammar**.

The term *grammar* can strike terror into the hearts of people. But you should note that there are two ways to go about writing grammatical rules. One is to tell people how they *should* speak (this is of course the domain of English teachers and copy-editors); we call these kinds of rules **prescriptive rules** (as they prescribe how people should speak according

---

[3] This is a bit of an oversimplification. We really have a "chicken and the egg" problem here. You can't know what data to study unless you have a hypothesis about what is important, and you can't have a hypothesis unless you have some basic understanding of the data. Fortunately, as working syntacticians this philosophical conundrum is often irrelevant, as we can just jump feet-first into both the hypothesis-forming and the data-analysis at the same time.

to some standard). Some examples of prescriptive rules include "never end a sentence with a preposition", "use *whom* not *who*" and "don't split infinitives". These rules tell us how we are supposed to use our language. The other approach is to write rules that describe how people *actually* speak, whether or not they are speaking "correctly". These are called **descriptive rules**. Consider for a moment the approach we're taking in this book. Which of the two types (descriptive or prescriptive) is more scientific? Which kind of rule is more likely to give us insight into how the mind uses Language? We focus on descriptive rules. This doesn't mean that prescriptive rules aren't important (in fact, in the problem sets section of this chapter you are asked to critically examine the question of descriptive vs. prescriptive rules), but for our purposes descriptive rules are more important. For an interesting discussion of the prescriptive/descriptive debate, see Pinker's (1995) book: *The Language Instinct*.

You now have enough information to answer General Problem Sets GPS1 & 2, as well as Challenge Problem Set CPS1 at the end of this chapter. For practice try Workbook Exercise WBE1 in chapter 1 of The Syntax Workbook, *an optional companion book to this text.*

Do Rules Really Exist?

Generative grammar claims to be a theory of cognitive psychology, so it's reasonable to ask whether formal rules *really* exist in the brain/minds of speakers. After all, a brain is a mass of neurons firing away, so how can formal mathematical rules exist up there? Remember, however, that we are attempting to *model* Language; we aren't trying to describe Language exactly. This question confuses two disciplines: psychology and neurology. Psychology is concerned with the mind, which represents the output and the abstract organization of the brain. Neurology is concerned with the actual firing of the neurons and the physiology of the brain. Generative grammar doesn't try to be a theory of neurology. Instead it is a model of the psychology of Language. Obviously, the rules per se don't exist in our brains, but they do model the external behavior of the mind. For more discussion of this issue, look at the readings in the further reading section of this chapter.

3.1 An Example of the Scientific Method as Applied to Syntax

Let's turn now to a real-world application of the scientific method to some language data. The following data concern the form of a specific kind of noun, called an *anaphor* (plural: *anaphors*; the phenomenon is called *anaphora*). These include the nouns that end with *-self* (e.g., *himself, herself, itself*). In chapter 5, we look at the distribution of anaphors in detail; here we'll only consider one superficial aspect of them. In the following sentences, as is standard in the syntactic literature, a sentence that isn't well-formed is marked with an *asterisk* (*) before it. For these sentences assume that *Bill* is male and *Sally* is female.

2) a) Bill kissed himself.
   b) *Bill kissed herself.
   c) Sally kissed herself.
   d) *Sally kissed himself.
   e) *Kiss himself.

To the unskilled eye, the ill-formed sentences in (2b and d) just look silly. It is obvious that Bill can't kiss herself, because Bill is male. However, no matter how matter-of-factly obvious this is, it is part of a bigger generalization about the distribution of anaphors. In particular, the generalization we can draw about the sentences in (2) is that an anaphor must agree in *gender* with the noun it refers to (its *antecedent*). So in (2a and b) we see that the anaphor must agree in gender with *Bill*, its antecedent. The anaphor must take the masculine form *himself*. The situation in (2c and d) is the same; the anaphor must take the form *herself* so that it agrees in gender with the feminine *Sally*. Note further that a sentence like (2e) shows us that anaphors must have an antecedent. An anaphor without an antecedent is unacceptable. A plausible hypothesis (or rule) given the data in (2), then, is stated in (3):

3) An anaphor must (i) have an antecedent and (ii) agree in gender (masculine, feminine, or neuter) with that antecedent.

The next step in the scientific method is to test this hypothesis against more data. Consider the additional data in (4):

4) a) The robot kissed itself.
   b) She knocked herself on the head with a zucchini.
   c) *She knocked himself on the head with a zucchini.
   d) The snake flattened itself against the rock.
   e) ?The snake flattened himself/herself against the rock.
   f) The Joneses think themselves the best family on the block.
   g) *The Joneses think himself the most wealthy guy on the block.
   h) Gary and Kevin ran themselves into exhaustion.
   i) *Gary and Kevin ran himself into exhaustion.

Sentences (4a, b, and c) are all consistent with our hypothesis that anaphors must agree in gender with their antecedents, which at least confirms that the hypothesis is on the right track. What about the data in (4d and e)? It appears as if any gender is compatible with the antecedent *the snake*. This appears, on the surface, to be a contradiction to our hypothesis. Think about these examples a little more closely, however. Whether sentence (4e) is well-formed or not depends upon your assumptions about the gender of the snake. If you assume (or know) the snake to be male, then *The snake flattened himself against the rock* is perfectly well-formed. But under the same assumption, the sentence *The snake flattened herself against the rock* seems very odd indeed, although it is fine if you assume the snake is female. So it appears as if this example also meets the generalization in (3); the vagueness about its well-formedness has to do with the fact that we are rarely sure what gender a snake is and not with the actual structure of the sentence.

Now, look at the sentences in (4f–i); note that the ill-formedness of (g) and (i) is not predicted by our generalization. In fact, our generalization predicts that sentence (4i) should be perfectly grammatical, since *himself* agrees in gender (masculine) with its antecedents *Gary* and *Kevin*. Yet there is clearly something wrong with this sentence. The hypothesis needs revision. It appears as if the anaphor must agree in gender and **number** with the antecedent. Number refers to the quantity of individuals involved in the sentence; English primarily distinguishes singular number from plural number. (5) reflects our revised hypothesis.

5) An anaphor must agree in gender and number with its antecedent.

If there is more than one person or object mentioned in the antecedent, then the anaphor must be plural (i.e., *themselves*).

Testing this against more data, we can see that this partially makes the right predictions (6a), but it doesn't properly predict the acceptability of sentences (6b–e):

6) a) People from Tucson think very highly of themselves.
 b) *I gave yourself the bucket of ice cream.
 c) I gave myself the bucket of ice cream.
 d) *She hit myself with a hammer.
 e) She hit herself with a hammer.

Even more revision is in order. The phenomenon seen in (6b–e) revolves around a grammatical distinction called **person**. Person refers to the perspective of the speaker with respect to the other participants in the speech act. **First person** refers to the speaker. **Second person** refers to the addressee. **Third person** refers to people being discussed that aren't participating in the conversation. Here are the English pronouns associated with each person: (**Nominative** refers to the *case* form the pronouns take when in subject position like *I* in "*I* love peanut butter"; *accusative* refers to the form they take when in object positions like *me* in "John loves *me*". We will look at case in much more detail in chapter 9, so don't worry if you don't understand it right now.)

7)

	Nominative		Accusative		Anaphoric	
	Singular	Plural	Singular	Plural	Singular	Plural
1	I	we	me	us	myself	ourselves
2	you	you	you	you	yourself	yourselves
3 masc	he		him		himself	
3 fem	she	they	her	them	herself	themselves
3 neut	it		it		itself	

As you can see from this chart, the form of the anaphor seems also to agree in person with its antecedent. So once again we revise our hypothesis (rule):

8) An anaphor must agree in person, gender and number with its antecedent.

With this hypothesis, we have a straightforward statement of the distribution of this noun type, derived using the scientific method. In the problem sets below, and in chapter 6, you'll have an opportunity to revise the rule in (8) with even more data.

You now have enough information to try WBE2, and CPS2 & 3.

3.2 Sources of Data

If we are going to apply the scientific method to syntax, it is important to consider the sources of our data. One obvious source is in collections of either spoken or written texts. Such data are called *corpora* (singular: *corpus*). There are many corpora available, including some searchable through the internet. For languages without a literary tradition or ones spoken by a small group of people, it is often necessary for the linguist to go and gather data and compile a corpus in the field. In the early part of the last century, this was the primary occupation of linguists, and it is proudly carried on today by many researchers.

The linguist Heidi Harley reports in her blog[4] on an example of using search engines to do linguistic analysis. Harley notes that to her ear, the

---

[4] http://heideas.blogspot.com/2005/10/scalar-adjectives-with-arguments.html.

expression *half full of something* sounds natural, but *half empty of something* does not. She does a comparison of *half empty* vs. *half full* and of *half empty of* vs. *half full of*. She finds that the ratio of *half full* to *half empty* without the *of* is roughly 1:1. The ratio of *half full of* to *half empty of* is approximately 149:1. This is a surprising difference. Harley was able to use the Web to show that a fairly subtle difference in acceptability is reflected in the frequency with which the expressions are used.

But corpus searches aren't always adequate for finding out the information syntacticians need. For the most part corpora only contain grammatical sentences. Sometimes the most illuminating information is our knowledge that a certain sentence is <u>un</u>grammatical (i.e., not a sentence of normal English), or that two similar sentences have very different meanings. Consider the pair of sentences in (9) as a starting point.

9)   a)   Doug blew the building up.
        b)   Doug blew up the building.

Most native speakers of English will accept both of these sentences as acceptable sentences, with a preference for (9b). They also know that while the first sentence (9a) is unambiguous, the second one has two meanings (He destroyed the building using explosives vs. he blew really hard with his lungs up the stairwell). The second of these meanings is a bit silly, but it's a legitimate interpretation of the sentence.

Now contrast the sentences in (9) with the similar pair in (10). In these forms I've replaced "the building" with the pronoun "it":

10)   a)   Doug blew it up.
        b)   Doug blew up it.

Here we find a different pattern of interpretation. (10a) is unambiguous just the way (9a) is, it refers to an act of explosion and cannot have an interpretation where Doug was blowing hard with his lungs up something. Sentence (10b), however, is a surprise. Unlike (9b), (10b) cannot have anything to do with explosives. It can only have the interpretation where Doug is blowing air up whatever "it" is. Recall that with (9) this "puff of air reading" was the silly or strange one. With a pronoun, however, it's the only available interpretation.

While corpora are unquestionably invaluable sources of data, they are only a partial representation of what goes on in the mind. More particularly, corpora often contain instances of only acceptable (or, more precisely, well-formed) sentences (sentences that sound "OK" to a native speaker). For example, the online *New York Times* contains very few ungrammatical sentences. Even corpora of naturalistic speech complete with the errors every speaker makes don't necessarily contain the data we need to test the falsifiable predictions of our hypotheses. So corpora are just not enough: there is no way of knowing whether a corpus has *all* possible forms of grammatical sentences. In fact, as we will see in the next few chapters, due to the productive nature of language, a corpus could *never* contain all the grammatical forms of a language, nor could it even contain a representative sample. To really get at what we know about our languages (remember syntax is a cognitive science), we have to know what sentences are *not* well-formed. That is, in order to know the range of acceptable sentences of English, Italian or Igbo, we *first* have to know what are *not* acceptable sentences in English, Italian or Igbo. This kind of negative information is very rarely available in corpora, which mostly provide grammatical, or well-formed, sentences.

Consider the following sentence:

11) *Who do you wonder what bought?

For most speakers of English, this sentence borders on word salad – it is not a good sentence of English. How do you know that? Were you ever taught in school that you can't say sentences like (11)? Has anyone ever uttered this sentence in your presence before? I seriously doubt it. The fact that a sentence like (11) sounds strange, but similar sentences like (12a and b) *do* sound OK is not reflected anywhere in a corpus:

12) a)   Who do you think bought the bread machine?
    b)   I wonder what Fiona bought.

Instead we have to rely on our knowledge of our native language (or on the knowledge of a native speaker consultant for languages that we don't speak natively). Notice that this is *not* conscious knowledge. I doubt there are many native speakers of English that could tell you why sentence (11) is terrible, but most can tell you that it is. This is subconscious knowledge. The trick is to get at and describe this subconscious knowledge.

The psychological experiment used to get this subconscious kind of knowledge is called the **grammaticality judgment task**. The judgment task involves asking a native speaker to read a sentence, and judge whether it is well-formed (grammatical), marginally well-formed, or ill-formed (unacceptable or ungrammatical).

There are actually several different kinds of grammaticality judgments. Both of the following sentences are ill-formed, but for different reasons:

13) a)   #The toothbrush is pregnant.
    b)   *Toothbrush the is blue.

Sentence (13a) sounds bizarre (cf. *the toothbrush is blue*) because we know that toothbrushes (except in the world of fantasy/science fiction or poetry) cannot be pregnant. The meaning of the sentence is strange, but the form is OK. We call this *semantic ill-formedness* and mark the sentence with a #. By contrast, we can glean the meaning of sentence (13b); it seems semantically reasonable (toothbrushes can be blue), but it is ill-formed from a structural point of view. That is, the determiner *the* is in the wrong place in the sentence. This is a *syntactically ill-formed* sentence. A native speaker of English will judge both these sentences as ill-formed, but for very different reasons. In this text, we will be concerned primarily with syntactic well-formedness.

You now have enough information to answer WBE 3 & 4, GPS 3, and CPS 4 & 5.

Judgments as Science?

Many linguists refer to the grammaticality judgment task as "drawing upon our native speaker intuitions". The word "intuition" here is slightly misleading. The last thing that pops into our heads when we hear the term "intuition" is science. Generative grammar has been severely criticized by many for relying on "unscientific" intuitions. But this is based primarily on a misunderstanding of the term. To the layperson, the term "intuition" brings to mind guesses and luck. This usage of the term is certainly standard. When a generative grammarian refers to "intuition", however, she is using the term to mean "tapping into our subconscious knowledge". The term "intuition" may have been badly chosen, but in this circumstance it refers to a real psychological effect. Intuition (as a grammaticality judgment) has an entirely scientific basis. It is replicable under strictly controlled experimental conditions (these conditions are rarely applied, but the validity of the task is well established). Other disciplines also use intuitions or judgment tasks. For example, within the study of vision, it has been determined that people can accurately judge differences in light intensity, drawing upon their subconscious knowledge (Bard et al. 1996). To avoid the negative associations with the term intuition, we will use the less loaded term *judgment* instead.

3.3 Competence vs. Performance

A related issue concerns the unacceptability of forms like (14). Native speakers will have to read this sentence a couple of times to figure out what it means.

14) #Cotton shirts are made from comes from India.

This kind of sentence (called a **garden path sentence**) is very hard to understand and process. In this example, the problem is that the intended reading has a noun, *cotton*, that is modified by a reduced relative clause: *(that) shirts are made from*. The linear sequence of *cotton* followed by *shirt* is ambiguous with the noun phrase *cotton shirts*. Note that this kind of relative structure is okay in other contexts; compare: *That material is the cotton shirts are made from*. Sentences like (14) get much easier to understand with really clear pauses (where … is meant to indicate a pause): *Cotton … shirts are made from … comes from India*. Or by insertion of a *that* which breaks up the potentially ambiguous *cotton shirts* sequence: *The cotton that shirts are made from comes from India*. What is critical about these garden path sentences is that, once one figures out what the intended meaning is, native speakers can identify them as grammatical sentences or at the very least as sentences that have structures that would otherwise be grammatical in them. The problem for us as linguists is that native speakers have a really hard time figuring out what the intended meaning for these sentences is on those first few passes!

A similar situation arises when we have really long sentences with complex syntactic relations. Look at (15). A first reading of this sentence will boggle your average speaker of English. But if you read it a couple of times, it becomes obvious what is intended. In fact, the sentence seems to be structured grammatically.

15) Who did Bill say Frank claimed that Mary seems to have been likely to have kissed?

The reason this sentence is hard to understand is that the question word *who* is very far away from where it gets interpreted (as the object of *kiss*), and what lies in between those two points is quite a lot of sophisticated embeddings and structure. But once you get a chance to think about it, it gets better and better as a sentence. The most famous example of this kind of effect is called **center embedding**. English speakers tolerate a small amount of stacking of relative clauses between subjects and verbs, so (16) – while a little clumsy – is still a good sentence for most speakers of English. We have some cheese, the kind that mice love, and it stinks. If you have trouble with this sentence put a big pause after *cheese* and before *stinks*.

16) Cheese mice love stinks.

But no pauses will fix a sentence in which we put another reduced relative right after *mice*, with the intended meaning that cheese which is loved by mice who are caught by cats is stinky:

17) #Cheese mice cats catch love stinks

This sentence is practically uninterpretable for English speakers. Chomsky (1965) argued that the problem here is not one of the grammar (as English grammar allows reduced relative clauses after subjects and before verbs), but instead either a constraint on short-term memory[5] or a constraint on our mental ability to break apart sentences as we hear them. The English *parsing* system – that is the system that breaks down sentences into their bits – has certain limits, and these limits are distinct from the limits on what it means to be "grammatical". Sentences (14), (15), and (16) are unacceptable to native speakers in a qualitatively different way than the ones in (13).

The distinction we've been looking at here is often known as the *competence/performance* distinction. When we speak or listen, we are performing the act of creating a piece of language output. This performance can be interrupted by all sorts of extraneous factors: we can be distracted or bored; we can cough or mumble our words; we can forget what we had previously heard; the noise of the bus driving past can blot out a crucial word. *Performance* refers to the kinds of language that are actually produced and heard. *Competence*, by contrast, refers to what we *know* about our language; it is unimpeded by factors that might muddy the waters of performance. So think about the really long complicated sentence in (15). The first time you read it, things like your memory and how complicated it was interfered with your ability to understand it. So the initial unacceptability of the sentence was due to a performance problem. But once you thought about it and stared at it a bit, you saw that it was actually a fairly standard grammatical sentence of English – just a really complicated one. When you did this you were accessing your competence in (or knowledge of) English grammar.

This takes us to a new point. Listen carefully to someone speak (not lecture or read aloud, but someone really speaking in a conversation). You'll notice that they don't speak in grammatical sentences. They leave stuff off and they speak in fragments. They start and they stop the same sentence a couple of times. Everyone does this, even the most eloquent among us. So much of what you hear (or see in spoken language corpora) consists of actually "ungrammatical" forms. Nevertheless, if you're a native English speaker, you have the ability to judge if a sentence is acceptable or not. These two tasks, understanding spoken conversational language and being able to judge the well-formedness of a sentence, seem to actually be different skills

---

[5] The working memory hypothesis is suspicious because speakers of languages like Japanese and German can understand the similar sentences in their languages without problem.

corresponding roughly to performance and competence. This harkens back to the Language/language distinction talked about above.

An analogy that might clarify these distinctions: imagine that you're a software engineer and you're writing a piece of computer code. First you run it on your own computer and it behaves beautifully. The output of the computer code is one kind of performance of the underlying competence. Then you run it on your little sister's ancient PC. The program doesn't perform as you expect. It's really slow. It crashes. It causes the fan to run continuously and the processor to overheat. Now you go back and look at the code. There are no errors in the code. It meets all the requirements of the computer language. So from the perspective of competence, your program is okay. The real problem here is not with your code, but with the machine you're running it on. The processor is too old, there isn't enough memory and you have a computer that tends to overheat. These are all performance problems.

So what does this mean for the linguist using grammaticality judgments as a tool for investigating syntax? It means that when using a judgment, you have to be really clear about what is causing the acceptability or unacceptability of the sentence. Is the sentence acceptable just because you have gleaned enough information from the conversational context (in which case we might consider it a performance effect)? If you hear a sentence that you judge as unacceptable, is it because someone was speaking too quickly and left out a word, or is it because the sentence really doesn't work as an English sentence at all? This distinction is very subtle, but it is one that syntacticians have to pay careful attention to as they do their work.

You now have enough information to answer CPS 6.

---

4. WHERE DO THE RULES COME FROM?

In this chapter we've been talking about our subconscious knowledge of syntactic rules, but we haven't dealt with how we get this knowledge. This is sort of a side issue, but it may affect the shape of our theory. If we know how children acquire their rules, then we are in a better position to develop a proper formalization of them. The way in which children develop knowledge is an important question in cognitive science. The theory of generative grammar makes some very specific (and very surprising) claims about this.

4.1 Learning vs. Acquisition

One of the most common misconceptions about Language is the idea that children and adults "learn" languages. Recall that the basic kind of knowledge we are talking about here is subconscious knowledge. When producing a sentence you don't consciously think about where to put the subject, where to put the verb, etc. Your subconscious language faculty does that for you. Cognitive scientists make a distinction in how we get conscious and subconscious knowledge. Conscious knowledge (like the rules of algebra, syntactic theory, principles of organic chemistry or how to take apart a carburetor) is *learned*. Subconscious knowledge, like how to speak or the ability to visually identify discrete objects, is *acquired*. In part, this explains why classes in the formal grammar of a foreign language often fail abysmally to train people to speak those languages. By contrast, being immersed in an environment where you can subconsciously acquire a language is much more effective. In this text we'll be primarily interested in how people acquire the rules of their language. Not all rules of grammar are acquired, however. Some facts about Language seem to be built into our brains, or *innate*.

You now have enough information to answer GPS 4.

4.2 Innateness: Language as an Instinct

If you think about the other types of knowledge that are subconscious, you'll see that many of them (for example, the ability to walk) are built directly into our brains – they are instincts. No one had to teach you to walk (despite what your parents might think!). Kids start walking on their own. Walking is an instinct. Probably the most controversial claim of Noam Chomsky's is that Language is also an instinct. Many parts of Language are built in, or *innate*. Much of Language is an ability hard-wired into our brains by our genes.

Obviously, particular languages are not innate. It is never the case that a child of Slovak parents growing up in North America who is never spoken to in Slovak grows up speaking Slovak. They'll speak English (or whatever other language is spoken around them). So on the surface it seems crazy to claim that Language is an instinct. There are very good reasons to believe, however, that a human facility for Language (perhaps in the form of a "Language organ" in the brain) is innate. We call this facility *Universal Grammar* (or *UG*).

4.3 The Logical Problem of Language Acquisition

What follows is a fairly technical proof of the idea that Language is at least plausibly construed as an innate, in-built system. If you aren't interested in this proof (and the problems with it), then you can reasonably skip ahead to section 4.4.

The argument in this section is that a productive system like the rules of Language probably could not be learned or acquired. Infinite systems are in principle, given certain assumptions, both unlearnable and unacquirable. Since we all have such an infinite system in our heads, we shouldn't have been able to acquire it. So it follows that it is built in. The argument presented here is based on an unpublished paper by Alec Marantz, but is based on an argument dating back to at least Chomsky (1965).

First here's a sketch of the proof, which takes the classical form of an argument by modus ponens:

> *Premise (i)*: Syntax is a productive, recursive and infinite system.
> <u>*Premise (ii):* Rule-governed infinite systems are unlearnable.</u>
> *Conclusion*: Therefore syntax is an unlearnable system. Since we have it, it follows that at least parts of syntax are innate.

There are parts of this argument that are very controversial. In the challenge problem sets at the end of this chapter you are invited to think very critically about the form of this proof. Challenge Problem Set 3 considers the possibility that premise (i) is false (but hopefully you will conclude that, despite the argument given in the problem set, the idea that Language is productive and infinite is correct). Premise (ii) is more dubious, and is the topic of Challenge Problem Set 4. Here, in the main body of the text, I will give you the classic versions of the support for these premises, without criticizing them. You are invited to be skeptical and critical of them if you do the Challenge Problem sets.

Let's start with premise (i). Language is a productive system. That is, you can produce and understand sentences you have never heard before. For example, I can practically guarantee that you have never heard the following sentence:

18) The dancing chorus-line of elephants broke my television set.

The magic of syntax is that it can generate forms that have never been produced before. Another example of this productive quality lies in what is called **recursion**. It is possible to utter a sentence like (19):

19) Rosie loves magazine ads.

It is also possible to put this sentence inside another sentence, like (20):

20) I think [Rosie loves magazine ads].

Similarly you can put this larger sentence inside of another one:

21) Drew believes [I think [Rosie loves magazine ads]].

and of course you can put this bigger sentence inside of another one:

22) Dana doubts that [Drew believes [I think [Rosie loves magazine ads]]].

and so on, and so on ad infinitum. It is always possible to embed a sentence inside of a larger one. This means that Language is a productive (probably infinite) system. There are no limits on what we can talk about. Other examples of the productivity of syntax can be seen in the fact that you can infinitely repeat adverbs (23) and you can infinitely add coordinated nouns to a noun phrase (24):

23) a) a very big peanut
    b) a very very big peanut
    c) a very very very big peanut
    d) a very very very very big peanut
        etc.

24) a) Dave left
    b) Dave and Alina left
    c) Dave, Dan, and Alina left
    d) Dave, Dan, Erin, and Alina left
    e) Dave, Dan, Erin, Jaime, and Alina left
        etc.

It follows that for every grammatical sentence of English, you can find a longer one (based on one of the rules of recursion, adverb repetition, or coordination). This means that language is at least countably infinite. This premise is relatively uncontroversial (however, see the discussion in Challenge Problem Set 5).

Let's now turn to premise (ii), the idea that infinite systems are unlearnable. In order to make this more concrete, let's consider an algebraic treatment of a linguistic example. Imagine that the task of a child is to determine the rules by which her language is constructed. Further, let's simplify the task, and say a child simply has to match up situations in the real world with utterances she hears.[6] So upon hearing the utterance

---

[6] The task is actually several magnitudes more difficult than this, as the child has to work out the phonology, etc., too, but for argument's sake, let's stick with this simplified example.

the cat spots the kissing fishes, she identifies it with an appropriate situation in the context around her (as represented by the picture).

25) "the cat spots the kissing fishes" =

Her job, then, is to correctly match up the sentence with the situation.[7] More crucially she has to make sure that she does *not* match it up with all the other possible alternatives, such as the things going on around her (like her older brother kicking the furniture or her mother making her breakfast, etc.). This matching of situations with expressions is a kind of mathematical relation (or function) that *maps* sentences onto particular situations. Another way of putting it is that she has to figure out the rule(s) that decode(s) the meaning of the sentences. It turns out that this task is at least very difficult, if not impossible.

   Let's make this even more abstract to get at the mathematics of the situation. Assign each sentence some number. This number will represent the input to the rule. Similarly we will assign each situation a number. The function (or rule) modeling language acquisition maps from the set of sentence numbers to the set of situation numbers. Now let's assume that the child has the following set of inputs and correctly matched situations (perhaps explicitly pointed out to her by her parents). The x value represents the sentence she hears. The y is the number correctly associated with the situation.

26) *Sentence* (input)   *Situation* (output)

x	y
1	1
2	2
3	3
4	4
5	5

---

[7] Note that this is the job of the child who is using Universal Grammar, not the job of UG itself.

Given this input, what do you suppose that the output where $x = 6$ will be?

6   ?

Most people will jump to the conclusion that the output will be 6 as well. That is, they assume that the function (the rule) mapping between inputs and outputs is $x = y$. But what if I were to tell you that in the hypothetical situation I envision here, the correct answer is situation number 126? The rule that generated the table in (20) is actually:

27) $[(x - 5)^*(x - 4)^*(x - 3)^*(x - 2)^*(x - 1)] + x = y$

With this rule, all inputs equal to or less than 5 will give an output equal to the input, but for all inputs greater than 5, they will give some large number.

When you hypothesized the rule was $x = y$, you didn't have all the crucial information; you only had part of the data. This seems to mean that if you hear only the first five pieces of data in our table then you won't get the rule, but if you learn the sixth you will figure it out. Is this necessarily the case? Unfortunately not: Even if you add a sixth line, you have no way of being sure that you have the right function until you have heard *all* the possible inputs. The important information might be in the sixth line, but it might also be in the 7,902,821,123,765th sentence that you hear. You have no way of knowing for sure if you have heard all the relevant data until you have heard them all. In an infinite system you can't hear them all, even if you were to hear 1 sentence every 10 seconds for your entire life. If we assume the average person lives to be about 75 years old, if they heard one new sentence every 10 seconds, ignoring leap years and assuming they never sleep, they'd have only heard about 39,420,000 sentences over their lifetime. This is a much smaller number than infinity. Despite this poverty of input, by the age of 5 most children are fairly confident with their use of complicated syntax. Productive systems are (possibly) unlearnable, because you never have enough input to be sure you have all the relevant facts. This is called *the logical problem of language acquisition*.

Generative grammar gets around this logical puzzle by claiming that the child acquiring English, Irish, or Yoruba has some help: a flexible blueprint to use in constructing her knowledge of language called **Universal Grammar**. Universal Grammar restricts the number of possible functions that map between situations and utterances, thus making language learnable.

You now have enough information to try CPS 7 & 8.

> **Statistical Probability or UG?**
> In looking at the logical problem of language acquisition you might be asking yourself, "Ok, so maybe kids don't get all the data, but perhaps they get enough to draw conclusions about what is the most likely structure of their grammar?" For example, we might conclude that a child learning English would observe the total absence of any sentences that have *that* followed by a trace (e.g., 22d), so after hearing some threshold of sentences they conclude that this sentence type is ungrammatical. This is a common objection to the hypothesis of UG. Unfortunately, this hypothesis can't explain why many sentence types that are extremely rare (to the point that they are probably never heard by children) are still judged as grammatical by the children. For example, English speakers rarely (if ever) produce sentences with seven embeddings (*John said that Mary thinks that Susan believes that Matt exclaimed that Marian claimed that Art said that Andrew wondered if Gwen had lost her pen*); yet speakers of English routinely agree these are acceptable. The actual speech of adult speakers is riddled with errors (due to all sorts of external factors: memory, slips of the tongue, tiredness, distraction, etc.). However, children do not seem to assume that any of these errors, which they hear frequently, are part of the data that determine their grammars.

4.4 Other Arguments for UG

The evidence for UG doesn't rely on the logical problem alone, however. There are many other arguments that support the hypothesis that at least a certain amount of language is built in.

An argument that is directly related to the logical problem of language acquisition discussed above has to do with the fact that we know things about the grammar of our language that we couldn't possibly have learned. Start with the data in (28). A child might plausibly have heard sentences of these types (the underline represents the place where the question word *who* might start out – that is, as either the object or the subject of the verb *will question*):

28) a)   Who do you think that Ciaran   will question _____ first?
    b)   Who do you think   Ciaran   will question _____ first?
    c)   Who do you think   _____   will question Seamus first?

The child has to draw a hypothesis about the distribution of the word *that* in English sentences. One conclusion consistent with these observed data is that the word *that* in English is optional. You can either have it or not.

Unfortunately this conclusion is not accurate. Consider the fourth sentence in the paradigm in (28). This sentence is the same as (28c) but with a *that*:

    d) *Who do you think that _____ will question Seamus first?

It appears as if *that* is only optional when the question word (*who* in this case) starts in object position (as in 28a and b). It is obligatorily absent when the question word starts in subject position (as in 28c and d) (don't worry about the details of this generalization). What is important to note is that *no one* has ever taught you that (28d) is ungrammatical. Nor could you have come to that conclusion on the basis of the data you've heard. The logical hypothesis on the basis of the data in (28a–c) predicts sentence (28d) to be grammatical. There is nothing in the input a child hears that would lead them to the conclusion that (28d) is ungrammatical, yet every English-speaking child knows it is. One solution to this conundrum is that we are born with the knowledge that sentences like (28d) are ungrammatical.[8] This kind of argument is often called the **underdetermination of the data** argument for UG.

    Most parents raising a toddler will swear up and down that they are teaching their child to speak and that they actively engage in instructing their child in the proper form of the language. The claim that overt instruction by parents plays any role in language development is easily falsified. The evidence from the experimental language acquisition literature is very clear: parents, despite their best intentions, do not, for the most part, correct ungrammatical utterances by their children. More generally, they correct the content rather than the form of their child's utterances (see for example the extensive discussion in Holzman 1997).

29) (from Marcus et al. 1992)
    Adult: Where is that big piece of paper I gave you yesterday?
    Child: Remember? I writed on it.
    Adult: Oh that's right, don't you have any paper down here, buddy?

---

[8] The phenomenon in (28) is sometimes called the **that-*trace* effect**. There is no disputing the fact that this phenomenon is not learnable. However, it is also a fact that it is not a universal property of all languages. For example, French and Irish don't seem to have the *that*-trace effect. Here is a challenge for those of you who like to do logic puzzles: If the *that*-trace effect is not learnable and thus must be biologically built in, how is it possible for a speaker of French or Irish to violate it? Think carefully about what kind of input a child might have to have in order to learn an "exception" to a built-in principle. This is a hard problem, but there is a solution. It may become clearer below when we discuss parameters.

When a parent does try to correct a child's sentence structure, it is more often than not ignored by the child:

30) (from Pinker 1995: 281 – attributed to Martin Braine)
    Child: Want other one spoon, Daddy.
    Adult: You mean, you want the other spoon.
    Child: Yes, I want other one spoon, please, Daddy.
    Adult: Can you say "the other spoon"?
    Child: Other … one … spoon.
    Adult: Say "other".
    Child: Other.
    Adult: "Spoon".
    Child: Spoon.
    Adult: "Other … spoon".
    Child: Other … spoon. Now give me other one spoon?

This humorous example is typical of parental attempts to "instruct" their children in language. When these attempts do occur, they fail. However, children still acquire language in the face of a complete lack of instruction. Perhaps one of the most convincing explanations for this is UG. In the problem set part of this chapter, you are asked to consider other possible explanations and evaluate which are the most convincing.

    There are also typological arguments for the existence of an innate language faculty. All the languages of the world share certain properties (for example they *all* have subjects and predicates – other examples will be seen throughout the rest of this book). These properties are called **universals** of Language. If we assume UG, then the explanation for these language universals is straightforward – they exist because all speakers of human languages share the same basic innate materials for building their language's grammar. In addition to sharing many similar characteristics, recent research into Language acquisition has begun to show that there is a certain amount of consistency cross-linguistically in the way children acquire Language. For example, children seem to go through the same stages and make the same kinds of mistakes when acquiring their language, no matter what their cultural background.

    Derek Bickerton (1984) has noted the fact that creole languages[9] have a lot of features in common with one another, even when they come from very diverse places in the world and spring forth from unrelated languages. For

---

[9] Creole languages are new languages that are formed when a generation of speakers starts using a trade language or pidgin as their first language and speak it natively in the home.

example, they all have SVO order; they all lack non-specific indefinite articles; they all use modals or particles to indicate tense, mood, and aspect, and they have limited verbal inflection, and many other such similarities. Furthermore these properties are ones that are found in the speech of children of non-creole languages. Bickerton hypothesizes that these properties are a function of an innate *language bioprogram*, an idea similar to Chomsky's Universal Grammar.

Finally, there are a number of biological arguments in favor of UG. As noted above, Language seems to be both human-specific and pervasive across the species. All humans, unless they have some kind of physical impairment, seem to have Language as we know it. This points towards it being a genetically endowed instinct. Additionally, research from neurolinguistics seems to point towards certain parts of the brain being linked to specific linguistic functions.

With very few exceptions, most generative linguists believe that some Language is innate. What is of controversy is how much is innate and whether the innateness is specific to Language, or follows from more general innate cognitive functions. We leave these questions unanswered here.

You now have enough information to try GPS 5 and CPS 9.

4.5 Explaining Language Variation

The evidence for UG seems to be very strong. However, we are still left with the annoying problem that languages differ from one another. This problem is what makes the study of syntax so interesting. It is also not an unsolvable one.

The fact that an inborn system should allow variation won't be a surprise to any biologist. Think about the color of your eyes. Every sighted person has eyes. Having eyes is clearly an inborn property of being a human (or being a mammal). I doubt that anyone would object to that characterization. Nevertheless we see both widespread variation in eye color, size, and shape among humans, and widespread variation in form and position among various mammalian species. A closer analog to language might be bird song. In 1962, Marler and Tamura observed dialect variation among the songs of white-crowned sparrows. The ability and motivation for these birds to vocalize is widely assumed to be innate, but the particular song they sing is dependent upon the input they hear.

One way in which languages differ is in terms of the words used in the language. The different words of different languages clearly have to be learned or memorized and are not innate. Other differences between languages must also be acquired. For example the child learning English must determine that its word order is subject-verb-object (SVO), but the child learning Irish determines the order is verb-subject-object (VSO) and the Turkish child figures out subject-object-verb (SOV) order. The explanation for this kind of fact will be explored in detail in chapter 6. Foreshadowing slightly, we'll claim there that differences in the grammars of languages can be boiled down to the setting of certain innate *parameters* (or switches) that select among possible variants. Language variation thus reduces to learning the correct set of words and selecting from a predetermined set of options.

Oversimplifying slightly, most languages put the elements in a sentence in one of the following word orders:

31) a) Subject Verb Object (SVO)   (e.g., English)
    b) Subject Object Verb (SOV)   (e.g., Turkish)
    c) Verb Subject Object (VSO)   (e.g., Irish)

A few languages use

    d) Verb Object Subject (VOS)   (e.g., Malagasy)

No (or almost no)[10] languages use

    e) Object Subject Verb (OSV)
    f) Object Verb Subject (OVS)

Let us imagine that part of UG is a parameter that determines the basic word order. Four of the options (SVO, SOV, VSO, and VOS) are innately available as possible settings. Two of the possible word orders are not part of UG. The child who is acquiring English is innately biased towards one of the common orders; when she hears a sentence like "Mommy loves Kirsten", if the child knows the meaning of each of the words then she might hypothesize two possible word orders for English: SVO and OVS. None of the others are consistent with the data. The child thus rejects all the other hypotheses. OVS is not allowed, since it isn't one of the innately available forms. This leaves SVO, which is the correct order for English. So children acquiring English will choose to set the word order parameter at the innately available SVO setting.

In his excellent book *The Atoms of Language*, Mark Baker inventories a set of possible parameters of language variation within the UG hypothesis.

---

[10] This is a matter of some debate. Derbyshire (1985) has claimed that the language Hixkaryana has object-initial order.

This is an excellent and highly accessible treatment of parameters. I strongly recommend this book for further reading on how language variation is consistent with Universal Grammar.

You now have enough information to try GPS 6 and CPS 10.

5. CHOOSING AMONG THEORIES ABOUT SYNTAX

There is one last preliminary we have to touch on before actually doing some real syntax. In this book we are going to posit many hypotheses. Some of these we'll keep, others we'll revise, and still others we'll reject. How do we know what is a good hypothesis and what is a bad one? Chomsky (1965) proposed that we can evaluate how good theories of syntax are using what are called the *levels of adequacy*. Chomsky claimed that there are three stages that a grammar (the collection of descriptive rules that constitute your theory) can attain in terms of adequacy.

If your theory only accounts for the data in a corpus (say a series of printed texts) and nothing more, it is said to be an *observationally adequate grammar*. Needless to say, this isn't much use if we are trying to account for the cognition of Language. As we discussed above, it doesn't tell us the whole picture. We also need to know what kinds of sentences are unacceptable, or ill-formed. A theory that accounts for both corpora and native speaker judgments about well-formedness is called a *descriptively adequate grammar*. On the surface this may seem to be all we need. Chomsky, however, has claimed that we can go one step better. He points out that a theory that also accounts for how children acquire their language is the best. He calls this an *explanatorily adequate grammar*. The simple theory of parameters might get this label. Generative grammar strives towards explanatorily adequate grammars.

You now have enough information to try GPS 7.

6. THE SCIENTIFIC METHOD AND THE STRUCTURE OF THIS TEXTBOOK

Throughout this chapter I've emphasized the importance of the scientific method to the study of syntax. It's worth noting that we're not only going to apply this principle to small problems or specific rules, but we'll also apply it in a more global way. This principle is in part a guide to the way in which the rest of this book is structured.

In chapters 2–5 (the remainder of Part 1 of the book) we're going to develop an initial hypothesis about the way in which syntactic rules are formed. These are the phrase structure rules (PSRs). Chapters 2 and 3 examine the words these rules use, the form of the rules, and the structures they generate. Chapters 4 and 5 look at ways we can detail the structure of the trees formed by the PSRs.

In chapters 6–9 (Part 2 of the book), we examine some data that present problems for the simple grammar presented in Part 1. When faced with more complicated data, we revise our hypotheses, and this is precisely what we do. We develop a special refined kind of PSR known as an X-bar rule. X-bar rules are still phrase structure rules, but they offer a more sophisticated way of looking at trees. This more sophisticated version also needs an additional constraint known as the "theta criterion", which is the focus of chapter 8.

In chapters 10–13 (Part 3) we consider even more data, and refine our hypothesis again, this time adding a new rule type: the transformation (we retain X-bar, but enrich it with transformations). Part 4 of the book (chapters 14–18) refines these proposals even further.

With each step we build upon our initial hypothesis, just as the scientific method tells us to. I've been teaching with this proposal–revision method of theory construction for a couple of years now, and every now and then I hear the complaint from a student that we should just start with the final answer (i.e. the revised hypotheses found in the later chapters in the book). Why bother learning all this "other" "wrong" stuff? Why should we bother learning phrase structure rules? Why don't we just jump straight into X-bar theory? Well, in principle, I could have constructed a book like that, but then you, the student, wouldn't understand *why* things are the way they are in the latter chapters. The theory would appear to be unmotivated, and you wouldn't understand what the technology actually does. By proposing a simple hypothesis early on in the initial chapters, and then refining and revising it, building new ideas onto old ones, you not only get an understanding of the motivations for and inner workings of our theoretical premises, but you get practice in working like a real linguist. Professional linguists, like all scientists, work from a set of simple hypotheses and revise them in light of predictions made by the hypotheses. The earlier versions of the theory aren't "wrong" so much as they need refinement and revision. These early versions represent the foundations out of which the rest of the theory has been built. This is how science works.

7. CONCLUSION

In this chapter, we've done very little syntax but talked a lot about the assumptions underlying the approach we're going to take to the study of sentence structure. The basic approach to syntax that we'll be using here is generative grammar; we've seen that this approach is scientific in that it uses the scientific method. It is descriptive and rule-based. Further, it assumes that a certain amount of grammar is built in and the rest is acquired.

IDEAS, RULES, AND CONSTRAINTS INTRODUCED IN THIS CHAPTER

i)   *Syntax*: The level of linguistic organization that mediates between sounds and meaning, where words are organized into phrases and sentences.

ii)   *Language (capital L)*: The psychological ability of humans to produce and understand a particular language. Also called the *Human Language Capacity* or *i-Language*. This is the object of study in this book.

iii)   *language (lower-case l)*: A language like English or French. These are the particular instances of the human Language. The data sources we use to examine Language are languages. Also called *e-language*.

iv)   *Generative Grammar*: A theory of linguistics in which grammar is viewed as a cognitive faculty. Language is generated by a set of rules or procedures. The version of generative grammar we are looking at here is primarily the *Principles and Parameters approach* (P&P) touching occasionally on *Minimalism.*

v)   *The Scientific Method*: Observe some data, make generalizations about that data, draw a hypothesis, test the hypothesis against more data.

vi)   *Falsifiable Prediction*: To prove that a hypothesis is correct you have to look for the data that would prove it *wrong*. The prediction that might prove a hypothesis wrong is said to be falsifiable.

vii)   *Grammar*: Not what you learned in school. This is the set of rules that generate a language.

viii)   *Prescriptive Grammar*: The grammar rules as taught by so-called "language experts". These rules, often inaccurate descriptively, prescribe how people should talk/write, rather than describe what they actually do.

ix)   *Descriptive Grammar*: A scientific grammar that describes, rather than prescribes, how people talk/write.

x)   *Anaphor*: A word that ends in *-self* or *-selves* (a better definition will be given in chapter 5).

xi)   *Antecedent*: The noun an anaphor refers to.

xii)   *Asterisk (*)*: The mark used to mark syntactically ill-formed (unacceptable or ungrammatical) sentences. The hash mark, pound, or number sign (#) is used to mark semantically strange, but syntactically well-formed, sentences.

xiii)   *Gender (grammatical)*: Masculine vs. Feminine vs. Neuter. Does not have to be identical to the actual sex of the referent. For example, a dog might be female, but we can refer to it with the neuter pronoun *it*. Similarly, boats don't have a sex, but are grammatically feminine.

xiv)   *Number*: The quantity of individuals or things described by a noun. English distinguishes singular (e.g., *a cat*) from plural (e.g., *cats*). Other languages have more or less complicated number systems.

xv)   *Person*: The perspective of the participants in the conversation. The speaker or speakers (*I, me, we, us*) are called the **first person**. The addressee(s) (*you*) is called the **second person**. Anyone else (those not involved in the conversation) (*he, him, she, her, it, they, them*) is referred to as the **third person**.

xvi)   *Case*: The form a noun takes depending upon its position in the sentence. We discuss this more in chapter 11.

xvii)   *Nominative*: The form of a noun in subject position (*I, you, he, she, it, we, they*).

xviii)   *Accusative*: The form of a noun in object position (*me, you, him, her, it, us, them*).

xix)   *Corpus (pl. Corpora)*: A collection of real-world language data.

xx)   *Native Speaker Judgments (Intuitions)*: Information about the subconscious knowledge of a language. This information is tapped by means of the grammaticality judgment task.

xxi)   *Semantic Judgment*: A judgment about the meaning of a sentence, often relying on our knowledge of the context in which the sentence was uttered.

xxii)   *Syntactic Judgment*: A judgment about the form or structure of a sentence.

xxiii)   *Garden Path Sentence:* A sentence with a strong ambiguity in structure that makes it hard to understand.

xxiv)   *Center Embedding:* A sentence in which a relative clause consisting of a subject and a verb is placed between the main clause subject and verb. E.g., *The house [Bill built] leans to the left.*

xxv)   *Parsing:* The mental tools a listener uses to process and understand a sentence.

xxvi) *Competence*: What you know about your language.

xxvii) *Performance*: The real-world behaviors that are a consequence of what you know about your language.

xxviii) *Learning*: The gathering of conscious knowledge (like linguistics or chemistry).

xxix) *Acquisition*: The gathering of subconscious information (like language).

xxx) *Innate*: Hard-wired or built-in, an instinct.

xxxi) *Recursion*: The ability to embed structures iteratively inside one another. Allows us to produce sentences we've never heard before.

xxxii) *Universal Grammar (UG)*: The innate (or instinctual) part of each language's grammar.

xxxiii) *The Logical Problem of Language Acquisition*: The proof that an infinite system like human language cannot be learned on the basis of observed data – an argument for UG.

xxxiv) *Underdetermination of the Data*: The idea that we know things about our language that we could not have possibly learned – an argument for UG.

xxxv) *Universal*: A property found in all the languages of the world.

xxxvi) *Bioprogram Hypothesis:* The idea that creole languages share similar features because of an innate basic setting for language.

xxxvii) *Observationally Adequate Grammar*: A grammar that accounts for observed real-world data (such as corpora).

xxxviii) *Descriptively Adequate Grammar*: A grammar that accounts for observed real-world data and native speaker judgments.

xxxix) *Explanatorily Adequate Grammar*: A grammar that accounts for observed real-world data and native speaker judgments and offers an explanation for the facts of language acquisition.

FURTHER READING: Baker (2001b), Barsky (1997), Bickerton (1984), Chomsky (1965), Jackendoff (1993), Pinker (1995), Sampson (1997), Uriagereka (1998)

GENERAL PROBLEM SETS

GPS1. PRESCRIPTIVE RULES
[Creative and Critical Thinking; Basic]
In the text above, we claimed that descriptive rules are the primary focus of syntactic theory. This doesn't mean that prescriptive rules don't have their uses. What are these uses? Why do societies have prescriptive rules?

GPS2. OBLIGATORY SPLIT INFINITIVES
[Creative and Critical Thinking, Analysis; Intermediate]
The linguist Arnold Zwicky has observed[11] that the prescription not to split infinitives can result in utterly ungrammatical sentences. The adverb *soon* can be reasonably placed before the infinitive (a) or after it (b) and, for most native speakers of English, also in the split infinitive (c):

a)   I expect soon to see the results.
b)   I expect to see the results soon.
c)   I expect to soon see the results.

Zwicky notes that certain modifiers like *more than* or *already* when used with a verb like *to double,* obligatorily appear in a split infinitive construction (g). Putting them anywhere else results in the ungrammatical[12] sentences (d–f):

d)   *I expect more than to double my profits.
e)   *I expect to double more than my profits.
f)   *I expect to double my profits more than.
g)   I expect to more than double my profits.

Explain in your own words what this tells us about the validity of prescriptive rules such as "Don't split infinitives". Given these facts, how much stock should linguists put in prescriptive rules if they are following the scientific method?

GPS3. JUDGMENTS
[Application of Skills; Intermediate]
All of the following sentences have been claimed to be ungrammatical or unacceptable by someone at some time. For each sentence,

i)   indicate whether this unacceptability is due to a prescriptive or a descriptive judgment, and
ii)   for all descriptive judgments indicate whether the ungrammaticality has to do with syntax or semantics (or both).

One- or two-word answers are appropriate. If you are not a native speaker of English, enlist the help of someone who is. If you are not familiar with the *prescriptive* rules of English grammar, you may want to consult a writing guide or English grammar or look at Pinker's *The Language Instinct.*

a)   Who did you see in Las Vegas?
b)   You are taller than me.
c)   My red is refrigerator.

---

[11] http://itre.cis.upenn.edu/~myl/languagelog/archives/000901.html.
[12] To be entirely accurate, (d) and (e) aren't wholly ill-formed; they just can't mean what (g) does. (d) can mean "I expect something else too, not just to double my profits" and (e) can mean "I expect to double something else too, not just my profits." The * marks of ungrammaticality are for the intended reading identical to that of (g).

d)   Who do you think that saw Bill?
e)   Hopefully, we'll make it through the winter without snow.
f)   My friends wanted to quickly leave the party.
g)   Bunnies carrots eat.
h)   John's sister is not his sibling.

GPS4. LEARNING VS. ACQUISITION
[Creative and Critical Thinking; Basic]
We have distinguished between learning and acquiring knowledge. Learning is conscious; acquisition is automatic and subconscious. (Note that acquired things are *not* necessarily innate. They are just subconsciously obtained.) Other than language, are there other things we acquire? What other things do we learn? What about walking? Or reading? Or sexual identity? An important point in answering this question is to talk about what kind of evidence is necessary to distinguish between learning and acquisition.

GPS5. UNIVERSALS
[Creative and Critical Thinking; Intermediate]
Pretend for a moment that you don't believe Chomsky and that you don't believe in the innateness of syntax (but only *pretend*!). How might you account for the existence of universals (see definition above) across languages?

GPS6. INNATENESS
[Creative and Critical Thinking; Intermediate]
We argued that some amount of syntax is innate (inborn). Can you think of an argument that might be raised against innateness? (It doesn't have to be an argument that works, just a plausible one.) Alternately, could you come up with a hypothetical experiment that could *disprove* innateness? What would such an experiment have to show? Remember that cross-linguistic variation (differences between languages) is *not* an argument against innateness or UG, because UG contains parameters that allow variation within the set of possibilities allowed for in UG.

GPS7. LEVELS OF ADEQUACY
[Application of Skills; Basic]
Below, you'll find the description of several different linguists' work. Attribute a level of adequacy to them (state whether the grammars they developed are observationally adequate, descriptively adequate, or explanatorily adequate). Explain *why* you assigned the level of adequacy that you did.

a)   Juan Martínez has been working with speakers of Chicano English in the barrios of Los Angeles. He has been looking both at corpora (rap music, recorded snatches of speech) and working with adult native speakers.

b) Fredrike Schwarz has been looking at the structure of sentences in eleventh-century Welsh poems. She has been working at the national archives of Wales in Cardiff.

c) Boris Dimitrov has been working with adults and corpora on the formation of questions in Rhodopian Bulgarian. He is also conducting a longitudinal study of some two-year-old children learning the language to test his hypotheses.

CHALLENGE PROBLEM SETS

Challenge Problem Sets are special exercises that either challenge the presentation of the main text or offer significant enrichment. Students are encouraged to complete the other problem sets before trying the Challenge Sets. Challenge Sets can vary in level from interesting puzzles to downright impossible conundrums. Try your best!

CHALLENGE PROBLEM SET 1: PRESCRIPTIVISM
[Creative and Critical Thinking; Challenge]
The linguist Geoff Pullum reports[13] that he heard Alex Chadwick say the sentence below on the National Public Radio Show "Day to Day". This sentence has an interesting example of a split infinitive in it:

> But still, the policy of the Army at that time was not to send – was specifically to **not** send – women into combat roles.

Here, Mr. Chadwick corrects himself from not splitting an infinitive (*was not to send*) to a form where the word *not* appears between *to* and *send*, thus creating a classic violation of this prescriptive rule. One might wonder why he would correct the sentence in the wrong direction. Pullum observes that the two versions mean quite different things. *The policy was not to send women into combat* means that it was not the policy to send women into combat (i.e. negating the existence of such a policy). The sentence with the split infinitive by contrast, means that there was a policy and it was that they didn't send women into combat. It's a subtle but important distinction in the discussion. Note that putting the *not* after *send* would have rendered the sentence utterly unintelligible. With this background in mind, provide an argument that linguists should probably ignore prescriptive rules if they're trying to model real human language.

CHALLENGE PROBLEM SET 2: ANAPHORA
[Creative and Critical Thinking, Data Analysis; Challenge]
In this chapter, as an example of the scientific method, we looked at the distribution of anaphora (nouns like *himself, herself,* etc.). We came to the following conclusion about their distribution:

---

[13] http://itre.cis.upenn.edu/~myl/languagelog/archives/002180.html.

An anaphor must agree in person, gender, and number with its antecedent.

However, there is much more to say about the distribution of these nouns (in fact, chapter 5 of this book is entirely devoted to the question).

Part 1: Consider the data below. Can you make an addition to the above statement that explains the distribution of anaphors and antecedents in the very limited data below?

a) Geordi sang to himself.
b) *Himself sang to Geordi.
c) Betsy loves herself in blue leather.
d) *Blue leather shows herself that Betsy is pretty.

Part 2: Now consider the following sentences:[14]

e) Everyone should be able to defend himself/herself/themselves.
f)   I hope nobody will hurt themselves/himself/?herself.

Do these sentences obey your revised generalization? Why or why not? Is there something special about the antecedents that forces an exception here, or can you modify your generalization to fit these cases?

CHALLENGE PROBLEM SET 3: YOURSELF
[Creative and Critical Thinking; Challenge]
In the main body of the text we claimed that all anaphors need an antecedent. Consider the following acceptable sentence. This kind of sentence is called an "imperative" and is used to give orders.

a) Don't hit yourself!

Part 1: Are all anaphors allowed in sentences like (a)? Which ones are allowed there, and which ones aren't?

Part 2: Where is the antecedent for *yourself*? Is this a counterexample to our rule? Why is this rule an exception? It is easy to add a stipulation to our rule; but we'd rather have an explanatory rule. What is special about the sentence in (a)?

CHALLENGE PROBLEM SET 4: CONSTRUCT AN EXPERIMENT
[Creative and Critical Thinking; Challenge]
Linguists have observed that when the subject of a sentence is close to the verb, the verb will invariably agree with that subject.

a)   She is dancing
b)   They are dancing
c)   The man is dancing
d)   The men are dancing

---

[14] Thanks to Ahmad Lotfi for suggesting this part of the question.

But under certain circumstances this tight verb–subject agreement relation is weakened (sentence taken from Bock and Miller 1991).

e)   The readiness of our conventional forces are at an all-time low.

The subject of the sentence *readiness* is singular but the verb seems to agree with the plural *forces*. The predicted form is:

f)   The readiness of our conventional forces is at an all-time low.

One hypothesis about this is that the intervening noun (*forces*) blocks the agreement with the actual subject noun *readiness*.

        Construct an experiment that would test this hypothesis. What kind of data would you need to confirm or deny this hypothesis? How would you gather these data?

CHALLENGE PROBLEM SET 5: JUDGMENTS[15]
[Data Analysis and Application of Skills; Challenge]
Consider the following sentences:
a)   i.   The students met to discuss the project.
        ii.   The student met to discuss the project.
        iii.   The class met to discuss the project.
b)   i.   Zeke cooked and ate the chili.
        ii.   Zeke ate and cooked the chili.
c)   i.   He put the clothes.
        ii.   He put in the washing machine.
        iii.   He put the clothes in the washing machine.
        iv.   He put in the washing machine the clothes.
d)   i.   I gave my brother a birthday present.
        ii.   I gave a birthday present to my brother.
        iii.   That horror movie almost gave my brother a heart attack.
        iv.   That horror movie almost gave a heart attack to my brother.
e)   Where do you guys live at?
f)   i.   It is obvious to everybody that Tasha likes Misha.
        ii.   The fact that Tasha likes Misha is obvious to everybody.
        iii.   Who is it obvious that Tasha likes?[16]
        iv.   Who is the fact that Tasha likes obvious?

Some of these sentences would be judged acceptable by all (or nearly all) speakers of English, while other sentences would be judged unacceptable by at least some speakers. Find at least five native English speakers and elicit an acceptability judgment for each of these sentences (present the sentences to your speakers orally, rather than having them read them off the

---

[15] This problem set is thanks to Matt Pearson.

[16] The intended meaning for (iii) and (iv) is "Who is the person such that it is obvious that Tasha likes that person?" Or paraphrased another way: "It's obvious that Tasha likes somebody. Who is that somebody?"

page). Give the results of your elicitation in the form of a table. Discuss how your consultants' reactions compare with your own native speaker judgments. If a sentence is judged unacceptable by most or all speakers, what do you think is the source of the unacceptability? Choose from the options listed below, and briefly explain and justify each choice. Are there any sentences for which it is difficult to determine the reason for the unacceptability, and if so, why?

- The sentence is **ungrammatical** in the linguistic sense: It would not be produced by a fully competent native speaker of English under any context, and is unlikely to be uttered except as a performance error. It should be marked with a *.
- The sentence is **marginally grammatical**. One could imagine a native speaker saying this sentence, but it seems less than perfect syntactically, and should probably be marked with a **?** or **??**.
- The sentence is fully grammatical in the linguistic sense, but only in *some* varieties of English. It is likely to be treated as 'incorrect' or 'poor style' by some speakers because it belongs to a **stigmatized variety** (an informal or colloquial register, or a non-standard dialect), and is not part of formal written English. We might choose to indicate this with a **%**.
- The sentence is syntactically well-formed, but **semantically anomalous**: It cannot be assigned a coherent interpretation based on the (normal) meanings of its component words, and should be marked with a **#**.

CHALLENGE PROBLEM SET 6: COMPETENCE VS. PERFORMANCE
[Creative and Critical Thinking; Extra Challenge]
Performance refers to a set of behaviors; competence refers to the knowledge that underlies that behavior. We've talked about it for language, but can you think about other cognitive systems or behaviors where we might see examples of this distinction? What are they? Grammaticality judgments work for determining the competence underlying language; how might a cognitive scientist explore competence in other domains?

CHALLENGE PROBLEM SET 7: IS LANGUAGE REALLY INFINITE?
[Creative and Critical Thinking; Extra Challenge]
> [***Note to instructors***: this question requires some background in either formal logic or mathematical proofs.]

In the text, it was claimed that because language is recursive, it follows that it is infinite. (This was premise (i) of the discussion in section 4.3.) The idea is straightforward and at least intuitively correct: if you have some well-formed sentence, and you have a rule that can embed it inside another structure, then you can also take this new structure and embed it inside another and so on and so on. Intuitively this leads to an infinitely large number of possible sentences. Pullum and Scholz (2005) have claimed that one formal version of this intuitive idea is either circular or a contradiction.

Here is the structure of the traditional argument (paraphrased and simplified from the version in Pullum and Scholz). This proof is cast in such a way that the way we count the number of sentences is by comparing the number of words in the sentence. If for *any* (extremely high) number of words, we can find a longer sentence, then we know the set is infinite. First some terminology:

➢   *Terminology:* call the set of well-formed sentences *E*. If a sentence *x* is an element of this set we write *E(x)*.
➢   *Terminology:* let us refer to the length of a sentence by counting the number of words in it. The number of words in a sentence is expressed by the variable *n*. There is a special measurement operation (function) which counts the number of words. This is called μ. If the sentence called *x* has 4 words in it then we say $\mu(x) = 4$.

Next the formal argument:

Premise 1: There is at least one well-formed sentence that has more than zero words in it.
$$\exists x[E(x) \ \& \ \mu(x) > 0]$$
Premise 2: There is an operation in the PSRs such that any sentence may be embedded in another with more words in it. That means for any sentence in the language, there is another longer sentence. (If some expression has the length *n*, then some other well-formed sentence has a size greater than *n*).
$$\forall n \ [\exists x[E(x) \ \& \ \mu(x) = n]] \rightarrow [\exists y[E(y) \ \& \ \mu(y) > n]]$$

Conclusion: Therefore for every positive integer *n*, there are well-formed sentences with a length longer than *n* (i.e., the set of well-formed English expressions is at least countably infinite):
$$\therefore \forall n \ [\exists y[E(y) \ \& \ \mu(y) > n]]$$

Pullum and Scholz claim that the problem with this argument lies with the nature of the set E. Sets come of two kinds: there are finite sets which have a fixed number of elements (e.g. the set {a, b, c, d} has 4 and exactly 4 members). There are also infinite sets, which have an endless possible number of members (e.g., the set {a, b, c, ... } has an infinite number of elements).

Question 1: Assume that E, the set of well-formed sentences, is finite. This is a contradiction of one of the two premises given above. Which one? Why is it a contradiction?

Question 2: Assume that E, the set of well-formed sentences, is infinite. This leads to a circularity in the argument. What is the circularity (i.e., why is the proof circular)?

Question 3: If the logical argument is either contradictory or circular what does that make of our claim that the number of sentences possible in a language is infinite? Is it totally wrong? What does the proof given immediately above really prove?

Question 4: Given that E can be neither a finite nor an infinite set, is there any way we might recast the premises, terminology, or conclusion in order not to have a circular argument and at the same time capture the intuitive insight of the claim? Explain how we might do this or why it's impossible. Try to be creative. There is no "right" answer to this question. Hint: one might try a proof that proves that a subset of the sentences of English is infinite (and by definition the entire set of sentences in English is infinite) or one might try a proof by contradiction.

Important notes:
1) Your answers can be given in English prose; you do not need to give a formal mathematical answer.
2) Do not try to look up the answer in the papers cited above. That's just cheating! Try to work out the answers for yourself.

CHALLENGE PROBLEM SET 8: ARE INFINITE SYSTEMS REALLY UNLEARNABLE?
[Creative and Critical Thinking; Challenge]
In section 4.3, you saw the claim that if language is an infinite system then it must be unlearnable. In this problem set, you should aim a critical eye at the premise that infinite systems can't be learned on the basis of the data you hear.

While the extreme view in section 4.3 is logically true, consider the following alternative possibilities:

a) We as humans have some kind of "cut-off mechanism" that stops considering new data after we've heard some threshold number of examples. If we don't hear the crucial example after some period of time we simply assume it doesn't exist. Rules simply can't exist that require access to sentence types so rare that you don't hear them before the cut-off point.

b) We are purely statistical engines. Rare sentence types are simply ignored as "statistical noise". We consider only those sentences that are frequent in the input when constructing our rules.

c) Child-directed speech (motherese) is specially designed to give you precisely the kinds of data you need to construct your rule system. The child listens for very specific "triggers" or "cues" in the parental input in order to determine the rules.

Question 1: To what extent are (a), (b), or (c) compatible with the hypothesis of Universal Grammar? If (a), (b) or (c) turned out to be true, would this mean that there was no innate grammar? Explain your answer.

Question 2: How might you experimentally or observationally distinguish between (a), (b), (c) and the infinite input hypothesis of 4.3? What kinds of evidence would you need to tell them apart?

Question 3: When people speak, they make errors. (They switch words around, they mispronounce things, they use the wrong word, they stop mid-sentence without completing what they are saying, etc.) Nevertheless children seem to be able to ignore these errors and still come up with the right set of rules. Is this fact compatible with any of the alternative hypotheses: (a), (b), or (c)?

CHALLENGE PROBLEM SET 9: INNATENESS AND PRESCRIPTIVISM?
[Creative and Critical Thinking; Challenge]
Start with the assumption that Language is an instinct. How is this an argument against using prescriptive rules?

CHALLENGE PROBLEM SET 10: LEARNING PARAMETERS: PRO-DROP
[Critical Thinking, Data Analysis; Challenge]
Background: Among the Indo-European languages there are two large groups of languages that pattern differently with respect to whether they require a pronoun (like *he, she, it*) in the subject position, or whether such pronouns can be "dropped". For example, in both English and French, pronouns are required. Sentences without them are usually ungrammatical:

a) He left   b) *Left
c) Il est parti   (French)   d) *est parti   (French)
    he is gone
    "he left"

In languages such as Spanish and Italian, however, such pronouns are routinely omitted (1s = first person, singular):

e) Io telefono   f) telefono   (Italian)
    I call.1s   call.1s
    "I call (phone)"   "I call"

Question 1: Now imagine that you are a small child learning a language. What kind of data would you need to know in order to tell if your language was "pro-drop" or not? (Hint: Does the English child hear sentences both with and without subjects? Does the Italian child? Are they listening for sentences with subjects or without them?)

Question 2: Assume that one of the two possible settings for this parameter (either your language is pro-drop or it is not) is the "default" setting. This default setting is the version of the parameter one gets if one doesn't hear the right kind of input. Which of the two possibilities is the default?

Question 3: English has imperative constructions such as:

g) Leave now!

Why doesn't the English child assume on the basis of such sentences that English is pro-drop?

chapter 2

Parts of Speech

Learning Objectives

After reading chapter 2 you should walk away having mastered the following ideas and skills:

1. Distinguish between distributional and semantic definitions of parts of speech.
2. Identify a part of speech by its distribution.
3. Identify cases of complementary distribution.
4. Know the difference between an open-class and a closed-class part of speech.
5. Explain the difference between lexical and functional categories.
6. Identify different subcategories using feature notations.
7. Identify plural nouns, mass nouns and count nouns and distinguish them with features.
8. Explain the difference between predicates and arguments.
9. Categorize verbs according to their argument structure (intransitive, transitive, ditransitive) and represent this using features.

Syntax: A Generative Introduction, Third Edition. Andrew Carnie.
© 2013 Andrew Carnie. Published 2013 by John Wiley & Sons, Inc.

0. WORDS AND WHY THEY MATTER TO SYNTAX

It goes without saying that sentences are made up of words, so before we get into the syntactic meat of this book, it's worth looking carefully at different kinds of words.

What is most important to us here is the word's **part of speech** (also known as **syntactic category** or **word class**). The most common parts of speech are **nouns, verbs, adjectives, adverbs,** and **prepositions** (we will also look at some other, less familiar parts of speech below). Parts of speech tell us how a word is going to function in the sentence. Consider the sentences in (1). Notice that we can substitute various words that are of the type *noun* for the second word in the sentence:

1) a) The *man* loved peanut butter cookies.
   b) The *puppy* loved peanut butter cookies.
   c) The *king* loved peanut butter cookies.

However, we cannot substitute words that aren't nouns:[1]

2) a) *The *green* loved peanut butter cookies.
   b) *The *in* loved peanut butter cookies.
   c) *The *sing* loved peanut butter cookies.

The same holds true for larger groups of words (the square brackets [...] mark off the relevant groups of words).

3) a) *[John]* went to the store.
   b) *[The man]* went to the store.
   c) *[Quickly walks] went to the store.

4) a) *[Norvel]* kissed the Blarney stone.
   b) *[To the washroom] kissed the Blarney stone.

If we have categories for words that can appear in certain positions and categories for those that don't, we can make generalizations (scientific ones) about the behavior of different word types. This is why we need parts of speech in syntactic theory.

---

[1] Remember, the * symbol means that a sentence is syntactically ill-formed.

1. DETERMINING PART OF SPEECH

1.1 The Problem of Traditional Definitions

If you were taught any grammar in school, you may have been told that a noun is a "person, place, or thing", or that a verb is "an action, state, or state of being". Alas, this is a very over-simplistic way to characterize various parts of speech. It also isn't terribly scientific or accurate. The first thing to notice about definitions like this is that they are based on semantic criteria. It doesn't take much effort to find counterexamples to these semantic definitions. Consider the following:

5) The *destruction* of the city bothered the Mongols.

The meaning of *destruction* is *not* a "person, place, or thing". It is an action. By semantic criteria, this word should be a verb. But in fact, native speakers unanimously identify it as a noun. Similar cases are seen in (6):

6) a) *Sincerity* is an important quality.
    b) the *assassination* of the president
    c) *Tucson* is a great place to live.

Sincerity is an attribute, a property normally associated with adjectives. Yet in (6a), *sincerity* is a noun. Similarly in (6b) *assassination*, an action, is functioning as a noun. (6c) is more subtle. The semantic property of identifying a location is usually attributed to a preposition; in (6c) however, the noun *Tucson* refers to a location, but isn't itself a preposition. It thus seems difficult (if not impossible) to rigorously define the parts of speech based solely on semantic criteria. This is made even clearer when we see that a word can change its part of speech depending upon where it appears in a sentence:

7) a) Gabrielle's *mother* is an axe-murderer.   (N)
    b) Anteaters *mother* attractive offspring.   (V)
    c) Wendy's *mother* country is Iceland.   (Adj)

The situation gets even muddier when we consider languages other than English. Consider the following data from Warlpiri:

8) Wita-ngku ka   maliki wajilipinyi.
    small-SUBJ AUX dog   chase.PRES
    "The small (one) is chasing the dog."

In this sentence, we have a thing we'd normally call an adjective (the word *wita* "small") functioning like a noun (e.g., taking subject marking). Is this a noun or an adjective?

It's worth noting that some parts of speech don't lend themselves to semantic definitions at all. Consider the sentence in (9). What is the meaning of the word *that*?

9)   Mikaela said that parts of speech intrigued her.

If parts of speech are based on the meaning of the word, how can we assign a part of speech to a word for which the meaning isn't clear?[2]

Perhaps the most striking evidence that we can't use semantic definitions for parts of speech comes from the fact that you can know the part of speech of a word without even knowing what it means:

10) The yinkish dripner blorked quastofically into the nindin with the pidibs.

Every native speaker of English will tell you that *yinkish* is an adjective, *dripner* a noun, *blorked* a verb, *quastofically* an adverb, and *nindin* and *pidibs* both nouns, but they'd be very hard pressed to tell you what these words actually mean. How then can you know the part of speech of a word without knowing its meaning? The answer is simple: The various parts of speech are not semantically defined. Instead they depend on where the words appear in the sentence and what kinds of affixes they take. Nouns are things that appear in "noun positions" and take "noun suffixes" (endings). The same is true for verbs, adjectives, etc. Here are the criteria that we used to determine the parts of speech in sentence (10):

11) a) yinkish   between *the* and a noun
                           takes *-ish* adjective ending
    b) dripner   after an adjective (and *the*)
                           takes *-er* noun ending
                           subject of the sentence
    c) blorked   after subject noun
                           takes *-ed* verb ending
    d) quastofically   after a verb
                           takes *-ly* adverb ending
    e) nindin   after *the* and after a preposition
    f) pidibs   after *the* and after a preposition
                           takes *-s* noun plural ending

---

[2] Be careful here: the *function* of the word is clear (it is used to subordinate clauses inside of sentences) but it doesn't have an obvious *meaning* with respect to the real world.

The part of speech of a word is determined by its place in the sentence and by its morphology, *not* by its meaning. In the next section, there is a list of rules and distributional criteria that you can use to determine the part of speech of a word.

1.2 Distributional Criteria

The criteria we use for determining part of speech then aren't based on the meanings of the word, but on its **distribution**. We will use two kinds of distributional tests for determining part of speech: morphological distribution and syntactic distribution.

First we look at **morphological distribution**; this refers to the kinds of affixes (prefixes and suffixes) and other morphology that appear on a word. Let's consider two different types of affixes. First, we have affixes that make words out of other words. We call these affixes **derivational morphemes**. These suffixes usually result in a different part of speech from the word they attach to. For example, if we take the word *distribute* we can add the derivational suffix *-(t)ion* and we get the noun *distribution*. The *-(t)ion* affix thus creates nouns. Any word ending in *-(t)ion* is a noun. This is an example of a morphological distribution. A similar example is found with the affix *-al*, which creates adjectives. If we take *distribution*, and add *-al* to it, we get the adjective *distributional*. The *-al* ending is a test for being an adjective. Derivational affixes make a word a particular category; by contrast **inflectional morphemes** don't *make* a word into a particular category, but instead only *attach* to certain categories. Take for example the superlative suffix *-est*. This affix only attaches to words that are already adjectives: *big, biggest* (cf. *dog, *doggest*). Because they are sensitive to what category they attach to, inflectional suffixes can also serve as a test for determining part of speech category.

The other kind of test we use for determining part of speech uses **syntactic distribution**. Syntactic distribution refers to what other words appear near the word. For example, nouns typically appear after determiners (articles) such as *the*, although they need not do so to be nouns. We can thus take appearance after *the* to be a test for noun-hood.

Something to Think About: Circularity
In section 1 of this chapter, it was claimed that we needed parts of speech to help us determine where in the sentence a word appeared. So for example, we know that verbs and adjectives in English don't function as the subjects of sentences. Above we have given one test for part of speech category in terms of the word's distribution in the sentence. Here's something to think about. Have we created a circular argument: category determines position in the sentence and the position in the sentence determines category? Is this really circular? Does it matter?

2. THE MAJOR PARTS OF SPEECH: N, V, ADJ, AND ADV

Having determined that we are going to use distributional criteria for determining the part of speech of a word, we'll now turn to some tests for particular lexical items. We'll limit ourselves to the major classes of noun (N), verb (V), adjective (Adj), and adverb (Adv). We'll look at other parts of speech in later sections.

One thing that you'll notice is that these are specific to English. Every language will have its own distributional criteria. For each language linguists have to develop lists like the ones below.[3]

A final word of qualification is in order. Not every test will work in every situation, so it is usually best to use multiple morphological and syntactic tests for any given word if you can.

2.1 Nouns

Derivational Suffixes: In English, nouns often end in derivational endings such as -ment (basement), -ness (friendliness), -ity (sincerity), -ty (certainty), -(t)ion (devotion), -ation (expectation), -ist (specialist), -ant (attendant), -ery (shrubbery), -ee (employee), -ship (hardship), -aire (billionaire), -acy (advocacy), -let (piglet), -ling (underling), -hood (neighborhood), -ism (socialism), -ing (fencing).

Inflectional Suffixes: Nouns in English don't show much inflection, but when pluralized can take suffixes such as -s (cats), -es (glasses), -en (oxen), -ren (children), -i (cacti), -a (addenda).

---

[3] The lists in this section are based on the discussions of English morphology found in Katamba (2004) and Harley (2006).

Note that the following endings have homophonous usage with other parts of speech: -*ing*, -*s*, '*s*, -*er*, -*en*, but also sometimes are found on nouns.

Syntactic Distribution: Nouns often appear after determiners such as *the*, *those*, *these* (e.g., *these peanuts*), and can appear after adjectives (*the big peanut*). Nouns can also follow prepositions (*in school*). All of these conditions can happen together (*in the big gymnasium*). Nouns can appear as the subject of the sentence (we will define subject rigorously in a later chapter): *The syntax paper was incomprehensible*; or as the direct object: *I read the syntax paper*. Nouns can be negated by *no* (as opposed to *not* or *un-*): *No apples were eaten.*

One easy way to see if something is a noun is to see if you can replace it with another word that is clearly a noun. So if we want to see if the word *people* is a noun or not, we can substitute another word we know for sure to be a noun, e.g., *John* in *I saw people running all over the place* vs. *I saw John running all over the place).*

2.2 *Verbs*

Derivational Suffixes: Verbs often end in derivational endings such as -*ate* (*dissipate*), and -*ize*/-*ise* (*regularize*).

Inflectional Suffixes: In the past tense, verbs usually take an -*ed* or -*t* ending. In the present tense, third person singular (*he, she, it*), they usually take the -*s* ending. Verbs can also take an -*ing* ending in some aspectual constructions, (*she was walking*) and most take either an -*en* or an -*ed* suffix when they are passivized (more on passivization in later chapters): *the ice cream was eaten.*

Note that the following endings have homophonous usage with other parts of speech: -*ing*, -*s*, -*en*, -*ed.*

Syntactic Distribution: Verbs can follow auxiliaries and modals such as *will*, *have, having, had, has, am, be, been, being, is, are, were, was, would, can, could, shall, should, may, must*, and the special non-finite marker *to*. Verbs follow subjects, and can follow adverbs such as *often* and *frequently*. Verbs can be negated with *not* (as opposed to *no* and *un-*[4]).

2.3 *Adjectives*

Derivational Suffixes: Adjectives often end in derivational endings such as -*ing* (*the dancing cat*), -*ive* (*indicative*), -*able* (*readable*), -*al* (*traditional*),

---

[4] There are verbs that begin with *un-*, but in these circumstances *un-* usually means "reverse", not negation.

-ate (intimate), -ish (childish), -some (tiresome), -(i)an (reptilian), -ful (wishful), -less (selfless), -ly (friendly).

Inflectional Suffixes: Adjectives can be inflected into a comparative form using *-er* (alternately they follow the word *more*). They can also be inflected into their superlative form using *-est* (alternately they follow the word *most*). Adjectives are typically negated using the prefix *un-* (in its sense meaning "not", not in its sense meaning "undo").

Note that the following affixes have homophonous usage with other parts of speech: *-ing, -er, -en, -ed, un-, -ly*.

Syntactic Distribution: Adjectives can appear between determiners such as *the, a, these*, etc. and nouns (*the big peanut*). They also can follow the auxiliary *am/is/are/was/were/be/been/being* (warning: this distribution overlaps with verbs). Frequently, adjectives can be modified by the adverb *very* (warning: this distribution overlaps with adverbs).

You now have enough information to try CPS 1 & 2.

2.4 Adverbs

Derivational Suffixes: Many adverbs end in *-ly*: *quickly, frequently*, etc.

Inflectional Suffixes: Adverbs generally don't take any inflectional suffixes. However, on rare occasions they can be used comparatively and follow the word *more*: *She went more quickly than he did.* Adverbs typically don't take the prefix *un-* unless the adjective they are derived from does first (e.g., *unhelpfully* from *unhelpful*, but **unquickly, *unquick*).

Syntactic Distribution: The syntactic distribution of adverbs is most easily described by stating where they can't appear. Adverbs can't appear between a determiner and a noun (**the quickly fox*) or after the verb *is* and its variants.[5] They can really appear pretty much anywhere else in the sentence, although typically they appear at either the beginning or the end of the clause/sentence. Frequently, like adjectives, they can be modified by the adverb *very*.

You now have enough information to answer WBE 1 & 2 and GPS 1–6.

---

[5] In some prescriptive variants of English, there is a limited set of adverbs that can appear after *is*. For example, *well* is prescriptively preferred over *good*, in such constructions as *I am well* vs. *I am good* (referring to your state of being rather than the acceptability of your behavior). Most speakers of American English don't allow any adverbs after *is*.

Adjectives and Adverbs: Part of the Same Category?
Look carefully at the distributions of adjectives and adverbs. There is a great deal of overlap between them. Adverbs typically take *-ly*; however, there are a number of clear adjectives that take this suffix too (e.g., *the friendly cub*). Both Adj and Adv can be modified by the word *very*, and they both have the same basic function in the grammar – to attribute properties to the items they modify. In fact, the only major distinction between them is syntactic: Adjectives appear inside NPs, while adverbs appear elsewhere. This kind of phenomenon is called *complementary distribution*. (Where you get an adjective vs. an adverb is entirely predictable.) When two elements are in complementary distribution in linguistics, we normally think of them as variants of the same basic category. For example, when two sounds in phonology are in complementary distribution, we say they are allophones of the same phoneme. We might extend this analysis to parts of speech: There is one "supercategory" labeled "A" that has two subcategories in it (allo-parts-of-speech, if you will): Adj and Adv. In this book we'll stick with the traditional Adj and Adv categories, simply because they are familiar to most people. But you should keep in mind that the category A (including both adjectives and adverbs) might provide a better analysis and might be better motivated scientifically.

3. OPEN VS. CLOSED; LEXICAL VS. FUNCTIONAL

3.1 *Open vs. Closed Parts of Speech*

Some parts of speech allow you to add neologisms (new words). For example, imagine I invented a new tool especially for the purpose of removing spines from cacti, and I called this tool a *pulfice*. This kind of word is easily learned and adopted by speakers of English. In fact, we might even predict that speakers would take *pulfice* and develop a verb *pulficize*, which means to remove cactus spines using a *pulfice*. New words may be coined at any time, if they are open class (e.g., *fax, internet, grody*). By contrast there are some parts of speech that don't allow new forms. Suppose I wanted to describe a situation where one arm is under the table and another is over the table, and I called this new preposition *uvder*: *My arms are uvder the table*. It's fairly unlikely that my new preposition, no matter how useful it is, will be adopted into the language. Parts of speech that allow new members are said to be *open class*. Those that don't (or where coinages are very rare) are *closed class*. All of the cases that we've looked at so far have been open class parts of speech.

3.2 Lexical vs. Functional

The open/closed distinction is similar to (but not identical to) another useful distinction in parts of speech. This is the distinction between lexical and functional parts of speech. *Lexical* parts of speech provide the "content" of the sentence. Nouns, verbs, adjectives, and adverbs are all lexical parts of speech. *Functional* parts of speech, by contrast, provide the grammatical information. Functional items are the "glue" that holds a sentence together. One way to tell if a lexical item is functional or lexical is to see if it is left behind in "telegraphic speech" (that is, the way a telegram would be written; e.g., *Brian bring computer! Disaster looms!*). Functional categories include determiners, prepositions, complementizers, conjunctions, negation, auxiliaries, and modals. We will detail some of these below in section 3.3.

You now have enough information to answer WPS 3, GPS 7, and CPS 3.

3.3 Some Functional (Closed) Categories of English

We'll survey here some of the main functional categories of English. This list is by no means complete. While it is possible to provide distributional definitions for various functional parts of speech, because they are closed class there are relatively few members of each class, so it's possible to simply list most of them.

We'll start our categorization with *prepositions* (abbreviated P). Prepositions appear before nouns (or more precisely, noun phrases). English prepositions include the following:

12) *Prepositions of English* (P): to, from, under, over, with, by, at, above, before, after, through, near, on, off, for, in, into, of, during, across, without, since, until.

The class of *determiners* (D) is a little broader. It contains a number of subcategories including articles, quantifiers, numerals, deictics, and possessive pronouns. Determiners appear at the very beginning of English noun phrases.

13) *Determiners of English* (D)
    a)   *Articles:* the, a, an
    b)   *Deictic articles:* this, that, these, those, yon

   c)   *Quantifiers:*[6] every, some, many, most, few, all, each, any, less, fewer, no
   d)   *(Cardinal) numerals:* one, two, three, four, etc.
   e)   *Possessive pronouns:*[7] my, your, his, her, its, our, their
   f)   *Some wh-question words:* which, whose

You now have enough information to answer WBE 4 & 5.

Are Numerals of Category D or Adj?

Cardinal numerals, in phrases like *two books*, seem to function like quantifiers like *all* or *few* at least in terms of their function as counting elements. In the case of *one big book*, the *one* can stand in place of an obligatory determiner (normally we'd require a determiner like *a* or *the* -- leaving off the determiner makes the phrase ungrammatical (**big book*). This suggests, then, that numerals are of category D. However, consider the case of *these two books*. In this phrase, the numeral functions more like an adjective, in that it appears between the deictic article *these* and the noun. What category are numerals? That's a difficult question to answer, and one that requires more theoretical tools than I can give you in this book, at this stage in your learning at least. I tell my own students that for the purposes of doing assignments in this book either analysis is plausible, and possibly both situations exist.

Conjunctions (Conj) are words that connect two or more phrases together on an equal level:

14) *Conjunctions of English* (Conj): and, or, nor, neither ... nor, either ... or

The class of *complementizers* (C) also connects structures together, but they embed one clause inside of another instead of keeping them on an equal level:

15) *Complementizers of English* (C): that, for, if, whether

One of the most important categories that we'll use is the category of *tense* (T). For the moment we will *not* include tense suffixes such as *-ed* and *-s* in this class, and treat those as parts of verbs (we will revisit this issue in chapter 9). Instead, the category T consists of auxiliaries, modals, and

---

[6] Not all quantifiers can be determiners. For example, the quantifiers *lot* and *least* cannot function in this capacity (and are a noun and an adjective, respectively).

[7] The possessive forms *mine, yours, hers, theirs,* and *ours* are nouns, as are some uses of *his* and *its* (when there is no other noun in the NP).

the non-finite tense marker. In the older syntactic literature, the category T is sometimes called Infl (inflection) or Aux (Auxiliary). We'll use the more modern T.

16) *Tense categories of English* (T)
   Auxiliaries: have/has/had, am/is/are/was/were, do/does/did
   Modals: will, would, shall, should, can, could, may, might, must
   Non-finite tense marker: to

There is one special category containing only one word: *not,* which we'll call **negation** (Neg). There are other categories that express negation (e.g., the determiners *no, any,* and the noun *none*). We'll reserve the category Neg for the word *not,* however.

You now have enough information to answer WBE 6 & 7, GPS 8–10, and CPS 4.

---

4. SUBCATEGORIES AND FEATURES

You may have noticed that in sections 2 and 3, I hinted that each major part of speech category may have subtypes. For example, we listed six different kinds of D (articles, deictics, quantifiers, numerals, possessive pronouns, *wh*-pronouns) and three kinds of T (auxiliaries, modals, and the non-finite marker). The technical term for these subtypes is **subcategories**. For the most part, we are going to be interested in the main part of speech categories (N, V, Adj, Adv, P, D, Conj, C, T, and Neg), but sometimes we will want to refer to the subcategories.

One way to mark subcategories is through the use of **features**. Consider the case of T. To distinguish among the subcategories we can appeal to the features [±modal] and [±non-finite]:

17) Auxiliary[8] $T_{[-modal, -nonfinite]}$
   Modal $T_{[+modal, -nonfinite]}$
   to $T_{[+modal, +nonfinite]}$

One set of possible values of these features is missing ([-modal, +nonfinite]). We might similarly distinguish among tense forms using features like [±past] etc. So *was* is [+past]; *is* is [-past] etc.

---

[8] Auxiliaries are marked here as [−nonfinite], but they can of course appear in non-finite clauses like *I want to be dancing.* When they do so, however, they aren't marking the non-finite nature of the clause – the particle *to* is. The feature [±nonfinite] is meant to indicate what function the word has, not where the word can appear.

Similarly we can distinguish among the various kinds of determiner using features like [±wh], [±quantifier], [±deictic], etc. The details of this kind of analysis aren't crucial to the grammar fragments you are given in this book, as long as you understand the basic concept behind using features to mark subcategories.[9] In the rest of this section, we look at some of the subcategories of N, V, and P that will be of use to us in the rest of the book.

I'm not going to discuss subcategories of Adj and Adv, although they exist. In a grey textbox above, I've suggested that Adj and Adv are themselves subcategories of a larger category A. We also find many subcategories *within* the Adj and Adv categories. Some of these distinctions are explored in problem sets at the end of the chapter.

4.1 *Subcategories of Nouns*

We can slice the pie of English nouns apart along several dimensions including plural vs. singular, proper vs. common, pronoun vs. lexical noun, and count vs. mass noun.

First let's distinguish along the line of ***plurality***. English nouns can be either singular or plural. The distinction between singular and plural is usually morphologically marked with one of the plural endings like -*s* or -*es* (although it need not be, as in *mice* or *deer*). Most singular nouns in English require a D;[10] plural ones do not require a D, although they allow one:

18) a)   *Cat ate the spider.
    b)   The cat ate the spider.
    c)   Cats ate the spider.
    d)   The cats ate the spider.

We mark this distinction with the feature [±PLURAL].

Closely related to the plural/singular distinction is the ***count*** vs. ***mass*** noun distinction. Count nouns represent individual, "countable" elements. For example, *apple* is a count noun. "Mass nouns" usually can't be counted in the same way. For example *sincerity* and *air* are mass nouns. There are two easy distributional tests to distinguish between mass and count nouns. Mass nouns take the quantifier *much*, while count nouns take *many*.

---

[9] If you are interested in the details of what a system with a fully specified feature structure system might look like, have a look at Carnie (2011). But be warned that the theoretical framework outlined there is not completely compatible with the one discussed in this book.

[10] However, see the discussion of count vs. mass nouns below.

19) a)   many apples
    b)   *much apples/apple[11]
    c)   *many sincerity
    d)   *many air
    e)   much sincerity
    f)   much air

Like plurals, mass nouns generally don't require a determiner, but count nouns do:

20) a)   *I ate apple.
    b)   I ate the apple.
    c)   I ate sugar.
    d)   I ate the sugar.
    e)   He is filled with sincerity.
    f)   I doubt his sincerity.

We distinguish between count and mass nouns using the feature [±count].

Next, let us distinguish between *proper names* and *common nouns*. Proper names are nouns like *Andrew Carnie*. Common nouns are all other nouns. For the most, part proper names resist taking determiners:

21) a)   Andrew Carnie   b)   *the Andrew Carnie

There are some exceptions to this generalization. For example, when referring to a family it's common to say *the Smiths*. In other languages, proper names can take determiners. For example, in some dialects of Spanish, it is okay to say *La Rosamaria* "the Rosemary". If necessary, we can distinguish proper names from common nouns using the feature [±PROPER], although this feature is less useful than the others.

Finally let's look at the subcategories of *pronouns* and *anaphors*. These classes differ from the others in that they are closed. They never allow determiners or adjectival modification.

22) a)   he   b)   himself
    c)   *the he   d)   *the himself
    e)   *big he   f)   *big himself

Pronouns belong to the class [+PRONOUN, −ANAPHOR]. Anaphors are [+PRONOUN, +ANAPHOR]. All other nouns are [−PRONOUN, −ANAPHOR].

---

[11] Many native speakers of English will be able to "force" a reading onto *much apple*. But what they are doing is using *apple* as a mass noun (referring to the state of being an apple or the totality of apples in the universe). It is often possible to force a mass reading on count nouns, and a count reading on mass nouns (e.g., a water).

You now have enough information to do WBE 8 & 9 and GPS 11.

The Special Case of Possessive Pronouns

Possessive pronouns are an especially tricky case. They clearly function semantically like nouns. So for example, *Susan's father* might be the same person as *her father*, where *her* refers to Susan. In chapter 5, you'll see cases where possessive pronouns behave like pronouns with respect to a phenomenon called binding. But in other regards, possessive pronouns actually behave more like determiners: they are in complementary distribution with determiners (**the her book*). They appear at the beginning of the noun phrase. This gives possessive pronouns the flavor of a determiner. So are possessive pronouns a subcategory of noun or a subcategory of determiners? That's a really tricky question. Once you learn about head movement in chapter 9, you might consider an analysis where they start out as nouns and become determiners via the mechanism of head movement. But for the first part of this book, it's probably easier just to treat them as determiners, because they normally appear in the same syntactic positions as determiners.

4.2 *Subcategories of Verbs*

There are really two major ways in which we can divide up verbs into subcategories. One is along the lines of tense/finiteness (i.e., whether the verb is *left, leaves, (will) leave* or *(to) leave*). We're going to leave these distinctions aside until chapter 9, although I hope it is obvious by now how we'd use features to distinguish among them, even if the precise features we'd use aren't defined yet. The other way to divvy up verbs is in terms of the number of noun phrases (NPs) and prepositional phrases (PPs) or clauses (CPs) they require. This second kind of division is known as ***argument structure***.

In order to discuss argument structure, we first need to define some basic terms. If you took grammar in school, you probably learned that "every sentence has a subject and a predicate." Under your schoolroom definitions, the subject is usually the first noun phrase (that is, the first noun and all things that go along with it), and the predicate is everything else in the sentence. So for example, in (23) the subject is *the dastardly phonologist*, and the predicate would be *stole the syntactician's lunch*.

23) [The dastardly phonologist][stole the syntactician's lunch].
     subject   *predicate*   *(traditional definitions)*

The definition of subject isn't too bad (we'll refine it later though), but syntacticians use the term "predicate" *entirely differently*. The syntactician's definition of predicate is based on the mathematical notion of a "relation". The **predicate** defines the relation between the individuals being talked about and the real world – as well as among themselves. The entities (which can be abstract) participating in the relation are called **arguments**. To see how this works, look at the following example:

24) Gwen hit the baseball.

There are two arguments in this example, *Gwen* and *the baseball*. These are elements in the world that are participants in the action described by the sentence. The predicate here is *hit*. *Hit* expresses a relation between the two arguments: more precisely, it indicates that the first argument (*Gwen*) is applying some force on the second argument (*the baseball*). This may seem patently self-evident, but it's important to understand what is going on here on an abstract level. This usage of the terms predicate and argument is identical to how they are used in formal logic.

　　We can speak about any particular predicate's **argument structure**. This refers to the number of arguments that a particular predicate requires. Another name for argument structure is **valency**. Take, for example, predicates that take only one argument (i.e., they have a valency of 1). These are predicates like *smile, arrive, sit, run*, etc. The property of transitivity refers to how many arguments follow the verb. In predicates with a valency of 1, no arguments follow the verb (the single argument *precedes* the verb), so these predicates are said to be **intransitive**. Predicates that take two obligatory arguments have a valency of 2; some examples are *hit, love, see, kiss, admire*, etc. These predicates are said to be **transitive**, because they have a single argument after the verb (the other argument precedes the verb). Finally predicates that take three arguments have a valency of 3. *Put* and *give* are the best examples of this class. These predicates have two arguments after the verb so are said to be **ditransitive**.

25)

Transitivity	Valency	Example
Intransitive	1 argument	smile, arrive
Transitive	2 arguments	hit, love, kiss
Ditransitive	3 arguments	give, put

In determining how many arguments a predicate has, we only consider the obligatory NPs and PPs. Optional ones are never counted in the list of arguments. Only obligatory elements are considered arguments.

Predicates not only restrict the number of arguments that appear with them, they also restrict the categories of those arguments. A verb like *ask* can take either an NP or a clause (embedded sentence = CP) as a complement:

26) a) I asked [NP the question].
    b) I asked [CP if you knew the answer].

But a verb like *hit* can only take an NP complement:

27) a) I hit [NP the ball].
    b)*I hit [CP that you knew the answer].

With these basics in mind, we can set up a series of features based on how many and what kind of arguments a verb takes.

Let's start with intransitives. These require a single NP subject. We'll mark this with the feature [NP __] where the underscore represents where the verb would go in the sentence. An example of such a verb would be *leave*.

Most transitive verbs require an NP object, so we can mark these with the feature [NP __ NP]. An example of this is the verb *hit*, seen above in (27). Verbs like *ask* (see 26 above), *think, say,* etc. allow either an NP object or a CP (embedded clause) object. We can mark this using curly brackets {} and a slash. {NP/CP} means "a choice of NP or CP". So the feature structure for predicates like this is [NP __ {NP/CP}].

Ditransitive verbs come in several major types. Some ditransitives require two NP objects (the first is an indirect object, the other a direct object). The verb *spare* is of this category. It does not allow an NP and a PP:

28) a) I spared [NP him] [NP the trouble].
    b) *I spared [NP the trouble] [PP to him].

This category of ditransitive is marked with the feature [NP __ NP NP]. The opposite kind of ditransitive is found with the verb *put*. *Put* requires an NP and a PP:

29) a) *I put [NP the box] [NP the book].
    b) I put [NP the book] [PP in the box].

This kind of ditransitive takes the feature [NP __ NP PP]. We also have ditransitives that appear to be a combination of these two types and allow either an NP or a PP in the second position:

30) a) I gave [NP the box] [PP to Leah].
    b) I gave [NP Leah] [NP the box].

Did You Run the Race?

The claim that only obligatory arguments are found in argument structure is not as straightforward as it sounds. Consider the verb *run*. It has both an intransitive use *(I ran)* and a transitive use *(I ran the race)*. A similar problem is raised by languages that can drop the subject argument (e.g. Spanish and Italian) and by imperative sentences in English *(Go home now!)*. The subject is still an argument in these constructions, even though you can't hear it. In cases like the verb *run*, we'll simply claim that there are two verbs *to run*: one that takes an object and one that doesn't.

These have the feature [NP ___ NP {NP/PP}]. Finally we have ditransitives that take either two NPs, or one NP and one CP, or an NP and a PP:

31) a) I told [$_{NP}$ Daniel] [$_{NP}$ the story].
    b) I told [$_{NP}$ Daniel] [$_{CP}$ that the exam was cancelled].
    c) I told [$_{NP}$ the story] [$_{PP}$ to Daniel].

Verbs like *tell* have the feature [NP ___ NP {NP/PP/CP}].

The following chart summarizes all the different subcategories of verb we've discussed here:

32)

Subcategory	Example
V$_{[NP\_]}$ (intransitive)	*leave*
V$_{[NP\_NP]}$ (transitive type 1)	*hit*
V$_{[NP\_\{NP/CP\}]}$ (transitive type 2)	*ask*
V$_{[NP\_NP\,NP]}$ (ditransitive type 1)	*spare*
V$_{[NP\_NP\,PP]}$ (ditransitive type 2)	*put*
V$_{[NP\_NP\,\{NP/PP\}]}$ (ditransitive type 3)	*give*
V$_{[NP\_NP\,\{NP/PP/CP\}]}$ (ditransitive type 4)	*tell*

There are other types of verbs that we haven't listed here. We'll introduce similar features as we need them.

You can now try WBE 10, GPS 12, and CPS 5–8.

5. CONCLUSION

In this chapter, we've surveyed the parts of speech categories that we will use in this book. We have the lexical parts of speech N, V, Adj, and Adv, and the functional categories D, P, C, Conj, Neg, and T. Determining part of speech is done not by traditional semantic criteria, but by using morphological and syntactic distribution tests. We also looked at distributional evidence for various subcategories of nouns and verbs, and represented these distinctions as feature notations on the major categories.

IDEAS, RULES, AND CONSTRAINTS INTRODUCED IN THIS CHAPTER

i) *Parts of Speech (a.k.a. Word Class, Syntactic Categories)*: The labels we give to constituents (N, V, Adj, Adv, D, P, C, T, Neg, Conj). These determine the position of the word in the sentence.

ii) *Distribution*: Parts of speech are determined based on their distribution. We have both *morphological distribution* (what affixes are found on the word) and *syntactic distribution* (what other words are nearby).

iii) *Complementary Distribution*: When you have two categories and they never appear in the same environment (context), you have complementary distribution. Typically complementary distribution means that the two categories are subtypes of a larger class.

iv) Parts of speech that are *Open Class* can take new members or coinages: N, V, Adj, Adv.

v) Parts of speech that are *Closed Class* don't allow new coinages: D, P, Conj, C, T, Neg, and the pronoun and anaphor subcategories of N.

vi) *Lexical Categories* express the content of the sentence. N (including pronouns), V, Adj, Adv.

vii) *Functional Categories* contain the grammatical information in a sentence: D, P, Conj, T, Neg, C.

viii) *Subcategories*: The major parts of speech can often be divided up into subtypes. These are called subcategories.

ix) *Feature Notations* on major categories are a mechanism for indicating subcategories.

x) *Plurality* refers to the number of nouns. It is usually indicated in English with an -*s* suffix. Plural nouns in English do not require a determiner.

xi) *Count vs. Mass*: Count nouns can appear with determiners and the quantifier *many*. Mass nouns appear with *much* and usually don't have articles.

xii)   The *Predicate* defines the relation between the individuals being
         talked about and some fact about them, as well as relations among
         the arguments.

xiii)   *Argument Structure*: The number of arguments that a predicate
         takes.

xiv)   The *Arguments* are the entities that are participating in the predicate
         relation.

xv)   *Intransitive*: A predicate that takes only one argument.

xvi)   *Transitive*: A predicate that takes two arguments.

xvii)   *Ditransitive*: A predicate that takes three arguments.

FURTHER READING: Baker (2003), Grimshaw (1990), Harley (2006), Katamba
(2004), Levin (1993), Williams (1983)

GENERAL PROBLEM SETS

GPS1. NOUNS

[Application of Skills; Basic]

Identify all the nouns in the following passage from *The Adventures of
Sherlock Holmes* by Sir Arthur Conan Doyle.[12] You can ignore pronouns like
I, he, my, whom, her, and *me* – although these are, of course, nouns as well.

> The lamps had been lit, but the blinds had not been drawn, so
> that I could see Holmes as he lay upon the couch. I do not
> know whether he was seized with compunction at that moment
> for the part he was playing, but I know that I never felt more
> heartily ashamed of myself in my life than when I saw the
> beautiful creature against whom I was conspiring, or the grace
> and kindliness with which she waited upon the injured man.
> And yet it would be the blackest treachery to Holmes to draw
> back now from the part which he had entrusted to me. I
> hardened my heart, and took the smoke-rocket from under my
> ulster. After all, I thought, we are not injuring her. We are but
> preventing her from injuring another.

GPS2. VERBS

[Application of Skills; Basic]

Using the passage above in question 1, identify all the verbs. Do not
worry about modals and auxiliary verbs. So ignore *had, been, could,
do, was, would, be,* and *are* (all of which are of category T).

---

[12] Taken from the open source version at http://www.gutenberg.org/.

GPS3. ADJECTIVES AND ADVERBS

[Application of Skills; Basic]
Using the passage above in question 1, identify all the adjectives and adverbs.

GPS4. PREPOSITIONS

[Application of Skills; Basic]
Using the passage above in question 1, identify all the prepositions.

GPS5. PART OF SPEECH 1[13]

[Application of Skills; Basic]
Identify the main parts of speech (i.e., <u>N</u>ouns, <u>V</u>erbs, <u>Adj</u>ectives/<u>Adv</u>erbs, and <u>P</u>repositions) in the following sentences. Treat hyphenated words as single words:

a) The old rusty pot-belly stove has been replaced.
b) The red-haired assistant put the vital documents through the new efficient shredder.
c) The large evil leathery alligator complained to his aging keeper about his extremely unattractive description.
d) I just ate the last piece of chocolate cake.

GPS6. NOOTKA

[Application of Skills; Intermediate]
Consider the following data from Nootka (data from Sapir and Swadesh 1939), a language spoken in British Columbia, Canada, and answer the questions that follow.

a) Mamu:k-ma qu:ʔas-ʔi.
   working-PRES man-DEF
   "The man is working."

b) Qu:ʔas-ma mamu:k-ʔi.
   man-PRES working-DEF
   "The working one is a man."

(The : mark indicates a long vowel. ʔ is a glottal stop. *PRES* in the second line means "present tense", *DEF* means "definite determiner" (the).)

Questions about Nootka:
1) In sentence a, is *Qu:ʔas* functioning as a verb or a noun?

---

[13] Problem set contributed by Sheila Dooley-Collberg.

2) In sentence a, is *Mamu:k* functioning as a verb or a noun?
3) In sentence b, is *Qu:ʔas* a verb or a noun?
4) In sentence b, is *Mamu:k* a verb or a noun?
5) What criteria did you use to tell what is a noun in Nootka and what is a verb?
6) How does this data support the idea that there are no semantic criteria involved in determining the part of speech?

GPS7. GENDER NEUTRAL PRONOUNS
[Creative and Critical Thinking; Basic]
Most standard varieties of English don't have a gender-neutral singular pronoun that can refer to humans (other than the very awkward "one"). There have been numerous attempts to introduce gender-neutral singular human pronouns into English. The following list is a subset of the ones found on John Chao's gender-neutral pronoun FAQ:[14]

> *ae, ar, co, e, em, ems, en, es, et, ey, fm, ha, hann, he'er, heesh, heir, hem, her'n,*
> *herim, herm, hes, hesh, heshe, hey, hez, hi, himer, hir, hirem, hires, hirm, his'er,*
> *his'n, hisher, hizer, ho, hom, hse, hymer, im, ip, ir, iro, jhe, le, lem, na, ne, ner, nim,*
> *on, per, po, rim, s/he, sap, se, sem, ser, sheehy, shem, shey, shim, sie, sim, ta, tem,*
> *term, tey, thim, thon, uh, ve, vim, vir, vis, xe, z, ze, zie, zim, zir.*

None of these have caught on. Instead, the otherwise plural *they/them/ their/themselves* is usually felt to be more natural by native speakers. Why have the above forms not caught on, but instead we have co-opted a plural pronoun for this usage?

GPS8. FUNCTIONAL CATEGORIES
[Application of Skills; Basic]
The following is an extract from the preface to Captain Grose's *Dictionary of the Vulgar Tongue* (1811) (from the open source Gutenberg project):

> The propriety of introducing the university slang will be readily admitted; it is not less curious than that of the College in the Old Bailey, and is less generally understood. When the number and accuracy of our additions are compared with the price of the volume, we have no doubt that its editors will meet with the encouragement that is due to learning, modesty, and virtue.

---

[14] http://www.aetherlumina.com/gnp/index.html.

For every word in this paragraph identify its part of speech, and mark whether each part of speech is a lexical or functional part of speech and whether the part of speech is open or closed.

GPS9. FUNCTIONAL CATEGORIES
[Creative and Critical Thinking; Intermediate]
Interjections are functional items, in that they express a grammatical notion (such as the speaker's agreement or attitude with respect to the thing being said), but are they closed class? Is it possible to make up new interjections?

GPS10. PART OF SPEECH 2
[Application of Skills; Intermediate]
Consider the following selection from *Jabberwocky*, a poem by Lewis Carroll (From *Through the Looking-Glass and What Alice Found There*, 1872):

> 'Twas brillig, and the slithy toves
> Did gyre and gimble in the wabe;
> All mimsy were the borogoves,
> And the mome raths outgrabe.

> "Beware the Jabberwock, my son!
> The jaws that bite, the claws that catch!
> Beware the Jubjub bird, and shun
> The frumious Bandersnatch!"

> He took his vorpal sword in hand:
> Long time the manxome foe he sought –
> So rested he by the Tumtum tree
> And stood awhile in thought.

> And, as in uffish thought he stood,
> The Jabberwock, with eyes of flame,
> Came whiffling through the tulgey wood,
> And burbled as it came.

For each underlined word, indicate its part of speech (word class), and for Ns, Vs, Adjs, and Advs, explain the *distributional* criteria by which you came up with that classification. If the item is a closed class part of speech, indicate that. Do not try to use a dictionary. Most of these words are nonsense words. You will need to figure out what part of speech they are according to what suffixes and prefixes they take, along with where they appear relative to other words.

GPS11. SUBCATEGORIES OF NOUNS

[Application of Knowledge; Basic]

For each of the nouns below put a + sign in the box under the features that they have. Note that some nouns might have a plus value for more than one feature. The first one is done for you. Do not mark the minus (–) values, or the values for which the word is not specified; mark only the plus values!

Noun	PLURAL	COUNT	PROPER	PRONOUN	ANAPHOR
cats	+	+			
milk					
New York					
they					
people					
language					
printer					
himself					
wind					
lightbulb					

GPS12. SUBCATEGORIES OF VERBS

[Application of Knowledge; Intermediate]

For each of the verbs below, list whether it is intransitive, transitive or ditransitive and list which features it takes (see the list in (32) as an example). In some cases they may allow more than one feature (e.g., the verb *eat* is both [NP __ NP] and [NP ___]). Give an example for each feature:

> *spray, sleep, escape, throw, wipe, say, think, begrudge (or grudge), thank, pour, send, promise, kiss, arrive*

CHALLENGE PROBLEM SETS

CHALLENGE PROBLEM SET 1: -IAN AND -ISH

[Critical and Creative Thinking; Challenge]

In the text we claimed that the suffixes *-ian* and *-ish* mark adjectives. Consider the following sentences:

a) The Canadian government uses a parliamentary system of democracy.
b) The Canadian bought himself a barbeque.
c) The prudish linguist didn't enjoy looking at the internet.

d) We keep those censored copies of the book hidden to protect the sensibilities of the prudish.

What should we make the words ending in -ish and -ian in sentences (b) and (d)? Are they adjectives? If not, how can we account for the fact that these words end in -ish and -ian? There are many possible answers to this question.

CHALLENGE PROBLEM SET 2: NOMINAL PRENOMINAL MODIFIERS[15]

[Critical and Creative Thinking; Challenge]

Part 1: By the syntactic distributional criteria given to you in the text, what part of speech should the underlined words in the following examples be?

a) the <u>leather</u> couch
b) the <u>water</u> spout

Part 2: By contrast, what do the following facts tell us about the parts of speech of *leather* and *water*?

a) the leather
b) the water
c) ?the very leather couch (cf. the very red couch)
d) ?the very water spout (cf. the very big spout)
e) *The more leather couch / *The leatherer couch (cf. the bigger couch)
f) *The more water spout
g) *The waterest spout

CHALLENGE PROBLEM SET 3: INTENSIFIERS

[Application of Knowledge; Challenge]

English has a subcategory of adverbs called **intensifiers**. This class includes *very, rather, too* (when used before an adjective), *quite, less, nearly, partly, fully, mostly,* and *sometimes*.

Question 1: Is this subcategory an open class part of speech or a closed class part of speech? Explain your answer.

Question 2: Describe the distribution of this subcategory. In particular describe where it can appear relative to other adverbs (and adjectives). Can other adverbs appear in this environment?

---

[15] Thanks to Jack Martin for suggesting this problem set.

CHALLENGE PROBLEM SET 4: COMPLEMENTARY DISTRIBUTION
[Critical Thinking; Challenge]
In a grey textbox in section 2.4, it's argued that adjectives and adverbs are in complementary distribution and thus might be part of the same super-category A. Are N and V in complementary distribution? What about Adv and V? What about N and Adj? Create examples to show whether these categories are in complementary distribution. If any are in complementary distribution with the others what does this tell us about the parts of speech? Next consider whether any functional categories are in complementary distribution with lexical categories.

CHALLENGE PROBLEM SET 5: SUBCATEGORIES OF ADVERBS
[Application of Skills and Knowledge; Challenge]
Your goal in this problem set is to develop a set of subcategories for adverbs. Consider the following adverbs. When doing these tests don't put any extra stress or focus on the adverb – try to say the sentence naturally without emphasizing the adverbs. Also, don't put extra pauses before or after any of the adverbs.

> *luckily, earnestly, intently, hopefully, probably, certainly, frequently, patiently, always, completely, almost, again, evidently, frankly, demandingly, yesterday, necessarily*

Part 1: For each adverb determine:
1) Can it appear before the subject? (e.g., *Unbelievably, I don't know any pixies.*)
2) Can it appear between the T (e.g., *will, have, is, can*) and the verb? (e.g., *I have often wondered about the existence of pixies.*)
3) Can it appear after the object? Or at the end of the sentence? (e.g., *Pixies eat mushrooms vigorously.*)
4) Can it appear between an object and a PP in a ditransitive (e.g., *I put the book carefully on the table.*)
(Note: these adverbs may appear in several of these positions.)

Part 2: Group the adverbs together into subcategories based on your answers to part 1.

Part 3: Within each group you may find more subtle orderings. For example, within the subcategory of adverbs that can appear between auxiliaries and verbs there may be an ordering of adverbs. Try putting multiple adverbs in each position. What are the orderings you find?

CHALLENGE PROBLEM SET 6: SUBCATEGORIES OF ADJECTIVES

[Application of Knowledge; Challenge]

Just as there are positional differences among adverbs (see Challenge Problem Set 3), we find an ordering of adjectives with respect to each other. Below is a list of adjectives. Pair each adjective with every other adjective and see which must come first in a noun phrase. Try to come up with a general ordering among these adjectives. (Although in the text I've told you to include numerals with the class of determiners, I've listed them here as adjectives. For the rest of the book treat them as determiners.)

big, young, blue, desperate, two, scaly, thick

One word of caution: it is sometimes possible to put some adjectives in any order. However, many of these orders are only possible if you are using the adjective contrastively or emphatically. For example, you can say *the old rubber sneaker* with a normal non-contrastive meaning, but *the rubber old sneaker* is only possible when it has a contrastive emphatic meaning (*the RUBBER old sneaker as opposed to the leather one*). Don't let these contrastive readings interfere with your subcategorization.

CHALLENGE PROBLEM SET 7: ANIMACY

[Application of Knowledge; Challenge]

Part 1: The term animacy refers to whether something is alive or not. We haven't included any animacy restrictions in our subcategorization of verbs or nouns in the main body of the text. Consider the following data:

a) Susan bought some flowers for her mother.
b) Susan bought her mother some flowers.
c) Susan bought some flowers for her birthday.
d) *Susan bought her birthday some flowers.

Construct feature structures to explain the ungrammaticality of (d). Hint: you'll need to use choice brackets { } to do this.

Part 2: Observe the following limited data from Spanish (taken from Legate 2005). When do you use the dative marker *a* in Spanish? How would you encode this with a feature structure for the verb *vimos*?

e)   Vimos a Juan
       saw.1pl DAT Juan
       "We saw Juan"

f)   Vimos la casa   de Juan
       saw.1pl the house   of Juan
       "We saw Juan's house"

CHALLENGE PROBLEM SET 8: IMPLICIT ARGUMENTS[16]
[Creative Thinking; Challenge]
Above we claimed that the verb *give* requires either an NP and a PP or two
NPs (i.e. *Dave gave a punchbowl to Andrew* and *Dave gave Andrew a
headache*). But consider sentences like the following:

1) I gave blood.
2) I don't give a darn.
3) Andy gives freely of his time.
4) Dan gave his life.

Each of these might lead us to conclude that *give* requires fewer arguments
than we have claimed. Are these simply counterexamples to the claim that
give is of subcategory $V_{[NP \_\_\_ NP \{NP/PP\}]}$ or is something more complicated
going on here?

   A related but slightly different issue arises with sentences like those in
(5) and (6).

5) Dan gives to charity.
6) Sorry, I gave last week.

Will your solution for 1–4 work for these examples too?

---

[16] Thanks to Dave Medeiros for suggesting this problem set.

Constituency, Trees, and Rules

Learning Objectives

After reading chapter 3 you should walk away having mastered the following ideas and skills:

1. Be able to explain what a constituent is.
2. Show whether a string of words is a constituent or not.
3. Using phrase structure rules, draw the trees for English sentences.
4. Explain and apply the Principle of Modification.
5. Produce paraphrases for ambiguous sentences and draw trees for each meaning.
6. Using data, be able to extract a set of phrase structure rules for another language.
7. Define recursion and give an example.

0. INTRODUCTION

Syntax is about the study of sentence *structure*. So let's define what we mean by "structure." Consider the sentence in (1):

1) The student loved his syntax assignments.

Syntax: A Generative Introduction, Third Edition. Andrew Carnie.
© 2013 Andrew Carnie. Published 2013 by John Wiley & Sons, Inc.

One way to describe this sentence is as a simple linear string of words. Certainly this is how it is represented on the page. We could describe the sentence as consisting of the words *the, student, loved, his, syntax,* and *assignments* in that order. As you can probably figure out, if that were all there was to syntax, you could put down this book here and not bother with the next fifteen chapters. But that isn't all there is to syntax. The statement that sentence (1) consists of a linear string of words misses several important generalizations about the internal structure of sentences and how these structures are represented in our minds. In point of fact, we are going to claim that the words in sentence (1) are grouped into units (called **constituents**) and that these constituents are grouped into larger constituents, and so on until you get a sentence.

Notice that on a purely intuitive level, certain words seem to be closely related to one another. For example, the word *the* seems to be tied more to the meaning of *student* than it is to *loved* or *syntax*. A related intuition can be seen by looking at the sentences in (2).

2) a) The student loved his phonology readings.
    b) The student hated his morphology professor.

Compare these sentences to (1). You'll see right away that the relationship between *the student* and *his syntax assignments* in (1) and *the student* and *his phonology readings* in (2a) is the same. Similarly, the relation between *the student* and *his morphology professor* in (2b), while of a different kind (hating instead of loving), is similar: There is one entity (*the student*) who is either hating or loving another entity (*his syntax assignments, his phonology readings* or *his morphology professor*). In order to capture these intuitions (the intuition that certain words are more closely connected than others, and the intuitions about relationships between words in the sentence), we need a more complex notion. The notions we use to capture these intuitions are **constituency** and **hierarchical structure**. The idea that *the* and *student* are closely related to one another is captured by the fact that we treat them as part of a bigger unit that contains them, but not other words. We have two different ways to represent this bigger unit. One of them is to put square brackets around units:

3) [the student]

The other is to represent the units with a group of lines in what is called a tree structure:

4)   ⟋⟍
     the student

These bigger units are called **constituents**. An informal definition for a constituent is given in (5):

5) *Constituent*: A group of words that function together as a unit.

Constituency is the most important and basic notion in syntactic theory. Constituents form the backbone of the rest of this book. They capture the intuitions mentioned above. The "relatedness" is captured by membership in a constituent. As we will see it also allows us to capture the relationships between constituents exemplified in (1).

Constituents don't float out in space. Instead they are embedded one inside another to form larger and larger constituents. This is *hierarchical structure*. Foreshadowing the discussion below a bit, here is the structure we'll develop for (1):

6)

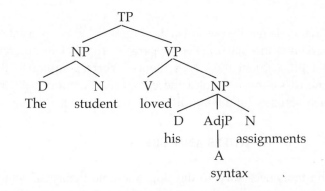

This is a typical hierarchical *tree structure*. The sentence constituent (represented by the symbol TP) consists of two constituents: a subject *noun phrase* (NP) [*the student*] and a predicate phrase or *verb phrase* (VP) [*loved his syntax assignments*]. The subject NP in turn contains a *noun* (N) *student* and a *determiner* (or article) (D) *the*. Similarly the VP contains a *verb* (V), and an object NP [*his syntax assignments*]. The object NP is further broken down into three bits: a determiner *his*, an adjective *syntax*, and a noun *assignments*. As you can see this tree has constituents (each represented by the point where lines come together) that are inside other constituents. This is hierarchical structure. Hierarchical constituent structure can also be represented with brackets. Each pair of brackets ([ ]) represents a constituent. We normally put the label of the constituent on the left member of the pair. The **bracketed diagram** for (6) is given in (7):

7) [$_{TP}$[$_{NP}$[$_D$The][$_N$student]][$_{VP}$[$_V$loved][$_{NP}$[$_D$his][$_{AdjP}$[$_{Adj}$syntax]][$_N$assignments]]]].

As you can see, bracketed diagrams are much harder to read, so for the most part we will use tree diagrams in this book. However, sometimes bracketed diagrams have their uses, so you should be able to translate back and forth between trees and bracketed diagrams.

The Psychological Reality of Constituency

In the 1960s, Merrill Garrett and his colleagues showed that constituency has some reality in the minds of speakers. The researchers developed a series of experiments that involved placing a click in a neutral place in the stream of sounds. People tend to perceive these clicks not in the place where they actually occur, but at the edges of constituents. The italicized strings of words in the following sentences differ only in how the constituents are arranged.

i)   [In her *hope of marrying*]   *An/na was impractical.*
                                 ↑
ii) [Harry's *hope of marrying An/na*]   *was impractical.*
                                      ↑

Syntactic constituency is marked with square brackets [ ]; the placement of the click is marked with a slash /. People perceive the click in different places (marked with a ↑) in the two sentences, corresponding to the constituent boundaries – even though the click actually appears in the same place in each sentence (in the middle of the word *Anna*).

---

1. RULES AND TREES

Now we have the tools necessary to develop a simple theory of sentence structure. We have a notion of constituent, which is a group of words that functions as a unit, and we have labels (parts of speech) that we can use to describe the parts of those units. Let's put the two of these together and try to develop a description of a possible English sentence. In generative grammar, generalizations about structure are represented by rules. These rules are said to "generate" the tree. So if we draw a tree a particular way, we need a rule to generate that tree. The rules we are going to consider in this chapter are called ***phrase structure rules*** (PSRs) because they generate the phrase structure tree of a sentence.

1.1 Noun Phrases (NPs)

Let's start with the constituents we call noun phrases (or NPs) and explore the range of material that can appear in them. The simplest NPs contain only a noun (usually a proper noun [+proper], pronoun [+pron], mass noun [−count] or a plural noun [+plural]):

8) a) John   b) water   c) cats

Our rule must minimally generate NPs that contain only an N. The format for PSRs is shown in (9a); we use X, Y, and Z here as variables to stand for any category. (9b) shows our first pass at an NP rule:

9) a)   XP   →   X Y Z
            ↑   ↑   ↑
        the label   *"consists of"*   *the elements that make up*
        for the constituent   *the constituent*

    b) NP → N

This rule says that an NP is composed of (written as →) an N. This rule would generate a tree like (10):

10)   NP
        |
        N

There are many NPs (e.g., those that are [+count]) that are more complex than this of course:

11) a) the box
    b) his binder
    c) that pink fluffy cushion

We must revise our rule to account for the presence of determiners:

12) a) NP → D N

This generates a tree like:

    b)   NP
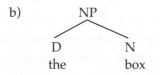
            D   N
            the   box

Compare the NPs in (8) and (11): You'll see that determiners are optional. This being so, we must indicate their optionality in the rule. We do this with parentheses ( ) around the optional elements:

13) NP → (D) N

Nouns can also be optionally modified by adjectives, so we will need to revise our rule as in (14) (don't worry about the "P" in AdjP yet, we'll explain that below).

14) a) the big box   b) his yellow binder

15) NP → (D) (AdjP) N

Nouns can also take prepositional phrase (PP) modifiers (see below where we discuss the structure of these constituents), so once again we'll have to revise our rule:

16) a)   the big box of crayons
    b)   his yellow binder with the red stripe

17) NP → (D) (AdjP) N (PP)

For concreteness, let's apply the rule in (17):

18)

        NP
    ┌────┬────┬──────┐
    D   AdjP N   PP[1]
   the   △   box   △
        big   of crayons

The NP constituent in (18) consists of four subconstituents: D, AdjP, N and PP.

For the moment, we need to make one more major revision to our NP rule. It turns out that you can have more than one adjective and more than one PP in an English NP:

19) The [Adjp big] [Adjp yellow] box [pp of cookies] [pp with the pink lid].

In this NP, the noun *box* is modified by *big, yellow, of cookies*, and *with the pink lid*. The rule must be changed then to account for this. It must allow more than one adjective and more than one PP modifier. We indicate this with a +, which means "repeat this category as many times as needed":

20) NP → (D) (AdjP+) N (PP+)

We will have cause to slightly revise this rule in later sections of this chapter and later chapters, but for now we can use this rule as a working hypothesis.

You now have enough information to try CPS 1–3.

1.2 Adjective Phrases (AdjPs) and Adverb Phrases (AdvPs)

Consider the following two NPs:

21) a)   the big yellow book
    b)   the very yellow book

---

[1] I'm using a triangle here to obscure the details of the PP and AdjP. Students should avoid using triangles when drawing trees, as you want to be as explicit as possible. I use it here only to draw attention to other aspects of the structure.

On the surface, these two NPs look very similar. They both consist of a determiner, followed by two modifiers and then a noun. But consider what modifies what in these NPs. In (21a) *big* modifies *book*, as does *yellow*. In (21b) on the other hand, only *yellow* modifies book; *very* does not modify *book* (**very book*) – it modifies *yellow*. On an intuitive level then, the structures of these two phrases are actually quite different. (21a) has two adjective constituents that modify the N, whereas (21b) has only one [*very yellow*]. This constituent is called an adjective phrase (AdjP). The rule for the adjective phrase is given in (22a):

22) a) AdjP → (AdvP) Adj

b)

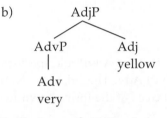

This will give us the following structures for the two NPs in (21):

23) a)

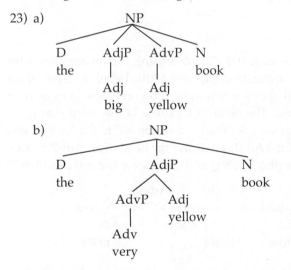

So despite their surface similarity, these two NPs have radically different structures. In (23a) the N is modified by two AdjPs, in (23b) by only one. This leads us to an important restriction on tree structures:

24) *Principle of Modification (informal):* Modifiers are always attached within the phrase they modify.

The adverb *very* modifies *yellow*, so it is part of the *yellow* AdjP in (23b). In (23a) by contrast, *big* doesn't modify *yellow*, it modifies *book*, so it is attached directly to the NP containing *book*.

A very similar rule is used to introduce AdvPs:

25) AdvP → (AdvP) Adv

26) very quickly

27)

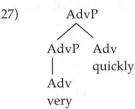

Here is a common mistake to avoid: Notice that the AdvP rule specifies that its modifier is another AdvP: AdvP → (AdvP) Adv. The rule does NOT say *AdvP → (Adv) Adv, so you will never get trees of the form shown in (28):

28)

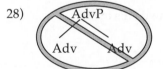

You might find the tree in (27) a little confusing. There are two Advs and two AdvPs. In order to understand that tree a little better, let's introduce a new concept: **heads**. We'll spend much more time on heads in chapters 6 and 7, but here's a first pass: The head of a phrase is the word that gives the phrase its category. For example, the head of the NP is the N, the head of a PP is the P, the head of the AdjP is Adj and the head of an AdvP is Adv. Let's look first at an adjective phrase (29a) and compare it to a complex AdvP:

29) a)

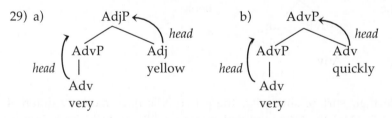

In (29a), the heads should be clear. The adverb *very* is the head of the adverb phrase and the adjective *yellow* is the head of AdjP. In (29b) we have the same kind of headedness, except both elements are adverbs. *Very* is the head of the lower AdvP, and *quickly* is the head of the higher one. We have two adverbs, so we have two AdvPs – **each has its own head**.

With this in mind, we can explain why the "very" AdvP is embedded in the AdjP. Above we gave a very informal description of the Principle of Modification. Let's try for a more precise version here:

30) **Principle of Modification** (revised): If an XP (that is, a phrase with some category X) modifies some head Y, then XP must be a sister to Y (i.e., a daughter of YP).

31)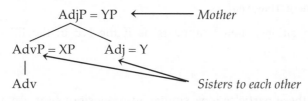

The diagram in (31) shows you the relations mentioned in the definition in (30). If we take the AdjP to be the **mother,** then its **daughters** are the AdvP and the head Adj. Since AdvP and Adj are both daughters of the same mother, then we say they are **sisters.** In (30) X and Y are variables that stand for any category. If one XP (AdvP) modifies some head Y (Adj), then the XP must be a sister to Y (i.e., the AdvP must be a sister to the head Adj), meaning they must share a mother. You'll notice that this relationship is asymmetric: AdvP modifies Adj, but Adj does *not* modify AdvP.

You now have enough information to try WBE 1 and GPS 1.

1.3 Prepositional Phrases (PPs)

The next major kind of constituent we consider is the prepositional phrase (PP). Most PPs take the form of a preposition (the head) followed by an NP:

32) a) [PP to [NP the store]]
    b) [PP with [NP an axe]]
    c) [PP behind [NP the rubber tree]]

The PP rule appears to be:

33) a) PP → P NP

    b)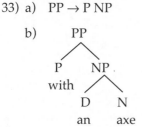

In the rule we've given here, the NP in the PP is obligatory. There may actually be some evidence for treating the NP in PPs as optional. There is a class of prepositions, traditionally called particles, that don't require a following NP:

34) a) I haven't seen him *before*.
    b) I blew it *up*.
    c) I threw the garbage *out*.

If these are prepositions, then it appears as if the NP in the PP rule is optional:

35) PP → P (NP)

Even though all these particles look similar to prepositions (or are at least homophonous with them), there is some debate about whether they are or not. As an exercise you might try to think about the kinds of phenomena that would distinguish particles from prepositions without NPs.

You now have enough information to try WBE 2 and GPS 2 & 3.

1.4 Verb Phrases (VPs)

Next we have the category headed by the verb: the verb phrase (VP). Minimally a VP consists of a single verb. This is the case of intransitives ($V_{[NP\_\_]}$):

36) a) VP → V
    b) Ignacious [$_{VP}$ left].

    c)   VP
                     |
                     V
                    left

Verbs may be modified by adverbs (AdvPs), which are, of course, optional:

37) a) Ignacious [$_{VP}$ left quickly].
    b) VP → V (AdvP)

    c)   VP

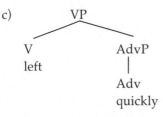

        V   AdvP
       left |
                       Adv
                      quickly

Interestingly, many of these adverbs can appear on either side of the V, and you can have as many AdvPs as you like:

38) a) Ignacious [$_{VP}$ quickly left].
    b) Ignacious [$_{VP}$ [$_{AdvP}$ deliberately] [$_{AdvP}$ always] left [$_{AdvP}$ quietly] [$_{AdvP}$ early]].
    c) VP → (AdvP+) V (AdvP+)

39)

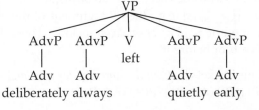

You'll recall from chapter 2 that there is a subcategory of verbs that can take an NP object (the transitive V$_{[NP\_NP]}$); these NPs appear immediately after the V and before any AdvPs:

40) a) VP → (AdvP+) V (NP) (AdvP+)
    b) Bill [$_{VP}$ frequently kissed *his mother-in-law*].
    c) Bill [$_{VP}$ kissed *his mother-in-law* quietly]. (cf. *Bill [$_{VP}$ kissed quietly *his mother-in-law*].)

41)

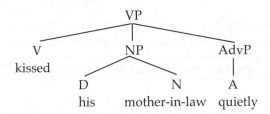

It is also possible to have two NPs in a sentence, for example with a double object verb like *spare* (V$_{[NP\_NP\,NP]}$). Both these NPs must come between the verb and any AdvPs:

42) I spared [$_{NP}$ the student] [$_{NP}$ any embarrassment] [$_{AdvP}$ yesterday].

Note that you are allowed to have a maximum of only two argument NPs. For this reason, we are not going to use the Kleene plus (+) which allows you to have as many as you like. Instead we are going to simply list both NPs in the rule:

43) a) VP → (AdvP+) V (NP) (NP) (AdvP+)

b)
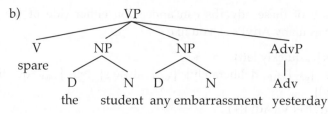

Verbs can be modified by PPs as well. These PPs can be arguments as in ditransitive verbs of the type V[_NP _ NP PP] (e.g., the PP argument of the verb *put*) or they can be simple modifiers like *for a dollar* below. These PPs can appear either after an adverb or before it.

44) a) Bill [_VP frequently got his buckets [_PP *from the store*] [_PP *for a dollar*]].
    b) VP → (AdvP+) V (NP) (NP) (AdvP+) (PP+) (AdvP+)

c)
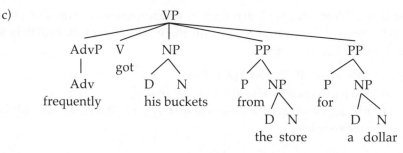

The rule in (44b) is nearly our final VP rule for this chapter; we'll need to make one further adjustment to it once we look at the structure of clauses.

You now have enough information to try WBE 3, GPS 4, and CPS 4.

1.5 Clauses

Thus far, we have NPs, VPs, APs, and PPs, and we've seen how they can be hierarchically organized with respect to one another. One thing that we have not accounted for is the structure of the sentence (or more accurately *clause*).[2] A clause consists of a subject NP and a VP. The label we use for clause is TP (which stands for tense phrase).[3]

45) [_TP [_NP Bill] [_VP frequently got his buckets from the store for a dollar]].

This can be represented by the rule in (46):

---

[2] We'll give a proper definition for clause in a later chapter.
[3] In other books you might find sentences labeled as S or IP. S and IP are essentially the same thing as TP. We'll use TP here since it will make the transition to X-bar theory (in chapter 6) a little easier.

46) TP → NP VP

A tree for (45) is given in (47):

47)
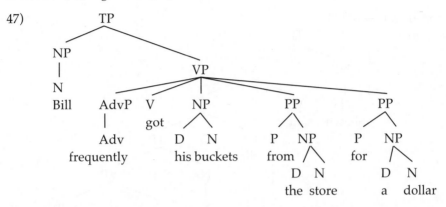

TPs can also include other items, including (unsurprisingly) elements of the category T, such as modal verbs and auxiliary verbs like those in (48):

48) a) Cedric *might* crash the longboat.
   b) Gustaf *has* crashed the semi-truck.

It may surprise you that we won't treat these as verbs. The reason for this will become clear in later chapters. Note that the T in the TP is optional.

49) TP → NP (T) VP

A tree showing the application of this rule is given in (50):

50)
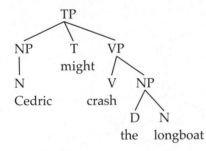

Clauses don't always have to stand on their own. There are times when one clause is embedded inside another:

51) [TP Shawn said [TP he decked the janitor]].

In sentence (51) the clause *he decked the janitor* lies inside the larger main clause. Often embedded clauses are introduced by a complementizer like *that* or *if:*

52) [$_{TP}$ Shawn said [$_{CP}$ [$_C$ that] [$_{TP}$ he decked the janitor]]].

We need a special rule to introduce complementizers (C):

53) a)   CP → (C) TP
    b)

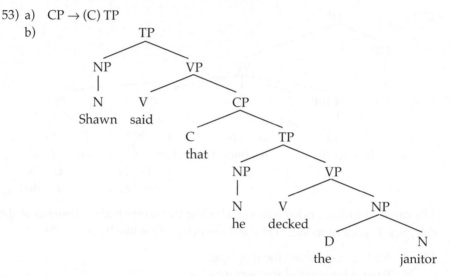

For the moment we will assume that *all* embedded clauses are CPs, whether or not they have a complementizer. We'll show evidence for this in chapter 7. This means that a sentence like *Shawn said he decked the janitor* will have a CP in it even though there is no complementizer *that*.

54)

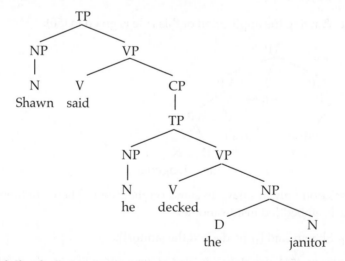

Embedded clauses appear in a variety of positions. In (54), the embedded clause appears in essentially the same slot as the direct object. Embedded clauses can also appear in subject position:

55) [_{TP} [_{CP} That he decked the janitor] worried Jeff].

Because of this we are going to have to modify our TP and VP rules to allow embedded clauses. Syntacticians use curly brackets { } to indicate a choice. So {NP/CP} means that you are allowed *either* an NP or a CP but not both. The modification to the TP rule is relatively straightforward. We simply allow the choice between an NP and a CP in the initial NP:

56) a) TP → {NP/CP} (T) VP

   b)

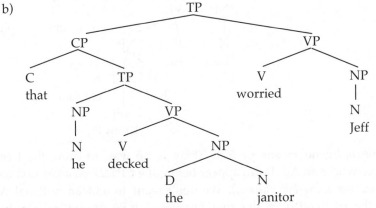

The revised VP rule requires a little more finesse. First observe that in verbs that allow both an NP and a CP (V_[NP_ NP {NP/CP}] such as *ask*), the CP follows the NP but precedes the PP (in the following sentence *yesterday* and *over the phone* should be interpreted as modifying *ask*, not *ate*), essentially in the position of the second NP in the rule:

57) Naomi asked [_{NP} Erin] [_{CP} if [_{TP} Dan ate her Kung-Pao chicken]] yesterday over the phone.

This gives us the rule :

58) a) VP → (AdvP+) V (NP) ({NP/CP}) (AdvP+) (PP+) (AdvP+)

b)

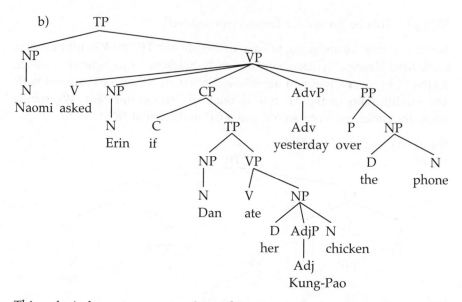

This rule is by no means perfect. There is no way to draw the tree for sentences where an AdvP can appear before the CP (*Naomi asked Erin quietly if Dan ate her Kung-Pao chicken*). We don't want to add an optional AdvP before the ({CP/NP}) in the rule because AdvPs cannot appear before the NP. For the moment, we'll go with the VP rule as it is written, although we return to the issue in chapter 6.

The last revision we have to make to our PSRs is to add the CP as a modifier to NPs to account for cases like (59).

59) a) [NP The fact about Bill [CP that he likes ice-cream]] bothers Natasha.
    b) NP → (D) (AdjP+) N (PP+) (CP)
    c)

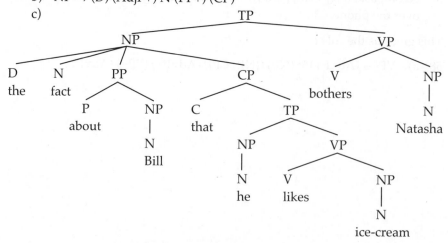

Relative Clauses

In addition to the CPs that modify Ns as in the above cases, there is another kind of CP modifier to an N. This is called a *relative clause*. We aren't going to include relative clauses in our rules yet. This is because they often contain what is called a "gap" or a place where some part of the clause is missing. For example:

i)   The man [whose car I hit _____ last week] sued me.

The underscore in the sentence indicates where the gap is – the object of the verb *hit* is in the wrong place. It should be where the underscore is. Corresponding to the gap we also have the *wh*-word *whose* and the noun *car*. These are appearing at the beginning of the clause. Because of these gaps and fronted *wh*-elements, we aren't going to worry about the internal structure of these clauses until chapter 12.

Here's a challenge: relative clauses actually appear in a different position than the CPs that follow nouns like *the fact*. Can you figure out what the difference is? (Hint: it has to do with the relative position of the CP and the PP in the NP rule.)

1.6   Coordination (Conjunction)

One type of constituent that we haven't yet considered is the coordinated or conjoined constituent. This is a constituent like those in (60) below, where we have two elements with identical categories that are joined together with words like *and, or, but, nor*, etc.

60) a)   the [blue and red] station wagon
    b)   I saw [these dancers and those musicians] smoking something suspicious.
    c)   I am [drinking lemonade and eating a brownie].
    d)   [I've lost my wallet or I've lost my mind.]
    e)   We went [through the woods and over the bridge].

The coordination in (a) combines two adjectives into a single modifier, (b) combines two NPs, (c) combines two VPs, (d) two sentences and (e) two PPs. Coordination seems to be able to join together two identical categories and create a new identical category out of them. In order to draw trees with conjunction in them, we need two more rules. These rules are slightly different than the ones we have looked at up to now. These rules are not category-specific. Instead they use a variable (X). This X can stand for N or V or A or P, etc. Just like in algebra, it is a variable that can stand for different categories. We need two rules, one to conjoin phrases (*[The Flintstones] and [the Rubbles]*) and one to conjoin words (*the [dancer] and [singer]*):

61) a) XP → XP conj XP
    b) X → X conj X

These result in trees like the following for the phrases and sentences in (60).

62) a)

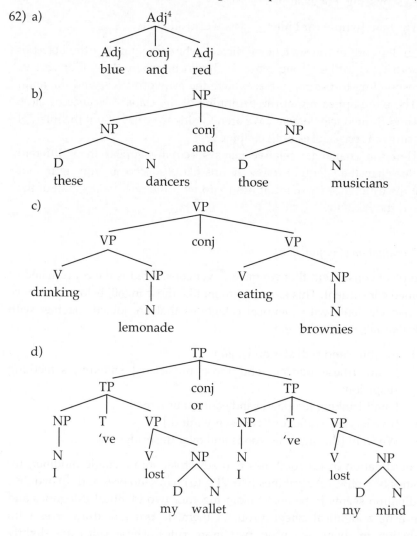

---

[4] This could also have been drawn with a conjoined AdjP since the category of red and blue is ambiguous between a head word and a phrase:

[AdjP [AdjP blue] and [AdjP red]]

e)

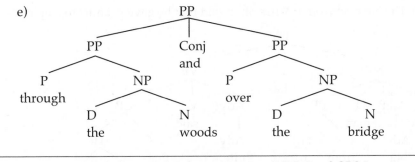

You now have enough information to try WBE 4 and GPS 5.

1.7 Summary

In this section we've been looking at the PSRs needed to generate trees that account for English sentences. As we'll see in later chapters, this is nothing but a first pass at a very complex set of data. It is probably worth repeating the final form of each of the rules here:

63) a) CP → (C) TP
    b) TP → {NP/CP} (T) VP
    c) VP → (AdvP+) V (NP)({NP/CP}) (AdvP+) (PP+) (AdvP+)
    d) NP → (D) (AdjP+) N (PP+) (CP)
    e) PP → P (NP)
    f) AdjP → (AdvP) Adj
    g) AdvP → (AdvP) Adv
    h) XP → XP conj XP
    i) X → X conj X

These rules account for a wide variety of English sentences. It's quite a complicated set, but it captures the basic generalizations about the constituency of English. Later, in Chapter 6, we'll propose a simplified set of rules that isn't quite so stipulative. A sentence using each of the rules in (63) is shown in (64):

64) The big man from NY has often said that he gave peanuts to elephants.

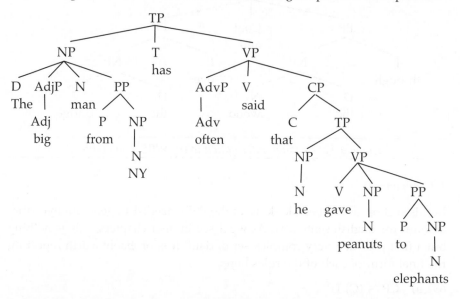

Recursion

Notice the following thing: The TP rule has a VP under it. Similarly, the VP rule can take a CP under it, and the CP takes a TP. This means that the three rules can form a loop and repeat endlessly:

i)   Fred said that Mary believes that Susan wants that … etc.

This property, called *recursion*, accounts partially for the infinite nature of human language. Because you get these endless loops, it is possible to generate sentences that have never been heard before.

2. HOW TO DRAW A TREE

You now have the tools you need to start drawing trees. You have the rules, and you have the parts of speech. I suspect that you'll find drawing trees much more difficult than you expect. It takes a lot of practice to know which rules to apply and apply them consistently and accurately to a sentence. You won't be able to draw trees easily until you literally do dozens of them. Drawing syntactic trees is a learned skill that needs lots of practice, just like learning to play the piano.

There are actually two ways to go about drawing a tree. You can start at the bottom and work your way up to the TP, or you can start with the TP and work your way down. Which technique you use depends upon your individual style. For most people who are just starting out, starting at the bottom of the tree with the words works best. When you become more practiced and experienced you may find starting at the top quicker. Below, I give step-by-step instructions for both of these techniques.

2.1 Bottom-up Trees

This method for tree drawing often works best for beginners. Here are some (hopefully helpful) steps to go through when drawing trees.

1. Write out the sentence and identify the parts of speech:

   D   Adv Adj N   V   D   N
   The very small boy kissed the platypus.

2. Identify what modifies what. Remember the modification relations. If the word modifies something then it is contained in the same constituent as that thing.

Very modifies *small.*	*Very small* modifies *boy.*
The modifies *boy.*	*The* modifies *platypus.*
The platypus modifies *kissed.*	

3. Start linking together items that modify one another. It often helps to start at the right edge. Always start with adjacent words. If the modifier is modifying a noun, then the rule you must apply is the NP rule:

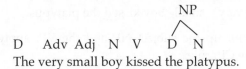

   D   Adv Adj N   V   D   N
   The very small boy kissed the platypus.

   Similarly if the word that is being modified is an adjective, then you must apply the AdjP rule:

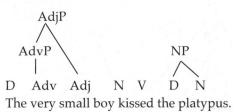

   D   Adv Adj   N   V   D   N
   The very small boy kissed the platypus.

4. Make sure you apply the rule *exactly* as it is written. For example the AdjP rule reads AdjP → (AdvP) Adj. This means that the Adv must have an AdvP on top of it before it can combine with the Adj.

5. Keep applying the rules until you have attached all the modifiers to the modified constituents. Apply one rule at a time. Work from right to left (from the end of the sentence to the beginning). Try doing the rules in the following order:

   a) AdjPs & AdvPs   b) NPs & PPs
   c) VPs   d) TP
   e) If your sentence has more than one clause in it, start with the most embedded clause.

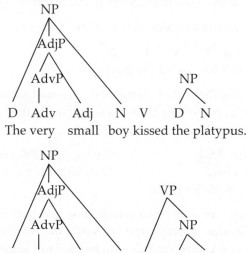

6. When you've built up the subject NP and the VP, apply the TP (and if appropriate the CP) rule:

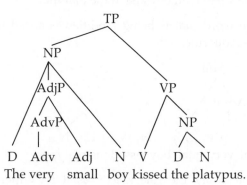

7. *This is the most important step of all*: Now go back and make sure that your tree is really generated by the rules. Check each level

in the tree and make sure your rules will generate it. If they don't, apply the rule correctly and fix the structure.

8.   Some important considerations:
    a)   Make sure that everything is attached to the tree.
    b)   Make sure that every category has only *one* line immediately on top of it (it can have more than one under it, but only one immediately on top of it).
    c)   Don't cross lines.
    d)   Make sure all branches in the tree have a part of speech label.
    e)   Avoid triangles.

Skill at tree drawing comes only with practice. At the end of this chapter are a number of sentences that you can practice on. I also encourage you to try some of the trees in the workbook. Use the suggestions above if you find them helpful. Another helpful idea is to model your trees on ones that you can find in this chapter. Look carefully at them, and use them as a starting point. Finally, don't forget: Always check your trees against the rules that generate them.

To Line or Not?

In many works on syntax you will find trees that have the word connected to the category with a line, rather than writing the word immediately under its category as we have been doing. This is a historical artifact of the way trees used to be constructed in the 1950s. The lines that connect elements in trees mean "created by a phrase structure rule." There are no phrase structure rules that connect words with their categories (i.e., there is no rule V → *kissed*), so technically speaking any line between the word's category and the word is incorrect.

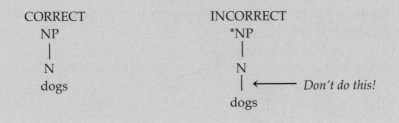

2.2 *The Top-down Method of Drawing Trees*

Most professional syntacticians use a slightly quicker means of drawing trees. Once you are practiced at identifying the structure of trees, you will probably want to use this technique. But be warned, sometimes this technique can lead you astray if you are not careful.

1. This method starts out the same way as the other: write out the sentence and identify the parts of speech.

D Adv Adj N V D N
The very small boy kissed the platypus.

2. Next draw the TP node at the top of the tree, with the subject NP and VP underneath:

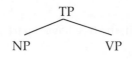

D Adv Adj N V D N
The very small boy kissed the platypus.

3. Using the NP rule, flesh out the subject NP. You will have to look ahead here. If there is a P, you will probably need a PP. Similarly, if there is an Adj, you'll need at least one AdjP, maybe more. Remember the Principle of Modification: elements that modify one another are part of the same constituent.

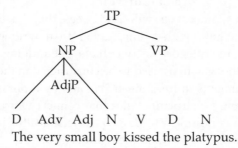

D Adv Adj N V D N
The very small boy kissed the platypus.

4. Fill in the AdvPs, AdjPs and PPs as necessary. You may need to do other NPs inside PPs.

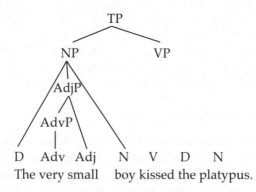

D Adv Adj N V D N
The very small boy kissed the platypus.

5. Next do constituents inside the VP, including object NPs, and any APs and PPs inside them.

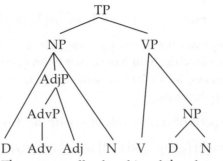

6. Again, the most important step is to go back and make sure that your tree obeys all the rules, as well as the golden rule of tree structures.

Again, I strongly recommend that you start your tree drawing using the bottom-up method, but after some practice, you may find this latter method quicker.

Tree Drawing Software
There are some software tools that can help you draw trees. There are many such programs, but I particularly recommend two:
>   http://www.ece.ubc.ca/~donaldd/treeform.htm
>   http://www.yohasebe.com/rsyntaxtree/

Both these programs will generate graphics files that can be pasted into most word processors.

2.3 Bracketed Diagrams

Sometimes it is preferable to use the bracketed notation instead of the tree notation. This is especially true when there are large parts of the sentence that are irrelevant to the discussion at hand. Drawing bracketed diagrams essentially follows the same principles as tree drawing (see 2.1 or 2.2 above). The exception is that instead of drawing to lines connecting at the top, you put square brackets on either side of the constituent. A label is usually put on the left member of the bracket pair as a subscript.

65)   NP

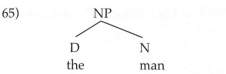

D   N
the   man   = [$_{NP}$[$_D$ the] [$_N$ man]]

Both words and phrases are bracketed this way. For each point where you have a group of lines connecting, you have a pair of brackets.

To see how this works, let's take our sentence from sections 2.1 and 2.2 above and do it again in brackets:

1.   First we mark the parts of speech, this time with labeled brackets:

[$_D$ The] [$_{Adv}$ very] [$_{Adj}$ small] [$_N$ boy] [$_V$ kissed] [$_D$ the] [$_N$ platypus].

2.   Next we apply the AP, NP, and PP rules:
[$_D$ The] [$_{AdvP}$[$_{Adv}$ very]] [$_{Adj}$ small] [$_N$ boy] [$_V$ kissed] [$_D$ the] [$_N$ platypus].
[$_D$ The] [$_{AdjP}$[$_{AdvP}$[$_{Adv}$ very]] [$_{Adj}$ small]] [$_N$ boy] [$_V$ kissed] [$_D$ the] [$_N$ platypus].
[$_{NP}$[$_D$ The]][$_{AdjP}$[$_{AdvP}$[$_{Adv}$ very]][$_{Adj}$ small]][$_N$ boy]] [$_V$ kissed] [$_D$ the] [$_N$ platypus].
[$_{NP}$[$_D$ The]][$_{AdjP}$[$_{AdvP}$[$_{Adv}$ very]][$_{Adj}$ small]][$_N$ boy]][$_V$ kissed][$_{NP}$[$_D$the][$_N$platypus]].

3.   Now the VP and TP rules:

[$_{NP}$[$_D$The]][$_{AdjP}$[$_{AdvP}$[$_{Adv}$very]][$_{Adj}$small]][$_N$boy]][$_{VP}$[$_V$kissed][$_{NP}$[$_D$the][$_N$platypus]]].
[$_{TP}$[$_{NP}$[$_D$The]][$_{AdjP}$[$_{AdvP}$[$_{Adv}$very]][$_{Adj}$small]][$_N$boy]][$_{VP}$[$_V$kissed][$_{NP}$[$_D$the]
    [$_N$platypus]]]].

You now have enough information to try WBE 5 and GPS 6.

3. MODIFICATION AND AMBIGUITY

Syntactic trees allow us to capture another important fact about syntactic structure: Sentences often are ambiguous. Let's start with the following sentence:

66) The man killed the king with the knife.

This sentence turns out to have more than one meaning, but for the moment consider only the least difficult reading for it (the phrase in quotes that follows is called a *paraphrase*): "the man used the knife to kill the king." Remember the Principle of Modification:

67) *Principle of Modification* (revised): If an XP (that is, a phrase with some category X) modifies some head Y, then XP must be a sister to Y (i.e., a daughter of YP).

In this first meaning, the PP *with the knife* modifies *killed*, so the structure will look like (68):

68)

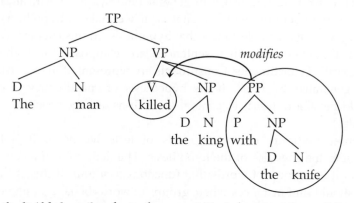

[*With the knife*] describes how the man killed the king. It modifies the verb *killed*, so it is attached under the VP.

Now consider a paraphrase of the other meaning of (66). "the king with the knife was killed by the man (who used a gun)." This meaning has the PP *with the knife* modifying *king*, and thus attached to the NP:

69)

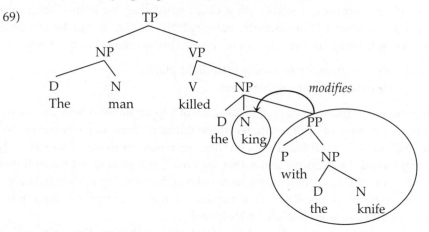

These examples illustrate an important property of syntactic trees. Trees allow us to capture the differences between ambiguous readings of the same surface sentence.

You now have enough information to try WBE 6 and GPS 7 & 8.

4. CONSTITUENCY TESTS

In chapter 1, we held linguistics in general (and syntax specifically) up to the light of the scientific method. That is, if we make a hypothesis about something, we must be able to test that hypothesis. In this chapter, we have proposed the hypothesis that sentences are composed of higher-level groupings called constituents. Constituents are represented in tree structures and are generated by rules. If the hypothesis of constituency is correct, we should be able to test it in general (as well as test the specific instances of the rules).

In order to figure out what kinds of tests we need, it is helpful to reconsider the specifics of the hypothesis. The definition of a constituent states that it is a group of words that functions as a unit. If this is the case, then we should find instances where groups of words behave as single units. These instances can serve as tests for the hypothesis. In other words, they are **tests for constituency**. There are a lot of constituency tests listed in the syntactic literature. We are going to look at only four here: replacement, stand-alone, movement, and coordination.

First, the smallest constituent is a single word, so it follows that if you can replace a group of words with a single word then we know that group forms a constituent. Consider the italicized NP in (70). It can be replaced with a single word (in this case a pronoun). This is the **replacement** test.

70) a) *The man from NY* flew only ultra-light planes.
    b) *He* flew only ultra-light planes.

There is one important caveat to the test of replacement: There are many cases in our rules of optional items (those things marked in parentheses like the AdjP in NP → (D) (AdjP+) N). When we replace a string of words with a single word, how do we know that we aren't just leaving off the optional items? To avoid this problem, we have to keep the meaning as closely related to the original as possible. This requires some judgment on your part. None of these tests is absolute or foolproof.

The second test we will use is the **stand-alone** test (sometimes also called the **sentence fragment** test). If the words can stand alone in response to a question, then they probably constitute a constituent. Consider the sentence in (71a) and repeated in (71b). We are going to test for the constituency of the italicized phrases.

71) a) Paul *ate at a really fancy restaurant*.
    b) Paul *ate at* a really fancy restaurant.

If we ask the question "What did Paul do yesterday afternoon?" we can answer with the italicized group of words in (74a), but not in (74b):

72) a)   Ate at a really fancy restaurant.
    b)   *Ate at.

Neither of these responses is proper English in prescriptive terms, but you can easily tell that (74a) is better than (74b).

   Movement is our third test of constituency. If you can move a group of words around in the sentence, then they form a constituent – because you can move them as a unit. Some typical examples are shown in (73). *Clefting* (73a) involves putting a string of words between *It was* (or *It is*) and a *that* at the beginning of the sentence. *Preposing* (73b) (also called *pseudoclefting*) involves putting the string of words before a *is/are what* or *is/are who* at the front of the sentence. We discuss the *passive* (73c) at length in chapters 9 and 11. Briefly, it involves putting the object in the subject position, the subject in a "by phrase" (after the word *by*) and changing the verb form (for example from *kiss* to *was kissed*).

73) a)   Clefting: It was [a brand new car] that he bought.
                            (from *He bought a brand new car*)

    b)   Preposing: [Big bowls of beans] are what I like.
                            (from *I like big bowls of beans*)

    c)   Passive: [The big boy] was kissed by [the slobbering dog].
                            (from *The slobbering dog kissed the big boy*)

Again, the movement test is only reliable when you keep the meaning roughly the same as in the original sentence.

   Finally, we have the test of *coordination* (also called *conjunction*). Coordinate structures are constituents linked by a conjunction like *and* or *or*. Only constituents of the same syntactic category can be conjoined:

74) a)   [John] and [the man] went to the store.
    b)   *John and very blue went to the store.

If you can coordinate a group of words with a similar group of words, then they form a constituent.

You now have enough information to try GPS 9 & 10 and CPS 5 & 6.

When Constituency Tests Fail

Unfortunately, sometimes it is the case that constituency tests give false results (which is one of the reasons we haven't spent much time on them in this text). Consider the case of the subject of a sentence and its verb. These do not form a constituent. However, under certain circumstances you can conjoin a subject and verb to the exclusion of the object:

i)   Bruce loved and Kelly hated phonology class.

Sentence (i) seems to indicate that the verb and subject form a constituent, which they don't. As you will see in later chapters, it turns out that things can move around in sentences or be deleted. This means that sometimes the constituency is obscured by other factors. For this reason, to be sure that a test is working correctly you have to apply more than one test to a given structure. Always perform at least two different tests to check constituency, as one alone may give you a false result.

5. CONSTITUENCY IN OTHER LANGUAGES

The rules and processes we have seen so far describe a significant chunk (but by no means all) of English sentence constituent structures. In this section, we investigate the ways in which languages vary from one another with respect to phrase structure. We'll also look at languages that appear to have no phrase structure at all as well as languages with very free word order, and conclude with some tips for doing foreign language problems.

5.1 Head Ordering[5]

As discussed above, the **head** of a phrase is the word that gives its category to the phrase. So prepositions are the heads of prepositional phrases, nouns are the heads of noun phrases, etc. English tends towards having the heads of phrases on the left of phrases. Prepositions come before the NPs they are associated with, complementizers come before the clause they modify, etc. Leaving aside adjectives, adverbs and determiners, which mess up the picture a bit, it is also the case that nouns come before prepositional modifiers, and verbs come before noun phrase and prepositional phrase modifiers. Therefore we often say that English is *left-headed*. But other languages exhibit different headedness properties.

---

[5] Much of the data in this section is taken from the World Atlas of Language Structures Online (http://wals.info).

There are many languages where the predominant order has heads on the right (i.e., are *right-headed*). Take for example the sentence in (75) from Lezgian, a Caucasian language spoken in Azerbaijan (data from Haspelmath 1993: 218). In this language prepositions (or more accurately postpositions) come after their noun phrase.

75)   duxturrin   patariw   fena.
        doctors   to   go.PAST
        "She went to doctors."

The phrase structure rule for Lezgian PPs is given in (76), where the head P follows the NP rather than preceding it.

76)   PP → NP P

In English adjectives appear before the noun they modify, but in French, for example (77), they typically follow the noun they modify. So we would use a rule like that in (78).

77)   les   gars   beaux
        the.PL   guys   handsome.PL
        "The handsome guys"

78)   NP → (D) N (AdjP+)

In English, object NPs follow the verb they are associated with, but in many languages, including Japanese, the object comes before the verb as in (79) (Kuno 1973: 10). A partial phrase structure rule (leaving out the adverbs and PPs) for the Japanese VP is given in (80).

79)   John-ga   tegami-o   yonda.
        John-SUBJ   letter-OBJECT   read.PAST
        "John read the letter."

80)   VP → (NP) V

Even in the order of the subject and the VP (predicate), we find major differences among languages. For example, in Nias, a language spoken in Sumatra, the subject of the sentence follows both the verb and its object:

81)   Irino   vakhe   inagu.
        cook   rice   mother.1S.POSS
        "My mother cooked rice."

So the right half of the sentence rule is the reverse of that in English:

82)   TP → VP NP

To summarize what we've seen in this section, phrase structure rules can vary between languages. Often this is an effect of headedness. Japanese and Lezgian for example, tend to put their heads on the right-hand side of the phrase. But the patterns can be subtler and involve more variation than this. What remains the same among all these cases is that one is usually able to describe the sentence structure of basic clauses using variations on our phrase structure rules. This is a very strong claim, and there are at least two kinds of language that challenge it: (i) languages where sentences seem to be largely composed of single, very heavily inflected, words and (ii) languages with apparently free word order. These two kinds of languages are the topics of the next two sections.

5.2 Languages without Phrase Structure and Free Word Order Languages

There are many languages in the world in which it appears that there are no sentences. Instead, one finds very complicated words. Take for example Nahuatl (spoken in Mexico), where we find sentences like that in (83) (data from Merlan 1976: 184):

83)   Nimictomimaka.
         "I'll give you money."

Languages like this are called **polysynthetic** languages. At first blush one might think that the existence of such forms means that phrase structure is not universal to the world's languages. A more careful investigation suggests that this might be an oversimplification, however. If you have ever taken a course in morphology, you'll know that even in English words are structured entities. One speculation syntacticians have about polysynthetic languages is that "words" like that in (83) are actually syntactically complex. The basic idea is that the rules that govern syntactic form in some languages are similar to the rules that govern word form in other languages.

Another challenge to the idea that much syntactic structure can be captured using phrase structure comes from languages with relatively free word order. Take the famous case of the Australian language Warlpiri (data from Hale 1983). In this language the verb and the noun phrases can appear in any order, as long as the auxiliary particle (in 84, *ka*) appears in the second position in the sentence.

84) a) Ngarrka-ngku ka   wawirri   panti-rni.
         man-ERG   AUX   kangaroo   spear-NONPAST
         "The man is spearing the kangaroo."

    b) Wawarri ka panti-rni ngarrka-ngku.
    c) Panti-rni ka ngarrka-ngku panti-rni.   ... and so on.

If you've ever taken lessons in Latin, you'll know that something similar is true in that language as well. One can find all of the following possible word orders:

85) a) Mīlitēs   urbem dēlēbunt.
        Soldiers   city   destroy.FUT.3PL
        "The soldiers will destroy the city."

    b) Mīlitēs dēlēbunt urbem.
    c) Urbem mīlitēs dēlēbunt.
    d) Urbem dēlēbunt mīlitēs.
    e) Dēlēbunt mīlitēs urbem.
    f) Dēlēbunt urbem mīlitēs.

Sentence (85a) was the most normal order (subject object verb, i.e. TP → NP VP, VP → (NP) V), but all the other orders were possible too.

What do we make of languages that exhibit freedom in word order? In the past 15 or so years, linguists such as the Persian linguist Simin Karimi and the Hungarian linguist Katalin É. Kiss have shown that these orders aren't really "free". In fact, with each ordering there is a special semantics applied. For example, in Latin (and Persian) the thing that comes first in the sentence is most typically the "topic" of the sentence. Topics are the old information in the sentence or the information that follows from previously understood discourse. So for example, we'd use sentences (85c and d) when we had been talking about some particular city immediately before uttering this sentence. Other times the order can be affected by emphasis (known as contrastive focus), where an especially important idea contrasted with other ideas is drawn into highlight. Often these focuses (or foci) are put at the beginning of sentences. Sometimes there is a complex interplay between topic and focus structures.

In each language that exhibits "free" word order, we find that there is one "neutral" order. Typically this is the order used when a sentence has no special topic or focus and is used "out of the blue". In Latin this is SOV. The neutral orders can typically be created by phrase structure rules. The various word orders determined by topic and focus are created by a special kind of rule called a "transformational rule". We return to transformational rules in later chapters in this book, and to both polysynthetic and non-configurational languages in chapter 18.

5.3 Doing Foreign Language Problem Sets

Often, linguistic examples from languages other than English will take the following form (example from Sinhala – a language spoken in Sri Lanka; data from Lehmann 1978):

86) Jōn   ballavə däkka. ←──────────── *Actual language data*
    John   dog   saw ←──────────── *Word-by-word gloss*
    "John saw the dog."   ←──────────── *Idiomatic translation*

There are three lines: the actual data, a word-by-word gloss and an idiomatic translation into English. Of these, the most important for doing the problem set is the second line – the word-by-word gloss. The glosses are lined up word for word (and sometimes morpheme for morpheme) with the foreign language on the line above. This line tells you (1) what each word in the foreign language example means, and more importantly, (2) the order of the words in the foreign language. When trying to determine the phrase structure of a foreign language or the behavior of a word or phrase, this is the line to look at! (However, when drawing trees and citing examples in your answer, it is considered more respectful of the language to use the actual foreign language words.) Remember: *don't* do an analysis of the idiomatic translation of the sentence, because then you are only doing an analysis of English!

Here's a more complete paradigm of Sinhala, along with a series of typical problem set questions:

87) Jōn   ballavə däkka.
    John   dog   saw
    "John saw the dog."

88) Jōn   janēle iñdəla ballavə däkka.
    John   window from dog   saw
    "John saw the dog from the window."

89) Jōn   eyāge taḍi   ballavə däkka.
    John   his   big   dog   saw
    "John saw his big dog."

a) Assume there is an AdjP rule: AdjP → Adj. What is the NP rule?
b) What is the PP rule of Sinhala?
c) What is the VP rule of Sinhala? (Assume all non-head material is optional.)
d) What is the TP rule of Sinhala?
e) Draw the tree for sentences (88) and (89).

The first step in analyzing a language like this is to determine the parts of speech of each of the words. Be very careful here. Do not assume because English has certain categories that the language you are looking at has the same categories; however, all other things being equal you can assume that there will be some parallels (unless we have evidence to the contrary):

90) Jōn   ballavə däkka.
    John   dog   saw
    N   N   V

91) Jōn   janēle   iñdəla ballavə däkka.
    John   window   from   dog   saw
    N   N   P   N   V

92) Jōn   eyāge   taḍi   ballavə däkka.
    John   his   big   dog   saw
    N   D   Adj   N   V

Next let's answer question (a). We can observe from sentence (90) that an NP in Sinhala (just like in English) can be an N by itself (e.g., *Jōn*). This means that anything other than the noun has to be optional. Consider now the sentence in (92); from the literal English translation we can tell that the words meaning "big" and "his" modify the word "dog", and are thus part of the NP headed by "dog". We're told in (a) to assume that there is an AdjP rule (AdjP → Adj), and we are treating the word for "his" as a determiner. Thus it follows that the Sinhala NP rule is at least the following: NP → (D) (AdjP) N. You'll notice that the order of elements in this rule is the same as the order of elements in the Sinhala sentence.

You should also note that the PP meaning "from the window" does not modify the N, so is not part of the NP rule at this point. Since it modifies the V, it will be part of the VP rule.

Question (b) asks us about the PP rule. We have one P in the data – the word meaning "from" in sentence (91). Pay careful attention here. This P appears between two nouns; but the noun associated with the P is the one meaning "window". This means that the P in Sinhala *follows* the NP; so the rule is PP → NP P. We have no evidence if the NP here is optional.

The VP rule is next in (c). Sentence (91) is the most informative here. Looking at what would be in the VP in English, we have the PP meaning "from the window" and the NP meaning "dog". These both precede the V. This is true in sentences (90) and (92) too. The PP is clearly optional, but there is no evidence in the data about whether the NP is or not. However, you are told to assume that "all non-head material is optional." So the rule is VP → (PP) (NP) V.

Finally we have the TP rule. Like English, the subject NP precedes the VP. So the rule is TP → NP VP. We have no evidence for a T node so we have not posited one.

Here are the trees for (91) and (92).

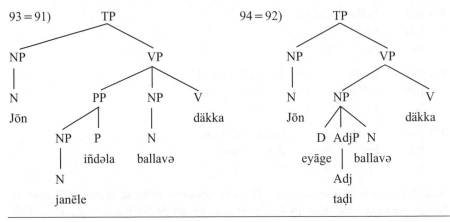

You now have enough information to try WBE 7–11, GPS 11–15, and CPS 7

---

6. SUMMARY AND CONCLUSION

We've done a lot in this chapter. We looked at the idea that sentences are hierarchically organized into constituent structures. We represented these constituent structures in trees and bracketed diagrams. We also developed a set of rules to generate those structures. We looked at constituency tests that can be used to test the structures. And finally we looked at the way constituent structure can vary across languages.

IDEAS, RULES, AND CONSTRAINTS INTRODUCED IN THIS CHAPTER

i)   *Constituent*: A group of words that function together as a unit.
ii)   *Hierarchical Structure*: Constituents in a sentence are embedded inside of other constituents.
iii)   *Syntactic Trees and Bracketed Diagrams*: These are means of representing constituency. They are generated by rules.
iv)   *English Phrase Structure Rules*
       a) CP → (C) TP
       b) TP → {NP/CP} (T) VP

c)   VP → (AdvP+) V (NP) ({NP/CP}) (AdvP+) (PP+) (AdvP+)
d)   NP → (D) (AdjP+) N (PP+) (CP)
e)   PP → P (NP)
f)   AdjP → (AdvP) Adj
g)   AdvP → (AdvP) Adv
h)   XP → XP conj XP
i)   X → X conj X

v)   *Head*: The word that gives its category to the phrase.

vi)   *Recursion*: The possibility of loops in the phrase structure rules
        that allow infinitely long sentences, and explain the creativity
        of language.

vii)   *The Principle of Modification*: If an XP (that is, a phrase with some
        category X) modifies some head Y, then XP must be a sister to Y (i.e.,
        a daughter of YP).

viii)   *Constituency Tests*: Tests that show that a group of words
        functions as a unit. There are four major constituency tests given
        here: *movement, coordination, stand-alone,* and *replacement*.

FURTHER READING: Carnie (2011), Chomsky (1957, 1965)

GENERAL PROBLEM SETS

GPS1. TREES: NPS, ADJPS AND ADVPS
[Application of Skills; Basic]
Draw the trees for the following AdjPs, AdvPs, and NPs:
a) very smelly   b) too quickly
c) much too quickly   d) very much too quickly
e) the old shoelace
f) the soggy limp spaghetti noodle *[assume* spaghetti = *Adj]*
g) these very finicky children

GPS2. TREES II: ENGLISH PPS
[Application of Skills; Basic]
Draw the trees for the following English NPs and PPs:
a) the desk with the wobbly drawer
b) in my black rubber boots *[assume* rubber = *Adj]*
c) that notebook with the scribbles in the margin
d) the pen at the back of the drawer in the desk near the bright yellow
    painting

GPS3. STARBUCKESE
[Critical and Creative Thinking; Basic]
In standard English, one can't put a PP before a head noun that the preposition modifies. For example, the NP in (a) is completely ungrammatical.

a)   *The with milk coffee.

But there is a major chain of coffee stores whose employees seem to allow a different ordering of elements in NPs:

b)   A venti with room Americano.[6]

Let's call this dialect Starbuckese. Starbuckese also appears to allow *with soy* and *with skim* to precede the head noun. The phenomenon might also be seen in certain fixed phrases like *at issue content*, *in house lawyer* and *over the counter medicine*, which are not limited to the employees of ubiquitous coffee dispensaries.[7]
     What changes would you have to make to the English phrase structure rules to allow Starbuckese NPs like (b) above?

GPS4. TREES III: THE VICES OF VPS
[Application of Skills; Intermediate]
Draw the trees for the following English VPs:
a)   snores   b)   eats burgers
c)   always smokes in the car   d)   drinks frequently in the car
e)   smokes in the car frequently   f)   smokes cigars in the car
g)   sent Gregory a dirty email on Friday

GPS5. TREES IV: COORDINATION
[Application of Skills; Intermediate]
Draw the trees for the following English coordinations:
a)   buttons and bows
b)   to and from the house
c)   very big and ugly *(note: this is ambiguous and could have 2 trees; try to draw them both!)*
d)   kiss and hug your dad *(this is a VP)*
e)   kiss your dad and hug your mom *(this is a VP)*
f)   He likes cookies and he hates crumbcake.

---

[6] For those not familiar with this chain: *venti* is the size; an *Americano* is an espresso with hot water; and *with room* means that they leave space for you to add milk.
[7] Thanks to my linguistically oriented Facebook® friends who came up with all these examples.

GPS6. ENGLISH

[Application of Skills and Knowledge; Basic to Advanced]
Draw phrase structure trees *and* bracketed diagrams for each of the following sentences. Indicate all the categories (phrase (e.g., NP) and word level (e.g., N)) on the tree. Use the rules given above in the "Ideas" summary of this chapter. Be careful that items that modify one another are part of the same constituent. Treat words like *can, should, might,* and *was* as instances of the category T (tense). (Sentences d–h are from Sheila Dooley.)

a) The kangaroo hopped over the truck.
b) I haven't seen this sentence before.   *[before is a P, haven't is a T]*
c) Susan will never sing at weddings.   *[never is an Adv]*
d) The officer carefully inspected the license.
e) Every cat always knows the location of her favorite catnip toy.
f) The cat put her catnip toy on the plastic mat.
g) The very young child walked from school to the store.
h) John paid a dollar for a head of lettuce.
i) Teenagers drive rather quickly.
j) A clever magician with the right equipment can fool the audience easily.
k) The police might plant the drugs in the apartment.
l) Those Olympic hopefuls should practice diligently daily.
m) The latest research on dieting always warns people about the dangers of too much cholesterol.
n) That annoying faucet was dripping constantly for months.
o) Marian wonders if the package from Boston will ever arrive.
p) I said that Bonny should do some dances from the Middle East.
q) That Dan smokes in the office really bothers Alina.
r) The belief that syntactic theory reveals the inner structure of sentences emboldened the already much too cocky professor.

GPS7. AMBIGUITY I

[Application of Skills and Knowledge; Basic]
Consider the two trees below in (A) and (B). These abstractly represent the structure of the sentences below them. Determine whether each sentence has the structure in (A), the structure in (B), or both! (A triangle indicates that the structure below that node is not important to the question.)

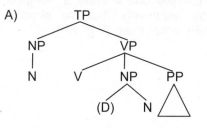

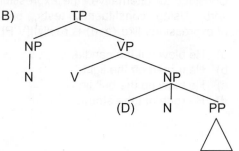

1) I bought the parrot in the store
2) I put the milk in the fridge

3) I mailed the sweater to Mary
4) They chased the man with the car
5) I knew the man with the brown hair

GPS8. AMBIGUITY II
[Application of Knowledge and Skills; Basic to Intermediate]
The following English sentences are all ambiguous. Provide a paraphrase (a sentence with roughly the same meaning) for each of the possible meanings, and then draw (two) trees of the *original* sentence that distinguish the two meanings. Be careful not to draw the tree of the paraphrase. Your two trees should be different from one another, where the difference reflects which elements modify what. (For sentence (b) ignore the issue of capitalization.) You may need to assume that *old* and *seven* can function as adverbs. Sentences (c), (d), (e), and (f) are ambiguous newspaper headlines taken from http://www.fun-with-words.com/ambiguous_headlines.html.

a)   John said Mary went to the store quickly.
b)   I discovered an old English poem.
c)   Two sisters reunited after 18 years in checkout counter
d)   Enraged cow injures farmer with ax
e)   Hospitals are sued by seven foot doctors
f)   Dealers will hear car talk after noon

GPS9. STRUCTURE
[Application of Knowledge; Intermediate]
In the following sentences a sequence of words is marked as a constituent with square brackets. State whether or not it is a real constituent, and what criteria (that is constituency tests) you applied to determine that result.

a)   Susanne gave [the minivan to Petunia].
b)   Clyde got [a passionate love letter from Stacy].

GPS10. ENGLISH PREPOSITIONS
[Critical Thinking; Intermediate]
In the text, we claimed that perhaps the NP in PPs was optional, explaining why we can say *He passed out*, where the preposition *out* has no object. Consider an alternative: the expression *[passed out]* is really a "complex" verb. Using constituency tests, provide arguments that the structure of expressions like (a–d) is really [[V P] NP] rather than: [V [P NP]].

a)   He blew out the candle.
b)   He turned off the light.
c)   He blew up the building.
d)   He rode out the storm.

GPS11. SWEDISH NPS

[Application of Skills and Knowledge; Basic]
Consider the following data from Swedish. (If you speak Swedish, please confine yourself to this data; do *not* try to include definite forms, e.g., the umbrella.) You may wish to review section 5.4.2 before attempting this problem. (Data courtesy of Sheila Dooley.)

a) folk   "people"
b) ett paraply   "an umbrella"
c) tre paraplyer   "three umbrellas"
d) ett äpple   "an apple"
e) ett rött paraply   "a red umbrella"
f) ett gult äpple   "a yellow apple"
g) ett mycket fint paraply   "a very fine umbrella"
h) ett gammalt fint paraply   "a fine old umbrella"
i) ett rött paraply med ett gult handtag   "a red umbrella with a yellow handle"

1) Assume the Adv rule of Swedish is AdvP → Adv. What is the AdjP rule?
2) Are determiners obligatory in Swedish NPs?
3) Are AdjPs obligatory in Swedish NPs?
4) What is the PP rule for Swedish?
5) Are PPs obligatory in Swedish NPs?
6) What is the NP rule for Swedish?
7) Draw the trees for (g), (h), and (i).
8) Give the bracketed diagrams for (f) and (i).

GPS12. BAMBARA

[Application of Skills; Basic]
Consider the following data from Bambara, a Mande language spoken in Mali. (The glosses have been slightly simplified.) Pay careful attention to the second line, where the word order of Bambara is shown. (Data from Koopman 1992.)

a) A   kasira.
    he cried
    "He cried."

b) Den   ye   ji   min.
    child   PAST   water   drink
    "The child drank water."

c) N sonna a ma.
    I agreed it to
    "I agreed to it."

Answer the following questions about Bambara. Do not break apart words in your analysis.

1) Do you need a T category in Bambara?
2) Do you need a D category in Bambara?

3) What is the NP rule for Bambara? (You do not need any AdjP or PPs in the rule.)
4) What is the PP rule for Bambara?
5) What is the VP rule for Bambara?
6) What is the TP rule for Bambara? (Keep in mind your answers to the above questions; be consistent.)
7) Draw trees for (a), (b), and (c) using your rules.
8) Draw bracketed diagrams for (b) and (c).

GPS13. HIXKARYANA
[Application of Skills; Basic/Intermediate]
Look carefully at the following data from a Carib language from Brazil (the glosses have been slightly simplified from the original). In your analysis do not break apart words. (Data from Derbyshire 1985.)

a) Kuraha   yonyhoryeno   biyekomo.
   bow   made   boy
   "The boy made a bow."

b) Newehyatxhe   woriskomo komo.
   take-bath   women   all
   "All the women take a bath."

c) Toto   heno komo   yonoye kamara.
   person   dead all   ate   jaguar
   "The jaguar ate all the dead people."

Now answer the following questions about Hixkaryana:

1) Is there any evidence for a determiner category in Hixkaryana? Be sure to consider quantifier words (like *some* and *all*) as possible determiners.
2) Posit an NP rule to account for Hixkaryana. (Be careful to do it for the second line in these examples, the word-by-word gloss, not the third line.) Assume there is an AdjP rule: AdjP ⟶ Adj.
3) Posit a VP rule for Hixkaryana.
4) Posit a TP rule for Hixkaryana.
5) What is the part of speech of *newehyatxhe*? How do you know?
6) Draw the trees for (a) and (c) using the rules you posited above. (Hint: if your trees don't work, then you have probably made a mistake in the rules.)
7) Give bracketed diagrams for the same sentences.

GPS14. DUTCH
[Application of Skills; Intermediate]
Consider the following sentences of Dutch. (Data from Ferdinand de Haan.)

a) De man in de regenjas is naar Amsterdam gegaan.
   the man in the raincoat is to   Amsterdam going
   "The man in the raincoat is going to Amsterdam."

b)   De man heeft een gele   auto met een aanhanger gekocht.
     the man has   a   yellow car with a   trailer   bought
     "The man has bought a yellow car with a trailer."

c)   De vrouw   heeft een auto gekocht.
     the woman has   a   car bought
     "The woman has bought a car."

d)   Jan is vertrokken.
     John is gone
     "John left."

1)   Assume an AdjP rule, AdjP → Adj; what is the NP rule of Dutch?
2)   What is the PP rule of Dutch?
3)   What is the VP rule of Dutch? (Assume that *is* and *heeft* are of the
     category T and are not part of the VP.)
4)   What is the TP rule for Dutch?
5)   Draw the trees for (a) and (b).

GPS15. LIVONIAN
[Application of Skills; Intermediate]
Consider the following sentences of Livonian,[8] a highly endangered
language spoken in Latvia. It belongs to the Finnic language family. I've
simplified some of the glosses here for pedagogical reasons.

1)   Min   kovāl   sõbrā   mõļtõb
     my   smart   friend paint
     "My smart friend is painting."

2)   Līvõd   lapst   jūobõd kõļimtõ
     Livonian   children   drink   juice
     "(The) Livonian children are drinking juice."

3)   Nänt   vanāāma   kutsūb mēḑi   kuodāj sillõ
     their   grandmother   invite us   house into
     "Their grandmother is inviting us into the house."

Now answer the following questions:
a)   Assume that possessive pronouns are determiners. Are determiners
     optional or obligatory in Livonian NPs?
b)   Assume the following rule exists in Livonian: AdjP → Adj. Now what is
     the NP rule of Livonian?
c)   What is the PP rule of Livonian?
d)   What is the VP rule of Livonian?
e)   What is the TP rule of Livonian?

---

[8] Examples adapted from: Boiko, Kersti (2000) *Līvõ Kēļ*. Līvõd Īt. Many thanks to
Uldis Balodis for his help constructing this problem set.

f) Using the rules you figured out above, draw the trees for sentences (1), (2) and (3).

CHALLENGE PROBLEM SETS

CHALLENGE PROBLEM SET 1: QUANTIFIERS
[Critical Thinking; Challenge]
Our NP rule only allows one determiner. How can we deal with NPs like (a), (b), and (c), but still rule out NPs like (d)?

a) the two CDs
b) the many reasons
c) all the books
d) *the those books

CHALLENGE PROBLEM SET 2: ICELANDIC
[Data analysis and Critical Thinking; Challenge]
This problem set builds on Challenge Problem Set 1. Consider the complex NP given in (a):[9]

a) allir hinir   litlu   sniglarnir   mínir   fjórir
    all   other   little   snails.the   my   four
    "all my other four little snails"

Leaving aside the definite ("the") marking on the noun, think about all the things in this NP that fall under the category of determiner as we defined it in chapter 2. How might we explain how all of these are possible in this NP? Hint: think about the possibility that phrase structure rules might refer to subcategories.

CHALLENGE PROBLEM SET 3: POSSESSIVE NPS
[Critical Thinking; Challenge]
Part 1: Our NP rule reads NP → (D) (AdjP+) N (PP+) (CP). Consider the following NPs. What problem do these NPs cause our rule?

a) Patrick's box
b) the man's box

Part 2: Consider the following data:

c) *Patrick's the box
d) *the man's the box

---

[9] Data from Norris (2011).

How might you revise the NP rule to account for NPs like (a) and (b), keeping in mind that a possessive NP (like *Patrick's*) cannot appear in the same NP as a determiner? Given the rule you develop, draw the tree for (b).

CHALLENGE PROBLEM SET 4: NOMINAL ADVERBIALS
[Critical Thinking and Data Analysis; Challenge]
In the text we observed that NPs must appear adjacent to the verb in VPs; they cannot come after a post-verbal AdvP:

a) *Shannon kissed quietly the kitten.
b) Shannon kissed the kitten quietly

However, there appears to be a class of nouns that can appear in this position. These are nouns expressing quantities of time:

c) Shannon left quietly *every day*.

Other examples are *last year, every day, each week*.

Part 1: How do we know that these constituents are NPs and not AdvPs? (Pay attention to what can modify the N.)

Part 2: Is there a way to incorporate such NPs into our PSR system? Explain your answer.

CHALLENGE PROBLEM SET 5: CONSTITUENCY TESTS[10]
[Application of Knowledge; Challenge]
Do the words in boldface in the following sentence form a *single* constituent? That is, is there a *[Barbie and Ken kissing]* constituent? How do you know? Use all the tests available to you.

   Barbie and Ken were seen by everyone at the party **kissing**.

A couple of things may help you in this problem. (1) Remember that constituents can be inside other constituents. (2) This sentence is a passive, which means that some movement has happened, so don't let the fact that there is other stuff in between the two bits throw you off.

CHALLENGE PROBLEM SET 6: USING CONSTITUENCY TESTS[11]
[Application of Knowledge; Challenge]
Consider the following sentence.

a) Juliet says that Romeo lies to his parents a lot.

Part 1: Note that this sentence is ambiguous as to which verb the adverb *a lot* modifies. Paraphrase the two interpretations in your own words.

Part 2: Draw two phrase structure trees for this sentence each corresponding

---

[10] Sheila Dooley is the source of this problem set.
[11] Thanks to Yosuke Sato for this problem set.

to one of its meanings you stated in part 1.

Part 3: Recall that VP-constituency can be established by using VP-preposing. Sentence (b) shows that *eat apples* is a VP constituent. A string that can be preposed by VP-preposing qualifies as VP.

b)   Eat apples, Julian does every day.

Explain why the VP-preposed version of sentence (b) given in (c) is not ambiguous anymore.

c)   Lie to his parents a lot, Juliet says that Romeo does.

Part 4: Explain why the following VP-preposed version of sentence (b) is still ambiguous.

d)   Lie to his parents, Juliet says that Romeo does a lot.

CHALLENGE PROBLEM SET 7: WHY ARE OVS LANGUAGES RARE?
[Application of Knowledge; Challenge]
Given the basic units of subject NPs (S), object NPs (O), and verbs (V), there are logically 6 possible word orders of the world's languages: SOV, SVO, VSO, VOS, OSV, and OVS. Of these possible orders, the first two are very common, the second two are found throughout the world but are much rarer, and the last two are almost unheard of. (The exceptions seem to be limited to a set of Carib languages spoken in South America.) Tomlin (1986) claims that 45% of the world's languages are SOV, 42% are SVO, 9% are VSO, 3% are VOS, and less than 1% of the world's languages exhibit OSV or OVS. Let's concentrate on the rare OVS order.

Part 1. What would the TP and VP phrase structure rules for an OVS language look like?

Part 2. Do phrase structure grammars make any predictions about the frequency of word orders? In other words, is there any reason that OVS languages should be rare if they are possible in a phrase structure notation? Does our grammatical system correctly predict that object-initial languages should be so very rare?

Part 3. Are there any common word orders that phrase structure grammars predict would not exist? (Assume that subjects are always the NP introduced by the TP rule, and objects are always introduced by the VP rule, and that you can't cross lines in a tree.)

chapter 4

Structural Relations

Learning Objectives

After reading chapter 4 you should walk away having mastered the following ideas and skills:

1. Identify dominance in a tree.
2. Distinguish dominance from immediate dominance.
3. Understand the relationship between exhaustive domination and constituency.
4. Identify precedence in a tree.
5. Understand the constraint against crossing lines.
6. Identify c-command in a tree.
7. Distinguish symmetric from asymmetric c-command.
8. Identify different government relations.
9. Define structurally subject, object, oblique, object of a preposition and indirect object.

0. INTRODUCTION

In chapter 3, we developed the notion of constituency. Constituents are groups of words that function as single units. In order to systematically identify these, we proposed a set of rules. These rules generate trees, which in turn represent constituency. Take a careful look at any tree in the last chapter and you'll notice that it is a collection of labels and lines; within this

Syntax: A Generative Introduction, Third Edition. Andrew Carnie.
© 2013 Andrew Carnie. Published 2013 by John Wiley & Sons, Inc.

collection of labels there is an organization. In particular, various parts of the tree are organized hierarchically with respect to one another. A collection of lines and labels with an internal organization like syntactic trees is a geometric object. It isn't a geometric object like a circle or a square, but nonetheless it has bits that are spatially organized with respect to one another. If syntactic trees are geometric objects, they can be studied and described mathematically – the focus of this chapter. This chapter differs from all the others in this book. You won't see many sentences or phrases here, and there is very little data. This chapter is about the purely formal properties of trees. But don't think you can skip it. The terminology we develop here is a fundamental part of syntactic theory and will play an important role in subsequent chapters.

> **Why Study the Geometry of Trees?**
>
> It is worth considering whether it is necessary to concern ourselves with the mathematics of tree diagrams. There are actually two very good reasons why we should do this. First, by considering the geometry of trees, we can assign names to the various parts and describe how the parts relate to one another. For example, in the last chapter we were only able to give a vague definition of the term *constituent*. In this chapter, we'll be able to give a precise description. Second, it turns out that there are many syntactic phenomena that make explicit reference to the geometry of trees. One of the most obvious of these refers to anaphors. Anaphors can only appear in certain positions in the geometry of the tree. The distribution of anaphors and other types of nouns is the focus of the next chapter.

1. THE PARTS OF A TREE

Let's start with a very abstract tree drawing:

1)

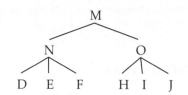

This tree would be generated by the rules in (2):

2) M → N O
    N → D E F
    O → H I J

You can check this by applying each of the rules to the tree in (1). I'm using an abstract tree here because I don't want the content of each of the nodes to interfere with the underlying abstract mathematics. (But if you find this confusing, you can substitute TP for M, NP for N, VP for O, etc., and you'll see that this is just a normal tree.) Now we can describe the various parts of this tree. The lines in the tree are called **branches**. A formal definition of branch is given in (3), and the branches are marked in (4):

3) *Branch:* A line connecting two parts of a tree.

4)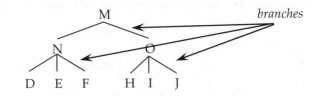

The end of any branch is called a **node**. Both ends are called nodes. For example, N and F are both called nodes of a branch. Any time two or more branches come together, this is also called a node:

5) *Node:* The end of a branch.

A node with two or more branches below it is said to be **branching**; a node that has a single branch below it is said to be **non-branching**.

Nodes in a tree are labeled. In the tree above, M, N, O, D, E, F, H, I, J are the *labels* for the nodes that make up the tree. This is very abstract of course. In the last chapter, we looked at the various parts of speech (N, V, A, P, etc.) and the phrasal categories associated with them (NP, VP, AP, PP, etc.). These are the labels in a real syntactic tree.

6) *Label:* The name given to a node.

There are actually different kinds of nodes that we'll want to make reference to. The first of these is called the **root node**. The root node doesn't have any branch on top of it. There is only ever one root node in a sentence. (The term root is a little confusing, but try turning the trees upside down and you'll see that they actually do look like a tree (or a bush at least). In the trees we looked at in the last chapter, the root node was almost always the TP (sentence) node.

7) *Root node (preliminary):* The node with no line on top of it.

At the opposite end of the tree are the nodes that don't have any lines underneath them. If the tree analogy were to really hold up, we should call these "leaves." More commonly, however, these are called **terminal nodes**.

8) *Terminal node (preliminary):* Any node with no branch underneath it.

Any node that isn't a terminal node is called a ***non-terminal node***:

9) *Non-terminal node (preliminary):* Any node with a branch underneath it.

Notice that the root node is also a non-terminal node by this definition. After we add some definitions in the next chapter, we'll have reason to reformulate the definitions of root, terminal and non-terminal nodes, but for now these should give you the basic idea. In (10), we have a tree where the root node, the terminal nodes, and the non-terminal nodes are all marked.

10)

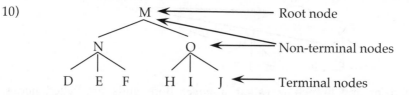

In this tree, M is the root node. M, N, and O are non-terminals, and D, E, F, H, I, and J are terminal nodes.

We now have all the terms we need to describe the various parts of a tree. The lines are called branches. The ends of the lines are called nodes, and each of the nodes has a label. Depending upon where the node is in the tree, it can be a root node (the top), a terminal (the bottom), or a non-terminal (any node except the bottom). Next we turn to a set of terms and descriptions that will allow us to describe the relations that hold between these parts. Because we are talking about a tree structure here, these relations are often called ***structural relations***.

You now have enough information to try WBE 1.

---

2. DOMINATION

2.1 Domination

Some nodes are higher in the tree than others. This reflects the fact that trees show a hierarchy of constituents. In particular, we want to talk about nodes that are higher than one another *and* are connected by a branch. The relation that describes two nodes that stand in this configuration is called *domination*. A node that sits atop another and is connected to it by a branch is said to dominate that node.

11) *Domination:*[1] Node A dominates node B if and only if A is higher up in the tree than B and if you can trace a line from A to B going only downwards.

In (12), M dominates all the other nodes (N, O, D, E, F, H, I, J). N dominates D, E, and F, and O dominates H, I, and J. O does not dominate F, as you can see by virtue of the fact that there is no branch connecting them.

12)

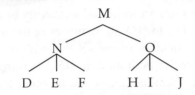

Domination is essentially a containment relation. The phrasal category N contains the terminal nodes D, E, and F. Containment is seen more clearly when the tree is converted into a bracketed diagram:

13) [$_M$ [$_N$ D E F] [$_O$ H I J]]

In (13) the brackets associated with N ([$_N$ D E F]) contain the nodes D, E, and F. The same holds true for O which contains H, I, and J. M contains both N and O and all the nodes that they contain. So domination is a technical way of expressing which categories belong to larger categories.

You now have enough information to try WBE 2 and GPS 1 & 2.

2.2 Exhaustive Domination

In the last chapter, we developed an intuitive notion of constituent. The relation of domination actually allows us to be a little more rigorous and develop a formal notion of constituency. In order to do this, we need another definition, *exhaustive domination*:

14) *Exhaustive domination*: Node A exhaustively dominates a *set* of terminal nodes {B, C, ..., D}, provided it dominates all the members of the set (so that there is no member of the set that is not dominated by A) *and* there is no terminal node G dominated by A that is not a member of the set.

---

[1] The definition given here is actually for proper domination (an irreflexive relation). Simple domination is usually reflexive (nodes dominate themselves). For the most part linguists are interested in proper domination rather than simple domination, and they use the term "domination" to mean "proper domination" as we do here. Domination is sometimes also called *dominance*.

This is a rather laborious definition. Let's tease it apart by considering an example.

15)

What we are concerned with here is a *set* of nodes and whether or not a given node dominates the entire set. Sets are indicated with curly brackets {}. Start with the set of terminal {B, C, D}. In (15) all members of the set {B, C, D} are dominated by A; there is no member of the set that isn't dominated by A. This satisfies the first part of the definition in (15). Turning to the second part, A *only* dominates these terminal nodes and no other terminals. There is no node G dominated by A that is not a member of the set. This being the case we can say of the tree in (15) that A exhaustively dominates the set {B, C, D}. Let's turn to a different tree now.

16)

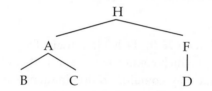

Again let's consider whether A exhaustively dominates the set {B, C, D}. In (16), one member of the set, D, is not dominated by A. Thus the set {B, C, D} is *not* exhaustively dominated by A. The reverse situation is seen in (17):

17)

While it is the case that in (17), B, C, and D are all immediately dominated by A, there is also the node G, which is not a member of the set {B, C, D}, so the set {B, C, D} is not exhaustively dominated by A (although the set {B, C, D, G} is). On a more intuitive level, exhaustive domination holds between a set of nodes and their mother. Only when the entire set (and only that set) are immediately dominated by their mother can we say that the mother exhaustively dominates the set.

Look carefully at the structures in (15), (16), and (17). In (15) you'll see that the set {B, C, D} forms a constituent (labeled A). In (17), that set does not form a constituent (although the set is part of a larger constituent in that tree). In (17), there is no sense in which B, C, and D form a unit that excludes G. It seems then that the notion of constituency is closely related to the relation of exhaustive domination. This is reflected in the following formal definition of a constituent:

18) *Constituent*: A set of terminal nodes exhaustively dominated by a particular node.

If we look at the tree in (16) again, you can see that each constituent meets this definition. The set of nodes exhaustively dominated by A is {B, C}, which is the set of terminals that make up the A constituent. Similarly, the constituent F is made up of the set {D}, which is exhaustively dominated by F; finally, H exhaustively dominates {B, C, D} (remember the definition is defined over *terminals*, so A and F don't count) which is the constituent that H represents.

Before turning to some other structural relations, it is important to look at one confusing piece of terminology. This is the distinction between *constituent* and *constituent of*. A constituent, as defined in (18), is a set of nodes exhaustively dominated by a single node. A **constituent of**, by contrast, is a *member* of the constituent set. Consider the tree in (19):

19)

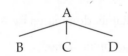

Here we have the constituent A, which exhaustively dominates the set {B, C, D}. Each member of this set is called a "constituent of A." So B is a constituent of A. "Constituent of" boils down to domination. A dominates B; therefore B is a constituent of A:

20) *Constituent of*: B is a constituent of A if and only if A dominates B.

You now have enough information to try WBE 3 and GPS 3.

2.3 Immediate Domination

Domination is actually quite a general notion: In (21), M dominates all of the nodes under it.

21)

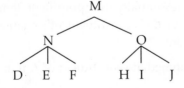

In certain circumstances we might want to talk about relationships that are smaller and more local. This is the relationship of **immediate domination.**

A node immediately dominates another if there is only one branch between them.

22) *Immediately dominate*: Node A immediately dominates node B if there is no intervening node G that is dominated by A, but dominates B. (In other words, A is the first node that dominates B.)

In (21), M dominates all the other nodes in the tree, but it only immediately dominates N and O. It does not immediately dominate any of the other nodes because N and O intervene.

There is an informal set of terms that we frequently use to refer to immediate domination. This set of terms is based on the fact that syntactic trees look a bit like family trees. If one node immediately dominates another, it is said to be the ***mother***; the node that is immediately dominated is called the ***daughter***. In the tree above in (21), N is D's mother and D is N's daughter. We can even extend the analogy (although this is pushing things a bit) and call M D's grandmother.

23) *Mother*: A is the mother of B if A immediately dominates B.

24) *Daughter:* B is the daughter of A if B is immediately dominated by A.

Closely related to these definitions is the definition of ***sister***:

25) *Sisters:* Two nodes that share the same mother.

With this set of terms in place we can now redefine our definitions of root nodes, terminal nodes, and non-terminals a little more rigorously:

26) *Root node (revised)*: The node that dominates everything, but is dominated by nothing. (The node that is no node's daughter.)

27) *Terminal node (revised)*: A node that dominates nothing. (A node that is not a mother.)

28) *Non-terminal node (revised)*: A node that dominates something. (A node that is a mother.)

We defined "constituent" in terms of domination, and from that we derived the "constituent of" relation (essentially the opposite of domination). We can also define a local variety of the "constituent of" relation that is the opposite of immediate domination:

29) *Immediate constituent of*: B is an immediate constituent of A if and only if A immediately dominates B.

This ends our discussion of the vertical axis of syntactic trees. Next we consider horizontal relations.

You now have enough information to try WBE 4 and GPS 4.

3. Precedence

Syntactic trees don't only encode the hierarchical organization of sentences, they also encode the linear order of the constituents. Linear order refers to the order in which words are spoken or written (left to right if you are writing in English). Consider the following rule:

30) M → A B

This rule not only says that M dominates A and B and is composed of A and B. It also says that A must precede B in linear order. A must be said before B, because it appears to the left of B in the rule. The relation of "what is said first" is called *precedence*.[2] In order to define this rigorously we have to first appeal to a notion known as *sister precedence*:

31) *Sister precedence*: Node A sister-precedes node B if and only if both are immediately dominated by the same node, and A appears to the left of B.

The ordering in this definition follows from the order of elements within a phrase structure rule. If A is to the left of B in a phrase structure rule M → A B, then A and B are immediately dominated by M, and are in the relevant order by virtue of the ordering within that rule. With this basic definition in mind we can define the more general precedence relation:

32) *Precedence*: Node A precedes node B if and only if neither A dominates B nor B dominates A *and* A (or some node dominating A) sister-precedes B or (some node dominating B).

This definition is pretty complex, so let's break it apart. The first bit of the definition says "neither A dominates B nor B dominates A." The reason for this should be obvious on an intuitive level. Remember, domination is a containment relation. If A contains B, there is no obvious way in which A could be to the left of B. Think of it this way. If you have a box, and the box has a ball in it, you can't say that the box is to the left of the ball. That is physically impossible. The box surrounds the ball. The same holds true for domination. You can't both dominate and precede/follow.

The second part of the definition says "A or some node dominating A sister-precedes B or some node dominating B." This may seem like an overly complex way to say "to the left," but there is a good reason we phrase it like this. This has to do with the fact that the terminals of a tree don't float out in

---

[2] Thanks to Dave Medeiros for helpful discussion of these notions.

space. Rather they are dominated by other nodes that might precede or follow themselves and other nodes. Consider the following tree drawn by a sloppy tree-drawer:

33)

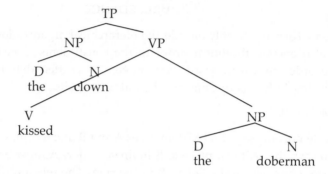

In this sloppily drawn tree, the verb *kissed* actually appears to the *left* of the noun *clown*. However, we wouldn't want to say that *kissed* precedes *clown*; this is clearly wrong. The sentence is said "The clown kissed the doberman," where *kissed* follows *clown*. We guarantee this ordering by making reference to the material that dominates the nodes we are looking at. Let A = *clown* and B = *kissed*. Let's substitute those into the definition:

34) [$_N$ *clown*] or some node dominating [$_N$ *clown*] (in this case NP) sister-precedes [$_V$ *kissed*] or some node dominating [$_V$ *kissed*] (in this case VP).

This means that [$_N$ *clown*] precedes [$_V$ *kissed*], because NP precedes VP. Note that precedence holds over <u>all</u> nodes, not just terminals. So [$_N$ *clown*] also precedes [$_{NP}$ *the doberman*].

   The second clause of the definition also allows us to explain an important restriction on syntactic trees: **You cannot allow branches to cross.** Trees like (35) are completely unacceptable (they are also impossible to generate with phrase structure rules – try to write one and you'll see).

35)

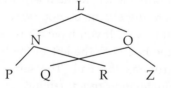

In this tree, Q is written to the left of R, apparently preceding R, but by the definition of precedence given above, this tree is ruled out. Q is to the left of R, but O *which dominates* Q is not. In other words, you can't cross branches. Another way of phrasing this is given in (36):

36) *No crossing branches constraint*: If one node X precedes another node Y, then X and all nodes dominated by X must precede Y and all nodes dominated by Y.

Just as in the domination relation, where there is the special local definition called "immediate domination," there is a special local form of precedence called ***immediate precedence***:

37) *Immediate precedence:* A immediately precedes B if there is no node G that follows A but precedes B.

Consider the string given in (38) (assume that the nodes dominating this string meet all the criteria set out in (32)):

38)   A   B   G

In this linear string, A immediately precedes B, because A precedes B and there is nothing in between them. Contrast this with (39):

39)   A   G   B

In this string, A does ***not*** immediately precede B. It does precede B, but G intervenes between them, so the relation is not immediate.

You now have enough information to try WBE 5 & 6, GPS 5 & 6, and CPS 1.

4. C-COMMAND

Perhaps the most important of the structural relations is the one we call *c-command*. Although c-command takes a little getting used to, it is actually the most useful of all the relations. In the next chapter, we'll look at the phenomenon of ***binding***, which makes explicit reference to the c-command relation. C-command is defined intuitively in (40) and more formally in (41):

40) *C-command (informal)*: A node c-commands its sisters and all the daughters (and granddaughters and great-granddaughters, etc.) of its sisters.

41) *C-command (formal)*: Node A c-commands node B if every[3] node dominating A also dominates B, and neither A nor B dominates the other.

---

[3] The usual requirement on c-command is that every ***branching*** node dominating A also dominates B. This additional branching requirement isn't necessary given the irreflexive definition of domination (i.e. proper domination) that we've given above. However, students may run into the branching definition in other works.

Look at the tree in (42). The node A c-commands all the nodes in the circle. It doesn't c-command any others:

42)

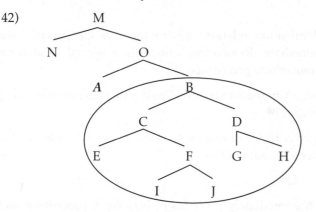

That is, A c-commands its sister (B) and all the nodes dominated by its sister (C, D, E, F, G, H, I, J). Consider now the same tree without the circle, and look at the nodes c-commanded by G:

43)

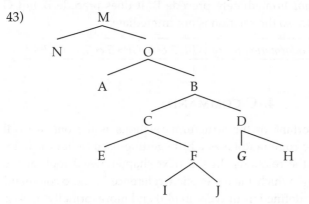

G c-commands *only* H (its sister). Notice that it does not c-command C, E, F, I, or J. C-command is a relation that holds among sisters and among aunts and their nieces and the descendants of their nieces. It *never* holds between cousins or between a mother and daughter.

You now have enough information to try GPS 7 and CPS 2.

There are various kinds of c-command. The first of these is when two nodes c-command one another. This is called **symmetric c-command** and is defined in (44):

44) *Symmetric c-command*: A symmetrically c-commands B if A c-commands B *and* B c-commands A.

This relation holds only between sisters. The other kind of c-command is the kind that holds where an aunt c-commands her nieces and the descendants of her nieces. This is called (unsurprisingly) *asymmetric c-command*:

45) *Asymmetric c-command:* A asymmetrically c-commands B if A c-commands B but B does *not* c-command A.

Consider again the tree in (42); N and O symmetrically c-command each other (as do all other pairs of sisters). However, N asymmetrically c-commands A, B, C, D, E, F, G, H, I, and J, since none of these c-command N.

You now have enough information to try WBE 7 and GPS 8.

Just as we had local (immediate) versions of domination and precedence, there is a local version of c-command. This is typically called *government*[4] (rather than immediate c-command). There are a number of different definitions for government. If you look back at our definitions for immediate precedence and immediate domination, you'll see that in both cases the locality (i.e., the closeness) of the relationship was defined by making reference to a potential intervening category. So for domination, some node A immediately dominates B provided there is no intermediate node G that A dominates and that dominates B. In (46a) there is no node between A and B, so A immediately dominates B. In (46b), by contrast, G is in between them, so A does not immediately dominate B.

46)   a)   A   b)   A
                  | |
                  B   G
                                          |
                                          B

The same idea played a role in precedence. In (47a), A immediately precedes B because there is nothing between them; in (47b) A precedes B, but it doesn't immediately precede B, because G intervenes.

47)   a)   M   b)   M

---

[4] Technically speaking, government isn't just immediate c-command; it also expresses a licensing relationship (that is, it has or had the special status of a constraint on the grammar). In this book, this licensing function isn't going to be used, so we're going to concentrate on the structural relationship part of the definition only.

Government is similarly defined:

48) *Government (first version):*[5] Node A governs node B if A c-commands B, and there is no node G, such that G is c-commanded by A and G asymmetrically c-commands B.

To see this at work, look at the tree in (49):

49)

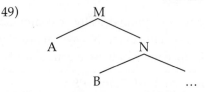

In this tree, A governs B. It c-commands B, and there is no node that c-commands B that A also c-commands. (You should note that A also governs N under this definition, A c-commands N, and there is no node that N c-commands that also c-commands A. The reverse is also true: N governs A because the relationship between A and N is symmetric c-command. B does not govern A, because B does not c-command A.) Contrast this with the tree in (50):

50)

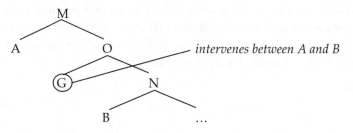

intervenes between A and B

Here A does not govern B, because the node G intervenes (or more precisely, A c-commands G and G c-commands B, thus violating the definition).

   Government is often "relativized" to the particular kind of element that's doing the government. For example, if the governor (the element doing the governing) is a phrase (an NP, a VP, etc.), then what count as interveners are only other phrases, not heads like N, V, etc. In (51) the AP *phrase-governs*[6] B. G and M don't count as interveners, even though they both are c-

---

[5] The definition of government that I've given you here is problematic if you allow trees with more than two branches under each node (when that happens the third node inadvertently acts as an intervener). In chapter 5, you will be introduced to X-bar theory, which has strictly binary branching trees. The problem with this definition disappears once you have binary trees. Thanks to Martha McGinnis for pointing this out to me.

[6] In the syntactic literature, this is more usually called **antecedent government** (which has an additional constraint called coindexing on it and is defined over particular

commanded by AP and they both c-command B. This is because they are not phrases – they are heads. GP and BP don't count as interveners either, because they don't command B; they dominate it.

51)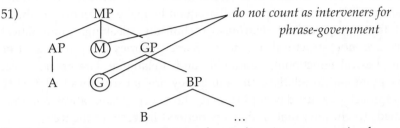

Similarly, if the governor is a head (**head-government**), then phrasal interveners don't count:

52)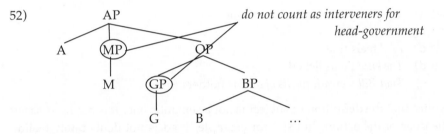

In (52), MP and GP do not count as interveners for A head-governing B because they are phrases. M and G don't count because they don't c-command B.[7] With this in mind, we can revise the definition:

53) *Government*
Node A governs node B if A c-commands B and there is no node G such that G is c-commanded by A and G asymmetrically c-commands B.
- *Phrase-government*: If A is a phrase, then G must also be a phrase.
- *Head-government*: If A is a head (word), G must also be a head.

In recent years, government has to a greater or lesser degree fallen out of fashion. Instead local relations previously linked to government are often determined by what is called the specifier–head relation. However, it is important to know what government is, because many influential papers in syntax refer to this relation.

You now have enough information to try WBE 8 and GPS 9 & 10.

categories – so NP antecedent governs another coindexed NP, provided there is no intervening c-commanding NP that also is c-commanded by the first). This is a refinement that we won't pursue here because it is rarely used anymore.
[7] These don't c-command B only if the branching requirement on c-command does not hold.

5. GRAMMATICAL RELATIONS

In addition to the structural relations that hold among items in a tree, there are some traditional grammatical terms that can be defined structurally. These are useful terms, and we will frequently make reference to them. We call these *grammatical relations*. Technically speaking, grammatical relations are not structural relations. Some theories of grammar (for example, Lexical-Functional Grammar and Relational Grammar) posit primitive grammatical relations (meaning they are not structurally defined). In the approach we are developing here, however, grammatical relations are defined structurally; that is, they are defined in terms of the tree.

In English the subject is always the NP or CP that appears before the verb or auxiliary:

54) a)   *The puppy* licked the kitten's face.
    b)   *It* is raining.
    c)   *Fred* feels fine.
    d)   *The kitten* was licked.
    e)   *That Bill's breath smells of onions* bothers Erin.

Notice that the definition of subject is not a semantic one. It is not necessarily the doer of the action. In (54c) for example, Fred is not deliberately feeling fine. In sentence (54d), the kitten is the one being licked, not the licker. Different semantic types[8] of noun phrases appear to be allowed to function as the subject. There is a straightforward structural definition of the *subject*:

55) *Subject (preliminary)*: NP or CP daughter of TP

In later chapters, we will have cause to refine this definition somewhat, but for now, this will do.

Next we have the ***direct object*** of the verb and the ***object of a preposition***. Examples of these are seen in (56) and (57), respectively:

56) *Direct object*
    a)   Susan kissed *the clown's nose*.
    b)   Cedric danced *a jolly jig*.
    c)   Dale said *that the lawn was overgrown*.

57) *Object of a preposition*
    a)   Gilgamesh cut the steak with *a knife*.
    b)   We drove all the way to *Buenos Aires*.

---

[8] In chapter 8, we will look at different semantic types of noun phrases. These types are called ***thematic relations***.

Preliminary definitions of these are given in (58) and (59); again we will have reason to revise these in later chapters.

58) *(Direct) object (preliminary)*: NP or CP daughter of a VP
59) *Object of preposition*: NP daughter of PP

To see these definitions at work consider the following tree. The NP *Les* is the daughter of TP, and is thus the subject. The NP *Paula* is a daughter of the VP headed by the transitive verb *kissed*, so *Paula* is the direct object. *Tuesday* is the NP daughter of a PP, thus the object of a preposition.

60)

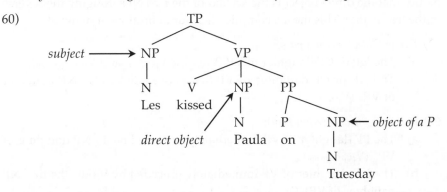

In addition to direct objects, when you have a ditransitive verb like *give* or *put* you also have an indirect object. The **indirect object** in English shows up in two places. It can be the PP that follows the direct object:

61)

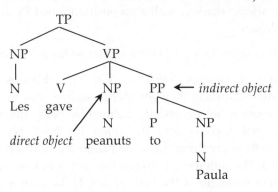

It can also be the *first* NP after the verb when the verb takes two NPs:

62)

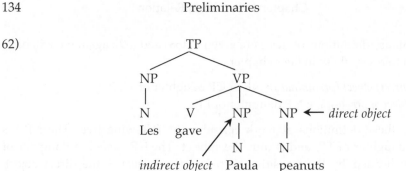

Notice that the direct object is the second of the two NPs, roughly the reverse of the tree in (61). This means complicating our definitions somewhat:

63) *Direct Object (second pass):*
   a) The NP or CP daughter of VP ($V_{[NP\_NP]}$, $V_{[NP\_CP]}$ and $V_{[NP\_NP\,PP]}$).
   b) The NP or CP daughter of VP that is preceded by an NP daughter of VP. ($V_{[NP\_NP\,\{NP/CP\}]}$)

64) *Indirect Object (preliminary):*
   a) The PP daughter of VP immediately preceded by an NP daughter of VP. ($V_{[NP\_NP\,PP]}$)
   b) The NP daughter of VP immediately preceded by V (i.e., the first NP daughter of VP). ($V_{[NP\_NP\,\{NP/CP\}]}$)

In addition to subjects, objects, and indirect objects, you may also occasionally see reference made to **obliques**. In English, obliques are almost always marked with a preposition. The PPs in the following sentence are obliques:

65) John tagged Lewis [PP *with a regulation baseball*][PP *on Tuesday*].

In many languages, such as Finnish, obliques aren't marked with prepositions, instead they get special suffixes that mark them as oblique. So obliqueness is not necessarily defined by being marked by a preposition – that is just a convenient definition for now. Notice that obliques can structurally show up in the same position as indirect objects (compare (66a) to (66b)). The difference between the two is in whether the PP is part of the argument structure of the verb or not. If the verb is of type $V_{[NP\_NP\,PP]}$ like *give*, then the PP is an indirect object, but if the verb is of type $V_{[NP\_NP]}$ (where the PP isn't specified by the feature), like *eat*, then the PP is an oblique.

66) a)

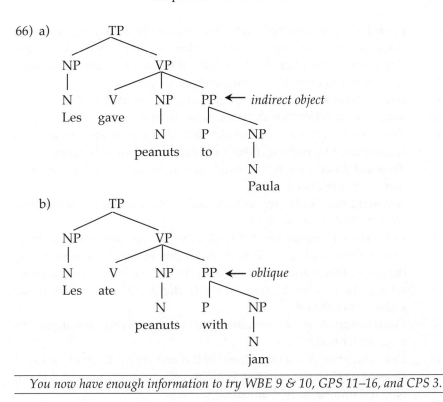

6. SUMMARY AND CONCLUSIONS

This chapter has been a bit different from the rest of this book. It hasn't been about Language per se, but rather about the mathematical properties of the system we use to describe language. We looked at the various parts of a syntactic tree and then at the three relations that can hold between these parts: domination, precedence, and c-command. In all the subsequent chapters of this book, you'll find much utility for the terms and the relations described here.

IDEAS, RULES, AND CONSTRAINTS INTRODUCED IN THIS CHAPTER
i)   *Branch*: A line connecting two parts of a tree.
ii)   *Node*: The end of a branch.
iii)   *Label*: The name given to a node (e.g., N, NP, TP, etc.).
iv)   *(Proper) Domination*: Node A dominates node B if and only if A is higher up in the tree than B and if you can trace a branch from A to B going only downwards.

v)   *Immediate Domination*: Node A immediately dominates node B if
        there is no intervening node G that is dominated by A, but
        dominates B. (In other words, A is the first node that dominates B.)

vi)   A is the *Mother* of B if A immediately dominates B.

vii)   B is the *Daughter* of A if B is immediately dominated by A.

viii)   *Sisters*: Two nodes that share the same mother.

ix)   *Root Node (revised)*: The node that dominates everything, but
        is dominated by nothing. (The node that is no node's daughter.)

x)   *Terminal Node (revised)*: A node that dominates nothing. (A node
        that is not a mother.)

xi)   *Non-terminal Node (revised)*: A node that dominates something.
        (A node that is a mother.)

xii)   *Exhaustive Domination*: Node A exhaustively dominates a *set* of
        terminal nodes {B, C, ..., D} provided it dominates all the members of
        the set (so that there is no member of the set that is not dominated by
        A) *and* there is no terminal node G dominated by A that is not
        a member of the set.

xiii)   *Constituent*: A set of terminal nodes exhaustively dominated by
        a particular node.

xiv)   *Constituent of*: A is a constituent of B if and only if B dominates A.

xv)   *Immediate Constituent of*: A is an immediate constituent of B if and
        only if B immediately dominates A.

xvi)   *Sister Precedence*: Node A sister-precedes node B if and only if both
        are immediately dominated by the same node, and A appears to
        the left of B.

xvii)   *Precedence*: Node A precedes node B if and only if neither A
        dominates B nor B dominates A *and* A or some node dominating A
        sister-precedes B or some node dominating B.

xviii) *No Crossing Branches Constraint*: If node X precedes another node
        Y then X and all nodes dominated by X must precede Y and all
        nodes dominated by Y.

xix)   *Immediate Precedence*: A immediately precedes B if there is no node
        G that follows A but precedes B.

xx)   *C-command (informal)*: A node c-commands its sisters and all
        the daughters (and granddaughters, and great-granddaughters, etc.)
        of its sisters.

xxi)   *C-command (formal)*: Node A c-commands node B if every node
        dominating A also dominates B *and* neither A nor B dominates
        the other.

xxii)   *Symmetric C-command*: A symmetrically c-commands B if A
        c-commands B *and* B c-commands A.

xxiii) **Asymmetric C-command**: A asymmetrically c-commands B if A c-commands B but B does *not* c-command A.

xxiv) **Government**: Node A governs node B if A c-commands B, and there is no node G such that G is c-commanded by A and G asymmetrically c-commands B.

- **Phrase-government**: If A is a phrase, then the categories that count for G in the above definition must also be phrases.
- **Head-government**: If A is a head (word), then the categories that count for G in the above definition must also be heads.

xxv) **Subject** *(preliminary)*: NP or CP daughter of TP.

xxvi) **Object of Preposition** *(preliminary)*: NP daughter of PP.

xxvii) **Direct Object**:
a) With verbs of type $V_{[NP\_NP]}$, $V_{[NP\_ CP]}$ and $V_{[NP\_ NP PP]}$, the NP or CP daughter of VP.
b) With verbs of type $V_{[NP \_ NP \{NP/CP\}]}$, an NP or CP daughter of VP that is preceded by an NP daughter of VP.

xxviii) **Indirect Object** *(preliminary)*:
a) With verbs of type $V_{[NP\_ NP PP]}$, the PP daughter of VP immediately preceded by an NP daughter of VP.
b) With verbs of type $V_{[NP \_ NP \{NP/CP\}]}$, the NP daughter of VP immediately preceded by V (i.e., the first NP daughter of VP).

xxix) **Oblique**: any NP/PP in the sentence that is not a subject, direct object of a preposition, direct object, or indirect object.

FURTHER READING: Barker and Pullum (1990), Carnie (2010), Chomsky (1975), Higginbotham (1985), Reinhart (1976, 1983)

GENERAL PROBLEM SETS

GPS1. TREES
[Application of Skills; Basic to Intermediate]
Using the rules we developed in chapter 3, draw the trees for the following sentences. Many of the sentences are ambiguous. For those sentences draw *one* possible tree, indicating the meaning by providing a paraphrase.

a) The big man from New York loves bagels with cream cheese.
b) Susan rode a bright blue train from New York.
c) The plucky platypus kicked a can of soup from New York to Tucson.
d) John said Martha sang the aria with gusto.
e) Martha said John sang the aria from *La Bohème*.
f) The book of poems with the bright red cover stinks.
g) Louis hinted Mary stole the purse deftly.
h) The extremely tired students hated syntactic trees with a passion.

i)   Many soldiers have claimed bottled water quenches thirst best.
j)   Networking helps you grow your business.

GPS2. DOMINATION
[Application of Skills; Basic]
Study the following tree carefully and then answer the questions about it
that follow:

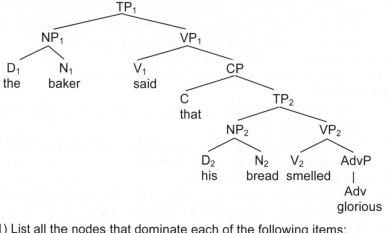

1) List all the nodes that dominate each of the following items:
    a) D_1 *the*   b) D_2 *his*   c) N_1 *baker*   d) N_2 *bread*
    e) V_1 *said*   f) V_2 *smelled* g) Adv *glorious*   h) C *that*
    i) TP_1 (if there are any)   j) TP_2 k) NP_1
    l) NP_2 m) VP_1 n) VP_2 o) CP
    p) AdvP
2)   What is the root node?
3)   List all the terminal nodes.
4)   List all the non-terminal nodes.
5)   List all the nodes that the following nodes dominate:
    a) VP_2 b) CP   d) NP_1

GPS3. EXHAUSTIVE DOMINATION
[Application of Skills; Intermediate]
Refer back to the tree for GPS2 to answer this question.

1)   In the tree, is the set of terminals {N_1, N_2} exhaustively dominated by
    a single node? If so, which one?
2)   In the tree, is the set {D_1, N_1} exhaustively dominated by a single node?
    If so, which one?
3)   In the tree, is the set {V_2, Adv} exhaustively dominated by a single node?
    If so, which one?
4)   In the tree, is the set {D_2, N_2, V_2, Adv} exhaustively dominated by a single
    node? If so, which one?

5) In the tree, is the set {D_1, N_1, V_1} exhaustively dominated by a single node? If so, which one?
6) In the tree, is the set {D_1} exhaustively dominated by a single node? If so, which one?
7) In the tree, is the set {C, D_2, N_2, V_2, Adv} exhaustively dominated by a single node? If so, which one?
8) What is the set of terminal nodes exhaustively dominated by VP_1?
9) Is the string *that his bread* a constituent? Explain your answer using the terminology of exhaustive domination.
10) Is the string *The baker said that his bread smelled glorious* a constituent? Explain your answer using the terminology of exhaustive domination.
11) Is NP_1 a constituent of TP_1?
12) Is NP_2 a constituent of TP_1?
13) Is NP_1 a constituent of TP_2?
14) Is NP_2 a constituent of TP_2?
15) Is V_2 a constituent of CP?
16) Is VP_2 a constituent of CP?
17) Are both Adv and AdvP constituents of VP_2?

GPS4. IMMEDIATE DOMINATION
[Application of Skills; Basic]
Go back to GPS2, study the tree again and answer the questions (1 a–p) as in GPS2, *except* limiting your answer to immediate domination instead of domination.

GPS5. PRECEDENCE
[Application of Skills; Basic]
Go back to GPS2, study the tree again and answer the questions (1 a–p) *except* changing domination to precedence (i.e., list all the nodes that precede D_1, etc.). For some elements there may be nothing that precedes them.

GPS6. IMMEDIATE PRECEDENCE
[Application of Skills; Basic]
Go back to GPS2, study the tree again and answer the questions (1 a–p) *except* changing domination to immediate precedence (i.e. list all the nodes that immediately precede D_1, etc.). For some elements there may be nothing that immediately precedes them.

GPS7. C-COMMAND
[Application of Skills; Basic]
Go back to GPS2, study the tree again and answer the following questions:
1) List all the nodes that the following nodes c-command:
   a) D_1 *the*   b) D_2 *his*   c) N_1 *baker*   d) N_2 *bread*
   e) V_1 *said*   f) V_2 *smelled* g) Adv *glorious*   h) C *that*

i) TP$_1$	j) TP$_2$	k) NP$_1$	l) NP$_2$
m) VP$_1$	n) VP$_2$	o) CP	p) AdvP

2) What nodes c-command TP$_2$?
3) What nodes c-command NP$_1$?
4) What nodes c-command C?

GPS8. SYMMETRIC AND ASYMMETRIC C-COMMAND
[Application of Skills; Basic/Intermediate]
Go back to GPS2, study the tree again and answer the following questions.
For some questions the answer may be "none":

1) List all the nodes that the following nodes symmetrically c-command (if there are any):

a) D$_1$ *the*	b) D$_2$ *his*	c) N$_1$ *baker*	d) N$_2$ *bread*
e) V$_1$ *said*	f) V$_2$ *smelled*	g) Adv *glorious*	h) C *that*
i) TP$_1$	j) TP$_2$	k) NP$_1$	l) NP$_2$
m) VP$_1$	n) VP$_2$	o) CP	p) AdvP

2) List all the nodes that the following nodes asymmetrically c-command (if there are any):

a) D$_1$ *the*	b) D$_2$ *his*	c) N$_1$ *baker*	d) N$_2$ *bread*
e) V$_1$ *said*	f) V$_2$ *smelled*	g) Adv *glorious*	h) C *that*
i) TP$_1$	j) TP$_2$	k) NP$_1$	l) NP$_2$
m) VP$_1$	n) VP$_2$	o) CP	p) AdvP

3) What nodes asymmetrically c-command V$_2$?
4) What nodes symmetrically c-command NP$_1$?
5) What nodes asymmetrically c-command C?
6) What nodes symmetrically c-command C?

GPS9. GOVERNMENT
[Application of Skills; Intermediate/Advanced]
Go back to GPS2, study the tree again and answer the following questions:

1) Does NP$_1$ govern VP$_2$? Why or why not?
2) Does NP$_1$ govern C *that*? Why or why not?
3) What nodes does N$_1$ govern?
4) Does V$_1$ head-govern V$_2$? Why or why not?
5) What node(s) does C *that* head-govern?
6) Does NP$_1$ phrase-govern AdvP? Why or why not?
7) Does VP$_2$ phrase-govern N$_2$? Why or why not?

GPS10. DRAW A TREE
[Application of Skills; Advanced]
Draw a single tree with the following properties:
a)   R is the root node
b)   B is a terminal node and precedes all other terminal nodes

c)   C dominates B
d)   C sister-precedes D
e)   {F, G, H} are exhaustively dominated by D
f)   F asymmetrically c-commands G and H
g)   E is immediately dominated by D
h)   F precedes E
i)   G sister precedes H

GPS11. GRAMMATICAL RELATIONS I
[Application of Skills; Intermediate]
Examine the following tree and then answer the questions that follow:

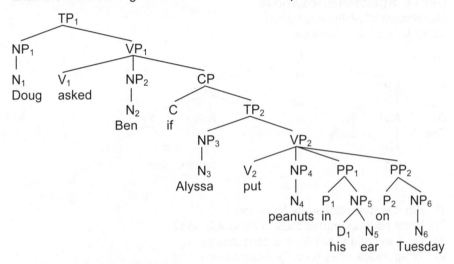

1) What is the subject of TP_1?
2) What is the subject of TP_2?
3) What is the object of P_1?
4) What is the object of P_2?
5) What is the direct object of VP_1?
6) What is the direct object of VP_2?
7) What is the indirect object of VP_1?
8) What is the indirect object of VP_2?
9) Is PP_2 an indirect object or an oblique? How can you tell?

GPS12. GRAMMATICAL RELATIONS II
[Application of Skills; Intermediate]
Go back to problem set 2, study the tree again and answer the following questions:

1) What is the subject of TP1?
2) What is the subject of TP2?
3) What is the object of VP1?
4) Does VP2 have an object?

GPS13. GRAMMATICAL RELATIONS III[9]
[Application of Skills and Data Analysis; Basic]
For each of the following sentences, identify the subject, the object (if there is one), the indirect object (if there is one), any objects of prepositions, the verb, and any obliques. Draw the tree for each sentence.

a)   It never rains violently in southern California.
b)   We should give the family dog another bath.
c)   The quiz show contestant bravely made a wild guess about the answer.

GPS14. STRUCTURAL RELATIONS[10]
[Application of Skills; Advanced]
Consider the following tree:

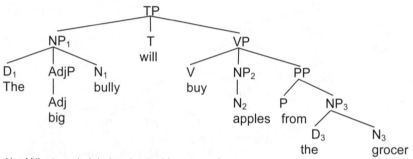

1)   What node(s) dominate N_3 *grocer*?
2)   What node(s) immediately dominate D_3 *the*?
3)   Do T *will* and V *buy* form a constituent?
4)   What nodes does N_1 *bully* c-command?
5)   What nodes does NP_1 *the big bully* c-command?
6)   What is V *buy*'s mother?
7)   What nodes does T *will* precede?
8)   List all the sets of sisters in the tree.
9)   What is the PP's mother?
10) Do NP_1 and VP asymmetrically c-command one another?
11) List all the nodes c-commanded by V.
12) What is the subject of the sentence?
13) What is the direct object of the sentence?
14) What is the object of the preposition?
15) Is NP_3 a constituent of VP?
16) What node(s) is NP_3 an immediate constituent of?
17) What node(s) does VP exhaustively dominate?
18) What is the root node?
19) List all the terminal nodes.

---

[9] Problem set contributed by Sheila Dooley.
[10] The idea for this problem set is borrowed from Radford (1988).

20) What immediately precedes N$_3$ *grocer*?

GPS15. TZOTZIL

[Data Analysis; Basic]
Tzotzil is a Mayan language spoken in Mexico. Consider the following sentences, then answer the questions that follow. Glosses have been simplified and the orthography altered from the original source. (Data from Aissen 1987.)

a) 'ispet lok'el 'antz   ti   t'ule.
   carry away woman the rabbit
   "The rabbit carried away (the) woman."

b) 'ibat xchi'uk smalal   li   Maruche.
   go with   her-husband the Maruche
   "(the) Maruche went with her husband." (Maruche is a proper name.)

c) Pas ti   'eklixa'une.
   built the church
   "The church was built."

1) What is the NP rule for Tzotzil?
2) What is the PP rule for Tzotzil?
3) What is the VP rule for Tzotzil?
4) What is the TP rule for Tzotzil?
5) What is the subject of sentence (b)?
6) Is [the church] a subject or an object of sentence (c)?
7) Does the verb precede the subject in Tzotzil?
8) Does the object precede the subject in Tzotzil?
9) Does the verb precede the object in Tzotzil?
10) Using the rules you developed above, draw the trees for (b) and (c).

GPS16. HIAKI

[Data Analysis; Intermediate]
Consider the data from the following sentences of Hiaki (also known as Yaqui), an Uto-Aztecan language from Arizona and Mexico. Data have been simplified. (Data from Dedrick and Casad 1999.)

a) Tékil   né-u   'aáyu-k.
   work   me-for is
   "There is work for me." (literally: "Work is for me.")

b) Hunáa'a yá'uraa hunáka'a hámutta nokriak.
   that   chief that   woman defend
   "That chief defended that woman."

c) Taáwe tótoi'asó'olam káamomólim híba-tu'ure.
   Hawk chickens   young   like
   "(The) hawk likes young chickens."

d) Tá'abwikasu   'áma   yépsak.
   different-person   there   arrived
   "A different person arrived there." (assume *there* is an adverb not a N)

Assume the rules AdjP → Adj and AdvP → Adv, and answer the following questions.

1) What is the NP rule for Hiaki?
2) Do you need a PP rule for Hiaki? Why or why not?
3) What is the VP rule for Hiaki?
4) What is the TP rule for Hiaki?
5) Using the rules you developed in questions 1–4, draw the tree for sentences (b, c, d).
6) What is the subject of sentence (b)?
7) Is there an object in (d)? If so, what is it?
8) What node(s) does *hunáa'a* c-command in (b)?
9) What node(s) does *hunáa'a yá'uraa* c-command in (b)?
10) What does *'áma* precede in (d)?
11) What node immediately dominates *káamomólim* in (c)?
12) What nodes dominate *káamomólim* in (c)?
13) What node immediately precedes *káamomólim* in (c)?
14) What nodes precede *káamomólim* in (c)?
15) Does *káamomólim* c-command *táawe* in (c)?
16) Do *hunáka'a* and *hámutta* symmetrically c-command one another in (b)?

CHALLENGE PROBLEM SETS

CHALLENGE PROBLEM SET 1: DISCONTINUOUS CONSTITUENTS
[Critical Thinking; Challenge]
Consider the following data:

a) A woman entered who was eating a chocolate enchilada.
b) The man that Bill said that Mary disliked loves beef waffles.

With sentence (a) assume that the relative clause *[who was eating a chocolate enchilada]* is a modifier of *the woman*. Assume that *the man* is both the direct object of the verb *disliked* and the subject of the verb *loves*. Is it possible to draw trees for these sentences without crossing lines? Explain why or why not.

CHALLENGE PROBLEM SET 2: NEGATIVE POLARITY ITEMS
[Critical Thinking; Challenge]
There is a class of phrase, such as [a red cent] and [a single thing], that are called negative polarity items (NPI). These are only allowed in sentences with a negative word like *not*. So for example, in sentences (a) and (c)

the NPI is fine. In the (b) and (d) sentences, however, the sentence is at best strange.

a) I didn't have a red cent.
b) *I had a red cent.   *(ungrammatical with idiomatic reading)*
c) I didn't read a single book the whole time I was in the library.
d) *I read a single book the whole time I was in the library.

It turns out that sentences with NPIs not only must have a word like *not*, they also have to be in a particular structural relationship with that *not* word. On the basis of the following sentences figure out what that relationship is. There are two possible answers consistent with this data. Assume that *not* and *n't* are dominated by the VP node.

e) I did not have a red cent.
f) *A red cent was not found in the box.

What kind of data would you need to decide between the two possible answers to this question?

CHALLENGE PROBLEM SET 3: IRISH
[Data Analysis and Critical Thinking; Challenge]
Consider the following data from Modern Irish Gaelic:

a) Phóg   Liam   Seán.   b) Phóg   Seán   Liam.
    kissed William   John   Kissed John   William
    "William kissed John."   "John kissed William."

c) Phóg   an fear   an mhuc.   d) Chonaic mé an mhuc mhór.
    kissed the man   the pig   Saw   I   the pig big
    "The man kissed the pig."   "I saw the big pig."

e) Rince   an bhean.
    Danced   the woman
    "The woman danced."

On the basis of this data answer the following questions:
1) What is the AdjP rule in Irish (if there is one)? Constrain your answer to the data here.
2) Write the NP rule for Irish, being sure to mark optional things in parentheses.
3) Can you write a VP rule for Irish? Assume that if you have a VP then object NPs (like *William* in (b) and *the big pig* in (d)) *must* be part of the VP, and that subject NPs (like *John* in (b) and *I* in (d)) are *never* part of VPs. Is it possible to keep those assumptions and not cross lines? ***If you can't, then don't posit a VP***.
4) If you don't have a VP rule for Irish, then how do we define direct object in this language?
5) What is the TP rule for Irish?
6) Using the rules you developed, draw trees for sentences (c), (d) and (e).

chapter 5

Binding Theory

Learning Objectives

After reading chapter 5 you should walk away having mastered the following ideas and skills:

1. Identify and distinguish R-expressions, pronouns and anaphors.
2. Understand antecedent and anaphor.
3. Distinguish coindexing from binding.
4. Define and apply binding to a tree.
5. Apply principles A, B, C to a tree.
6. Identify binding domains.

0. INTRODUCTION

Let's leave syntax for a moment and consider some facts about the meaning of NPs in English. There are some NPs that get their meaning from the context and discourse around them. For example, in the sentence in (1), the meaning of the word *Felicia* comes from the situation in which the sentence is uttered:

1) Felicia wrote a fine paper on Zapotec.[1]

---

[1] Zapotec is a language spoken in southern Mexico.

Syntax: A Generative Introduction, Third Edition. Andrew Carnie.
© 2013 Andrew Carnie. Published 2013 by John Wiley & Sons, Inc.

If you heard this sentence said in the real world, the speaker is assuming that you know who Felicia is and that there is somebody called Felicia who is contextually relevant. Although you may not have already known that she wrote a paper on Zapotec, this sentence informs you that there is some paper in the world that Felicia wrote, and it's about Zapotec. It presupposes that there is a paper in the real world and that this paper is the meaning of the phrase *a fine paper on Zapotec*. Both *a fine paper on Zapotec* and *Felicia* get their meaning by referring to objects in the world.[2] This kind of NP is called a *referring expression* (or *R-expression*):

2)   *R-expression*: An NP that gets its meaning by referring to an entity in the world.

The vast majority of NPs are R-expressions. But it is by no means the case that all NPs are R-expressions. Consider the case of the NP *herself* in the following sentence:

3)   Heidi bopped *herself* on the head with a zucchini.

In this sentence, *Heidi* is an R-expression and gets its meaning from the context, but *herself* must refer back to *Heidi*. It cannot refer to Arthur, Miriam, or Andrea. It must get its meaning from a previous word in the sentence (in this case *Heidi*). This kind of NP, one that obligatorily gets its meaning from another NP in the sentence, is called an *anaphor* (as we saw in chapter 1).

4)   *Anaphor*: An NP that obligatorily gets its meaning from another NP in the sentence.

Typical anaphors are *himself, herself, themselves, myself, yourself, ourselves, yourselves*, and *each other*.

> **Types of Anaphors**
> There are actually (at least) two different kinds of anaphors. One type is the *reflexive pronouns* like *herself, himself*, and *themselves*. The other kind are called *reciprocals*, and include words like *each other*. For our purposes, we'll just treat this group like a single class, although there are minor differences between the distributions of reflexives and reciprocals.

There is yet another kind of NP. These are NPs that can optionally get their meaning from another NP in the sentence, but may also optionally

---

[2] This is true whether the world being referred to is the actual world, or some fictional imaginary world created by the speaker/hearer.

get it from somewhere else (including context or previous sentences in the discourse). These NPs are called ***pronouns***.[3] Look at the sentence in (5):

5) Art said that he played basketball.

In this sentence, the word *he* can optionally refer to Art (i.e., the sentence can mean "Art said that Art played basketball") or it can refer to someone else (i.e., "Art said that Noam played basketball"). Typical pronouns include: *he, she, it, I, you, me, we, they, us, him, her, them, his, her, your, my, our, their,* and *one*. A definition of pronoun is given in (6):

6) *Pronoun*: An NP that may (but need not) get its meaning from another word in the sentence.

Getting back to syntax, it turns out that these different semantic types of NPs can only appear in certain syntactic positions that are defined using the structural relations we developed in the last chapter. Anaphors, R-expressions, and pronouns can only appear in specific parts of the sentence. For example, an anaphor may not appear in the subject position of sentence:

7) *Herself bopped Heidi on the head with a zucchini.

The theory of the syntactic restrictions on where these different NP types can appear in a sentence is called **binding theory**. Binding theory makes reference to the structural relations we learned about in the previous chapter. This chapter thus will be your first exposure to why structural relations are so important to syntacticians.

You now have enough information to try WBE 1 and GPS 1.

---

1. THE NOTIONS *COINDEX* AND *ANTECEDENT*

We're going to start with the distribution of anaphors. First, we need some terminology to set out the facts. An NP that gives its meaning to another noun in the sentence is called the ***antecedent***:

---

[3] There is some discrepancy among linguists in the use of this term. Some linguists use the term ***pronominal*** instead of pronoun and use the term pronoun to cover both anaphors and pronominals. This distinction, while more precise, is confusing to the beginner, so for our purposes we'll just contrast pronouns to anaphors, and avoid the term pronominal.

8) *Antecedent*:[4] An NP that gives its meaning to another NP.

For example, in sentence (3) (repeated here as 9), the NP *Heidi* is the source of the meaning for the anaphor *herself*, so *Heidi* is called the antecedent:

9) Heidi bopped herself on the head with a zucchini.

    ↑   ↑

   antecedent   *anaphor*

We use a special mechanism to indicate that two NPs refer to the same entity. After each NP we write a subscript letter. If the NPs refer to the same entity, then they get the same letter. If they refer to different entities they get different letters. Usually we start (as a matter of tradition) with the letter *i* and work our way down the alphabet. These subscript letters are called *indices* or *indexes* (singular: *index*).

10) a)   [Colin]$_i$ gave [Andrea]$_j$ [a basketball]$_k$.
    b)   [Art]$_i$ said that [he]$_j$ played [basketball]$_k$ in [the dark]$_l$.
    c)   [Art]$_i$ said that [he]$_i$ played [basketball]$_k$ in [the dark]$_l$.
    d)   [Heidi]$_i$ bopped [herself]$_i$ on [the head]$_j$ with [a zucchini]$_k$.

In (10a), all the NPs refer to different entities in the world, so they all get different indexes. The same is true for (10b). Without the indices, this sentence is ambiguous; *he* can refer to Art or to someone else. But with indexing, we disambiguate this form. (10b) only has the meaning where *he* is not *Art*, but someone else – the pronoun *he* and *Art* have different indexes. The indexing in sentence (10c), by contrast, has *he* and *Art* referring to the same person. In this sentence, *Art* is the antecedent of the pronoun *he*, so they have the same index. Finally in (10d), the anaphor *herself* refers back to *Heidi* so they get the same index. Two NPs that get the same index are said to be *coindexed*. NPs that are coindexed with each other are said to *corefer* (i.e., refer to the same entity in the world).

11) *Coindexed*: Two NPs are said to be coindexed if they have the same index.

In (10c) *Art* and *he* are coindexed; in (10b) *Art* and *he* are not coindexed.

You now have enough information to try WBE 2.

---

[4] In Latin the prefix *ante* means "before". However, in the system we are developing here, antecedents do *not* need to precede the noun they give their meaning to (although they frequently do). In some cases the antecedent may follow the noun that it gives its meaning to: e.g., *Everyone who knows him loves Dan. Him* can get its meaning from *Dan*, even though *Dan* follows *him*.

2. BINDING

The notions of coindexation, coreference, and antecedence are actually quite general ones. They hold no matter what structural position an NP is in the sentence. It turns out, however, that the relations between an antecedent and a pronoun or anaphor must bear particular structural relations. Contrast the three sentences in (12).[5]

12) a)   Heidi$_i$ bopped herself$_i$ on the head with a zucchini.
   b)   [Heidi$_i$'s mother]$_j$ bopped herself$_j$ on the head with a zucchini.
   c)   *[Heidi$_i$'s mother]$_j$ bopped herself$_i$ on the head with a zucchini.

In particular notice the pattern of indexes on (12b) and (12c). These sentences show that, while the word *herself* can refer to the whole subject NP *Heidi's mother*, it can't refer to an NP embedded inside the subject NP, such as *Heidi*. Similar facts are seen in (13).

13) a)   [The mother of Heidi$_i$]$_j$ bopped herself$_j$ on the head with a zucchini.
   b)   *[The mother of Heidi$_i$]$_j$ bopped herself$_i$ on the head with a zucchini.

A Quick Note on Notation

Syntacticians will sometimes abbreviate two sentences that are otherwise identical, but have different indices. The two possible indices are separated by a slash (/) and the index that would make the sentence ungrammatical is marked with an asterisk (*). So the abbreviated form of the two sentences in (13) would be:

13′) [The mother of Heidi$_i$]$_j$ bopped herself$_{j/*i}$ on the head with a zucchini.

This means that the version of this sentence where *herself* is indexed j (i.e., coindexed with *[the mother of Heidi]$_j$*) is grammatical; but when it is indexed i (i.e., coindexed with *[Heidi]$_i$*) it is ungrammatical.

Look at the trees for (12a and b), shown in (14a and b) below, and you will notice a significant difference in terms of the position where the NP immediately dominating *Heidi* is placed.

---

[5] In order to account for these sentences we'll have to slightly modify our NP rule:

NP → ({D/NP's}) (AdjP+) N (PP+)

14) a) (=12a)

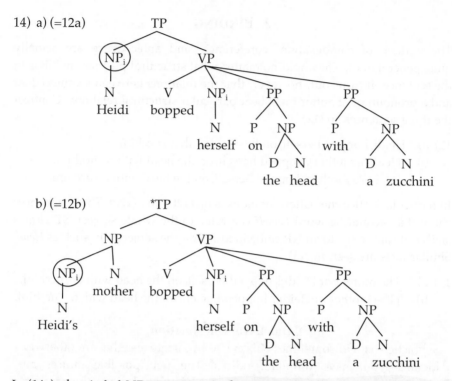

b) (=12b)

In (14a), the circled NP c-commands the NP dominating *herself*, but in (14b) it does not. It appears that the crucial relationship between an anaphor and its antecedent involves c-command. So in describing the relationship between an anaphor and an antecedent we need a more specific notion than simple coindexation. This is ***binding***:

15) *Binds*: A binds B if and only if A c-commands B *and* A and B are coindexed.

Binding is a special kind of coindexation. It is coindexation that happens when one of the two NPs c-commands the other. Notice that coindexation alone does not constitute binding. Binding requires *both* coindexation and c-command.

Now we can make the following generalization, which explains the ungrammaticality of sentences (16a) (=7) and (16b) (=12c):

16) a) (=7)   *Herself$_i$ bopped Heidi$_i$ on the head with a zucchini.
    b) (=12c) *[Heidi$_i$'s mother]$_j$ bopped herself$_i$ on the head with a zucchini.

In neither of these sentences is the anaphor bound. In other words, it is not c-commanded by the NP it is coindexed with. This generalization is called ***Binding Principle A***. Principle A determines the distribution of anaphors:

17) *Binding Principle A (preliminary)*: An anaphor must be bound.

Remember, bound means coindexed with an NP that c-commands it. If you look at the tree in (14b) you'll see that the anaphor *herself* and the NP *Heidi* are coindexed. However, they are not bound, since [NP *Heidi*] does not c-command [NP *herself*]. The same is true in the tree for (16a) (=7) shown in (18):

18)

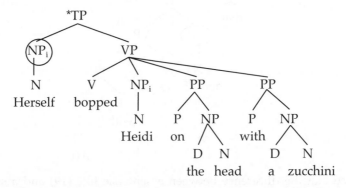

Even though the two NPs are coindexed, they do not form a binding relation, since the antecedent doesn't c-command the anaphor. You might think that *Heidi* binds *herself*, since the anaphor c-commands the antecedent.[6] But notice that this is not the way binding is defined. Binding is *not* a symmetric relationship. The **binder** (or antecedent) must do the c-commanding of the **bindee** (anaphor or pronoun), not the reverse.

You now have enough information to try WBE 3 & 4, GPS 2, and CPS 1.

---

3. LOCALITY CONDITIONS ON THE BINDING OF ANAPHORS

Consider now the following fact about anaphors:

19) *Heidi_i said that herself_i discoed with Art.
    (cf. Heidi_i said that she_i discoed with Art.)

A tree for sentence (19) is given below. As you can see from this tree, the anaphor is bound by its antecedent: [NP *Heidi*] c-commands [NP *herself*] and is coindexed with it. This sentence is predicted to be grammatical by the version of Principle A presented in (17), since it meets the requirement that anaphors be bound. Surprisingly, however, the sentence is ungrammatical.

---

[6] In fact, in this tree *herself* binds *Heidi*, and therein lies the problem; anaphors must be bound, they aren't the binders.

20)

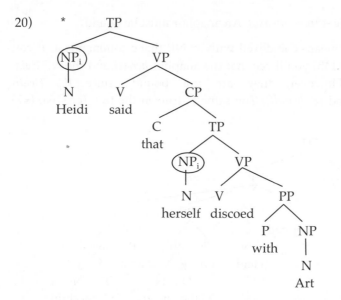

Notice that the difference between a sentence like (19) and a sentence like (12a) is that in the ungrammatical (19) the anaphor is in an embedded clause. The anaphor seems to need to find its antecedent in the same clause. This is called a *locality constraint*. The anaphor's antecedent must be near it or "local" in some way. The syntactic space in which an anaphor must find its antecedent is called a *binding domain*. For the moment let's just assume that the binding domain is the clause (TP).

21) *Binding domain*: The clause containing the NP (anaphor, pronoun, or R-expression).

Binding Domain

The definition we've given here for "binding domain" is clearly over-simplistic. For example, when there is an NP that contains an anaphor and an NP marked with 's, that NP seems to function as a binding domain:

i)   Heidi$_i$ believes any description of herself$_i$.
ii) *Heidi$_i$ believes Martha$_j$'s description of herself$_i$.
iii) Heidi$_i$ believes Martha$_j$'s description of herself$_j$.

The literature on this is extensive and beyond the scope of this chapter. But you should be aware that the definition given here needs extensive revision; we will return to this in chapter 17.

With this in mind, let's revise Principle A:

22) *Binding Principle A (revised)*: An anaphor must be bound in its binding domain.

You now have enough information to try WBE 5 and GPS 3.

---

4. The Distribution of Pronouns

Anaphors are not the only NP type with restrictions on their syntactic position. Pronouns can also be restricted in where they may appear:

23) a)   Heidi$_i$ bopped her$_j$ on the head with the zucchini.
    b)   *Heidi$_i$ bopped her$_i$ on the head with the zucchini.

Pronouns like *her* in the sentences in (23) may not be bound. (They may not be coindexed by a c-commanding NP.) The sentence in (23) may only have the meaning where the *her* refers to someone other than *Heidi*. Contrast this situation with the one in which the pronoun is in an embedded clause:

24) a)   Heidi$_i$ said [$_{CP}$ that she$_i$ discoed with Art].
    b)   Heidi$_i$ said [$_{CP}$ that she$_k$ discoed with Art].

In this situation, a pronoun may be bound by an antecedent, but it doesn't have to be. It can be bound, as in (24a), or not bound, as in (24b). Unlike the case of anaphors, which *must* be bound in a particular configuration, pronouns seem only to have a limitation on where they *cannot* be bound. That is, a pronoun cannot be bound by an antecedent that is a clause-mate (in the same immediate clause). You'll notice that this is exactly the opposite of where anaphors are allowed. This restriction is called **Principle B** of the binding theory. It makes use of the term free. *Free* is the opposite of bound.

25) *Free*: Not bound.
26) *Principle B*: A pronoun must be free in its binding domain.

Given that the binding domain is a clause, the ungrammaticality of (23b) is explained. Both *Heidi* and *her* are in the same clause, so they may not be bound to each other. The pronoun must be free. In (24) both indexings are allowed by Principle B. In (24b) the pronoun isn't bound at all (so is free within its binding domain). In (24a), the situation is a little trickier: The pronoun is bound, but it isn't bound within its binding domain (the embedded clause). Its binder lies outside the binding domain, so the sentence is grammatical.

You now have enough information to try WBE 6 and CPS 2 & 3.

---

5. THE DISTRIBUTION OF R-EXPRESSIONS

R-expressions have yet another distribution. R-expressions don't seem to allow any instances of binding at all, not within the binding domain and not outside it either.

27) a)   *Heidi$_i$ kissed Miriam$_i$.
   b)   *Art$_i$ kissed Geoff$_i$.
   c)   *She$_i$ kissed Heidi$_i$.
   d)   *She$_i$ said that Heidi$_i$ was a disco queen.

In none of these sentences can the second NP (all R-expressions) be bound by a c-commanding word. This in and of itself isn't terribly surprising, given the fact that R-expressions receive their meaning from outside the sentence (i.e., from the context). That they don't get their meaning from another word in the sentence (via binding) is entirely expected. We do have to rule out situations like (27), however. The constraint that describes the distribution of R-expressions is called *Principle C*.

28) *Principle C*: An R-expression must be free.

Notice that Principle C says nothing about a binding domain. Essentially R-expressions must be free everywhere. They cannot be bound at all.

You now have enough information to try WBE 7, GPS 4, and CPS 4–7.

A Common Mistake

Consider the sentence *She$_i$ loves Mary$_i$*. Which of the two NPs in this sentence is the antecedent? Common sense might tell us that *Mary* is. But common sense is wrong. The antecedent here is *she*. This is because *she* c-commands *Mary*, and not vice versa.

One easy way to avoid this mistake is not to think in terms of antecedent and anaphor/pronoun, but in terms of **binder** and **bindee**. The binder here is *she* because it is coindexed with *Mary* and c-commands *Mary*. *Mary* is the thing being bound (the bindee). Note that binding is typically an asymmetric relationship.

6. CONCLUSION

In this chapter, we looked at a very complex set of data concerning the distribution of different kinds of NPs. We saw that these different kinds of NPs can appear in different syntactic positions. A simple set of binding principles (A, B, and C) governs the distribution of NPs. This set of binding principles is built upon the structural relations developed in the last chapter.

In the next chapter, we are going to look at how we can develop a similarly simple set of revisions to the phrase structure rules. The constraints developed in this chapter have the shape of locality constraints (in that they require local, or nearness, relations between certain syntactic objects). In later chapters, we'll see a trend towards using locality constraints in other parts of the grammar.

The constraints developed in this chapter account for a wide range of data, but there are many cases that don't work. In particular there is a problem with our definition of binding domain. You can see some of these problems by trying some of the Challenge Problem Sets at the end of this chapter. We return to a more sophisticated version of the binding theory in chapter 17 in the last part of this book.

IDEAS, RULES, AND CONSTRAINTS INTRODUCED IN THIS CHAPTER

i) *R-expression*: An NP that gets its meaning by referring to an entity in the world.

ii) *Anaphor*: An NP that obligatorily gets its meaning from another NP in the sentence.

iii) *Pronoun*: An NP that may (but need not) get its meaning from another NP in the sentence.

iv) *Antecedent*: The element that binds a pronoun, anaphor or R-expression. When this element c-commands another coindexed NP, it is a *binder* of that NP.

v) *Index*: A subscript mark that indicates what an NP refers to.

vi) *Coindexed*: Two NPs that have the same index ($_i$, $_j$, $_k$, etc.) are said to be coindexed.

vii) *Corefer*: Two NPs that are coindexed are said to corefer (refer to the same entity in the world).

viii) *Binding*: A binds B if and only if A c-commands B *and* A and B are coindexed. A is the *binder*, B is the *bindee*.

ix) *Locality Constraint*: A constraint on the grammar, such that two syntactic entities must be "local" or near to one another.

x) *Binding Domain*: The clause (for our purposes).

xi) *Free*: Not bound.

xii) *The Binding Principles*
Principle A: An anaphor must be bound in its binding domain.
Principle B: A pronoun must be free in its binding domain.
Principle C: An R-expression must be free.

FURTHER READING: Aoun (1985), Chomsky (1980, 1981), Higginbotham (1980), Lasnik (1989), Reinhart (1976)

GENERAL PROBLEM SETS

GPS1. NP TYPES
[Application of Skills; Very Basic]
Identify the type of NP (anaphor, pronoun, R-expression) of each of the following:

> *their, each cat, folk dancing, oneself, each other, she, her, themselves*

GPS2. C-COMMAND AND BINDING
[Application of Skills; Basic]
Draw the trees for each of the following sentences, and for the bolded NPs indicate (i) whether there is a binding relationship between the two nouns, and (ii) if there is relationship, which noun is the binder and which is the element that is being bound. If there is no binding relationship, explain why (i.e., state which part of the definition of "binding" is not met). Note, this is not a question about the binding conditions (A, B, C) but about the definition of binding itself.

a) [The book about **[the president]**$_i$]$_k$ didn't bother **him**$_i$.
b) **[The book about [the president]**$_i$]$_k$ didn't bother **him**$_i$.
c) **[The book about [the president]**$_i$]$_k$ sold **itself**$_k$.
d) **[Andy**$_i$'s constant lack of effort]$_k$ dismayed **[his**$_i$ father]$_m$.
e) **[Andy**$_i$'s constant lack of effort]$_k$ dismayed **[his**$_n$ father]$_m$.

GPS3. BINDING DOMAIN
[Application of Skills; Basic]
Draw the tree for each of the following sentences. In your tree circle the binding domain for the boldfaced noun:

a) The students told **themselves** that the exam would include simple questions.
b) The students told their professor that **they** weren't worried about binding theory. *[Treat* weren't *as a T and* worried *as a V.]*
c) Michael said **the binding judgments** sounded wrong.

GPS4. BINDING PRINCIPLES
[Application of Skills and Data Analysis; Intermediate]
Explain why the following sentences are ungrammatical. For each sentence, say what the binding domain of the NP causing the problem is, whether it is c-commanded by its binder (antecedent), and name the binding condition that is violated.

a)   *Michael$_i$ loves him$_i$.
b)   *He$_i$ loves Michael$_i$.
c)   *Michael$_i$'s father$_j$ loves himself$_i$.
d)   *Michael$_i$'s father$_j$ loves him$_j$.
e)   *Susan$_i$ thinks that John should marry herself$_i$.
f)   *John thinks that Susan$_i$ should kiss her$_i$.

CHALLENGE PROBLEM SETS

CHALLENGE PROBLEM SET 1: WH-QUESTIONS
[Critical Thinking; Challenge]
What problem(s) does the following sentence raise for the binding theory as we have sketched it in this chapter? Can you think of a solution? (Hint: consider the non-question form of this sentence *John despises these pictures of himself.*)

Which pictures of himself$_i$ does John$_i$ despise?

Assume the following tree for this sentence:

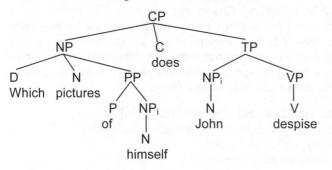

CHALLENGE PROBLEM SET 2: BINDING DOMAIN
[Critical Thinking; Challenge]
The following sentence with the assigned indexing is predicted by the theory we have given so far to be ungrammatical. But it is actually ok. Explain why our theory says this should be ungrammatical.

Andy$_i$ dismayed [**his$_i$** father]$_m$.

CHALLENGE PROBLEM SET 3: PERSIAN[7]
[Critical Thinking; Challenge]
Does the binding theory account for the following data? Explain. (*Râ* means "the" when following object NPs. 3SG means "third person singular.")

---

[7] This problem set was contributed by Simin Karimi.

a)   Jân$_i$ goft [$_{CP}$ ke [$_{TP}$ Mery$_k$ ketâb-â ro be xodesh$_{i/k}$ bargardune]].
     John said that   Mary book-PL râ to himself/herself return
     "John said that Mary (should) return the books to him/herself."

b)   Jân$_i$ goft [$_{CP}$ ke [$_{TP}$ Mery$_j$ ketâb-â ro be xodesh$_{i/j}$ barmigardune]].
     John said that   Mary book-PL râ to himself/herself return3SG.FUT
     "John said that Mary will return the books to him/herself."

Now consider (c) and (d): in these examples, xod "self" instead of xodesh
"himself" is used. How do you explain the contrast between (a and b) and
(c and d)? Note that (a and b) are taken from the spoken language, whereas
(c and d) represent the formal written variant.

c)   Jân$_i$ goft [ke [$_{TP}$ Mery$_k$ ketâb râ   barâye   xod$_{*i/k}$ bexânad]].
     John said that   Mary book râ   for   self   read3SG
     "John said that Mary (should) read the book to *himself/herself."

d)   Jân$_i$ goft [ke [$_{TP}$ Mery$_k$ ketâb râ   barâye xod$_{*i/k}$ negahdârad]].
     John said that Mary book râ   for   self   keep3SG
     "John said that Mary (should) keep the books for *himself/herself."

CHALLENGE PROBLEM SET 4: JAPANESE
[Data Analysis and Critical Thinking; Challenge]
Japanese has a number of items that can be called pronouns or anaphors.
One of these is zibunzisin. For the purposes of this assignment assume that
any noun that has the suffix -wa c-commands any other NP, and assume
that any noun that has the suffix -ga c-commands any NP with the suffix -o.
Consider the following data (data from Aikawa 1994):

a)   Johnwa$_i$ [$_{CP}$ [$_{TP}$ Maryga$_k$ zibunzisino$_{k/*i}$ hihansita] [$_C$ to]] itta.
     John   Mary   zibunzisin   criticized   that said
     "John said that Mary$_k$ criticized herself$_k$."
     "*John$_i$ said that Mary criticized himself$_i$."

Question 1: On the basis of only the data in (a) is zibunzisin an anaphor or
a pronoun? How can you tell?
     Now consider this sentence:

b)   Johnwa$_i$ [$_{CP}$ [$_{TP}$ zibunzisinga$_i$ Maryo korosita] [$_C$ to]] omotteiru.
     John   zibunzisin   Mary killed   that think
     "John thinks that himself killed Mary."
          (note: grammatical in Japanese.)

Question 2: Given this additional evidence, do you need to revise
your hypothesis from question 1? Is zibunzisin an anaphor, a pronoun
or something else entirely? How can you tell?
     One more piece of data:

c) *Johnwa$_i$ [$_{CP}$[$_{TP}$ zibunzisinga$_k$ Maryo$_k$ korosita] [$_C$ to]] omotteiru.
   John   zibunzisin   Mary   killed   that think
   "*John thinks that herself$_k$ killed Mary$_k$."

Question 3: Sentence (c) is a violation of which binding principle? (A, B, or C?) Which NP is binding which other NP in this sentence to cause the ungrammaticality?

CHALLENGE PROBLEM SET 5: COUNTEREXAMPLES?[8]
[Critical Thinking and Data Analysis; Challenge]
Each of the following examples is problematic for the binding theory we formulated above. Briefly explain why. For data from languages other than English, your answer should be based on the facts of the target language, and not the English translations. Assume that the Greek *idhio* is an anaphor and Dogrib *ye-* is a pronoun. How do these items behave differently from the English anaphors and pronouns?

a) I have no money on me.
b) John knew that there would be a picture of himself hanging in the post office.

c) *Modern Greek*
   O Yanis$_i$ ipe stin Katerina   oti i Maria aghapa ton idhio$_i$.
   John   said to Catherine   that Mary loves   himself
   "John$_i$ told Catherine that Mary loves him$_{i/*k}$."

d) *Dogrib*
   John   ye-hk'è   ha
   John   3SG(=him)-shoot   future
   "John$_i$ is going to shoot him$_{k/*i}$."

CHALLENGE PROBLEM SET 6: C-COMMAND OR PRECEDENCE?
[Critical Thinking and Data Analysis; Challenge]
In the text above, we proposed that binding required both c-command and coindexation. Consider an alternative: binding requires that the binder precedes (rather than c-commands) and is coindexed with the element that is bound. Which of these alternatives is right? How can you tell? You might consider data such as the following:

a) [$_{CP}$ [$_{CP}$ Although he$_i$ loves marshmallows,] [$_{TP}$ Art$_i$ is not a big fan of Smores]].
b) [$_{TP}$ [$_{NP}$ His$_i$ yearbook picture] gives Tom$_i$ the creeps].

Be very careful about this data. In particular, do *not* assume that an R-expression is automatically the binder. Pronouns can be binders

---

[8] This problem set was contributed by Betsy Ritter. The Dogrib data come from Saxon (1984).

for the purposes of binding theory and R-expressions might be bound (in which case they are ungrammatical by condition C).

CHALLENGE PROBLEM SET 7: IDENTITY STATEMENTS
[Critical Thinking; Challenge]
Sometimes the same person or thing can have different names. For example, the actress Marilyn Monroe was formerly known as Norma Jeane Baker. If R-expressions are subject to condition C, what problem do the following grammatical sentences have for our theory of binding?

a)   [Marilyn Monroe]$_i$ is [Norma Jeane Baker]$_i$.
b)   [Gene Simmons]$_i$ was originally named [Chaim Weitz]$_i$.
c)   [Hesperus]$_i$ is the same planetary object as [Phosphorus]$_i$.

How might we overcome this problem? (Hint: think about whether the indexing in (a–c) is appropriate or not.)

Part 2

The Base

chapter 6

X-bar Theory

Learning Objectives

After reading chapter 6, you should walk away having mastered the following ideas and skills:

1. Explain the motivation for simplifying the PSRs into X-bar theory.
2. Apply the notation of X-bar theory using variables.
3. Be able to draw a tree in X-bar theory.
4. Apply tests to distinguish complements from adjuncts.
5. Draw trees correctly placing modifiers as complements, adjuncts, and specifiers.
6. Describe the notion of a parameter.
7. Be able to correctly set the complement, adjunct, and specifier parameters for any foreign language data.

0. INTRODUCTION

As we saw in the last chapter, the theory of sentence structure that we've developed is quite powerful. It correctly predicts constituency and – along with structural relations and the binding theory – it also accounts for the structural restrictions on the interpretation of pronouns, anaphors, and R-expressions. This said, if we look a little more closely at sentence structure

Syntax: A Generative Introduction, Third Edition. Andrew Carnie.
© 2013 Andrew Carnie. Published 2013 by John Wiley & Sons, Inc.

in many languages, we see that our theory has some empirical inadequacies. (It can't account for all the data.) Consider, for example, the subject NP in the sentence in (1):

1)   [The big book of poems with the blue cover] is on the table.

The structure our NP rule NP → (D) (AdjP+) N (PP+) assigns to this is:

2)

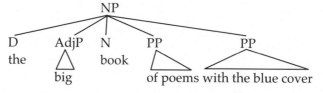

We can call this a *flat structure*. The PP *of poems* and the PP *with the blue cover* are on the same level hierarchically; there is no distinction between them in terms of dominance or c-command. In other words they are "flat" with respect to the head word *book*. From the point of view of constituency, we see that a number of tests point towards a more complicated structure. Consider first the constituency test of *replacement*. There is a particular variety of this process, called **one-*replacement***, that seems to target precisely a group of nodes that don't form a constituent in the tree in (2):

3)   I bought the big [book of poems with the blue cover] not the small [one].

Here, *one*-replacement targets *book of poems with the blue cover*. This group of words does not form a constituent in the tree in (2). Furthermore, *one*-replacement seems to be able to target other subgroups of words that similarly don't form constituents in (2):

4)   I bought the big [book of poems] with the blue cover, not the small [one] with the red cover.

These facts seem to point to a more deeply embedded structure for the NP:

5)

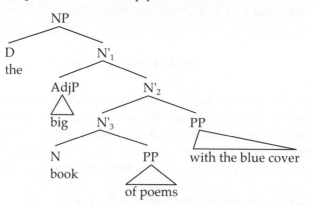

The *one*-replacement in (4) targets the node labeled N'$_3$. The *one*-replacement in (3) targets the node labeled N'$_2$. We have to change the NP slightly to get evidence for N'$_1$. If we change the determiner *the* to the determiner *that*, we can use *one*-replacement to target N'$_1$.

6) I want [$_{NP}$ this [$_{N'}$ big book of poems with the blue cover]] not [$_{NP}$ that [$_{N'}$ one]].

Similar evidence comes from conjunction:

7) Calvin is [the [dean of humanities] and [director of social sciences]].
8) Give me [the [blue book] and [red binder]].

We need these "intermediate" N' (pronounced "en-bar") categories to explain the items that are conjoined in these sentences.

   The flat structure seen in (2) is clearly inadequate and a more articulated structure is needed. This chapter is about these articulated trees. The theory that accounts for these is called **X-bar theory**.

   Before getting into the content of this chapter, a few bibliographic notes are in order. The first presentation of X-bar theory appeared in Chomsky (1970). Jackendoff's (1977) seminal book *X-bar Syntax* is the source of many of the ideas surrounding X-bar theory. Perhaps the most complete description of X-bar theory comes from an introductory syntax textbook (like this one). This is Radford's (1988) *Transformational Grammar: A First Course*. That textbook presents one of the most comprehensive arguments for X-bar theory. This chapter draws heavily on all three of these sources. If you are interested in reading a more comprehensive (although slightly out-of-date) version of X-bar theory, then you should look at Radford's book.

1. BAR-LEVEL PROJECTIONS

In order to account for the data seen above in the introduction, let us revise our NP rules to add the intermediate structure:

9) NP → (D) N'
10) N' → (AdjP) N'   *or*   N' (PP)
11) N' → N (PP)

These rules introduce a new character to our cast of nodes. This is the N' node. It plays the role of the intermediate constituent replaced by *one* above. The tree in (5) is repeated here showing how these rules (9–11) apply.

12)

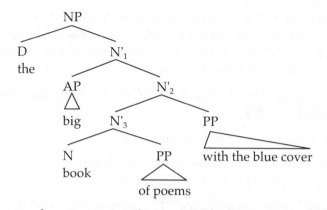

Rule (9) generates the NP node of this tree, with its daughters D and N'. The first version of rule (10) generates N'$_1$. The second version of rule (10) generates N'$_2$. Finally, the last rule (11) spells out N'$_3$ as N and its PP sister.

Equivalent Notations

The name "X-bar theory" comes from the original mechanism for indicating intermediate categories. N' was written as an N with a bar over the letter. This overbar or macron is the origin of the "bar" in the name of the theory. "X" is a variable that stands for any category (N, Adj, V, P, etc.). The following notations are all equivalent:

Phrase level	NP $= N'' = N'' = N^{max}$
Intermediate level	N' $= N'$
Word/Head level	N $= N°$

The same is true of all other categories as well (e.g., PP = P''= P''= P^{max}). Since overbars are hard to type, even with Unicode fonts, most people use a prime (') or apostrophe (') for the intermediate level and write the phrasal level as NP (or more rarely, N'').

We can now straightforwardly account for the *one*-replacement sentences. *One*-replacement is a process that targets the N' node:

13) One-*replacement:* Replace an N' node with *one.*

Without the intermediate N' node, we would have no way of accounting for *one*-replacement or conjunction facts. With N', explaining these sentences is easy, since there is more structure in each phrase.

The rule system in (9–11) has a number of striking properties (including the facts that it is binary branching and the first N' rule is iterative or self-recursive). We will return to these properties in a later section and show how they account for a number of surprising facts about the internal structure of phrases. First, however, let's see if any other categories also have intermediate structure.

1.1 V-bar

There is a similar process to *one*-replacement in the syntax of VPs. This is the process of **do-so-** (or **did-so-**) *replacement*. Consider first the VP in the following sentence, which has both an NP and a PP in it.

14) I [eat beans with a fork].

The rule we developed for VPs in chapter 3 generates the following flat tree:

15)

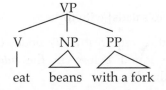

In this tree, there is no constituent that groups together the V and NP and excludes the PP. However, *do-so*-replacement targets exactly this unit:

16) I [eat beans] with a fork but Janet [does (so)] with a spoon.

Let's formalize this rule as:

17) Do-so-*replacement:* Replace a V' with *do so* (or *do* or *do so too* or *do too*).

For this to work we need the following rules:[1]

18) VP → V'
19) V' → V' (PP)   *or*   V' (AdvP)
20) V' → V (NP)

The tree structure for the VP in (14) will look like (21).

21)

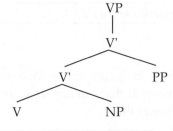

---

[1] The rule in (18) may appear a little mysterious right now (since it appears to introduce a vacuous structure) but we will have need of it in a later chapter. For the moment, just assume that it is necessary, and we will provide additional justification for it later.

Rule (18) generates the VP and the V' under it; the next rule (19) expands the top V' into another V' and a PP. Finally, the lower V' is expanded into V and NP by rule (20).

The rule of *do-so*-replacement seen in (17) targets the lower V' and replaces it with *do so*. Evidence for the higher V' comes from sentences like (22):

22) Kevin [ate spaghetti with a spoon] and Geordie [did so] too.

In this sentence, *did so* replaces the higher V' (which includes the V, the lower V', the NP, and the PP).

Similarly, conjunction seems to show an intermediate V' projection:

23) The chef [eats beans] and [serves salads] with forks.

The tree for a structure like this requires a V' node (a description of the conjunction rule can be found below in the **additional rules** in the Ideas section at the end of the chapter):

24)

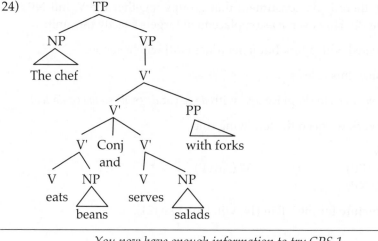

You now have enough information to try CPS 1.

1.2 Adj-bar and Adv-bar

The arguments for intermediate structure in AdjPs are a little trickier, as English seems to limit the amount of material that can appear in an AdjP. However, we do see such structure in phrases like (25):

25) the [very [[bright blue] and [dull green]]] gown

In this NP, *bright* clearly modifies *blue*, and *dull* clearly modifies *green*. One possible interpretation of this phrase (although not the only one) allows *very* to modify both *bright blue* and *dull green*. If this is the case then the structure must minimally look like (26).

26)

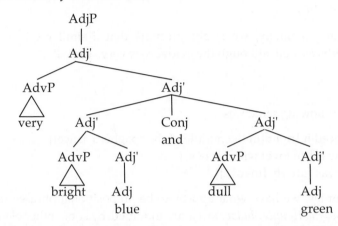

This must be the structure so that the AdvP can modify both *bright blue* and *dull green*.

Under certain circumstances, some adjectives appear to allow prepositional modifiers to follow them:

27) I am afraid/frightened of tigers.
28) I am fond of circus performers.

These post-adjectival PPs parallel the direct object of related verbs:

29) I fear tigers.
30) I like circus performers.

Consider now:

31) I am [[afraid/frightened of tigers] and [fond of clowns] without exception].

Under one reading of this sentence, *without exception* modifies both *afraid of tigers* and *fond of circus performers*. Again this would seem to suggest that the sentence has the constituency represented by the above bracketing, which points towards an intermediate category of Adj'.

There is also a replacement phenomenon that seems to target Adj's. This is *so*-replacement:

32) Bob is [very [serious about Mary]], but [less [so]] than Paul.

The adjective phrase here is *very serious about Mary*, but *so*-replacement only targets *serious about Mary*.

The rules that generate these structures are:

33) AdjP → Adj'
34) Adj' → (AdvP) Adj'
35) Adj' → Adj (PP)

For reasons of parsimony, we might presume that a similar set of rules governs adverbs as well, although the evidence is very scarce.

1.3 P-bar

Consider the following sentences:

36) Gwen placed it [right [in the middle of the spaghetti sauce]].
37) Maurice was [[in love] with his boss].
38) Susanna was [utterly [in love]].

In these examples, we have what appear to be prepositional phrases (*in the middle of the spaghetti sauce, in love*) that are modified by some other element: *right, with his boss,* and *utterly,* respectively. Note, however, that you can target smaller units within these large PPs with constituency tests:

39) Gwen knocked it [right [off the table] and [into the trash]].
40) Maurice was [[in love] and [at odds] with his boss].
41) Susanna was [utterly [in love]], but Louis was only [partly [so]].

Examples (39) and (40) show conjunction of the two smaller constituents. Example (41) is an example of *so*-replacement. Let us call the smaller constituent here P' on a parallel with N', Adj', and V'. The rules that generate PPs are given below:

42) PP → P'
43) P' → P' (PP)   *or*   (AdvP) P'
44) P' → P (NP)

With this, we complete our tour of intermediate structure. In developing our phrase structure system, we've managed to complicate it significantly. In the next section we look at ways to simplify the rule system yet capture all the constituency facts we've considered here.

2. GENERALIZING THE RULES: THE X-BAR SCHEMA

For each of the major phrase types (NPs, VPs, AdjPs, AdvPs, and PPs) we have come up with three rules, where the first and second rules serve to introduce intermediate structure. Let's repeat all the rules here. (Rules (48), (51), (54), and (57) are admittedly here simply by stipulation; we've seen no evidence for them. We're positing them now for reasons of parsimony with rule (45), but we'll see in the next chapter and the chapter that follows that the structures these rules introduce will be useful to us. Please allow me this one mysterious stipulation for the moment. I promise we'll return to the issue later in the book.)

45) NP → (D) N'
46) N' → (AdjP) N' *or* N' (PP)
47) N' → N (PP)
48) VP → V'
49) V' → V' (PP) *or* V' (AdvP)
50) V' → V (NP)
51) AdvP → Adv'
52) Adv' → (AdvP) Adv'
53) Adv' → Adv (PP)
54) AdjP → Adj'
55) Adj' → (AdvP) Adj'
56) Adj' → Adj (PP)
57) PP → P'
58) P' → P' (PP) *or* (AdvP) P'
59) P' → P (NP)

This is quite a complicated set, but seems to be more empirically motivated than the set of rules we set out in chapter 3. We can now ask, are we missing any generalizations here?

Indeed, we seem to be missing several. First, note that in all the rules above, the category of the rule is the same as the only element that is not optional. For example, in the NP rule, the element that isn't optional is N'. This is the same part of speech. Similarly, the only obligatory element in N' is either another N' or N. This is a very general notion in phrase structure; we call it headedness. All phrases appear to have **heads**. A head is the most prominent element in a phrasal category and gives its part of speech category to the whole phrase. Note that we don't have any rules of the form:

60) * NP → V AdjP

This rule not only seems meaningless, it is unattested in the system we've developed here. The requirement that phrases are headed is called *endocentricity*. The only obligatory element in a phrase is the head.

Second, note that with the exception of the determiner in the NP rule, all non-head material in the rules is both phrasal and optional. We never find rules of the form:

61) * V' → Adv V

With the exception of the determiner (an exception that we'll resolve in chapter 7), anything in an X-bar rule that isn't a head must be a phrase and optional.

Finally, notice that for each major category there are three rules, one that introduces the NP, VP, AdvP, AdjP, and PP, one that takes a bar level and repeats it (e.g., N' → N' (PP)), and one that takes a bar level and spells out the head (e.g., N' → N (PP)). We seem to be missing the generalization that for each kind of phrase, the *same kinds of rules* appear. X-bar theory is an attempt to capture these similarities among rules.

We can condense the rules we've proposed into a simple set. To do this we are going to make use of variables (like variables in algebra) to stand for particular parts of speech. Let X be a variable that can stand for any category N, V, Adj, Adv, P. XP is a catch-all term to cover NP, VP, AP, and PP. Similarly X' stands for N', V', Adj', Adv', and P', and X represents N, V, Adj, Adv, and P.

Using this variable notation we can capture the generalizations that we have missed. Let's start with the rules that introduce heads:

62) a) N' → N (PP)
    b) V' → V (NP)
    c) Adj' → Adj (PP)
    d) Adv' → Adv (PP)
    e) P' → P (NP)

By using the variable notation we can generalize across these rules with the single general statement:

63) X' → X (WP) (*to be revised*)

Both X and W here are variables for categories. This rule says that some bar level (on the left of the arrow) consists of some head followed by an optional, phrasal[2] element.

Now turn to the recursive N', A', V', and P' rules:

64) a) N' → (AdjP) N' *or* N' (PP)
    b) V' → V' (PP) *or* V' (AdvP)
    c) Adj' → (AdvP) Adj'
    d) Adv' → (AdvP) Adv'
    e) P' → P' (PP) or (AdvP) P'

---

[2] The D in the NP rule is, of course, not phrasal. This is a problem we will return to in the next chapter.

For each of these rules, a category with a single bar level is iterated (repeated), with some optional material either on the right or the left. Again using X as a variable, we can condense these into a single statement:

65) X' → (ZP) X' *or* X' (ZP) (*to be revised*)

Again the Xs here must be consistent in part of speech category. The material that is not the head (i.e., not X) must be phrasal and optional. Note that the categories of these non-head items are also indicated with variables (in this case: ZP).

Finally, let's consider the rules that introduce the topmost layer of structure:

66) a) NP → (D) N'
    b) VP → V'
    c) AdjP → Adj'
    d) AdvP → Adv'
    e) PP → P'

These rules can also be collapsed into a single rule:

67) XP → (YP) X' (*to be revised*)

We haven't motivated the existence of the YP here, except in the form of determiners. I know you're naturally suspicious of me saying "trust me on this" (and rightly so), but I promise we will resolve this in the next chapter.

The system we've come up with here is simple. We've reduced our phrase structure rules down to three general rules using variables: Because they use variables, these rules can generate the correct constituent structure of the sentences of English. This analysis isn't without problems, however. Before we turn to resolving these problems and drafting a final version of the X-bar rules, we need to introduce some new terminology.

3. COMPLEMENTS, ADJUNCTS, AND SPECIFIERS

Consider now the two prepositional phrases that are subconstituents of the following NP:

68) the book [PP of poems] [PP with the glossy cover]

Using the X-bar rules,[3] we can generate the following tree for this NP:

---

[3] Specific instructions on drawing trees using the X-bar rules can be found at the end of this chapter.

69)

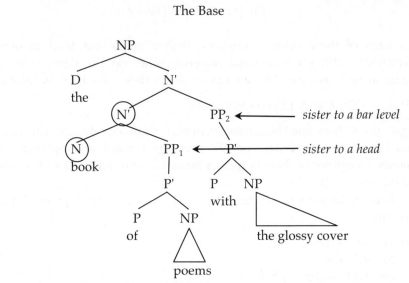

(I've used triangles in this tree to obscure some of the irrelevant details, but you should not do this when you are drawing trees until you have a confident grasp of how tree notation works.) You'll note that the two PPs in this tree are at different levels in the tree. The lower PP$_1$ is a sister to the head N (*book*), whereas the higher PP$_2$ is a sister to the N' dominating the head N and PP$_1$. You'll also notice that these two PPs were introduced by different rules. PP$_1$ is introduced by the rule:

70) X' → X (WP)

and PP$_2$ is introduced by the higher-level rule:

71) X' → X' (ZP)

An XP that is a sister to a head (N, V, A, or P) is called a **complement**. PP$_1$ is a complement. Complements roughly correspond to the notion "object" in traditional grammar. XPs that are sisters to single bar levels (N', V', A', or P') and are daughters of an X' are called **adjuncts**. PP$_2$ is an adjunct. Adjuncts often have the feel of adverbials or obliques and are typically optional additional information.

72) *Adjunct:* An XP that is a sister to a single bar level (N', V', A', or P') and a daughter of a single bar level (N', V', A', or P').

73) *Complement:* An XP that is a sister to a head (N, V, A, P), and a daughter of a single bar level (N', V', A', or P').

The rules that introduce these two kinds of XPs get special names:

74) *Adjunct rule:*   X' → X' (ZP)
75) *Complement rule:*   X' → X (WP)

A tree showing the structural difference between these is given below:

76)

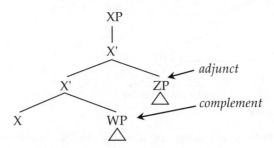

If there really are two different kinds of PP within an NP, then we expect that they will exhibit different kinds of behavior. It turns out that this is true: There are significant differences in behavior between adjuncts and complements.

3.1 Complements and Adjuncts in NPs

Take NPs as a prototypical example. Consider the difference in meaning between the two NPs below:

77) the book of poems
78) the book with a red cover

Although both these examples seem to have, on the surface, parallel structures (a determiner, followed by a noun, followed by a prepositional phrase), in reality they have quite different structures. The PP in (77) is a complement and has the following tree:

79)

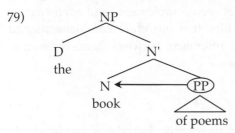

You'll note that the circled PP is a sister to N, so it is a complement. By contrast, the structure of (78) is:

80)

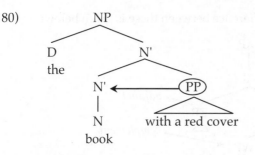

Here the PP *with a red cover* is a sister to N', so it is an adjunct. The difference between these two NPs is not one that you can *hear*. The difference between the two is in terms of the amount of structure in the tree. In (80), there is an extra N'. While this difference may at first seem abstract, it has important implications for the behavior of the two PPs. Consider first the meaning of our two NPs. In (77), the PP seems to complete (or complement) the meaning of the noun. It tells us what kind of book is being referred to. In (78), by contrast, the PP seems more optional and more loosely related to the NP. This is a highly subjective piece of evidence, but it corresponds to more syntactic and structural evidence too.

An easy heuristic (guiding principle) for distinguishing complements from adjunct PPs inside NPs is by looking at what preposition they take. In English, almost always (although there are some exceptions) complement PPs take the preposition *of*. Adjuncts, by contrast, take other prepositions (such as *from, at, to, with, under, on,* etc.). This test isn't 100 percent reliable, but will allow you to eyeball PPs and tell whether they are complements or adjuncts for the vast majority of cases. With this in mind, let's look at some of the other behavioral distinctions between complements and adjuncts.

Think carefully about the two rules that introduce complements and adjuncts. There are several significant differences between them. These rules are repeated here for your convenience:

81) *Adjunct rule:*   X' → X' (ZP)
82) *Complement rule:*   X' → X (WP)

First observe that because the complement rule introduces the head (X), the complement PP will always be adjacent to the head. Or more particularly, it will always be closer to the head than an adjunct PP will be. This is seen in the following data:

83) the book   [of poems]   [with a red cover]
         head   *complement*   *adjunct*

84) *the book   [with a red cover] [of poems]
         head   *adjunct*   *complement*

You can see how this is true if you look at the tree for sentence (83):

85)

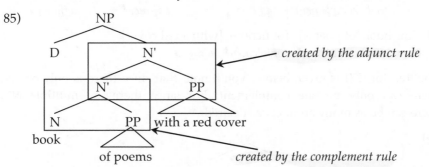

created by the adjunct rule

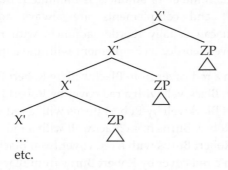

created by the complement rule

Since the adjunct rule takes an X'-level category and generates another X' category, it will always be higher in the tree than the output of the complement rule (which takes an X' and generates an X). Since lines can't cross, this means that complements will always be lower in the tree than adjuncts, and will always be closer to the head than adjuncts.

   There is another property of the rules that manifests itself in the difference between adjuncts and complements. The adjunct rule, as passingly observed above, is an iterative rule. That is, within the rule itself, it shows the property of recursion (discussed in chapter 3): On the left-hand side of the rule there is an X' category, and on the right-hand side there is another X'. This means that the rule can generate infinite strings of X' nodes, since you can apply the rule over and over again to its own output:

86)

```
                            X'
                          /    \
                        X'      ZP
                      /    \     △
                    X'      ZP
                  /    \     △
                X'      ZP
               ...       △
              etc.
```

The complement rule does not have this property. On the left side of the rule there is an X', but on the right there is only X. So the rule cannot apply iteratively. That is, it can only apply once within an XP. What this means for complements and adjuncts is that you can have any number of adjuncts (87), but you can only ever have one complement (88):

87) the book [of poems] [with a red cover] [from Blackwell] [by Robert Burns]
       head complement   adjunct   adjunct   adjunct

88) *the book [of poems] [of fiction] [with a red cover]
       head complement complement   adjunct

The tree for (87) is given below; you'll note that since there is only one N, there can only be one complement, but since there are multiple N's, there can be as many adjuncts as desired.

89)

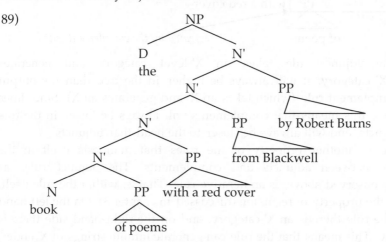

Related to the facts that the number of adjuncts is unlimited, but only one complement is allowed, and complements are always adjacent to the head, observe that you can usually reorder adjuncts with respect to one another, but you can never reorder a complement with the adjuncts:

90) a)   the book of poems with a red cover from Blackwell by Robert Burns
    b)   the book of poems from Blackwell with a red cover by Robert Burns
    c)   the book of poems from Blackwell by Robert Burns with a red cover
    d)   the book of poems by Robert Burns from Blackwell with a red cover
    e)   the book of poems by Robert Burns with a red cover from Blackwell
    f)   the book of poems with a red cover by Robert Burns from Blackwell
    g)   *the book with a red cover of poems from Blackwell by Robert Burns
    h)   *the book with a red cover from Blackwell of poems by Robert Burns
    i)   *the book with a red cover from Blackwell by Robert Burns of poems
          (etc.)

Note that adjuncts and complements are constituents of different types. The definition of adjuncthood holds that adjuncts are sisters to X'. Since conjunction (see **additional rules** at the end of this chapter) requires that you conjoin elements of the same bar level, you could not, for example, conjoin an adjunct with a complement. This would result in a contradiction: Something can't be both a sister to X' and X at the same time. Adjuncts can conjoin with other adjuncts (other sisters to X'), and complements can conjoin with other complements (other sisters to X), but complements cannot conjoin with adjuncts:

91) a)   the book of poems with a red cover and with a blue spine[4]
    b)   the book of poems and of fiction from Blackwell
    c)   *the book of poems and from Blackwell

There is one final difference between adjuncts and complements that we will examine here. Recall the test of *one*-replacement:

92) One-*replacement:* Replace an N' node with *one*.

This operation replaces an N' node with the word *one*. Look at the tree in (93):

93)

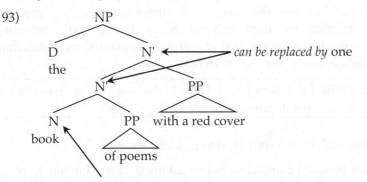

cannot be replaced by one

If you look closely at this tree you'll see that two possibilities for *one*-replacement exist. We can either target the highest N', and get:

94) the one

or we can target the lower N' and get:

95) the one with a red cover

But we cannot target the N head; it is not an N'. This means that *one* followed by a complement is ill-formed:

96) *the one of poems with a red cover[5]

---

[4] If this NP sounds odd to you, try putting emphasis on the *and*.
[5] Not everyone finds this NP ill-formed. There is at least one major US dialect that allows sentence (96). One possible explanation for this is that different dialects have different *one*-replacement rules. The dialect that finds this NP well-formed

Since complements are sisters to X and not X', they cannot stand next to the word *one*. Adjuncts, by definition, can.

So far in this chapter, we've covered a huge range of facts, so a quick summary is probably in order. In section 1, we saw that constituency tests pointed towards a more articulated structure for our trees than the one we developed in chapter 3. In section 2, we introduced the X' notation to account for this more complicated structure. In X-bar structure, there are three levels of categories. There are XPs, X's, and Xs. In this section – focusing exclusively on NPs – we introduced special terms for elements that are sisters to X' and X: *adjuncts* and *complements*. These two different kinds of modifier have different properties. Adjuncts but not complements can be iterated and reordered and can stand next to *one*. Complements, by contrast, must be located next to the head and can't be reordered. We also saw that we could conjoin complements with complements and adjuncts with adjuncts, but that we couldn't mix the two. All of these data provide support for the extra structure proposed in X-bar theory. In the next subsection, we'll briefly consider evidence that the complement/adjunct distinction holds for categories other than NP as well.

You can now try WBE 1 & 2, GPS 1–3, and CPS 2. You may want to read section 6 (on tree drawing) before attempting GPS 3.

3.2 Complements and Adjuncts in VPs, AdjPs, AdvPs, and PPs

The distinction between complements and adjuncts is not limited to NPs; we find it holds in all the major syntactic categories. The best example is seen in VPs. The direct object of a verb is a complement of the verb. Prepositional and adverbial modifiers of verbs are adjuncts:

97) I loved [the policeman] [intensely] [with all my heart].
     V   direct object   adverbial   PP phrase
          complement   *adjunct*   *adjunct*

---

allows either N or N' to be replaced. The dialect that finds this ill-formed (or at least odd), only allows N' to be replaced.

98)

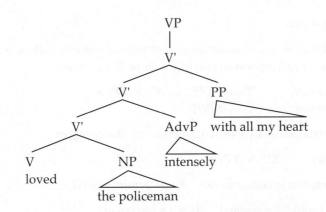

Direct objects must be adjacent to the verb, and there can only be one of them.

99) a) *I loved intensely the policeman with all my heart.
    b) *I loved the policeman the baker intensely with all my heart.

Did-so- (did-too-) *replacement* targets V'. Like *one*-replacement, this means that it can only apply before an adjunct and not before a complement:

100)   Mika loved the policeman intensely and
    a) Susan did so half-heartedly.
    b) *Susan did so the baker.

This is classic adjunct/complement distinction. In general, complements of all categories (N, V, A, P, etc.) are the semantic objects of the head. Consider for example all the complements below:

101) a) John fears dogs.   *(verb)*
    b) John is afraid of dogs.   *(adjective)*
    c) John has a fear of dogs. *(noun)*

In all these sentences, *(of) dogs* is a complement.

You now have enough information to try WBE 4 and GPS 4.

The evidence for the adjunct/complement distinction in adjective phrases and prepositional phrases is considerably weaker than that of nouns and verbs. Adverbs that modify adjectives have an adjunct flair – they can be stacked and reordered. Other than this, however, the evidence for the distinction in PPs and AdjPs comes mainly as a parallel to the NPs and VPs. This may be less than satisfying, but is balanced by the formal simplicity of having the same system apply to all categories.

3.3 *The Notion* Specifier

In the section 3.1 above, we introduced two structural notions: adjuncts and complements. These correspond to two of the three X-bar rules:

102) a) *Adjunct rule:*   X' → X' (ZP) *or* X' → (ZP) X'
      b) *Complement rule:*   X' → X (WP)

The third rule also introduces a structural position: the **specifier**.

103) *Specifier rule:*   XP → (YP) X'

We have only seen one specifier so far – the determiner in NPs:

104) [the]   [book] [of poems]   [with a red cover]
        specifier   *head*   *complement*   *adjunct*

105)

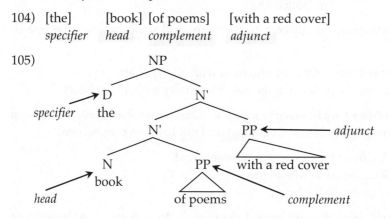

The specifier is defined as the daughter of XP and sister to X':

106) *Specifier:* An XP[6] that is a sister to an X' level, and a daughter of an XP.

We can show that specifiers are different from adjuncts and complements. Since the specifier rule is not recursive, you can only have one specifier:[7]

107) *the these red books

The specifier rule has to apply at the top of the structure. This means that the specifier will always be the leftmost element (in English anyway):

108) *boring the book

---

[6] If you are being observant you'll notice that the single example we have of a specifier is not a phrase, but a word (*the*), so it may seem odd to say XP here. We return to this issue in later chapters.

[7] One possible exception to this is the quantifier *all*, as in *all the books*. In the next chapter, we discuss the idea that determiners head their own phrase (called a DP), which might provide a partial explanation for this exception.

The above example also shows that specifiers can't be reordered with respect to other adjuncts or complements. As the final difference between specifiers and other types of modifier, specifiers can only be conjoined with other specifiers:

109) a)   two or three books
      b)   *two or boring books

On the surface, the usefulness of this position may seem obscure, since only determiners appear in it. But in later chapters we will have important uses for specifiers. (In particular, we will claim that they are the position where subjects are generated in a variety of categories.)

4. SOME DEFINITIONAL HOUSEKEEPING

With the refinements to the grammar we've made by adding X-bar theory to our system, we need to make some minor modifications to the rules and definitions that we introduced in previous chapters.

First, we need some terminology to describe the new parts of the phrase that we have added. We can refer to all the elements in an NP, for example, that are introduced (i.e. appear on the left side of the rule) by the three phrase structure rules as *projections* of the head. In the following tree, all the N's and the NP are said to be projections of the head N.

110)

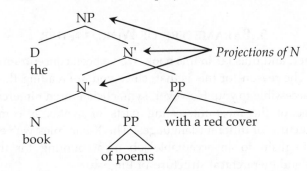

The NP is called the *maximal projection*; the N's are called *intermediate projections*.

Recall our definition of the Principle of Modification from chapter 3; a modifier must be a sister to the head it modifies:

111) *Principle of Modification* (old)
      If a YP (that is, a phrase with some category Y) modifies some head X, then YP must be a sister to X.

This definition no longer works for us. If you look at the tree in (110) you'll see that only the complement is actually a sister to the head. Modifiers that are adjuncts and specifiers aren't. To fix this we need to again revise the Principle of Modification:

111') **Principle of Modification** (revised)
       If a YP modifies some head X, then YP must be dominated by a projection of X (i.e., X' or XP).

By adding extra layers of structure we also need to revise our definitions of object and indirect object. In chapter 4, these relations are defined in terms of being immediately dominated by VP. But with the new X-bar structures these NPs aren't immediately dominated by VP anymore, so we need to change them so they are defined in terms of intermediate structure. This is easy to do for the direct object of transitive verbs:

112) **Direct Object** *(partly revised):*
       With verbs of type $V_{[NP\_NP]}$ and $V_{[NP\_CP]}$, the NP or CP sister to the V.

The definitions of indirect and direct objects in other types (e.g., ditransitives) are much harder. This is because our rules as stated only allow binary branching; only one complement is allowed. Yet for ditransitives we would ideally like to have two complements. This is a problem for X-bar theory. We will return to ditransitives and indirect objects in chapter 13.

5. PARAMETERS OF WORD ORDER

In this chapter, and thus far in this book, we've been concentrating primarily on English. The reason for this is that, since you are reading this book, it is a language accessible to you. However, syntacticians aren't interested only in English. One of the most interesting parts of syntax is comparing the sentence structure of different languages. The X-bar rules we've developed so far for English do an acceptable job of accounting for the order of constituents and hierarchical structure of English:

113) a) *Specifier rule:*   XP → (YP) X'
      b) *Adjunct rule:*   X' → X' (ZP) *or* X' → (ZP) X'
      c) *Complement rule:*   X' → X (WP)

They don't, however, account well for other languages. Consider the position of direct objects (complements) in Turkish. In Turkish, the complement precedes the head:

114) Hasan kitab-i oku-du.
     Hasan-SUBJ book-OBJ read-PAST
     "Hasan read the book."

If you look carefully at sentence (114) you notice that the word *kitabi* "book" precedes the word *okudu* "read".

Not all languages put the complement on the right-hand side like English. Not all languages put the specifier before the head either. Our rules, while adequate for English, don't really get at the syntactic structure of languages in general. Remember, syntax is the study of the mental representation of sentence structure, and since we all have the same basic grey matter in our brains, it would be nice if our theory accounted for both the similarities and the differences among languages.

X-bar theory provides us with an avenue for exploring the differences and similarities among languages. Let's start by generalizing our rules a little bit. Let's allow specifiers and adjuncts to appear on either side of the head:

115) a) *Specifier rule:*   XP → (YP) X' *or* XP → X' (YP)
     b) *Adjunct rule:*   X' → X' (ZP) *or* X' → (ZP) X'
     c) *Complement rule:*   X' → X (WP) *or* X' → (WP) X

Each of these rules has two options. The specifier/complement/adjunct can all appear on either side of their respective heads. Obviously, these rules are now too general to account for English. If these rules, as stated, were adopted straight up, they would predict the grammaticality of sentences like:

116) *[$_{NP}$ Policeman the] [$_{VP}$ Mary kissed].
     (meaning *The policeman kissed Mary.*)

It would be a bad thing to do this. At the same time, constituent orders like those of Turkish in fact exist, so this clearly is an option. Our theory must capture both facts: That the object–verb (OV) order is an option that languages use, and that it isn't the option used by English.

The way that generative syntacticians accomplish this is by claiming that the rules in (115) are the possibilities universally available to human beings. When you acquire a particular language you select *one* of the options in the rule, based upon the input you hear from your parents. Take, for example, the complement rule. In English, complements of verbs follow the verbal head. In Turkish, they precede the head. There are two options in the rule:

117) a) X' → X (WP)
     b) X' → (WP) X

The child learning English will adopt option (a). The child learning Turkish will adopt option (b). These options are called **parameters**. The proposal that word order is parameterized finds its origins in Travis (1984).

Here is an analogy that might help you understand this concept. Imagine that in your head you have a box of switches, just like the box of master breaker switches that controls the electricity in your house. These switches can be set *on* or *off*. The options in the X-bar rules are like these switches, they can be set in one direction or the other (and in some situations – such as adjuncts in English – allow both settings).

118)   X-bar parameters switch box

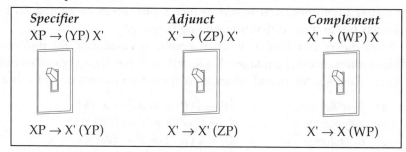

Specifier	*Adjunct*	*Complement*
XP → (YP) X'	X' → (ZP) X'	X' → (WP) X
XP → X' (YP)	X' → X' (ZP)	X' → X (WP)

When you are a child acquiring your language, you subconsciously set these switches, to tell you which version of the rules to use.

Notice that this gives us a very simple system for acquiring the word order of our languages. There are a finite set of possibilities, represented by the different settings of the parameters. English sets its complement parameter so that the complement follows the head. Turkish sets it the other way. The child only has to hear a small amount of data (perhaps even as little as one sentence) to know what side of the head complements go in their language. Once children have set the parameter, they can apply the right version of the rule and generate an unlimited number of sentences. In the problem sets at the end of this chapter, you have the opportunity of looking at some data from a variety of languages and determining how their X-bar parameters are set. For your reference, the English settings are given below:

119) a) *Specifier*   specifier on left, head on right (XP → (YP) X')
                          e.g., *the* book

      b) *Adjunct*   both options allowed (X'→ (ZP) X' and X' → X' (ZP))
                          e.g.,   *yellow* roses; books *from Poland*

      c) *Complement*   head on left, complement on right (X' → X (WP))
                          e.g.,   books *of poems*; John kissed *his mother.*

You now have enough information to try GPS 5 & 6 and CPS 3 & 4.

6. DRAWING TREES IN X-BAR NOTATION

6.1 Important Considerations in Tree Drawing

In this section, we'll run through the steps for drawing trees in X-bar notation. The basics of tree drawing that you learned in chapter 3 hold here too. However, some special principles apply to X-bar tree drawing:

i)   When identifying what modifies what, it is also important to know whether it is a complement, adjunct, or specifier. This is important because you have to know whether to make it a sister to the head, to an X', etc.

ii)   When linking material up, start with the modifiers closest to the head. Because X-bar structure is formulated the way it is, material closest to the head will be the most deeply embedded material – so it will have to attach to the head *first*.
      a) Identify the head.
      b) Attach the complement (must be a phrase!).
      c) Attach any adjuncts (which must be phrases themselves) working progressively away from the head. Each adjunct gets its own X' mother. (See points (iv) and (v) below for dealing with cases when you have either no adjuncts or have an adjunct on either side of the head.)
      d) When there are no more adjuncts, attach the specifier, if there is one. This gets an XP on top.
      e) Even if there is no specifier, put an XP on top of the projections. This indicates that there are no more modifiers of the head X.

iii) Keep in mind that none of the X-bar rules are optional. That is, they must all apply. This results in a fair amount of vacuous or non-branching structure. Even if the phrase has only a single word in it you will have *at least* the following structures:

120)   a) NP   b) VP   c) AdjP   d) AdvP   e) PP
          | | | | |
          N'   V'   Adj'   Adv'   P'
          | | | | |
          N   V   Adj   Adv   P
        Peter   left   red   badly   before

iv) Perhaps one of the most common errors of new syntacticians is in drawing trees for phrases with an adjunct but no complement. Consider the NP [notebook with a red cover]. *With a red cover* is an adjunct – that means that it has to be a sister to N' and a daughter to N' (by definition). This is seen in the following tree:

121)

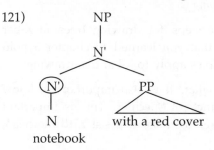

The circled N' here must be present in order to make the PP an adjunct. Be very careful to draw in these vacuous nodes that distinguish adjuncts from complements.

v) Another common issue that arises for new syntacticians is how to tree a sentence when there is an adjunct on either side of the head. Consider the sentence in (123):

122) Andy [_{VP} frequently eats sushi   with his boss].
                        adjunct   head complement   adjunct

We start by attaching the complement to the head:

123)

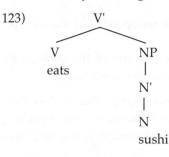

Our next step should be to attach an adjunct. But there are two adjuncts. Which one comes first? Interestingly, the answer is *either*. Two possible trees can come out of this VP:

124)   a)

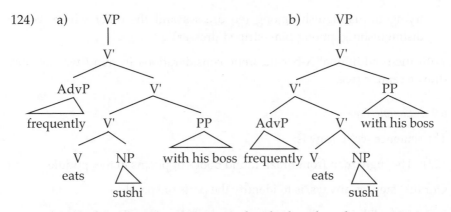

In (124a), the AdvP *frequently* is attached higher than the PP *with his boss*. In (124b), the PP is attached higher than the AdvP. Both of these trees are acceptable, because the adjunct rule iterates. This means that either version of it can appear in either order. Since we have two structures for this sentence you might wonder if there is any semantic ambiguity in this phrase. The distinction is subtle, but it is there. For (124a), we can identify a set of events of sushi-eating with the boss, and then we identify those events as occurring frequently. The meaning of (124b) is very subtly different: there is a set of frequent events of sushi-eating and we are identifying those as occurring with his boss. This distinction is a little easier to see in NPs:

125)   The red dress with the pink stripes

This can be treed two different ways:

126)   a)

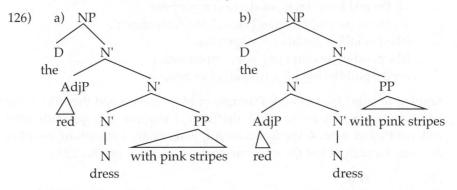

The first tree corresponds to a meaning where we are picking a red member out of the set of dresses with pink stripes. (126b) corresponds to the situation where we are picking a dress with pink stripes out of the set of red dresses. These two trees may pick out the same individuals in the world, but they do so in different contexts (one where we are trying to distinguish among red dresses and the other where we are distinguishing among pink-striped dresses).

With these additional X-bar-theoretic considerations in mind we can now draw a sample tree:

6.2 A Sample Tree

The sentence we'll draw is:

127)   The₁ ugly man from Brazil found books of poems in the₂ puddle.

Our first step, as always, is to identify the parts of speech:

128)   D   Adj N   P   N   V   N   P   N   P D   N
       The₁ ugly man from Brazil found books of poems in the₂ puddle.

Next, and most importantly, we have to identify what modifies or relates to what, and whether that modification is as an adjunct, complement, or specifier. This is perhaps the most difficult and tedious step, but it is also the most important. You will get better at this with practice. You can use the tests we developed above (stacking, coordination, etc.) to determine whether the modifier is a complement, adjunct, or specifier.

129)   [The₁] modifies [man] as a specifier.
       [ugly] modifies [man] as an adjunct.
       [Brazil] modifies [from] as a complement.
       [from Brazil] modifies [man] as an adjunct.
       [Poems] modifies [of] as a complement.
       [of Poems] modifies [books] as a complement.
       [books of poems] modifies [found] as a complement.
       [the₂] modifies [puddle] as a specifier.
       [the puddle] modifies [in] as a complement.
       [in the puddle] modifies [found] as an adjunct.

Keeping in mind the (revised) Principle of Modification and the strict X-bar structure, we next start to build the trees. I suggest you generally start with AdjPs and AdvPs. We have one Adj here. Note that nothing modifies this Adj. As such, it has the minimal structure given above in (120c).

130)   AdjP
                |
              Adj'
                |
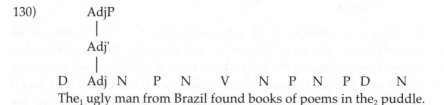
       D   Adj N   P   N   V   N   P   N   P D   N
       The₁ ugly man from Brazil found books of poems in the₂ puddle.

Next we do NPs and PPs. Again, we'll start on the right-hand side of the sentence. The first NP is *the puddle*. Be sure to apply all three of the NP rules here. Don't forget the N' node in the middle. The determiner is the specifier of the NP, so it must be the sister to N' and daughter of NP.

131)

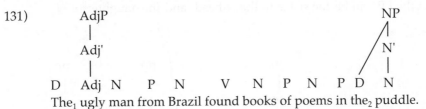

The₁ ugly man from Brazil found books of poems in the₂ puddle.

There are two nouns in this sentence that aren't modified by anything (*Brazil* and *poems*). Let's do these next. Even though they aren't modified by anything they get the full X-bar structure, with NP, N' and N. This is because the rules are *not* optional.

132)

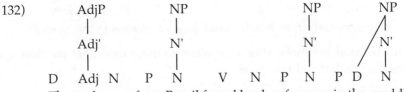

The₁ ugly man from Brazil found books of poems in the₂ puddle.

There are two more nouns in this sentence (*man* and *books*), but if you look carefully at our list of modifications (129), you'll see that they are both modified by PPs. So in order to do them, we have to first build our PPs. There are three Ps in this sentence (and hence three PPs); each of them takes one of the NPs we've built as a complement. The objects of prepositions are always complements. That means that they are sisters to P, and daughters of P':

133)

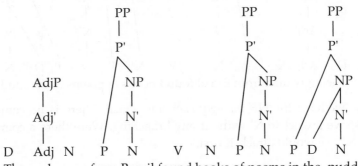

The₁ ugly man from Brazil found books of poems in the₂ puddle.

Now that we've generated our PPs, we'll go back to the two remaining NPs. Let's first observe that the PP *in the puddle* does **not** modify an N (it modifies the V *found*), so it is **not** attached at this stage. Now, turn to the N *books*. We start with the complement. *Of poems* is the complement meaning that the PP will be the sister to the N head, and the daughter of N'.

134)

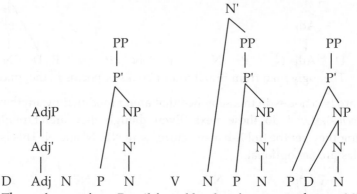

The₁ ugly man from Brazil found books of poems in the₂ puddle.

Nothing else modifies *books*. When there are no more modifiers we close off the projection with the phrase level:

135)

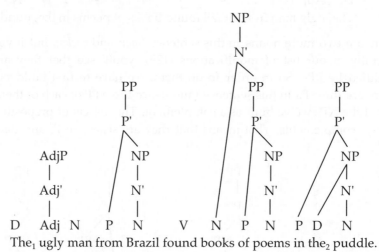

The₁ ugly man from Brazil found books of poems in the₂ puddle.

Finally, we have the NP *the ugly man from Brazil*. There is no complement here, so we project to N' without any branching. Were there a complement in the NP we would attach it first.

136)

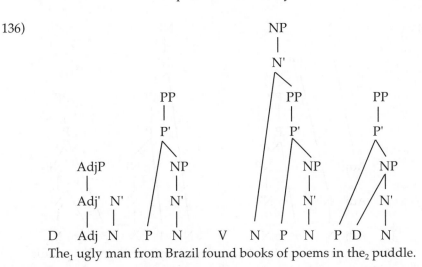

The₁ ugly man from Brazil found books of poems in the₂ puddle.

There are two adjuncts in this NP: *from Brazil* and *ugly*. As per point (v) (and see the trees in (126)), this can be treed two different ways. We can attach either adjunct first. I'll arbitrarily pick to attach the PP first here. Because it is an adjunct, it has to be a sister to N' and a daughter of N'. (Note the difference between this NP and *books of poems*.)

137)

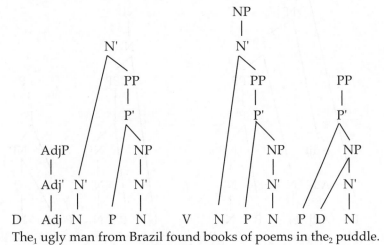

The₁ ugly man from Brazil found books of poems in the₂ puddle.

Next we attach the AdjP. Note that because it is an adjunct, it has to be sister to an N' and daughter of an N'. The N' it is a sister to is already in the tree (having been added in the previous step).

138)

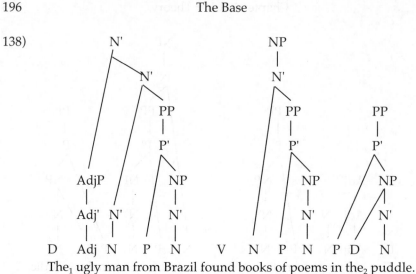

The₁ ugly man from Brazil found books of poems in the₂ puddle.

We're nearly finished with this NP. The determiner is a specifier, which is a daughter of NP and a sister to N'.

139)

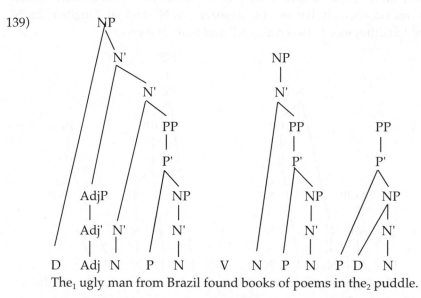

The₁ ugly man from Brazil found books of poems in the₂ puddle.

Now we turn to the VP. The verb *found* has two modifiers. *Books of poems* is a complement, and *in the puddle* is an adjunct. You should always start with the complement, and then follow with the adjuncts, because complements are closer to the head. Remember, complements are sisters to V, and adjuncts are sisters to V'. Notice that the complement NP, which is closer to the head, is attached lower than the adjunct PP. It is the sister to V and daughter of V'.

140)

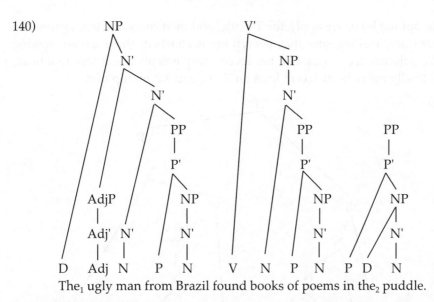

The₁ ugly man from Brazil found books of poems in the₂ puddle.

Now we attach the adjunct PP. It has to be a sister to V' (the one just created by the previous step) and daughter of a V' (which we will add here). Since there are no other modifiers of the V, we will also complete this phrase with the VP:

141)

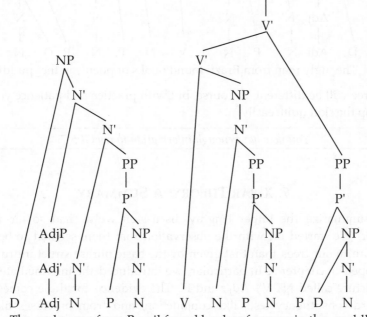

The₁ ugly man from Brazil found books of poems in the₂ puddle.

Last, but not least, we apply the TP rule, and then check the tree against the X-bar rules, making sure that: everything is attached; there are no crossing lines; adjuncts are sisters to a bar level; complements are sisters to a head; and finally every head has at least an X, X', and XP on top of it.

142)

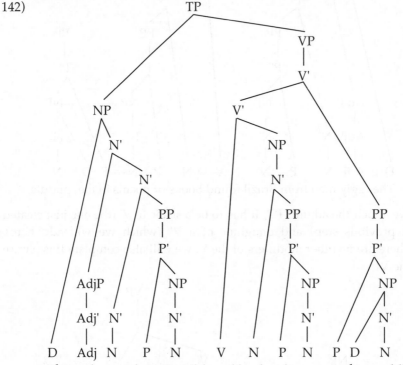

The₁ ugly man from Brazil found books of poems in the₂ puddle.

Each tree will be different, of course, but with practice and patience you will develop the skill quite easily.

You now have enough information to try GPS 7.

7. X-BAR THEORY: A SUMMARY

Let's summarize the rather lengthy discussion we've had so far in this chapter. We started off with the observation that there seemed to be more structure to our trees than that given by the basic phrase structure rules we developed in chapter 3. In particular, we introduced the intermediate levels of structure called N', V', Adj', and P'. The evidence for these comes from standard constituency tests like conjunction, and from processes like *one*-replacement and *do-so*-replacement. We also saw that material on different levels of structure behaved differently. Complements exhibit one set of behaviors and adjuncts a different set. Next we observed that our rules were failing to capture several generalizations about the data. First was the endocentricity generalization: all NPs have an N head, all AdjPs an Adj head, etc. There is no rule like *NP → V Adj. Next, there was the observation that all trees have three levels of structure. They all have specifiers (weak evidence here), adjuncts, and complements. In response to this, we proposed the following general X-bar-theoretic rules:

143) a) *Specifier rule:*   XP → (YP) X' *or* XP → X' (YP)
     b) *Adjunct rule:*   X' → X' (ZP) *or* X' → (ZP) X'
     c) *Complement rule:*   X' → X (WP) *or* X' → (WP) X

These rules use variables to capture cross-categorial generalizations. In order to limit the power of these rules, and in order to capture differences between languages, we proposed that the options within these rules were parameterized. Speakers of languages select the appropriate option for their language.

This is, you'll note, a very simple system. There are, of course, some loose ends, and in the next couple of chapters we'll try to tidy these up. First of all we have the problem of specifiers: we only have one specifier (the determiner). In the next chapter we'll suggest that in fact determiners aren't specifiers at all. Instead they are their own heads. Then we'll reserve specifier positions for something else: subjects. We'll also try to integrate our TP and CP rules into the system.

IDEAS, RULES, AND CONSTRAINTS INTRODUCED IN THIS CHAPTER

i)   *Specifier*: Sister to X', daughter of XP.
ii)   *Adjunct*: Sister to X', daughter of X'.
iii)   *Complement*: Sister to X, daughter of X'.
iv)   *Head*: The word that gives its category to the phrase.
v)   *Projection*: The string of elements associated with a head that bear the same category as the head (N, N', N', N', NP, etc.).
vi)   **Maximal Projection**: The topmost projection in a phrase (XP).
vii)   **Intermediate Projection**: Any projection that is neither the head nor the phrase (i.e., all the X' levels).
viii)   **One-*replacement***: Replacement of an N' node with *one*.
ix)   **Do-so-*replacement***: Replacement of a V' with *do so*.
x)   *Specifier Rule*:   XP → (YP) X' or XP →X' (YP)
xi)   *Adjunct Rule*:   X' → X' (ZP) or X' → (ZP) X'
xii)   *Complement Rule*: X' → X (WP) or X' → (WP) X

xiii)   *Additional Rules*:

CP → (C) TP   TP → NP (T) VP

XP → XP Conj XP   X' → X' Conj X'

X → X Conj X

xiv)   *Parameterization*: The idea that there is a fixed set of possibilities in terms of structure (such as the options in the X-bar framework), and people acquiring a language choose from among those possibilities.

xv)   *Principle of Modification* (revised): If a YP modifies some head X, then YP must be a sister to X or a projection of X (i.e., X' or XP).

FURTHER READING: Baltin and Kroch (1989), Borsley (1996), Carnie (1995, 2010), Chametzky (1996), Chomsky (1970), Jackendoff (1977), Kayne (1994), Lightfoot (1991), Speas (1990), Stowell (1981), Travis (1984)

GENERAL PROBLEM SETS

GPS1. COMPLEMENTS VS. ADJUNCTS in NPs
[Application of Skills; Basic]
Using the tests you have been given (reordering, adjacency, conjunction of likes, *one*-replacement) determine whether the PPs in the following NPs are complements or adjuncts. Give the examples that you used in constructing your tests. Some of the NPs have multiple PPs. Be sure to answer the question for every PP in the NP.

a)   A container [of flour]
b)   A container [with a glass lid]
c)   The collection [of figurines] [in the window]
d)   The statue [of Napoleon] [on the corner]
e)   Every window [in the building] [with a broken pane]

GPS2. ADJECTIVES
[Critical Thinking; Intermediate]
Are adjectives complements or adjuncts to the N? Use the tests you have been given to determine if adjectives are complements or adjuncts. Do NOT use the reordering test – it will not work because adjectives in English are strictly ordered by other principles. Also confine yourself to the adjectives listed below. (Other adjectives, such as *leather* in *leather shoes* or *chemistry* in *chemistry professor* behave differently. However, you can use these adjectives as interveners if you need to check adjacency to the head.)

   hot, big, red, tiny, ugly

GPS3. GERMAN NOUN PHRASES
[Data Analysis; Intermediate/Advanced]
Consider sentence (a) from German:[8]

a) Die schlanke Frau aus Frankreich isst   Kuchen mit Sahne.
    the thin   woman from France   eats cake   with cream
    "The thin woman from France eats cake with cream."

The following sentences are grammatical if they refer to the same woman
described in (a):

b) Die Schlanke aus Frankreich isst Kuchen mit Sahne.
    "The thin one from France eats cake with cream."

c) Die aus Frankreich isst Kuchen mit Sahne.
    "The one from France eats cake with cream."

d) Die Schlanke isst Kuchen mit Sahne.
    "The thin one eats cake with cream."

e) Die isst Kuchen mit Sahne.
    "She eats cake with cream."

Now consider sentences (f–i):

f) Die junge Koenigin von England liebte die Prinzessin.
    The young queen   of England loved the princess
    "The young queen of England loved the princess."

g) Die Junge liebte die Prinzessin.
    "The young one loved the princess."

h) Die liebte die Prinzessin.
    "She loved the princess."

i) *Die von England liebte die Prinzessin.
    "*The one of England loved the princess."

(*Native speakers of German should assume the judgments given even if
they don't agree with them.*)

Assume the following things, then answer the questions below:

   i)   *Der/Die* are always determiners, they are never nouns or pronouns.

   ii) *Schlanke* and *junge* are always adjectives, even in sentences (d)
   and (g) – **assume they never become nouns**. (Ignore the rules of
   German capitalization.)

1) Describe and explain the process seen in (a–e) and (f–i), being sure
    to make explicit reference to X-bar theory. What English phenomenon

---

[8] Thanks to Simin Karimi for providing the data for this question, and to Susi
Wurmbrand for clarifying the facts.

(discussed in this chapter) is this similar to? Make sure you analyze the *German* sentences not the English translations.

2) Draw the trees for sentences (a) and (f). Sentence (a) requires *two* different trees (important hint: the relevant ambiguity in (a) is inside the subject NP, _not_ in the position of the PP *mit Sahne*).

3) Explain the ungrammaticality of (i) in terms of X-bar theory. In particular explain the difference between it and sentence (c). Draw trees to explicate your answer.

GPS4. COMPLEMENTS AND ADJUNCTS IN VPS
[Application of Skills; Basic]
Using the tests you have been given (reordering, adjacency, conjunction of likes, *do-so*-replacement), determine whether the marked NPs, PPs and AdvPs in the following VPs are complements or adjuncts. Give the examples that you used in constructing your tests. Some of the VPs have multiple PPs and AdvPs. Be sure to answer the question for every PP, NP, and AdvP in the VP.

a) Erin [VP [AdvP never] keeps [NP her pencils] [PP in the correct drawer]].
b) Dan [VP walked [PP to New Mexico] [PP in the rain] [AdvP last year]].

GPS5. MALAGASY PARAMETER SETTINGS
[Application of Skills; Intermediate]
Consider the following data from Malagasy:

a) Nividy ny vary   no an'ny   ankizy   ny vehivavy
   bought the rice   for the   children   the woman
   "The woman bought the rice for the children."

b) Nividy vary   ny vehivavy
   bought rice   the woman
   "The woman bought rice."

c) Nametraka my mofo   ambony   ny latabatra   Rakoto
   put   the bread   on   the table   Rakoto
   "Rakoto put the bread on the table."

1) What is the complement parameter setting for Malagasy?
2) What is the adjunct parameter setting for Malagasy?
3) If determiners are specifiers, then what is the specifier parameter setting for Malagasy?
4) In the next chapter, we're going to argue that subject NPs are the specifiers of TP. If this is the case, then what is the specifier parameter setting for Malagasy?
5) Are your answers to (3) and (4) contradictory? How might you explain the contradiction?

GPS6. PARAMETERS
[Data Analysis; Basic to Intermediate]
Go back to the foreign language problems from chapters 3 and 4 (Hiaki, Irish, Bambara, Hixkaryana, Swedish, Dutch, Tzotzil) and see if you can determine the parameter settings for these languages. You may not be able to determine all the settings for each language. (Suggestion: put your answer in a table like the one below. English is done for you as an example.) Assume the following: Determiners are typical examples of specifiers; Adjectives and many PPs (although not all) are adjuncts. "Of" PPs and direct objects are complements. Be sure to check the complement/adjunct relation in all categories (N, Adj, Adv, V, P, etc.) if you can.

	Specifier	Adjunct	Complement
English	(YP) X'	Both	X (ZP)

GPS7. TREES
[Application of Skills; Basic to Advanced]
Draw the X-bar-theoretic trees for the following sentences. Treat possessive NPs like *Héloïse's* as specifiers. Several of the sentences are ambiguous; draw only one tree, but indicate using a paraphrase (or paraphrases) which meaning you intend by your tree.

a) Abelard wrote a volume of poems in Latin for Héloïse.
b) Armadillos from New York often destroy old pillowcases with their snouts. (NB: assume "their" is a determiner.)
c) People with boxes of old clothes lined up behind the door of the building with the leaky roof.
d) That automobile factories abound in Michigan worries me greatly.
e) No-one understands that phrase structure rules explain the little-understood phenomenon of the infinite length of sentences.
f) My favorite language is a language with simple morphology and complicated syntax.
g) Ivan got a noogie on Wednesday from the disgruntled students of phonology from Michigan.
h) The collection of syntax articles with the red cover bores students of syntax in Tucson.
i) The red volume of obscene verse from Italy shocked the puritan soul of the minister with the beard quite thoroughly yesterday.
j) The biggest man in the room said that John danced an Irish jig from County Kerry to County Tipperary on Thursday.
k) A burlap sack of potatoes with mealy skins fell on the professor of linguistics with the terrible taste in T-shirts from the twelfth story of the Douglass Building last Friday.
l) The bright green filing cabinet was filled to the brim with the most boring articles from a prestigious journal of linguistics with a moderately large readership.

CHALLENGE PROBLEM SETS

CHALLENGE PROBLEM SET 1: INTERMEDIATE STRUCTURE
[Application of Knowledge and Critical Thinking; Advanced/Challenge]
The following verb phrase is ambiguous in its structure:

Adam [$_{VP}$ frequently buys paintings from Natasha].

The ambiguity has to do with where [$_{AdvP}$ frequently] and [$_{PP}$ from Natasha] are attached in the string of V' categories. Note that the V' rule can be either V' → V' (PP) or V' → (AdvP) V' and these rules can apply in either order. Using the *do-so/did-so/did-too*-replacement test, provide some sentences that show that there is an ambiguity in structure here.

CHALLENGE PROBLEM SET 2: COMPLEMENT ADJPS?
[Data Analysis and Critical Thinking; Challenge]
You should do General Problem Set 2 above before attempting this problem.

Part 1: Consider the following adjectives:

leather (as in *leather shoe*), *chemistry* (as in *chemistry student*)

Using your tests for complements and adjuncts in NPs (adjacency, *one*-replacement, coordination of likes, only one complement – the test of reordering doesn't work since adjectives in English are ordered by other principles), decide whether these adjectives are functioning more like complements or adjuncts. Contrast them explicitly to adjectives such as *red* and *big*. Provide relevant examples to support your claim.

Part 2: Two analyses of these adjectives have been proposed. One is that they are complements (a); the other, more common, analysis is that these aren't adjectives at all, but are noun–noun compounds (notice that both *leather* and *chemistry* can function as nouns in their own right), as in (b).

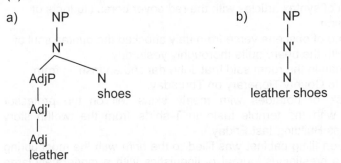

Which of these proposals is right? Try to come up with some arguments to distinguish between them. The following data may be helpful to you, but you should look for arguments beyond this data (i.e., come up with data of your own).

c)   plastic and leather shoes
d)   ?very leather shoes
e)   *very chemistry professor

CHALLENGE PROBLEM SET 3: AMBIGUOUS ADJPS?
[Data Analysis and Critical Thinking; Challenge]
Before trying this problem set you should try Challenge Problem Set 2 above.

Part 1: No matter what your answer to Challenge Problem Set 2 was above, assume for the moment that some AdjPs can function as adjuncts and others can function as complements. This requires that we modify our parameter settings for English. Propose a revised set of parameters for English to allow for the possibility that *chemistry* in *chemistry professor* is a complement. Note: your proposal must explain why in English object NP complements cannot appear before verbs but AdjP complements can appear before nouns (i.e., your proposal must account for why complement-head order is allowed in NPs but not in VPs).

Part 2: Consider the following ambiguous NP:

a)   the German teacher

It can mean either a teacher (say of math) who is German, or it can mean someone (of any nationality) who teaches the German language. Using the complement/adjunct distinction and the following data, explain this ambiguity in meaning. Pay attention to the meaning of *German* (whether it refers to the nationality or the subject) in each of the following sentences. Draw trees to explain your answer.

b)   the French German teacher
c)   the math and German teacher
d)   … not the American teacher but the German one

CHALLENGE PROBLEM SET 4: COMPLEMENTS TO ADJ HEADS[9]
[Critical Thinking and Application of Skills; Challenge]
Consider the word *sick*. This word seems to have two or more meanings. One meaning corresponds to the meaning "ill", as in *I feel sick*. The other meaning is something like "I've had enough", as in the expression *I am sick of it*. This second meaning seems to take a complement PP. The evidence for this is twofold: (1) To get this meaning of *sick* the complement must be present in the sentence. Otherwise we understand the physical meaning of *sick*. (2) The preposition that we find, *of*, is the most common preposition used with complement PP of adjectives and nouns. Judging from their

---

[9] Thanks to Leslie Saxon for contributing this problem set.

meanings and other properties, do any of the adjectives below regularly occur with complements?

delightful, familiar, sensitive, adjacent, full

chapter 7

Extending X-bar Theory to Functional Categories

0. INTRODUCTION

In the last chapter, we looked at a refinement of our phrase structure rules that not only accounted for intermediate structure, but also generalized patterns across categories. This refinement is X-bar theory:

Syntax: A Generative Introduction, Third Edition. Andrew Carnie.
© 2013 Andrew Carnie. Published 2013 by John Wiley & Sons, Inc.

1) a) *Specifier rule:*   XP → (YP) X' *or* XP → X' (YP)
    b) *Adjunct rule:*   X' → X' (ZP) *or* X' → (ZP) X'
    c) *Complement rule:*   X' → X (WP) *or* X' → (WP) X

These rules not only generate most of the trees we need for the sentences of the world's languages, they also capture the additional properties of hierarchical structure found within the major constituents. This said, you may have noticed that this system is far from perfect. First, there is the status of specifiers. In particular, the specifier rule we proposed above requires that the specifier be a phrase- (XP-)level category. However, the only instances of specifiers we've looked at are determiners, which appear *not* to be phrasal. In this chapter, we will look at determiners and specifiers and propose a new category that fits X-bar theory: a ***determiner phrase*** (DP). We will see that determiners are not specifiers. Instead, we'll claim that the specifier position is used to mark a particular grammatical function: that of subjects. You'll see that specifiers (of all categories) are where subjects go.

Another troubling aspect of the X-bar theory is the exceptional CP and TP rules that we have yet to incorporate into the system:

2) CP → (C) TP
    TP → NP (T) VP

These rules do not fit X-bar theory. In the X-bar rules in (1), you'll note that the only obligatory element is the head. In the sentence rules in (2), the opposite is true: the only optional element is the head itself. In this chapter, we will look at how we can modify these so that they fit into the more general pattern.

1. DETERMINER PHRASES (DPs)

In the last chapter, for lack of a better place to put them, we put determiners like *the, a, that, this, those,* and *these* in the specifiers of NPs. This, however, violates one of the basic principles underlying X-bar theory: All non-head material must be phrasal. Notice that this principle is a theoretical rather than an empirical requirement (i.e., it is motivated by the elegance of the theory and not by any data), but it is a nice idea from a mathematical point of view, and it would be good if we could show that it has some empirical basis.

One thing to note about determiners is that they are typically heads. Normally, there can only be one of them in an NP (this isn't true cross-linguistically, but for now let us limit ourselves to English):

3) *the that book

In other words, they don't seem to be phrasal. If our requirement says that the only thing that isn't a phrase in an NP is the N itself, then we have a problem. One solution, perhaps not obvious, to this is to claim that the determiner is not actually inside the NP. Instead, it heads its own phrasal projection. This was first proposed by Abney (1987):

4)   *Old view*   *DP hypothesis*

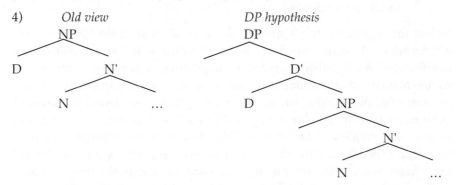

Determiners, in this view, are not part of the NP. Instead the NP is the complement to the determiner head. This solution solves the theoretical problem of the non-phrasality of the D, but we still need empirical evidence in its favor.

One piece of evidence comes from the behavior of genitive (possessive) NPs. There are two kinds of possessive NPs. The first is of less interest to us. This one is often called the *free genitive* or **of-genitive**:

5) a) the coat of the panther
    b) the roof of the building
    c) the hat of the man standing over there

The free genitive uses the preposition *of* to mark the possessive relation between the two NPs. More important in terms of evidence for DP is the behavior of the other kind of possessive: the **construct** or **'s-genitive**.

6) a) the panther's coat
    b) the building's roof
    c) the man standing over there's hat

There are a couple of important things to note about this construction. Notice first that the 's marker appears after the *entire* possessor NP. For example, it attaches to the whole phrase *the man standing over there* not just to the head *man* (7). This means that 's is not a suffix. Instead it seems to be a small word indicating possession. Next, note that it is in complementary distribution with (i.e., cannot co-occur with) determiners (8).

7) a) [the man standing over there]'s hat

   b) *the man's standing over there hat

8) a) *the building's the roof (cf. the roof of the building)
   b) *the panther's the coat (cf. the coat of the panther)

   c) *the man standing over there's the hat (cf. the hat of the man
       standing over there)

Unlike the *of*-genitive, the *'s*-genitive does not allow both the nouns to have
a determiner. In other words, *'s* and determiners are in complementary
distribution. As in other domains of linguistics, when two items are in
complementary distribution, they are instances of the same thing. (Take
for example, phonology, where when two phones are found in different
environments – in complementary distribution – then they are allophones
of the same phoneme.) Determiners like *the* and *'s* are different tokens of
the same type. Assuming that *'s* is a determiner, and assuming the DP
hypothesis holds true, we can now account for the positioning of the *'s*
relative to the possessor. The *'s* occupies the head D position, and
the possessor appears in its specifier (9–10)

9)

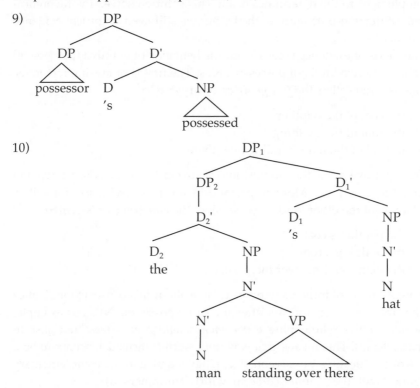

The possessor [*DP2 the man standing over there*] sits in the specifier of DP$_1$, which is headed by *'s*. So *'s* follows the whole thing. Notice that with our old theory, in which determiners are specifiers of NP, there is no way at all to generate *'s* as a determiner and to also have the possessor NP preceding it.

11)

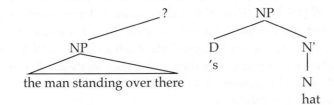

The X-bar rules don't provide any place to attach this pre-determiner NP if determiners are specifiers.

Notice that in the tree in (10) there is a specifier of DP$_1$ (filled by DP$_2$). Note further that this specifier is phrasal (projects to an XP). Which means that it meets with our requirement that all non-head material be phrasal.

You might ask if by moving determiners out of the specifier we have completely destroyed the empirical justification for the specifier rule. Actually, we haven't. Again if you look closely at the tree in (10) we still have a specifier, it just isn't D$_1$. Instead, it is the DP possessor (DP$_2$). Further, as we will see below, there are other related uses for the specifier positions. In particular, we will come to associate specifiers with subjects of various kinds of constituents.

You now have enough information to try WBE 1 & 2, GPS 1, and CPS 1 & 2.

---

2. A DESCRIPTIVE TANGENT INTO CLAUSE TYPES

A *clause* is essentially a *subject* (usually a DP that has the property indicated by the predicate; this is what the clause is about) and a *predicate phrase* (a group of words that assign a property to the subject). The most obvious kind of clause is the simple sentence. In the following examples, the subject is indicated in italics and the predicate phrase is in bold:

12) a)   *The boy* **ran**.
    b)   *Howard* is **a linguistics student**.

As we'll see below, there are many other kinds of clauses. But we can use this as a working definition.

A clause that stands on its own is called a *root, matrix,* or *main clause.* Sometimes, however, we can find examples of clauses within clauses. Examples of this are seen below:

13) a)   [Peter said [that Danny danced]].
    b)   [Bill wants [Susan to leave]].

In each of these sentences there are two clauses. In sentence (13a), there is the clause *(that) Danny danced*, which is inside the root clause *Peter said that Danny danced*. In (13b), we have the clause *Susan to leave*, which has the subject *Susan*, and the predicate phrase *(to) leave*. This is contained within the main clause *Bill wants Susan to leave*. Both of these clauses within clauses are called **embedded clauses**. Another name for embedded clause is **subordinate clause**. The clause containing the embedded clause is still called the **main** or **root clause**.

Embedded Clauses are Part of Main Clauses

A very common error among new syntacticians is to forget that embedded clauses are contained **within** main clauses. That is, when faced with identifying what the main clause is in a sentence like (i), most students will properly identify the embedded clause as *(that) Cathy loves him*, but will mistakenly claim that the main clause is only *Peter thinks*.

i)   Peter thinks that Cathy loves him.

This is completely incorrect. *Peter thinks* is not a constituent. The main clause is **everything** under the root TP node. So the main clause is *Peter thinks that Cathy loves him*. Be very careful about this.

    Using the TP and CP rules we developed in chapter 3, the structure of a root clause containing an embedded clause is given below (I've obscured the irrelevant details with triangles):

14)

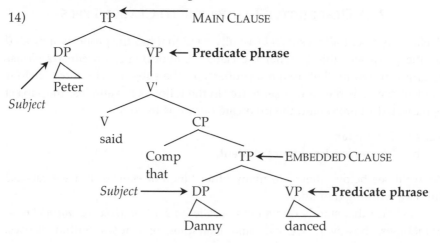

In addition to the distinction between main and embedded clauses, we can also distinguish among specifier, complement, and adjunct clauses. Here are some examples of *complement clauses*:

15) a)   Heidi said [that Art loves peanut butter].
    b)   Colin asked [if they could get a mortgage].

These complement clauses (CPs) are sisters to the verb, and thus complements. Clauses can also appear in adjunct positions. Relative clauses are one example of *adjunct clauses*:

16) [The man [I saw get into the cab]] robbed the bank.

The relative clause in (16) *[I saw get into the cab]* modifies the head *man*. *Specifier clauses* are ones that serve as the subject of a sentence (why these are specifiers will be made clear below):

17) a)   [[People selling their stocks] caused the crash of 1929].
    b)   [[For Mary to love that boor] is a travesty].

To summarize, we have two basic kinds of clauses, main and embedded. Embedded clauses are contained within main clauses. Further, there are three types of embedded clauses: specifier clauses, complement clauses, and adjunct clauses. This is summarized in the following table:

18)

Main clauses	Embedded clauses		
	specifier clauses	complement clauses	adjunct clauses

There is another way of dividing up the clause-type pie. We class clauses into two groups depending upon whether they are tensed or not. Clauses with predicates that are tensed are sometimes called (obviously) *tensed clauses*, but you may more frequently find them called *finite clauses*. Clauses without a tensed verb are called *tenseless* or *non-finite clauses* (sometimes also *infinitival clauses*).[1]

19) a)   I said [that Mary signed my yearbook].   *tensed or finite*
    b)   I want [Mary to sign my yearbook].   *tenseless or non-finite*

There are a number of tests for distinguishing finite from non-finite clauses. These tests are taken from Radford (1988). The embedded clause in sentence (20a) is tensed. The one in (20b) is untensed. I have deliberately selected

---

[1] In many languages, the form of a verb found in a non-finite clause is called the *infinitive*. In English, infinitives are often marked with the auxiliary *to*, as in *to sign*.

a verb that is ambiguous between tensed and untensed in terms of its morphology (suffixes) here as an illustration:

20) a) I know [you eat asparagus].   *finite*
    b) I've never seen [you eat asparagus].   *non-finite*

One way to tell if a clause is finite or not is to look for agreement and tense morphology on the verb. These include the *-s* ending associated with third person nouns (*he eats*) and the past tense suffixes like *-ed*. The above examples don't show any such suffixes. However, if we change the tense to the past a difference emerges:

21) a) I know you ate asparagus.   *finite*
    b) *I've never seen you ate asparagus.   *non-finite*

Finite clauses allow past tense morphology (the *ate* form of the verb *eat*); non-finite clauses don't. The same effect is seen if you change the person of the subject in the embedded clause. Third person subjects trigger the *-s* ending. This is allowed only in finite clauses.

22) a) I know he eats asparagus.   *finite*
    b) *I've never seen him eats asparagus.   *non-finite*

The case on the subject of the noun is often a giveaway for determining whether or not a clause is finite. Case refers to the notions **nominative** and **accusative** introduced in chapter 1, repeated here:

23)

	Nominative		Accusative		Anaphoric	
	Singular	Plural	Singular	Plural	Singular	Plural
1	I	we	me	us	myself	ourselves
2	you	you	you	you	yourself	yourselves
3 masc	he		him		himself	
3 fem	she	they	her	them	herself	themselves
3 neut	it		it		itself	

If the clause is finite, then a subject pronoun will take the nominative case form:

24) I know *he* eats asparagus.   *finite*

If the clause is non-finite then the subject will take the accusative form:

25) I've never seen *him* eat asparagus.   *non-finite*

One test that works most of the time, but is not as reliable as the others, is to see if the subject is obligatory. If the subject is obligatory, then the clause is finite. If the subject is optional, or is not allowed at all, then it is non-finite.

(Note: this test only works for English; in many languages, such as Spanish, subjects of finite clauses are optional.)

26) a) I think that he eats asparagus.   *finite*
        (cf. *I think that eats asparagus.)
    b) I want (him) to eat asparagus.   *non-finite*
        (cf. I want to eat asparagus.)

Another way to tell if a clause is finite or not is by looking at the complementizer. The complementizer *for* is only found with non-finite clauses. By contrast, *that* and *if* are only found with tensed clauses:

27) a) I wonder if he eats asparagus.   *finite*
    b) I think that he eats asparagus.   *finite*
    c) [For him to eat asparagus] is a travesty.   *non-finite*
    d) I asked for him to eat the asparagus.   *non-finite*

As a final test, we can note that finite and non-finite clauses take different kinds of T elements. The T in tensed clauses can contain auxiliaries and modals like *will, can, must, may, should, shall, is,* and *have*. By contrast the only auxiliary allowed in non-finite clauses is *to*.

28) a) I think [he *will* eat asparagus].
    b) I want him *to* eat asparagus. (cf. *I want him will eat asparagus.)

This last property gets at the heart of the distinction between finite and non-finite clauses. In structural terms the difference between a finite and a non-finite clause lies in terms of what kind of T the clause has. If a clause is finite it bears some tense feature (like [±PAST] or [±FUTURE]). If it is non-finite, it doesn't have any of these features. The question of how this works for clauses where there is no auxiliary we'll leave as a bit of a mystery for now, but will return to later in this chapter.

Let's summarize the discussion we've had thus far. We've been looking at a number of terms for describing various kinds of clauses. We defined clauses as a subject and a predicate phrase. We distinguished root or main clauses from embedded clauses. Embedded clauses come in three types: specifier clauses, complement clauses and adjunct clauses. The other dimension along which we can describe clauses is the finite/non-finite distinction.

With this terminology under our belts, we'll now turn to the structure of clauses, and see if we can make them fit better into X-bar theory.

You now have enough information to try WBE 3–8 and GPS 2–4.

---

3. COMPLEMENTIZER PHRASES (CPS)

We've observed that the TP rule and the CP rule stand out, since they don't fit X-bar theory. In X-bar theory, the head is always obligatory. This is not true of these two rules:

29) a)   CP → (C) TP
    b)   TP → DP (T) VP

In fact, it is a fairly trivial matter to change these rules into X-bar-theoretic format. Let us deal with the CP rule first. If we take X-bar theory to extend to CPs, we can assimilate the rule in (29a) to get a tree like that in (30):

30)

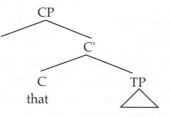

This CP structure has C as the head, a TP complement and an empty specifier position (this empty specifier position will become very important later for us when we do *wh*-movement in chapter 11).

We might ask how pervasive this rule is in our mental grammars. That is, do all clauses have CPs, or do only embedded clauses have CPs? On the surface, the answer to this question seems obvious: Only embedded clauses have CPs, since only embedded clauses appear to allow complementizers (31). However, there is evidence that all clauses, even root clauses like (31), require some kind of complementizer.

31) a)   John thinks that the asparagus is yummy.
    b)   *That the asparagus is yummy. (cf. Asparagus is yummy.)

32) Asparagus grows in California.

In particular, we'll claim that some sentences have null complementizers. Don't assume that I'm crazy. No matter how strange this proposal sounds, there is actually some good evidence that this is correct. The structure in (33) shows one of these null complementizers.

33)   [CP [C Ø [TP Asparagus grows in California]]]

The evidence for this claim comes from cross-linguistic comparison of questions among languages. In particular, we'll focus on *yes/no questions* (see chapter 9 for more discussion on these). These are questions that can be answered with either *yes*, *no*, or *maybe*. Examples of yes/no questions in English are given below:

34) a)   Did John leave?
    b)   Have you seen Louis?

In English, to form a yes/no question you either insert some form of the verb *do* (*do, does, did*) before the subject, or you invert the subject and the auxiliary (*You have seen Louis.* → *Have you seen Louis?*). This operation is called **subject-aux inversion** (more on this in chapter 9). In many other languages, however, yes/no questions are formed with a complementizer particle that precedes the verb. Take for example, Irish, which indicates yes/no questions with a special particle *Ar* (or its allomorph *An*):

35) Ar thit Seán?
     Q   fall John
     "Did John fall?"

Languages like English that use subject-aux inversion don't have special complementizer question particles. If a language has complementizer question particles, then it won't have subject-aux inversion. The phenomena are in complementary distribution. It seems reasonable to claim, then, that question complementizers and subject-aux inversion are part of the same basic phenomenon. In order to make this concrete, let's make the following proposal: There is a question complementizer particle in English, just like there is in Irish. The difference is that in English this complementizer particle is null (has no phonological content). We will represent this **null complementizer** with the symbol $\varnothing_{[+Q]}$. It has no phonological content, but it must be realized or pronounced someway. The way English satisfies this requirement is by moving T into the C head:

36)

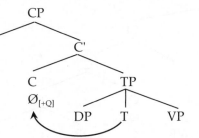

This results in the correct order, where the auxiliary (in T) now appears before the subject. By contrast, languages like Irish don't utilize this mechanism. Instead they have a particle that fills their [+Q] complementizer (like *Ar/An* in Irish).

English does, in fact, have an overt [+Q] complementizer, but it is only found in embedded questions. This complementizer is *if*. Unsurprisingly, subject-aux inversion is completely disallowed when *if* is present:

37) a)   Fabio asked if Claus had run a marathon.
    b)   *Fabio asked if had Claus run a marathon.
    c)   *Fabio asked had if Claus run a marathon.
    d)   ?Fabio asked had Claus run a marathon.

If occupies the [+Q] complementizer, so no subject-aux inversion is required (or allowed).

Given the existence of overt root complementizers in other languages and the evidence that subject-aux inversion patterns like these overt root complementizers, we can conclude that, for questions at least, there are complementizers (and CPs) present even in main clauses.

Of course, we haven't yet shown that non-question sentences have a root complementizer. For this, we need to add an extra step in the argument. You can only conjoin identical categories. If sentences showing subject-aux inversion use a null complementizer and if you can conjoin that question with a non-question (such as a statement), then that statement must also include a (null) complementizer and CP. It is indeed possible to conjoin a statement with a question:

38) [You can lead a horse to water] but [will it drink]?

Since the second clause here shows subject-aux inversion, we know there is a $\emptyset_{[+Q]}$ question complementizer present. By extension, we know that the clause it is conjoined with must *also* have a complementizer – this time, a non-question $\emptyset_{[-Q]}$. A CP can only be conjoined with another CP.

39)

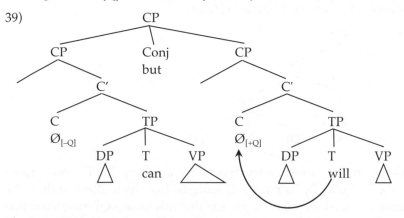

This is an argument for null complementizers attached to root clauses, even in simple statements. From this point forward, we will assume that there is a CP on top of every clause. For brevity's sake, I may occasionally leave this CP off my trees, but the underlying assumption is that it is always there. You should always draw it in when you are drawing your trees.

4. TENSE PHRASES (TPS)

The other rule that doesn't fit the X-bar pattern is our S rule:

40) TP → DP (T) VP

Assimilating this rule to X-bar theory results in a structure like the following:

41)

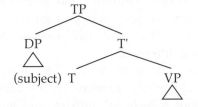

In this tree, the subject DP sits in the specifier of TP, and the VP is the complement. (This is our first clear instance where the notion of specifier corresponds to the notion of subject. We will consider some other cases below.) Again the problem here is that the element that we have designated as the head of the phrase (T) is apparently optional. In X-bar theory, heads are the only obligatory element.

In chapter 2, we equated T with auxiliary verbs. But we might ask what happens in clauses where there is no auxiliary: Is there a TP? Is there a T? Can we make the same claim we did for CPs that the C is obligatory? In order to answer this question, let's make the following observation: Tense inflection on a verb is in complementary distribution with auxiliaries (you never get both of them at the same time):

42) a) The roadrunner walks funny.
    b) The roadrunner is walking funny.
    c) *The roadrunner is walks/walkings funny.

Recall that when two elements are in complementary distribution then they are instances of the same category. This means that T can be realized both by auxiliaries and by inflectional endings on verbs. Similar evidence comes from coordination. Recall that you can only coordinate two items that are of the same category and bar level. In the following sentence, we are conjoining a T' that has an auxiliary with a T' that has a tensed verb. The tense inflection and auxiliary are italicized.

43) [$_{TP}$ I [$_T$[$_T$ kiss*ed* the toad] and [$_T$ *must* go wash my mouth now]]].

This evidence suggests that the two T's are identical in some deep sense. That is, they both involve a T node: one an auxiliary, the other a tense inflectional ending.

If you think about the basic order of the elements we seem to have argued ourselves into a corner. Auxiliaries appear on the left of verbs, and inflectional suffixes (like *-ed*, and *-s*) appear on the right:

44) a) He *will* go.
    b) He   go*es*.

There are other differences between auxiliaries and inflectional suffixes. For example, auxiliaries, but not suffixes, undergo subject-aux inversion. If we are to claim that inflectional suffixes and auxiliaries are both instances of T we have to account for these differences.

There are two possibilities out there in the literature. The older possibility, dating back to Chomsky's famous (1957) book, *Syntactic Structures*, is to claim that both inflectional suffixes and auxiliaries are indeed generated under T. They differ, however, in terms of whether they can stand alone or not. Auxiliaries are independent words and can stand alone. By contrast, suffixes like *-s* and *-ed* have to be attached to a verb. Much like the case of moving T to C in order to pronounce Ø$_{[+Q]}$, we might hypothesize that endings like *-s* and *-ed* can't be pronounced in isolation, so they move to attach to the verb. In particular they seem to lower onto the verb. The following tree shows how this would work for the simple sentence *He walked*. This sentence starts out as *[he -ed walk]* and then the *-ed* ending lowers to attach to the end of the verb:

45)   TP   *Affix Lowering Analysis*

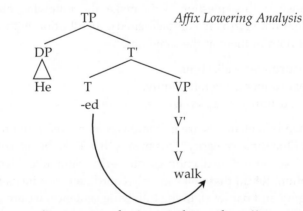

A more modern approach doesn't have the affixes generated in T. Instead, there are two tense markers, both of which are null: Ø$_{[PAST]}$ and Ø$_{[PRESENT]}$. The Ø$_{[PAST]}$ simply requires that its VP complement be in a past tense

(or preterite) form and Ø[PRESENT] requires that its VP complement be in a
present tense form.

46)   *Selectional Analysis*

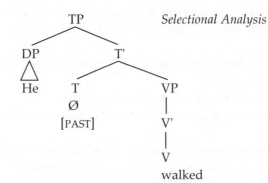

We look at how heads can place restrictions on their complements and
specifiers in the next chapter, and then we extend this more modern analysis
to the very complicated English auxiliary system in chapter 9.

You can now try WBE 9, GPS 5 & 6, and CPS 3.

IDEAS, RULES, AND CONSTRAINTS INTRODUCED IN THIS CHAPTER

i)   *Determiner Phrase (DP)*: D is not in the specifier of NP. D heads its
        own phrase: [DP [D' D NP]].
ii)   *Complementizer Phrase (CP)*: C is the head of CP and is obligatory
        in all clauses, although sometimes phonologically null:
        [CP [C' C TP]].
iii)   *Tense Phrase (TP)*: T is the head of TP and is obligatory in all
        clauses. Sometimes it involves lowering of the affix to the V.
        The subject DP occupies the specifier position: [TP DP_subject [T' T VP]].
iv)   *Free Genitive/of-Genitive*: Possessed of the possessor.
v)   *Construct Genitive/'s-Genitive*: Possessor 's possessed.
vi)   *Subject*: A DP that has the property indicated by the predicate
        phrase. What the sentence is about. In most sentences, this surfaces
        in the specifier of TP.
vii)   *Predicate Phrase*: A group of words that attributes a property to the
        subject. (In most sentences this is the VP, although not necessarily
        so.)
viii)   *Clause*: A subject and a predicate phrase (always a CP in our
        system).
ix)   *Root, Matrix, or Main Clause*: A clause (CP) that isn't dominated by
        anything.

x)   *Embedded Clause/Subordinate Clause*: A clause inside of another.

xi)   *Specifier Clause*: An embedded clause in a specifier position.

xii)   *Adjunct Clause*: An embedded clause in an adjunct position.

xiii)   *Complement Clause*: An embedded clause in a complement position.

xiv)   *Tenseless* or *Non-finite Clause*: A clause that isn't tensed (e.g., I want [*Mary to leave*]).

xv)   *Tensed* or *Finite Clause*: A clause that is tensed.

xvi)   *Yes/No Question*: A question that can be answered with a *yes*, a *no* or a *maybe*.

xvii)   *Subject-Aux Inversion*: A means of indicating a *yes/no* question. Involves movement of T to $\emptyset_{[+Q]}$ complementizer for morpho-phonological reasons.

xviii) *Affix Lowering*: An old analysis of how past and present tense suffixes get on the verb: The lowering of inflectional suffixes to attach to their verb. Now largely replaced by an analysis where T is null and selects for a VP complement that is correctly inflected.

FURTHER READING: Abney (1987), Chomsky (1991), Emonds (1980), Pollock (1989)

GENERAL PROBLEM SETS

GPS1. TREE DRAWING: DPS
[Application of Skills; Basic]
Draw the DP trees for the following phrases:

a) the kitten   b) the very orange kitten
c) the kitten's paw   d) the paw of the kitten
e) the kitten's mother's paw   f) the kitten's left paw

GPS2. SUBJECTS AND PREDICATE PHRASES
[Data Analysis; Basic]
In each of the following clauses identify the subject and the predicate phrase. Some sentences contain multiple clauses. Be sure to identify the subjects and predicate phrases of *all* clauses.

a) The peanut butter has got[2] moldy.
b) The duffer's swing blasted the golf ball across the green.
c) That Harry loves dancing is evidenced by his shiny tap shoes.
d) The Brazilians pumped the oil across the river.

---

[2] You may prefer *gotten* to *got* here. The choice is dialect-dependent.

GPS3. CLAUSE TYPES
[Data Analysis; Basic]
The following sentences are "complex" in that they contain more than one clause. For each sentence, identify each clause. Remember, main clauses include embedded clauses. Identify the complementizer, the T, and the subject of the clause; be sure to identify even *null* (Ø) complementizers and Ts with suffixes in them. State whether each clause is a finite clause or a non-finite clause.

a) Stalin may think that Roosevelt is a fool.
b) Lenin believes the Tsar to be a power-hungry dictator.
c) Brezhnev had said for Andropov to leave.
d) Yeltsin saw Chernyenko holding the bag.

GPS4. ENGLISH *THAT*[3]
[Critical Thinking; Basic]
Discuss the status of the word *that* in each of the following two sentences. Explain the differences between the two sentences. If you assign a different category status to *that* in each sentence, explain why. Draw the tree (use X-bar theory) for each of the sentences.

a) Robert thinks <u>that</u> students should eat asparagus.
b) Robert thinks <u>that</u> student should eat asparagus.

GPS5. TREES I
[Application of Skills; Basic to Intermediate]
Draw the trees for the following sentences. Use X-bar theory and show all CPs, DPs, and TPs.

a) The very young child walked from school to the store.
b) Linguistics students like phonetics tutorials.
c) John paid a dollar for a head of lettuce.
d) Teenagers drive rather quickly.
e) Martha said that Bill loved his Cheerios in the morning.
f) Eloise wants you to study a new language. [assume *to* = T]
g) For Maurice to quarrel with Joel frightened Maggie.
h) John's drum will always bother me.

GPS6. TREES II
[Application of Skills; Basic to Intermediate]
1) Go back to chapter 3, GPS 1 and GPS 2 and draw the trees using X-bar theory, including DPs.
2) Go back to chapter 3, GPS 6, and draw the trees using X-bar theory, including DPs, TPs, and CPs.

---

[3] Thanks to Eithne Guilfoyle for contributing this problem set.

3) Go back to chapter 4, GPS 1, and draw the trees using X-bar theory, including DPs, TPs, and CPs.

CHALLENGE PROBLEM SETS

CHALLENGE PROBLEM SET 1: HUNGARIAN DPS
[Data Analysis; Challenge]
In the text above, we argued that the structure of genitive constructions in English looks like:

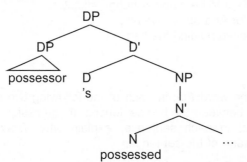

Consider the following data from Hungarian. Does the possessor DP appear in the same place as the English ones? Assume the determiners *az* and *a* modify the *possessed* noun, not the possessor. The ending on the word kalapom/kalapod/kalapja varies depending upon the possessor. This does not affect the answer to this question. (Data from Szabolcsi 1994.)

a) az én kalapom
    the I   hat-1SG
    "my hat"

b) a   te   kalapod
    the you hat-2SG
    "your hat"

Hungarian has another possessive construction, seen in (c).

c) Marinak a   kalapja
    Mary   the hat-3SG
    "Mary's hat"

Where is the possessor DP in (c)? Explain your answer.

CHALLENGE PROBLEM SET 2: NPI LICENSERS
[Data Analysis and Critical Thinking; Challenge]
The adverb *ever* is a negative polarity item. Negative polarity items must stand in a c-command relationship with a negative licenser. Assume that the properties of the head uniquely determine the properties of a phrase. Explain

how the following sentences are an argument for the subject being a DP
rather than an NP:

a) No man has ever beaten the centaur.
b) *Some man has ever beaten the centaur.
c) *Every man has ever beaten the centaur.

CHALLENGE PROBLEM SET 3: ENGLISH MODALS AND AUXILIARIES
[Data Analysis and Critical Thinking; Challenge]
In traditional grammar, two different kinds of T are found: modals and
auxiliaries. Modals include words like *can, must, should, would, could,
may, will* and in some dialects *shall*. Auxiliary verbs, by contrast, include
such words as *have* and *be*. In this book, we've treated both modals and
auxiliaries as T. An alternative is that only modals are really of category T,
and that auxiliaries are real verbs. Auxiliary and verb combinations are
actually a stacked set of VPs:

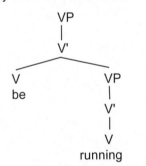

Construct an argument in favor of the idea that modals are of category T, but
auxiliaries are really verbs. Assume the following: You may have as many
V categories as you like, but there is only one T in any tensed clause's tree.

chapter 8

Constraining X-bar: Theta Theory

Learning Objectives

After reading chapter 8 you should walk away having mastered the following ideas and skills:

1) Distinguish between thematic relation and theta role.
2) Identify the thematic relations agent, theme, goal, source, experiencer, location, instrument, recipient, benefactor.
3) Explain how X-bar theory over-generates.
4) Explain the structure of the lexicon.
5) Draw the theta grids for a predicate.
6) Apply the theta criterion to a sentence as a filter to X-bar theory.
7) Distinguish sentences with expletive subjects from ones with theta-role-bearing subjects.
8) Explain the Extended Projection Principle and how it accounts for expletives.
9) Explain the ordering of the EPP with the theta criterion in the context of the model we are developing.

0. INTRODUCTION

In chapters 6 and 7, we developed a very simple and general theory of phrase structure: X-bar theory. Using only three rules, this theory accounts

Syntax: A Generative Introduction, Third Edition. Andrew Carnie.
© 2013 Andrew Carnie. Published 2013 by John Wiley & Sons, Inc.

for the distinction between adjuncts, complements, and specifiers. It incorporates the more articulated view of sentence hierarchy required by constituency tests, and it captures cross-categorial generalizations (i.e., the fact that all kinds of phrases – NPs, VPs, APs, PPs, CPs, DPs, and TPs – have the same basic properties). Most importantly, it allows us to draw trees for most of the sentences of any language.

This said, there is a significant problem with X-bar theory: it also generates sentences that are not acceptable or grammatical. Take for example the following pairs of grammatical and ungrammatical sentences:

1) a) Rosemary hates New York.
    b) *Rosemary hates.

2) a) Jennie smiled.
    b) *Jennie smiled the breadbox.

3) a) Traci gave the whale a jawbreaker.
    b) *Traci gave the whale.
    c) *Traci gave a jawbreaker.

Sentence (1b) should be perfectly acceptable (compare it to *Rosemary ran*). X-bar theory says that complements are optional. Therefore, direct objects, which are complements, should always be optional. The opposite type of fact is seen in the pair in (2). X-bar theory optionally allows a complement. So having a direct object here should be fine too. The same kind of effect is seen in (3), where both the direct object and indirect object are obligatory – contra X-bar theory.

What seems to be at work here is that certain verbs require objects and others don't. It appears to be a property of the *particular* verb. Information about the peculiar or particular properties of verbs is contained in our mental dictionary or **lexicon**. In this chapter, we'll look at how we can use the lexicon to constrain X-bar theory so that it doesn't predict the existence of ungrammatical sentences.

1. SOME BASIC TERMINOLOGY

In chapter 2, we discussed how different verb types take a different number of arguments. For example, an intransitive verb like *leave* takes a single DP, which is the subject. A transitive verb such as *hit* takes a DP subject and a DP object. Below are the subcategories we came up with in chapter 2 (substituting DP for NP):

4)

Subcategory	Example
$V_{[DP\_]}$ (intransitive)	*leave*
$V_{[DP\_\_DP]}$ (transitive type 1)	*hit*
$V_{[DP\_\_\{DP/CP\}]}$ (transitive type 2)	*ask*
$V_{[DP\_\_DP\,DP]}$ (ditransitive type 1)	*spare*
$V_{[DP\_\_DP\,PP]}$ (ditransitive type 2)	*put*
$V_{[DP\_\_DP\,\{DP/PP\}]}$ (ditransitive type 3)	*give*
$V_{[DP\_\_DP\,\{DP/PP/CP\}]}$ (ditransitive type 4)	*tell*

In addition to these restrictions, we also find semantic restrictions on what can appear in particular positions:

5) a) #My comb hates raisinettes.
    b) #A bolt of lightning killed the rock.

There is something decidedly strange about these sentences. Combs can't hate anything and rocks can't be killed. These semantic criteria are called **selectional restrictions**.

In the next section, we'll look at the theory of thematic relations, which is a particular way of representing selectional and subcategorizational restrictions.

2. THEMATIC RELATIONS AND THETA ROLES

One way of encoding selectional restrictions is through the use of what are called **thematic relations**. These are particular semantic terms that are used to describe the role that the argument plays with respect to the predicate. This section describes some common thematic relations (this list is by no means exhaustive, and the particular definitions are not universally accepted).

The initiator or doer of an action is called the **agent**. In the following sentences, *Ryan* and *Michael* are agents.

6) a) *Ryan* hit Andrew.
    b) *Michael* accidentally broke the glass.

Agents are most frequently subjects, but they can also appear in other positions.

Arguments that feel or perceive events are called *experiencers*. Experiencers can appear in a number of argument positions, including subject and object:

7) a) *Leah* likes cookies.
    b) *Lorenzo* saw the eclipse.
    c) Syntax frightens *Kenny*.

Experiencers are normally only found with verbs that involve a psychological component or express a notion that can be felt by a living being. For example, the subjects of verbs of perception (*see, perceive, hear, taste, feel, smell*, etc.), subjects and objects of verbs of emotion (*frighten, fear, dishearten*, etc.), and verbs of cognition (*know, understand*, etc.), among others can be experiencers. There is a temptation among new syntacticians to extend the notion "experiencer" to all sorts of arguments. For example, in the sentence *The rock fell on Terry*, does Terry experience the event? Of course he does, but he's not an "experiencer" in the technical sense we are using here. What about *the wall* in *The car hit the wall*? We want to limit the experiencer thematic relation to entities that can experience events, and only with predicates where the experience is a critical part of the meaning of the verb (like those listed above). In the end, as we'll see below, the exact thematic relations involved for a given predicate are not critical to the syntactic analysis we give these verbs, but it's good to be as precise as we possibly can be.

In some languages, the difference between agents and experiencers is marked grammatically on the nouns (usually as case markers), or sometimes with morphology on the verb. Take Korean[1] for example. If you have a verb like *culkew* which roughly means "enjoy", the normal morphology has the subject marked with dative case (8) – which is surprising since subjects typically take the nominative. This is the morphology typically associated with experiencer predicates.

8) Ku yeca-ekey   sopwung-i   culkew-ess-ta
    she.DAT   picnic-NOM   enjoy-PAST-DECL
    "She enjoyed the picnic."

But when the verb is marked with the suffix *eha*, meaning roughly "do", the case marking on the arguments shifts and the subject is marked with nominative case as in (9). Korean speakers report that sentences like (9) have a more agentive feel, and that the subject is overtly expressing her enjoyment, rather than just feeling it inside.

---

[1] Thanks to Hyun-Kyoung Jung for helpful discussion of these facts.

9) Ku yeca-ka sopwung-lul   culkew-eha-ess-ta
   she.NOM   picnic-ACC   enjoy-do-PAST-DECL
   "She enjoyed the picnic."

Entities that undergo actions or are moved, experienced, or perceived are called *themes*.

10) a) Alyssa kept *her syntax book*.
    b) The arrow hit *Ben*.
    c) The syntactician hates *phonology*.

The entity towards which motion takes place is called a *goal*. Goals may involve abstract motion.

11) a) Doug went *to Chicago*.
    b) *Dave* was given the piña colada mix.
    c) An evil thought struck *Dave*.

There is a special kind of goal called *recipient*. Recipients only occur with verbs that denote a change of possession:

12) a) Mikaela gave *Jessica* the book.
    b) *Daniel* received a scolding from Hanna.

The opposite of a goal is the *source*. This is the entity from which a motion originates:

13) a) *Bob* gave Steve the syntax assignment.
    b) Stacy came directly *from sociolinguistics class*.

The place where the action occurs is called the *location*:

14) a) Andrew is *in Tucson's finest apartment*.
    b) We're all *at school*.

The object with which an action is performed is called the *instrument*:

15) a) Chris hacked the computer apart *with an axe*.
    b) *This key* will open the door to the linguistics building.

Finally, the one for whose benefit an event took place is called the *beneficiary*:

16) a) He bought these flowers *for Aaron*.
    b) She cooked *Matt* dinner.

You now have enough information to try WBE 1–7 and GPS 1 & 2.

Notice that any given DP can have more than one thematic relation. In the following sentence, the DP *Jason* bears the thematic relations of agent and source (at the very least).

17) *Jason* gave the books to Anna.

There is no one-to-one relationship between thematic relations and arguments. However, linguists have a special construct called a **theta role** (or **θ role**) that does map one-to-one with arguments. Theta roles are bundles of thematic relations that cluster on one argument. In (17) above, *Jason* gets two thematic relations (agent and source), but only one theta role (the one that contains the agent and source thematic relations). Somewhat confusingly, syntacticians often refer to particular theta roles by the most prominent thematic relation that they contain. So you might hear a syntactician refer to the "agent theta role" of [DP *Jason*]. Strictly speaking, this is incorrect: Agent refers to a thematic relation, whereas the theta role is a bundle of thematic relations. But the practice is common, so we'll do it here. Remember, thematic relations are things like agent, theme, goal, etc., but theta roles are bundles of thematic relations assigned to a particular argument.

Let's now see how we can use these theta roles to represent the argument structure of a verb. Take a ditransitive verb like *place*. *Place* requires three arguments: a subject that must be an agent (the placer), a direct object, which represents the theme (the thing being placed), and an indirect object, which represents a location or goal (the thing on which the theme is being placed). Any variation from this results in ungrammaticality:

18) a)   John placed the flute on the table.
    b)   *placed the flute on the table.
    c)   *John placed on the table.
    d)   *John placed the flute.
    e)   *John placed the flute the violin on the table.[2]
    f)   *The rock placed the sky with the fork.
    g)   *John placed the flute the table.

Examples (18b–e) show that having either too many or too few arguments results in ungrammaticality. Example (18f) shows that using DPs with the wrong theta roles does the same (*the rock* can't be an agent; *the sky* can't be a theme – it can't be given to anyone; and *with the fork* is an instrument,

---

[2] This sentence would be okay if there were a conjunction between *the flute* and *the violin*. What does this tell us about what conjunction does to theta roles?

not a goal). (18g) shows us that the category of the argument is important (this we already knew from chapter 2) – the goal argument of the verb *place* must be a PP. It appears as if the verb *place* requires three arguments, that bear precisely the theta roles of agent (DP), theme (DP), and goal (PP). We represent this formally in terms of what is called a ***theta grid***.[3]

19)

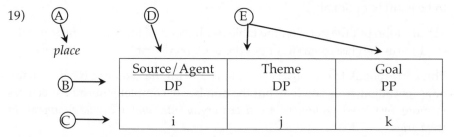

This grid consists of several parts. First of all, we have the name of the predicate (A). Next, for each argument that the predicate requires, there is a column (with two rows). Each of these columns represents a theta role. Notice that a column can have more than one thematic relation in it (but only one theta role). The number of columns corresponds exactly to the number of arguments the predicate requires. The first row (B) tells you the thematic relations and the categories associated with each of these theta roles. The second row (C) gives you what are called indices (singular: index) for each theta role. These are *not* the same as the indices in binding theory. When a predicate appears in an actual sentence, we mark the DP bearing the particular theta role with that index. Applying our grid to sentence (18), we get the following indexed sentence:

20) John$_i$ placed [the flute]$_j$ [on the table]$_k$.

The $_i$ index maps the agent theta role to *John*. The $_j$ index maps the theme theta role to *the flute*, etc.

Theta roles actually come in two types. The first is the ***external theta role*** (D). This is the one assigned to the subject. External theta roles are usually indicated by underlining the name of the theta role in the theta grid (e.g., Source/Agent in (19) The other kind are ***internal theta roles*** (E). These are the theta roles assigned to the object and indirect object. There is a semantic reason for the distinction between internal and external theta roles (see Marantz 1984 for extensive discussion), but we will leave that issue aside here. We will have use for the external/internal distinction in chapter 10,

---

[3] There are many ways to formalize theta grids, but I adopt here the indexing box method that Haegeman (1994) uses, since it seems to be the most transparent.

when we do DP movement. For now, however, you should simply indicate which argument is the subject by underlining its name.

If you look carefully at the theta grid in (19) you'll notice that it only contains a specifier (subject) and complements (direct object and indirect object). There are no adjuncts listed in the theta grid. Adjuncts seem to be entirely optional:

21) a)   John put the book on the table (with a pair of tongs).   *instrument*
    b)   (In the classroom) John put the book on the table.   *location*

This corresponds to our observation in chapter 6 that you can have as many or as few adjuncts as you like, but the number of complements and specifiers is more restricted. *Adjuncts are never arguments, and they never appear in theta grids.*

You can now try WBE 8 and GPS 3 & 4.

Up until now, we have been representing our grammar solely through the mechanism of rules (phrase structure, then X-bar rules). In order to stop X-bar rules from over-generating, we need a constraint. Constraints are like filters. They take the output of rules, and throw away any that don't meet the constraint's requirements. In essence, we are going to allow the X-bar rules to wildly over-generate, and produce ungrammatical sentences. Those sentences, however, will be thrown out by our constraint. The constraint we are going to use is called the **theta criterion**. The theta criterion ensures that there is a strict match between the number and types of arguments in a sentence and the theta grid.

22) *The Theta Criterion*
    a)   Each argument is assigned one and only one theta role.
    b)   Each theta role is assigned to one and only one argument.

This constraint requires that there is a strict one-to-one match between argument DPs and theta roles. You can't have more arguments than you have theta roles, and you can't have more theta roles than you have DPs. Furthermore, since theta roles express particular thematic relations, the arguments will have to be of appropriate semantic types for the sentence to pass the constraint.

Let's look at some examples to see how this works. Consider the verb *love*. It has the theta grid given in (23). I haven't written in the indices here, because we'll add them when we compare the grid to a particular sentence.

23) *love*

Experiencer	Theme
DP	DP

When a sentence containing the predicate *love* is produced, we apply indices to each of the arguments and match those arguments to theta roles in the grid. The sentence in (22) is grammatical with the correct number of arguments. It is matched to the theta grid in (23). There is a one-to-one matching between arguments and theta roles. So the theta criterion is satisfied, and the sentence is allowed to pass through the filter and surface.

24) Megan$_i$ loves Kevin$_j$.

25) *love*

Experiencer	Theme
DP	DP
i	j

Contrast this with the ungrammatical sentence in (24):

26) *Megan$_i$ loves.

This sentence lacks a theme argument, as seen in the following theta grid:

27) *love*

Experiencer	Theme
DP	DP
i	

The theme theta role is not assigned to an argument (there is no index in its lower box). This violates the second condition of the theta criterion: Every theta role is assigned to an argument. There is not a one-to-one matching of the theta roles to the arguments in this sentence. Since the theta criterion is violated, the sentence is filtered out (marked as ungrammatical). Notice, our X-bar rules *can* generate this sentence; it is ruled ungrammatical by our constraint.

The next sentence shows the opposite problem: A sentence with too many arguments.

28) *Megan$_i$ loves Jason$_j$ Kevin$_k$.

29) *love*

Experiencer	Theme	
DP	DP	
i	j	k

Here, the argument *Kevin* doesn't get a theta role. There are only two theta roles to be assigned, but there are three arguments. This violates the first part of the theta criterion: the requirement that every argument have a theta role. Again, the theta criterion filters out this sentence as ungrammatical.

To summarize, we can constrain the output of the X-bar rules using a semantic tool: theta roles. The theta criterion is a constraint or filter that rules out otherwise well-formed sentences. The theta criterion requires that there be a strict one-to-one matching between the number and kind of theta roles and the number and kind of arguments.

You now have enough information to try WBE 9, GPS 5, and CPS 1.

---

3. THE LEXICON

Let's take a step back from these details and look at the big picture. We have developed a model of grammar where we have three simple rules (the X-bar rules) that can generate a hierarchical constituent structure. These rules are constrained by the theta criterion, which uses the semantic notion of theta roles. Recall that our theory of syntax is meant to be a cognitive theory, so let's consider the question of where these rules and these theta roles are stored in the mind. Chomsky proposes that the part of the mind devoted to language is essentially divided into two parts. One part, which he calls the **computational component**, contains all the rules and constraints. This part of the mind does the work of building sentences and filtering out any ill-formed ones. The computational component can't work in a vacuum, however. It needs access to information about theta roles and the like. Chomsky claims that this information is stored in the **lexicon**, the other part of the human language faculty. The lexicon is your mental dictionary or list of words (and their properties). If you think about it, this is the obvious place for theta grids to be stored. Which theta role is assigned to which argument is a property of each predicate. It is information that must be associated with that predicate and that predicate only. The obvious place to store information about particular words (or more properly **lexical items**) is in the lexicon.

The lexicon contains all the irregular and memorized parts of language. Each lexical entry (dictionary entry) must contain at least the following information):

- the meaning of the word
- the syntactic category of the word (N, V, A, P, T, C, etc.)
- the pronunciation of the word

- exceptional information of all kinds (such as morphological irregularities)
- the theta grid (argument structure).

When you learn a new word, you memorize all this information.

On an abstract level we can diagram the grammatical system as looking something like:

30)

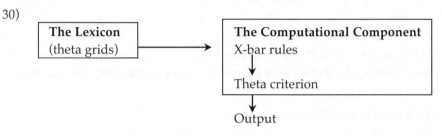

The lexicon feeds into the computational component, which then combines words and generates sentences. The fact that lexical information affects the form of the sentence is formalized in what we call the *Projection Principle*:

31) *The Projection Principle*
    Lexical information (such as theta roles) is syntactically represented at all levels.

4. EXPLETIVES AND THE EXTENDED PROJECTION PRINCIPLE

Before leaving the topic of the lexicon, I'd like to point out two special classes of predicates. Consider first the following "weather" verbs. These predicates don't seem to assign any theta roles:

32) a) It rained.
    b) It snowed.
    c) It hailed.

What theta role does the pronoun *it* get in these sentences? If you are having a problem figuring this out, ask yourself what *it* refers to in the above sentences. It appears as if *it* doesn't refer to anything. In syntax, we refer to pronouns like this as *expletive* or *pleonastic pronouns*. These pronouns don't get a theta role (which of course is a violation of the theta criterion – a point we will return to below). The theta grid for weather verbs is empty. They don't assign any theta roles.

There is another class of predicates that take expletive pronouns. These are predicates that optionally take a CP subject:

33) [$_{CP}$ That Bill loves chocolate] is likely.

The predicate *is likely* assigns one theta role. It takes one argument (the clause). (We will tentatively notate these clausal arguments with the theta role **proposition**, but will refine this in the next chapter.)

34) *is likely*

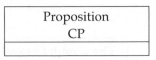

You'll note that in (34) the theta role is not underlined. This is because the clause bearing the theta role of proposition is a complement. This can be seen in the following example:

35) It is likely that Bill likes chocolate.

In this sentence, we again have an expletive *it*, which gets no theta role.

In order to maintain the theta criterion, we need to account for these expletive DPs without theta roles. Expletive pronouns usually appear in subject position. When *it* appears in other positions, it usually bears a theta role:

36) a)   I love *it*.   (*it* is a theme)
    b)   I put a book on *it*.   (*it* is a goal or location)

Expletives seem to appear where there is no theta marked DP (or CP) that fills the subject position. This is encoded in a revised version of the Projection Principle: The **Extended Projection Principle** (EPP):

37) *Extended Projection Principle* (EPP)
    All clauses must have subjects (i.e. the specifier of TP must be filled by a DP or CP) and lexical information is expressed at all levels.

The EPP works like the theta criterion. It is a constraint on the output of the X-bar rules. It requires that every sentence have a subject. Next, we must account for the fact that expletives violate the theta criterion.

One way of doing this is by claiming that expletives are not generated by the X-bar rules. Instead, they are inserted by a special *expletive insertion* rule:

38) *Expletive insertion rule*
    Insert an expletive pronoun into the specifier of TP.

This rule applies when there is no other subject. If there is no theta marked subject and no expletive subject, then the EPP will filter the sentence out.

The way in which we get around the theta criterion is by *ordering* the expletive insertion rule after the theta criterion has applied.

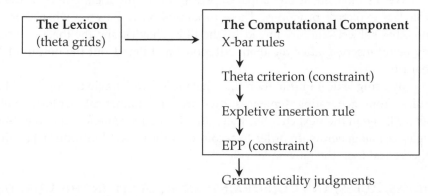

Since expletives are inserted *after* the theta criterion has applied, they can't be filtered out by it.

The model we've drawn here is very preliminary. In the next chapter, we will introduce a new kind of rule (the transformation – of which expletive insertion is a very special case) that will cause us to significantly revise this diagram.

Two Kinds of *It*

There are two *it* pronouns in English. One is the expletive found with weather verbs. The other is the neuter pronoun *it* found in sentences like:

i) It bit me on the leg.

If you contrast the *it* in (i) with the ones in the weather verbs, you'll see that the *it* in (i) does take a theta role (agent) and does refer to something (probably an insect or some other animal). Not every sentence with an *it* involves an expletive.

You now have enough information to try WBE 10, GPS 6, and CPS 2–5.

5. CONCLUSION

We started this chapter off with the observation that while X-bar rules capture important facts about constituency and cross-categorial generalizations, they over-generate (that is, they generate ungrammatical sentences). One way of constraining X-bar theory is by invoking lexical restrictions on sentences, such that particular predicates have specific argument structures, in the form of theta grids. The theta criterion rules out any sentence where the number and type of arguments don't match up one to one with the number and type of theta roles in the theta grid.

We also looked at one apparent exception to the theta criterion: theta-role-less expletive pronouns. These pronouns only show up when there is no other subject, and are forced by the EPP. They escape the theta criterion by being inserted after the theta criterion has filtered out the output of X-bar rules.

By using lexical information (like theta roles) we're able to stop the X-bar rules from generating sentences that are ungrammatical. Unfortunately, as we'll see in the next chapter, there are also many sentences that the X-bar rules *cannot* generate. In order to account for these, we'll introduce a further theoretical tool: the movement rule.

IDEAS, RULES, AND CONSTRAINTS INTRODUCED IN THIS CHAPTER

i)   *Selectional Restrictions*: Semantic restrictions on arguments.

ii)   *Thematic Relations*: Semantic relations between a predicate and an argument – used as a means of encoding selectional restrictions.

iii)   *Agent*: The doer of an action (under some definitions must be capable of volition).

iv)   *Experiencer*: The argument that perceives an event or state.

v)   *Theme*: The element that is perceived, experienced, or undergoing the action or change of state

vi)   *Goal*: The end point of a movement.

vii)   *Recipient*: A special kind of goal, found with verbs of possession

viii)   *Source*: The starting point of a movement.

ix)   *Location*: The place where an action or state occurs.

x)   *Instrument*: A tool with which an action is performed.

xi)   *Beneficiary*: The entity for whose benefit the action is performed.

xii)   *Proposition*: The thematic relation assigned to clauses.

xiii)   *Theta Role*: A bundle of thematic relations associated with a particular argument (DPs, PPs, or CPs).

xiv)   *Theta Grid*: The schematic representation of the argument structure of a predicate, where the theta roles are listed.

xv)   *External Theta Role*: The theta role associated with subjects.

xvi)   *Internal Theta Role*: The theta role associated with other arguments.

xvii)   *The Theta Criterion*:
        a) Each argument is assigned one and only one theta role.
        b) Each theta role is assigned to one and only one argument.

xviii) *Lexical Item*: Another way of saying "word". A lexical item is an entry in the mental dictionary.

xix)   *The Projection Principle*: Lexical information (like theta roles) is syntactically represented at all levels.

xx)   *Expletive (or Pleonastic) Pronoun*: A pronoun (usually *it* or *there*) without a theta role. Usually found in subject position.

xxi)   *Extended Projection Principle (EPP)*: All clauses must have subjects. Lexical information is syntactically represented.

xxii)   *Expletive Insertion*: Insert an expletive pronoun into the specifier of TP.

xxiii)   *The Lexicon*: The mental dictionary or list of words. Contains all irregular and memorized information about language, including the argument structure (theta grid) of predicates.

xxiv)   *The Computational Component*: The combinatorial, rule-based part of the mind. Where the rules and filters are found.

FURTHER READING: Gruber (1965), Haegeman (1994), Marantz (1984), Williams (1980, 1994)

GENERAL PROBLEM SETS

GPS1. IDENTIFYING THEMATIC RELATIONS
[Data Analysis and Application of Skills; Basic]
Part 1: Identify the thematic relations associated with each DP or embedded CP in the following sentences. Each DP or CP may have more than one thematic relation associated with it.

a)   Shannon sent Dan an email.
b)   Jerid thinks that Sumayya cooked some beef waffles for him.
c)   Stacy hit a baseball to Yosuke.
d)   Jaime danced a jig.
e)   Yuko rubbed the pizza with a garlic clove.
f)   It is raining in San Francisco.

Part 2: Draw the trees for (b–f). Use CPs, DPs, and TPs.

GPS2. WARLPIRI[4]
[Data Analysis; Basic]
Consider the following data from Warlpiri:

a)   Lungkarda   ka   ngulya-ngka   nguna-mi.
     bluetongue AUX   burrow-A   lie-NON.PAST
     "The bluetongue skink is lying in the burrow."

---

[4] The data for this problem set comes from Ken Hale via Barb Brunson.

b) Nantuwu   ka   karru-kurra   parnka-mi.
    horse   AUX   creek-B   run-NON.PAST
    "The horse is running to the creek."

c) Karli   ka   pirli-ngirli   wanti-mi.
    boomerang AUX   stone-C   fall-NON.PAST
    "The boomerang is falling from the stone."

d) Kurdu-ngku ka-jana pirli   yurutu-wana   yirra-rni.
    child-D   AUX   stone   road-E   put.NON.PAST
    "The child is putting stones along the road."

What is the meaning of *each* of the affixes (suffixes) glossed
with -A, -B, -C, -D, and -E? Can you relate these suffixes to thematic
relations? Which ones?

GPS3. THETA GRIDS
[Data Analysis; Basic]
For each of the sentences below identify each of the predicates (including
non-verbal predicates like *is likely*). Provide the theta grid for each.
Don't forget: include only arguments in the theta grid; DPs and PPs that are
adjuncts are not included. Index each DP, PP, CP argument with the theta
role it takes. Assume that there are two different verbs *give* (each with its
own theta grid) to account for (c) and (d); two different verbs *eat* (each with
its own theta grid) for (e) and (f); and two different verbs *ask* for (i) and (j).

a) The stodgy professor left with his teaching assistant.
b) I played a tune on my iPod.
c) Molly gave Calvin a kiss.
d) Mercedes gave a test to the students in the lecture hall.
e) Pangur ate a cat treat.
f) Susan ate yesterday at the restaurant.
g) Gwen saw a fire truck.
h) Gwen looked at a fire truck.
i) Michael asked a question.
j) Adam asked if Hyacinth likes pineapples.
k) It is sunny in the dining room.
l) I feel it is unfortunate that television is so vulgar these days.
m) That Angus hates sushi is mysterious.

GPS4. SINHALA[5]
[Data Analysis; Basic/Intermediate]
Two forms of the Sinhala verb appear in the data below and are identified
in the glosses as A or B. (Data from Gair 1970.)

---

[5] This problem is loosely based on one given to me by Barb Brunson. However,
the data and questions have been altered. The data in this version of the problem set
is taken directly from Gair, with some minor modifications to the glosses.

1) Provide a complete theta grid for each of the verbs in the following data. Be sure to primarily look at the second line of each piece of data, not the English translation.
2) Using indexes identify what theta role is assigned to each DP.
3) Discuss briefly (no more than two sentences) what kind of DP the suffix -ʈə attaches to.
4) What is the difference between *mamə* and *maʈə*? (Hint: the answer to this question is related to the answer to question (3).)
5) In terms of theta roles, what is the difference between the A and the B verb forms?

a) Mamə   kawi   kiənəwa.
   I   poetry   tell-A
   "I recite poetry."

b) Maʈə   kawi   kiəwenəwa.
   I   poetry   tell-B
   "I started reciting poetry (despite myself)."

c) Lamea   kataawə   ahanəwa.
   child   story   hear-A
   "The child listens to the story."

d) Lameaʈə   kataawə   æhenəwa.
   child   story   hear-B
   "The child hears the story."

e) Mamə   naʈənəwa.
   I   dance-A
   "I dance."

f) Maʈə   næʈəenəwa.
   I   dance-B
   "I dance (I can't help but do so)."

g) Hæmə irida   mə   mamə koləmbə yanəwa.
   every Sunday   EMPH   I   Columbo go-A
   "Every Sunday I deliberately go to Colombo."

h) Hæmə irida   mə   maʈə   koləmbə yæwenəwa.
   every Sunday   EMPH   I   Columbo go-B
   "Every Sunday I experience going to Colombo."

i) Malli   nitərəmə   aňḍənəwa.
   brother   always   cries-A
   "Brother always cries."

j) Malliʈə   nitərəmə   æňḍənəwạ.
   brother   always   cries-B
   "Brother always bursts out crying without control."

k)   Mamə   untə   baninəwa.
     I   them   scold-A
     "I deliberately scold them."

l)   Maṭə   untə   bænenəwa.
     I   them   scold-B
     "I experienced scolding them."

m)   Apiṭə   pansələ   peenəwa.
     we   temple   see-B
     "We saw the temple."

GPS5. THETA CRITERION
[Data Analysis; Intermediate]
Show how each of the following sentences is a violation of the theta criterion. Use theta grids to explain your answers.

a)   *Rosemary hates.
b)   *Jennie smiled the breadbox.
c)   *Traci gave the whale.
d)   *Traci gave a jawbreaker.
e)   *placed the flute on the table.
f)   *John placed on the table.
g)   *John placed the flute.
h)   *John placed the flute the violin on the table.
i)   *The rock placed the sky with the fork.
j)   *John placed the flute the table.

GPS6. EXPLETIVES
[Application of Knowledge; Intermediate]
In Suzette Haden Elgin's science fiction novel *Yonder Comes the Other End of Time* (Daw Books, New York 1986) there is a planet called Ozark, where magic is commonplace. Magic is performed by applying generative grammar rules to the real world. In the following passage, a group of magicians has just put up a wall around an entire kingdom, and a local magician and the hero (Coyote Jones from Earth) are discussing how it happened.

> "… And you understand how it's done?"
> "Certainly. Don't you?"
> Coyote admitted that he didn't understand it at all, and got an odd look for his candor. But as the two of them made their way back to Castle Smith, with Willow leading this time, the Magician of Rank explained it to him.
> "***It would be an Insertion Transformation***," he said, as casually as Coyote would have discussed the workings of his flyer. "No different, except in scale from causing a flower to appear where there wasn't one before or some such baby trick …"
> (Haden Elgin 1986: 159)

In the bold italic sentence above ("***It would be an insertion transformation***"), has the expletive insertion transformation applied? What evidence do you have for your claim? If not, how do you know (what's your evidence)? Be careful – the question is not whether they inserted a wall, but whether expletive insertion happened *in the bold-faced sentence* above!

CHALLENGE PROBLEM SETS

CHALLENGE PROBLEM SET 1: IRISH AND THE THETA CRITERION
[Data Analysis and Application of Skills; Challenge]
What problems does each of the following examples present for the theta criterion? (As a starting point, it may help to draw the theta grid for each verb and show what DP gets what role.) Please, not more than 3–4 sentences of discussion per example.

a) an fear   a   bhfaca mé é
    the man   who   saw   I   him
    "the man who I saw"

b) Rinceamar.
    dance.1PL
    "We danced."

c) Ba-mhaith liom   an teach   a   thógail.
    COND-good with-me   the house its building
    "I would like to build the house."

CHALLENGE PROBLEM SET 2: OBJECT EXPLETIVES
[Critical Thinking; Challenge]
In the text above, it was observed that theta-role-less expletives primarily appear in subject position. Consider the following sentence. Is *it* here an expletive?

    I hate it that you're always late.

How could you tell?

CHALLENGE PROBLEM SET 3: PASSIVES
[Data Analysis; Challenge]
Part 1: Write up the theta grids for the verbs in the following sentences. Assume there are two verbs *give* (give$_1$ is seen in (d), give$_2$ in (e)).

a) John bit the apple.
b) Susan forgave Louis.
c) The jockey rides the horse.
d) Phillip gave the medal to the soldier.
e) Phillip gave the soldier the medal.

Part 2: English has a suffix *-en* that, when attached to verbs, changes the structure of the sentence associated with them. This is called the **passive** morpheme. The following sentences are the passive equivalents of the sentences in part 1. The bracketed PPs starting with *by* are optional.

f)   The apple was bitten (by John).
g)   Louis was forgiven (by Susan).
h)   The horse was ridden (by the jockey).
i)   The medal was given to the soldier (by Phillip).
j)   The soldier was given the medal (by Phillip).

Describe in your own words what the *-en* passive suffix does to the theta grids of verbs. Pay careful attention to the last two examples, and to the optionality of the *by*-phrases.

CHALLENGE PROBLEM SET 4: HIAKI -WA[6]
[Data Analysis and Critical Thinking; Challenge]
Part 1: Consider the function of the suffix *-wa* in Hiaki (also known as Yaqui), a language spoken in Southern Arizona and Mexico. Look carefully at the data below, and figure out what effect this suffix has on the theta grids of Hiaki verbs. What English phenomenon is this similar to? (Data from Escalante 1990 and Jelinek and Escalante 2003.)

a)   Peo Huan-ta chochon-ak.[7]
      Pete John-ACC punch-PERF
      "Pete punched John."

a')   Huan chochon-wa-k.
      John punch-WA-PERF
      "John was punched."

b)   'Ume uusi-m uka kuchu-ta kuchi'i-m-mea bwa'a-ka.
      the children-PL the-ACC fish-ACC knife-PL-INST eat-PERF
      "The children ate the fish with knives."

b')   'U kuchu kuchi'i-m-mea bwa'a-wa-k.
      the fish knife-PL-INST eat-WA-PERF
      "The fish was eaten with knives."

c)   Peo bwiika.
      Pete sing
      "Pete is singing."

---

[6] Thanks to Heidi Harley for contributing this problem set.

[7] Sometimes when *-wa* attaches to a verb, the form of the root changes (usually /e/ becomes /i/). This is a morphophonological phenomenon that you don't need to worry about. ACC refers to accusative case, INST means instrument, and PERF means perfective aspect (aspect plays no role in the answer to this problem). There is no nominative suffix in Hiaki.

c') Bwiik-wa.
   sing-WA
   "Singing is happening." or "There is singing going on." or "Someone is singing."

Part 2: Not all verbs allow -*wa*. Consider the following pairs of sentences, which show verbs that don't allow -*wa*. In terms of theta grids, what do these sentences have in common with each other that differentiates them from the ones that allow -*wa* (above in part 1)?

a) 'U wikia chukte.
   the rope come.loose
   "The rope is coming loose."

a') *Chukti-wa.
   come.loose-WA
   "Coming loose is happening." or "There is coming loose going on." or "Something is coming loose."

b) 'U kaaro nasonte.
   the car damage
   "The car is damaged."

b') *Nasonti-wa.
   damage-WA
   "Damage is happening." or "There is damage going on." or "Something is getting damaged."

c) 'U kari veete-k.
   The house burn-PERF
   "The house burned."

c') *Veeti-wa-k.
   Burn-WA-PERF
   "Burning happened." or "There was burning going on." or "Something is getting burned."

d) 'U vachi bwase'e.
   The corn cook
   "The corn is cooking."

d') *Bwase'i-wa.
   cook-WA
   "Cooking happened." or "There was cooking going on." or "Something is being cooked."

Part 3: The data in (e) and (e') below might throw a wrench in the hypothesis you developed above in part 2. Explain why these data are problematic for your analysis in part 2.

e) Ume   uusim   sawaria-ta-mak   koko-n
    The.PL   children.PL   yellow.fever-ACC-with   die.PL-IMPF
    "The children were dying of yellow fever."

e') Sawaria-ta-mak   koko-wa-n
     Yellow.fever-ACC-with   die.pl-WA-*impf*
     "People were dying with yellow fever" or
     "There was dying with yellow fever."

CHALLENGE PROBLEM SET 5: ANTIPASSIVES
[Data Analysis and Critical Thinking; Challenge]
In many languages there is an operation that changes the theta grid of
certain verbs. This operation is called the ***antipassive***.

Part 1: Here is some data from Inupiaq, an Inuit language of Canada and
Alaska. Explain what adding the antipassive morpheme does to the theta
grid of the verb. Verbs in Inupiaq agree with both their subjects and their
objects. 3SUBJ-3OBJ means that the verb agrees with both a 3rd person
subject and a 3rd person object. 3 means that the verb only agrees
with a 3rd person subject. (Data from Seiler 1978.)

a) Aŋuti-m   umiaq   qiñig-aa   tirrag-mi.   *Active*
    man-ERG   boat-ABS   see-3SUBJ.3OBJ   beach-at
    "The man sees the boat at the beach."

b) Aŋun   (umiag-mik)   qiñiq-tuq   tirrag-mi.   *Antipassive*
    man-ABS   boat-INST   see-3   beach-at
    "The man sees (with a boat) at the beach."

Part 2: The following is some data from English. This might also be called
an antipassive construction. How is it similar or different from the Inupiaq
antipassive?

c) I ate a basket of apples.
d) I ate.

Auxiliaries and Functional Categories

Learning Objectives

After reading chapter 9 you should walk away having mastered the following ideas and skills:

1. Using theta grids, explain the restrictions that various kinds of C, T, and D nodes impose on their complements.
2. Learn to distinguish the various tense, aspect, voice, and mood properties of English verbal constructions.
3. Learn to identify the modals and various auxiliaries.
4. Identify participles, gerunds, bare forms, preterites, and present tense forms of verbs.
5. Demonstrate the similarities and differences between main verbs, auxiliaries, and modals.
6. Draw trees showing stacked VPs.
7. Discuss the properties of *do*-support.

0. INTRODUCTION

In chapter 8, we looked at how theta grids can be used to explain some restrictions on X-bar theory. X-bar theory, because it uses variables, can over-generate and create structures that don't exist in language. We saw that by looking at the semantic content of verbs (whether they took agents, or themes, etc.) as coded in theta grids and combined with the theta criterion, we were able to explain why verbs of various types don't appear with too many or too few arguments.

In this chapter, we're going to extend this analysis to a variety of functional items and auxiliary verbs, including complementizers and modals, as well as tense, aspectual, and voice auxiliaries. We'll also extend this to the nominal domain and look at various types of determiners. Using a system much like theta grids (but without reference to theta roles), we'll be able to explain the incredibly complex facts of the English auxiliary system.

1. COMPLEMENTIZERS

1.1 The Selection of Complementizers

As discussed at the end of chapter 7, there are many different kinds of complementizers. Some complementizers, such as English *that*, indicate that the clause that follows is a declarative. Others, like *if* or *whether*, mark the fact that the following clause is an embedded question. As discussed in chapter 2, certain verbs require that the clause that functions as their complement has particular properties. For example, the verb *think* in English requires that the clause that follows it be finite – compare (1a) to (1c and d) – and not a question – compare (1a) to (1e). The complement clause of *think* either lacks an overt complementizer (1b) or uses *that* (1a).

1) a)   I think that Art likes his beer.
   b)   I think Art likes his beer.
   c)   *I think for Art to like his beer.
   d)   *I think Art to like his beer.
   e)   *I think if Art likes his beer.

Now contrast *think* with verbs like *ordered* or verbs like *inquired*. *Order* can take either a finite or non-finite complement clause, but like *think*, can't take a question (2). *Inquire* can only take an interrogative complement clause.

2) a)   I ordered that Art drink his beer.
   b)   I ordered Art drink his beer.
   c)   ?I ordered for Art to drink his beer.
   d)   I ordered Art to drink his beer.
   e)   *I ordered if Art drink his beer.

3) a)   *I inquired that Art like his beer.
   b)   *I inquired Art likes his beer.
   c)   *I inquired for Art to like his beer.

d) *I inquired Art to like his beer.
e) I inquired if Art likes his beer.

Try substituting other verbs (such as *ask, want, think, believe, desire,* etc.) in the main clause and you'll see that there is significant diversity in what types of complement clauses these various verbs can take. We thus have a number of subcategories of verb that are sensitive to the kinds of CP that they take as arguments. This parallels the various subcategories of verb that were sensitive to the theta roles of DPs that we saw in the last chapter. We used theta grids in the previous chapter to capture those distinctions. In fact, towards the end of the last chapter we tentatively described the theta grid of the predicate *is likely* using the theta role of "proposition", which might be extended to verbs like *say* or *order*. We could presumably also introduce a theta role for "interrogatives", etc. On the surface this is a fine shorthand, but it misses the fact that these differences (unlike the semantic differences coded by thematic relations) are grammatical in nature and are expressed by functional items like complementizers and the like. Several times before in this book, I've hinted that the best solution for capturing these kinds of subcategories is to make use of features. Let's make that more explicit here.

Two Kinds of *If*

You'll note that the sentence in (1e) is ok if it is continued with a *then* clause: *I think if Art likes his beer, then we should get him some for his birthday.* The *if*-clause in this grammatical sentence is different than the one introduced by *if* in a question like *I asked if Art likes his beer.* The grammatical sentence noted above expresses a condition rather than an embedded question. For reasons of space, we won't really look at conditional *if*-clauses here. Nevertheless you should keep in mind that English has more than one complementizer *if*. One (as in (1e)) marks a question and is roughly equivalent to *whether.* The other, which is used in *if ... then* constructions, marks conditionals rather than questions and is not interchangeable with *whether.*

First we'll identify some of the complementizers we have in English (this list is not comprehensive – we'll propose more later in the book) and assign them feature values. The feature [±Q] corresponds to whether or not the complementizer introduces an embedded question. [–Q] replaces the "proposition" theta role that we used as shorthand in the last chapter. The feature [±finite] refers to whether or not the embedded clause is finite or non-finite. Assuming, as we argued in chapter 7, that every clause has a complementizer whether we hear it or not, I've included null complementizers here, all notated as Ø. The null complementizers are typically alternants of overt ones, so have the same features

4) a) that   [–Q, +FINITE]
    b) Ø_[-Q, +FINITE]   [–Q, +FINITE]
    c) for   [–Q, –FINITE]
    d) Ø_[-Q, -FINITE]   [–Q, –FINITE]
    e) if/whether   [+Q, +FINITE]

With these preliminary feature values in place we can now create grids for some of the verbs we discussed above. Since under X-bar theory CP is a projection of C, it has the same features as its head. So the theta grid for the verb *think* is given in (5).

5) *think*

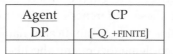

This grid requires that the external argument of *think* is a DP bearing the theta role with an agent thematic relation, and that the complement be a CP that is not an interrogative and is a finite clause. This is compatible with either a clause introduced by *that* (1a), or one introduced by the null complementizer in (4b), giving rise to the sentence in (1b). None of the rest of the complementizers are compatible with this restriction.

    Next let's turn to *order*, as in (2) above. *Order* requires that the complement clause not be a question, but is indifferent to whether the clause is finite or not. We can capture this indifference by not making any specification for the feature [±finite] and simply stating that the complement clause must be [–Q]:

6) *order*

Agent	CP
DP	[–Q]

This grid then allows either finite (2a and b) or non-finite embedded clauses (2c and d) as long as they aren't [+Q].

    Finally consider *inquire*. The primary condition on *inquire* is that the embedded clause be [+Q]. Whether or not that question must be finite or not is a little tricky. It depends upon whether or not you find the sentence *?I inquired to purchase a bikini* grammatical or not. Aside from the fact that I'm unlikely to buy a bikini, I find this sentence at least highly marked (i.e. ?), and probably completely unacceptable (*). For this reason, I'll tentatively stipulate that the complement CP for *inquire* be [+FINITE].

7) *inquire*

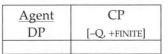

Agent	CP
DP	[–Q, +FINITE]

This will allow sentence (3e) but exclude all the others in (3).

You now have enough information to try WBE1 and GPS1.

1.2 Selection by Complementizers

The different kinds of complementizers themselves also select for different kinds of TP. Take, for example, the complementizer *that*; this C cannot have a TP headed by the infinitive marker *to*, which we claimed in chapter 7 was a T node (8). Any other kind of T category is ok.

8) a) *Heidi thinks that Andy to eat salmon-flavored candy bars.
    b) Heidi thinks that Andy is eating salmon-flavored candy bars.
    c) Heidi thinks that Andy has eaten salmon-flavored candy bars.
    d) Heidi thinks that Andy should eat salmon-flavored candy bars.
    e) Heidi thinks that Andy will eat salmon-flavored candy bars.
    f) Heidi thinks that Andy eats salmon-flavored candy bars.
    g) Heidi thinks that the salmon-flavored candy bars were eaten.

So *that* can appear with a progressive *be* auxiliary (8b), a perfect *have* auxiliary (8c), a modal auxiliary like *should* (8d), a future auxiliary like *will* (8e), a tensed verb (8f), and a passive *be* auxiliary (8g), but not *to*. We can capture this by making reference to a special feature, which we'll call [±INFINITIVE] (not to be confused with [±FINITE], which is a feature of complementizers). The T node *to* is marked as [+INFINITIVE], all the other T nodes are [–INFINITIVE], as specified in (9). (Recall that $\emptyset_{[PRES]}$ and $\emptyset_{[PAST]}$ are the null tense forms that take inflected verbs like *eats* and *ate* respectively.) With this feature in place we can specify the theta grid for that:

9) *that*

TP
[–INFINITIVE]

This grid will ensure that *that* will always take a TP that isn't *to*. In the exercises section of this chapter, you'll have the opportunity to explore the possibility that certain complementizers in other languages select for TPs based on features other than [±INFINITIVE].

You now have enough information to try WBE 2, GPS 2 & 3, and CPS 1.

2. DETERMINERS

In the last section, we saw how complementizers can select for certain kinds of TPs. We're now going to do the same here for determiners and the various kinds of complements they can take.

Let's start with two of the most common determiners in English, *the* and *a* (and its allomorph *an*). Both of these determiners can take a singular NP complement (10):

10) a) the muffin
    b) a muffin

But only *the* can take a plural complement (11a). *A/an* cannot (11b).

11) a) the muffins
    b) *a muffins

Let us assume there is a feature [±PLURAL]. The determiner *a/an* must be specified so that it won't take NPs headed by a [±PLURAL].

12) *a/an (to be revised)*

This theta grid ensures that *a/an* never can have a [+plural] complement. The determiner *the*, by contrast, allows either, so its theta grid will have no specification for the [±PLURAL] feature, thus allowing either variant to appear.

13) *the (to be revised)*

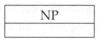

But the theta grids for *the* and *a/an* are actually a little more complicated than this. *The* can't appear with any old noun. For example, English *the* and *a/an* can't appear with most proper names (examples like *the Smiths* are an exception – try Challenge Problem Set 3 to see if you can work out how to accommodate that exception), nor can it appear with pronouns:

14) a) *The Andrew
    b) *The him

Let's distinguish proper names from common nouns with the feature [±PROPER] and pronouns from other nouns with the feature [±PRONOUN]. The data in (14) show us that we have to update the theta grids so that they only allow NPs with the negative version of these features.

15) a)   *a (final)*

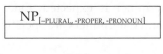

NP[-PLURAL, -PROPER, -PRONOUN]

b)   *the (to be revised)*

NP[-PROPER, -PRONOUN]

There is an interesting consequence of the system of selection we are developing here. In chapter 7, we suggested that all NPs, even ones without determiners or articles we can hear, actually have null determiners. The reason for this is because of the nature of the theta grids of verbs. Take, for example, the theta grid for the verb *strike*. This verb takes two DP arguments: one with an agent role and one with a theme role.

16) *strike*

Agent	Theme
DP	DP
i	k

This theta grid works fine for a sentence like (17a), but we have a challenge in (17b–d).

17) a)   The carpenter$_i$ struck the nail$_k$.
    b)   Franco$_i$ struck Adolph$_k$.
    c)   He$_i$ struck it$_k$.
    d)   Raindrops$_i$ struck rooftops$_k$.

The challenge is that the two arguments in (17b-d) don't appear to have determiners at all (and, for 17b and 17c, they *can't* have determiners!). So the arguments in these sentences plausibly look like NPs rather than DPs. Yet our theta grid for *strike* requires DPs and not NPs. One might think that you could fix this conflict by simply making the theta grid in (16) more complicated and allowing a choice of either a DP or an NP, so that the argument might be specified as {NP/DP} instead of just DP. However, if that were the case we couldn't explain why a sentence just like (17a), but without determiners, is completely unacceptable in English (i.e., *Carpenter struck nail). Such a sentence would be allowed if the theta grid allowed either NPs or DPs. So we're left with the uncomfortable conclusion that pronouns, proper names, and plurals must have determiners, but silent ones. This kind of conclusion inevitably makes new syntacticians dubious, and I can assure you it makes many more experienced syntacticians queasy too. However, it seems to be the most straightforward solution to this technical problem. But it actually also goes a long way to explain why proper names and pronouns *cannot* have a determiner. If these already have null determiners, then the absence of another determiner is expected. One possible version of this hypothesis is that these null determiners are specified as follows:

18) a) $\emptyset_{[+PROPER]}$

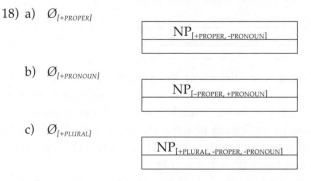

   b) $\emptyset_{[+PRONOUN]}$

   c) $\emptyset_{[+PLURAL]}$

A slightly more sophisticated analysis is developed in the problem sets in chapter 10.

Let's consider one additional simple example here (although you have the opportunity to try your hand at several other determiners in the problem sets and exercises). As we observed in chapter 2, the quantifier *many* can appear with (plural) count nouns (19a) and *much* appears with mass nouns (19b). The reverse is ungrammatical (19c and d).

19) a) many dogs
    b) much water
    c) *many waters (where *water* refers to the substance, not glasses of water)
    d) *much dog (where *dog* refers to a real dog, not the substance of doggy-hood.)

If we assume that nouns like *water* are [–COUNT] and nouns like *dog* are [+COUNT], then we can write theta grids for *much* and *many* that capture this restriction (20). The determiners *the* and *a/an* will also require a [+COUNT] feature.

20) a) *many*

NP$_{[+COUNT, +PLURAL, -PROPER, -PRONOUN]}$

b) *much*

$$\text{NP}_{[-\text{COUNT}, -\text{PLURAL}, -\text{PROPER}, -\text{PRONOUN}]}$$

You now have enough information to try WBE 3 & 4, GPS 4 & 5, and CPS 2–4.

Let's now look at another slightly more complicated case. Early on in this book, we claimed that only one determiner is allowed with most nouns, a fact that we explained a few paragraphs ago. But there actually are at least two exceptions to this. First we have the case of the quantifier *all*, which can appear with another determiner (21a). The other is the case of numerals, which can co-occur with *the* (21b).

21) a)   all the boys
    b)   the three boys

We'll deal with (21a) here, but I've left (21b) as a challenge for you to solve in Challenge Problem Set 5.

Sentence (21a) is a problem if determiners always take NPs as complements. We can solve this problem, however, if we presume that *all* can take another DP as a complement as in the tree in (22), where D_2 (*all*) takes a DP headed by D_1 (*the*) as a complement.

22)

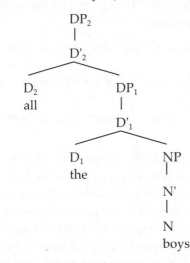

Such a structure would be licensed by a theta grid where *all* takes another DP as its complement, as in (23).

23) *all*

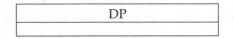

DP

There are some problems with this theta grid. Can you see them? These issues are explored in Challenge Problem Set 6.

You now have enough information to try CPS 5–7.

---

3. UNDERSTANDING TENSE, ASPECT, VOICE, AND MOOD

In section 4, we'll examine the tight interaction between the T node and the verbs it takes as complements. But first, we're going to take a brief descriptive tangent into the morphology and semantics of tense, aspect, voice, and mood in English. I'm taking the time to do this for two reasons. First, most students in North America and Britain have never received clear instruction on what the difference between these notions are. Second, they are very tightly bound together with the selectional properties of auxiliaries in English.

3.1 Tense

Tense refers to the time of an event relative to the time at which the sentence is either spoken or written. If I write or say *John left*, this entails that the act of John's leaving, **the event time**, happened before I wrote or said the sentence, **the assertion time**. We distinguish three tenses:

24) a)   *past tense*: the event time happened before the assertion time. e.g., *John danced.*
    b)   *present tense*: the event time is the same as the assertion time. e.g., *He likes ice cream.*
    c)   *future tense*: the event time is going to happen after the assertion time. e.g., *He will eat dinner.*

In English, the past tense is typically marked with an *-ed* suffix (e.g. the past tense of *dance* is *danced*) or the verb comes with a special past tense form (e.g. the past tense of *leave* is *left*). The form of a past tense verb whether it ends in an *–ed* or has a special form is called the **preterite**. The present tense is either unmarked (for 1st or 2nd person or plural subjects), e.g. *I hate beef waffles*, or marked with an *-s* suffix (in the 3rd person singular), e.g. *He hates beef waffles*. English is a strange language in that it doesn't have a regular inflected future tense. There are three strategies for overcoming this: two of them are the use of the modal and the use of the present tense to indicate a future action. In formal speech, the future is marked with the modal auxiliary *will* (*He will eat his beef waffles*). In less formal speech, the auxiliary *gonna* or *going to* is used (*I'm gonna eat my beef waffles*). Both of these strategies also imply that the action will definitely happen (or not, if combined with negation). The other strategy is to use a present tense to indicate future as in *I'm leaving here tomorrow*, where the present tense auxiliary *am* is used. These uses of the present tense to mark the future are called ***futurates***. In this book, we're going to concentrate on the simple cases of futures marked with *will*, but obviously a full account would have to explain *gonna* and futurates as well.

You now have enough information to try WBE 5.

3.2 Perfect Aspect

While tense is defined in terms of the relationship between the event time and the assertion time, **aspect** is a very different notion. Aspect is defined by making reference to some other point, typically other than the speech time, then looking at when the event happens relative to that reference point. Take for example sentence (25):

25) John had eaten his sandwich before I could get him his pickle.

The event of John eating his sandwich happened before a time that is distinct from when I wrote the sentence. In other words, it happened before I got him his pickle. The time of pickle-getting is a reference point, and John's eating happened before that.

The particular aspect found in (25) is called the **perfect**. The perfect happens when the time of the event occurs before the reference time. The perfect is always indicated in English by using the auxiliary *have* (or one of its variants forms: *has* or *had*) combined with a special form of the main verb known as the **participle**. This is sometimes inaccurately called the "past participle". We will avoid this term because there is nothing particularly "past" about participles – they can occur in the present and the future!

The participle in English can be formed four ways:

26) a)   by attaching an *-en* or *-n* suffix: *eat* → *eaten, fall* → *fallen*
    b)   by attaching an *-ed* suffix: *dance* → *danced, love* → *loved*
    c)   by using a special participial form: *drink* → *drunk, sing* → *sung*
    d)   by making no change at all: *hit* → *hit*

The method found in (26b) is especially confusing since the *-ed* suffix is often used to form the past tense as well. You can tell the difference between a participle and a past tense by the fact that the participle always appears with an auxiliary verb like *be, have,* or their variants.

27) a)   He danced   *past tense*
    b)   He has danced   *participle form of dance, found in the perfect aspect (cf.*
         He has fallen)

Identifying the perfect requires looking for two things. First you have to see if there is a *have/had/has* auxiliary. Second, you have to see if there is a participle. Abstractly then we can identify the sequence HAVE+PARTICIPLE as the defining characteristic of the perfect.

You now have enough information to try WBE 6.

The perfect aspect can be combined with each of the tenses. The aspect is marked by virtue of the fact that we have both a form of the verb *have* and a participle. The tense is indicated by the particular form of the verb *have*: In the past this verb shows up as *had*, in the present as *have* or *has*, and in the future as *will have*. In each of the following examples, we are using the participle of the verb *eat*: *eaten*.

28) a)   I had eaten the deep-fried muffins   *past perfect (pluperfect)*

         past   perfect

    b)   I have eaten the beef waffles   *present perfect*

         present perfect

    c)   I will have eaten the beef waffles   *future perfect*

         future   perfect

You now have enough information to try WBE 7.

3.3 Progressive Aspect

The second aspect we will look at is the **progressive**. The progressive aspect indicates an event that is ongoing in relation to the reference time. For example, imagine I say (29):

29) Jeff was dancing with Sylvia while Amy sat angrily at their table.

This means that there is some reference time that I have in mind (probably the time Amy was sitting at the table), and there was a co-occurrence between the reference time and the time of the dancing.

In English, the progressive aspect is always indicated by combining what is traditionally called the **present participle** form of the verb with some version of the auxiliary verb *be*. Present participles in English are always marked with -*ing*. In this book we're going to refer to present participles as *gerunds*. While this isn't exactly correct (the term "gerund" is more typically used to describe nouns that are homophonous with present participles), it allows us to avoid the confusing "present"/"past" participle terminology. We want to avoid these terms since both kinds of participle can appear with any tense. In English the form of the present participle is always identical to that of the gerund, so there is no harm in conflating the terms.

30)

Form	Traditional name	Name used in this book
ends in -*ing*	present participle	gerund
ends in -*en* (etc.)	past participle	participle

To indicate the progressive, the gerund is always combined with the auxiliary verb *be* or one of its variants (*was, were, am, is, are, be, being, been*). As in the perfect, the tense marking in progressives is typically indicated on the auxiliary. The progressive aspect is always presented in English by the pairing of the gerund with *be* (i.e., the progressive's formula is BE+GERUND).

You now have enough information to try WBE 8.

3.4 Voice

Voice refers to a phenomenon that changes the number of arguments and position of arguments that a verb uses. Consider a typical verb like *eat*. In an **active** sentence like *Calvin ate the beef waffles*, we can identify an agent (Calvin) – the subject of the sentence – and the eatee (the theme: *beef waffles*). In a **passive**, such as *The beef waffles were eaten*, the theme appears in subject position. The agent is either mentioned after a preposition (like *by Calvin*) or is omitted entirely.

In English, the passive voice is marked with a *be* auxiliary and the participle form of the verb: *The beef waffles **were eaten***. The formula for a passive is BE+PARTICIPLE (contrast this with the perfect, where the participle is combined with the verb *have*, and the progressive, where *be* is paired with a gerund). Active sentences bear no special marking.

You now have enough information to try WBE 9.

3.5 Combined Tense, Aspect, and Voice

Let's briefly summarize the patterns we've seen so far. We've distinguished three tenses (past, present, future), two aspects (perfect and progressive), and the passive voice. The marking of aspect and voice requires both an auxiliary and a special form of the verb that follows it:

31)

	Auxiliary verb	Following verb form
Perfect	have	participle (-en)
Progressive	be	gerund (-ing)
Passive voice	be	participle (-en)

It's possible to combine three rows in (31) to form very complex auxiliary verb strings:

32) The soup had been being eaten when it got spilled.

This is a past perfect progressive passive. Let's break (32) down into the relevant bits. Tense is indicated on the first auxiliary (*has* vs. *had*). The fact that the sentence is in the perfect aspect is indicated by a combination of the verb *had* and participle form (*-en*) of the next verb (*been*). The fact that the sentence also bears the progressive is indicated by the next *be* auxiliary (*been*) and the fact that the following verb is a gerund (*being*). Finally, the fact that the sentence is a passive is indicated by the last *being* auxiliary and the final main verb appearing in a participle form (*eaten*).

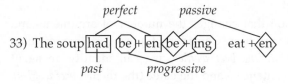

33) The soup had (be)+ en (be)+ ing   eat +en

The pattern here is complex, but surprisingly regular. There is an interleaving of tense, aspect markers, and voice marking, but the auxiliaries themselves appear in a strict order: tense > perfect > progressive > passive > main verbs.

One interesting part of the English auxiliary system is that it requires a combination of items to determine what aspect/voice is being represented. For example, the use of the participle does not by itself tell us if a particular aspect/voice is being used. The participle is used both in the perfect and in the passive. To distinguish the two, you have to see whether it is being used with the auxiliary *be* or the auxiliary *have*. Similarly, the auxiliary *be* by itself tells us nothing: when it is used with a gerund it is part of the marking of a progressive, but when it is used with a participle it marks the passive.

You now have enough information to try WBE 10.

3.6 Mood

We have only one more inflectional category to deal with. This is the category of **mood**. Mood refers to the speaker's perspective on the event – in particular, whether the event described is a possibility, a probability, a necessity, or an obligation. Typically speaking, mood is expressed through modal auxiliary verbs, although it can also be expressed through other means including adjectives (*it is possible that ...*), other auxiliaries or verbs (*Calvin has to eat his tuna*), or adverbs (*Possibly John will leave*).

The modals of English that express mood are:

34) *Modals of English*: can, could, may, might, would, shall, should, must, ought[1]

Modals have the following distributional properties. They always precede all other auxiliaries (35). They must precede negation (36). They can never take agreement inflection, like the third person suffix *-s* (37).

35) a) Jeff must have eaten the deep-fried muffin.
    b) *Jeff has must eaten the deep-fried muffin.

36) a) Jeff must not have eaten the deep-fried muffin.
    b) *Jeff not must have eaten the deep-fried muffin.

37) *Jeff musts eats a deep-fried muffin.

You now have enough information to try WBE 11 and GPS 6.

---

4. AUXILIARIES

With these fundamentals of different kinds of verbal morphology under our belts, we can turn to a syntactic description of how these notions are encoded into the grammar. In particular, we'll look at how we can use theta grids to express restrictions on ordering among the various tense, mood, aspect, and voice markers in English. First, however, we have to briefly discuss the difference between auxiliary uses of verbs like *be, have* and *do*, and main verb uses of the same verbs.

---

[1] Some people also characterize *dare, need,* and *has (to)* as modal verbs. These verbs express mood, but aren't modals because they require an infinitive complement. We leave them aside here. They have the syntax of main verbs. *Had better* might also be a modal, but because it's a phrase its status is controversial.

4.1 Main Verb vs. Auxiliary Verb Uses of be, have, *and* do

Consider the following sentences of English:

38) a) Calvin has a peanut.
    b) Susan has a cold.
    c) Bill had an accident.

39) a) Calvin has eaten a peanut.
    b) Frank has drunk too much.
    c) Bill has been dancing.

In terms of meaning, the verb *have* in (38) indicates **possession**. The possession can be concrete or it can be a bit more abstract (as in 38c). In each of these cases the verb *have* is followed by a DP. The sentences in (39) lack the semantics of possession and the syntactic structure is also different. In these forms *have* is followed by the participial form of the verb.

Next consider the following sentences:

40) a) Dane is a doctor.
    b) Jorge was the one.

41) a) Alex was eating the popsicle.
    b) Megan was sat on by her brother.

Sentence (41a) is the use of *be* (*was/is*) as part of a progressive sentence. Sentence (41b) is the use of *be* as part of a passive. In (40), by contrast, the verb *be* is used to indicate that the subject has a certain property or is identified with a particular role. It indicates membership in classes or expresses identity. These uses are known as **copular be**. The uses in (41), however, don't have these functions. Leaving aside the traditional description of gerunds as nouns (we will treat them mostly as verbs), the difference between (40) and (41) in terms of category is that the copular verb is followed by a noun and the progressive and passive usages are followed by verbal forms.

Next consider the following sentences that have the verb *do* (*did*). We're not really going to look carefully at this verb until the next chapter, but since it patterns with *be* and *have* with respect to differences we're discussing here, I'm including it here for completeness.

42) a) Catherine did her homework.   b) Calvin did a back flip.
43) a) Catherine did not eat.   b) Calvin did not do a back flip.

The distinction between (42) and (43) is a little more delicate and harder to describe. The *do* in (42) seems to mean something like "accomplish" or "perform". Some speakers might think the same thing is true of the *do* in

(43). But here things are subtler. No *do* is necessary in a simple declarative such as *Catherine ate*. But the *do* is required with a negation: *Catherine did not eat*. While the *do*s in (42) are followed by nouns, the *do*s in (43) are followed by (negated) verbs. Later, we'll claim that the *do* in (43) is "meaningless" – in the sense that it is present to support the tense morphology in the environment of negation. The fact that we can have two *do*s in a single sentence (43b) suggests that we have two verbs *do*: one to support tense and one to provide the meaning "accomplish/perform".

English appears to have multiple verbs *be*, at least two verbs *have*, and two verbs *do*. The ones in (38), (40) and (42) have the flavor of lexical verbs. The others are auxiliaries. To distinguish between each usage, from this point forward we'll annotate *be*, *have*, and *do* with subscript notations like be_{prog} (for progressive), be_{perf} (for perfect), etc.

44)

Name	Meaning	Subcategory
be_{cop}	Copula (identity/property)	Main verb
be_{prog}	Progressive	Auxiliary
be_{pass}	Passive	Auxiliary
$have_{poss}$	Possession	Main verb
$have_{perf}$	Perfect	Auxiliary
do_{main}	Accomplishment/performance	Main verb
do_{aux}	Supports tense before negation	Auxiliary

Next, we have to find evidence to support our hypothesis that there is a category distinction between main and auxiliary uses of these verbs. Recall the rule of subject-aux inversion that we discussed in chapter 7. This rule is used to indicate the presence of a *yes/no*-question. Now consider the following data:

45) a) Has Pangur eaten his tuna?   b) Is Pangur eating his tuna?
    c) Did Pangur eat his dinner?   d) *Ate Pangur his dinner?

Now contrast (45a) with (45d). Note that main verbs like ate can't undergo subject-auxiliary inversion, but auxiliaries can. Now, consider the following examples with what we've identified as "main verb" uses of *have* and *do*. This data represents the judgments of most North American speakers. Speakers of British English and many other dialects will probably disagree with the judgments given. For the purposes of this discussion, restrict yourself to the facts of American English as given in (46). (We leave aside *be* here, as it behaves differently.) The "main" verb uses of *do* and *have* cannot invert.

46) a)   *Has Calvin a bowl?   b)   *Did Calvin his homework?

Now consider the behavior of auxiliary verbs with respect to the negative word *not* (47).

47) a)   Angus is not leaving.
    b)   Calvin has not eaten his dinner.
    c)   Pangur did not play with his mouse.
    d)   *Calvin ate not his dinner.
    e)   *Pangur plays not with his mouse.[2]

Only auxiliary verbs and modals can appear before the word *not*. Main verbs like play and ate cannot appear before negation. The data in (48) shows that *have*$_{poss}$ and *do*$_{main}$ behave like main verbs and not like auxiliaries.

48) a)   *Calvin has not any catnip.
    b)   *Angus did not his homework.

You now have enough information to try WBE 12.

4.2 Modals vs. Auxiliaries

Modal verbs have a slightly different distribution than other auxiliaries like *have* or *be*. The discussion and exercises in this section are to help you figure out what that distribution is.

Auxiliaries like *be* and *have* take inflectional suffixes just like verbs. This includes tense morphology such as *-ed*, agreement morphology like *-s* and the suffixes that turn them into participles and gerunds (*-en* and *-ing*). They can be negated with *not*. They follow modals, the infinitive marker *to*, and, to a greater or lesser degree, other auxiliaries too. All of this suggests that they have some verbal properties, perhaps making them a special subcategory of verbs. Up until now, we've treated them as T nodes. But these facts give us pause to reconsider that analysis.

Unlike auxiliaries, modals like *can* and *should* do not take verbal inflectional endings[3] (**Jeff musts*). They also do not follow *not* (49b), nor

---

[2] Assume here that there is no continuation of this sentence with something like "… *but with his ball*". This sentence is ungrammatical without such a completion.

[3] In some works, you'll see the claim that *could* is the past tense of *can*; *would* is the past tense of *will*; *should* is the past tense of *shall*; *might* is the past tense of *may*, etc. I don't share these authors' intuition that there is past tense inflection here. The modals *could, should, would,* and *might*, in fact, all have a vaguely futurate feel to me. The difference between *can* and *could*, for example, does not seem to be an expression of

follow other modals (49c) or auxiliaries (49d) or the infinitive marker *to* (49e). Where *have* and *be* can combine with other auxiliaries, it appears as if you can only have one modal and it must be first in the string of verbal inflection.

49) a) I should not eat plums.
    b) *I have not should eat plums.
    c) *I must can eat plums.
    d) *I have should eat plums.
    e) *I want to should eat plums.

Recall from section 3 above that tense morphology must be also on the first element in the string of auxiliaries. It appears then that modal verbs are in complementary distribution with tense elements. This being the case, we can claim that they are instances of the category T (even though they don't identify any of past, present, future).

Might Could

Most speakers of English only allow one modal in a sentence. However, speakers from the South Eastern United States often allow a combination of *might* and *could*: %He might could leave. There is some evidence to suggest that this is actually a compound: Only these two modals can combine; they must be in this order, and for many speakers no adverb can appear between them, so this might not be a counter-example to our claim that modals are single words in the T head.

Some support for this idea comes from the distribution of the future tense marker *will. Will* has the same distribution as modals. It has to precede negation (50a and b) and it is in complementary distribution with the modal verbs: It is impossible to have a single clause that has both a modal and a future tense marker in it (50c and d).

50) a) Calvin will not eat the beef waffles.
    b) *Calvin not will eat the beef waffles.
    c) *Calvin could will eat the beef waffles.
    d) *Calvin will could eat the beef waffles.

Another property that *will* shares with modals is that the verb that follows it must not bear any tense or agreement inflection. The following verb is always in its "bare" form (51) without any inflectional suffixes.

51) a) I ate deep-fried muffins.
    b) He always eats deep-fried muffins.

---

tense, but clearly an expression of mood: *Can* expresses an ability whereas *could* expresses a possibility.

   c)   *I might ate deep-fried muffins.
   d)   *He always might eats deep-fried muffins.
   e)   I/he might eat deep-fried muffins.
   f)   He will eat deep-fried muffins.
   g)   *He will eats deep-fried muffins

These data show us two things: (i) The tense particle *will* patterns just like a modal, and (ii) when a modal is present, no tense morphology is present. This suggests that modals are indeed, against first appearances, of the category T.

We now conclude that *will* and modals are of category T, but what then are we to make of *have* and *be*. These verbs can follow negation (although they can also precede it), they do bear tense, and they can appear with other verbal items, including modals. So what are they? The other obvious candidate for category for these auxiliaries is category V – in contradiction to what we argued in chapter 2. In fact, there's good reason to think that auxiliaries are sometimes V and sometimes appear in T. We want to find some significant way to capture the idea that modals are distinct from auxiliaries in some ways (e.g., always precede negation), but similar to them in others (can undergo subject–auxiliary inversion for example). Similarly, we'll want to capture the fact that auxiliaries are similar to verbs in some ways (show tense inflection, can follow negation, etc.) but different from them in others (for example can undergo subject–auxiliary inversion). We'll return to this issue seriously next chapter.

For now, let's think about how we can encode the facts about modals that we've already discussed. There can only be one modal, and if one is present there can be no other tense marking in the clause. This is consistent with the fact that there is only one T node in any given clause. But we also need to encode that modal verbs require that the verb below them must not bear any tense morphology. This is actually quite easy to do using the technology of theta grids (see the appendix to this chapter for an alternative view). All we have to do is create a feature that describes the class of structures that modals can take as complements. We use a new kind of feature here, where the value of the feature is something other than ±. We want to be able to describe the form of the complement to the modal, which is always bare. This feature is [FORM *bare*]. We can posit similar features for participles [FORM *participle*], gerunds [FORM *gerund*], and tensed forms [FORM *preterite*] and [FORM *present*]. Let's take a few different verbs as examples, and see how these features translate as particular verb forms.

52)

[FORM *bare*]	[FORM *participle*]	[FORM *gerund*]	[FORM *preterite*]	[FORM *present*]
eat	eaten	eating	ate	eat/eats
dance	danced	dancing	danced	dance/dances
bite	bitten	biting	bit	bite/bites
take	taken	taking	took	take/takes
lay	laid	laying	laid	lay/lays
be	been	being	was/were	is/am/are
have	had	having	had	has/have

With modals, the complement always appears in one of the forms in the first column. So we can specify in the theta grid for a modal like *should* that the complement be a V with the feature [FORM *bare*]:

53) *should*

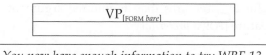

$$VP_{[FORM\ bare]}$$

You now have enough information to try WBE 13.

A tree for a sentence using *should* is given in (54). You'll notice that complement to the T is a VP with a verb in its bare form.

54)

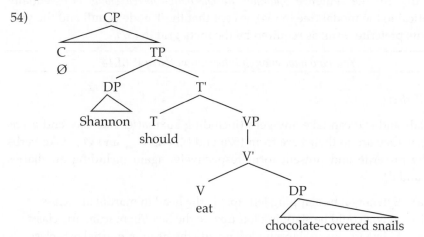

4.3 Past and Present Tense Marking in English

There is, of course, one major hitch in our claim that modals are of category T: present and past tense marking in English appears on *verbs*. This is no minor problem. But the use of the FORM feature gives us a way out.

Let us propose that there is a category T present in every sentence, even when we don't have a modal or *will*. This will require you to take a leap of faith, but consider for the moment the possibility that there are present tense and past tense equivalents to *will*, but that they have no phonological content, that is, they are totally silent. Let's call these $\emptyset_{pres}$ and $\emptyset_{past}$ (where $\emptyset$ is meant to invoke the idea of a silent word). It's ok to be suspicious of the idea of silent words, but note that English, like many languages, makes significant use of the absence of morphology to express content. So for example, the plurals of the nouns *deer* and *sheep* are *deer* and *sheep*. Similarly, the first and second person endings on verbs in English are typically silent too: *I walk_, you walk_* (cf. *she walks*). So perhaps silent words aren't quite such a stretch after all. The consequence of this is that the tense in a sentence like *Calvin ate the beef waffles* isn't in *ate*, but in the silent $\emptyset_{past}$ that precedes it.

55) a)   Calvin $\emptyset_{past}$ ate the beef waffles
    b)   Calvin can   eat the beef waffles

The theta grid for $\emptyset_{past}$ requires that its internal argument be headed by a verb with the feature [FORM *preterite*].

56) $\emptyset_{past}$

The tree for the sentence *Shannon ate chocolate-covered snails* is essentially identical to the modal tree in (54), except that the T node is null and the verb is in its preterite form, as required by the theta grid in (57).

You now have enough information to try WBE14.

4.4 Perfects

Modals and *will* can take any verb (including auxiliaries like *have* and *be*) as long as they are in their bare form (57a and b), and $\emptyset_{past}$ and $\emptyset_{pres}$ take verbs in the preterite and present form respectively, again including auxiliaries (57c and d).

57) a)   Sylvia will be slapping Jeff upside the head in martial arts class.
    b)   Sylvia could be slapping Jeff upside the head in martial arts class.
    c)   Sylvia $\emptyset_{past}$ was slapping Jeff upside the head in martial arts class.
    d)   Sylvia $\emptyset_{pres}$ is slapping Jeff upside the head in martial arts class.

Notice that what follows these T nodes is an auxiliary. This auxiliary has to be of category V because T always selects for a VP. Recall from section 3 above that if there are multiple auxiliaries, modals come first followed by any perfect auxiliaries. Let's make this more precise: *Have*$_{perf}$ can precede a main verb (58a), it can precede a progressive auxiliary (58b), and it can precede a passive auxiliary (58c). However, it can't precede another perfect auxiliary (58d) or a modal (58e).

58) a)   The cat had eaten.
   b)   The cat had been eating.
   c)   The tuna had been eaten.
   d)   *The cat had haven eaten.
   e)   *The cat had musten eat.

We can conclude then, that the *have*$_{perf}$ auxiliary selects for a V complement (explaining why a T, like *must*, is excluded) and that VP must be [–PERFECT] to explain why (d) is excluded, and must also be participial in form. We can capture this with the following theta grid:

59) *have*$_{perf}$

The tree for (58a) is given in (60) and the tree for (58b) is given in (61).

60)

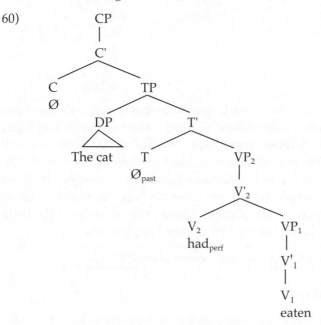

61)

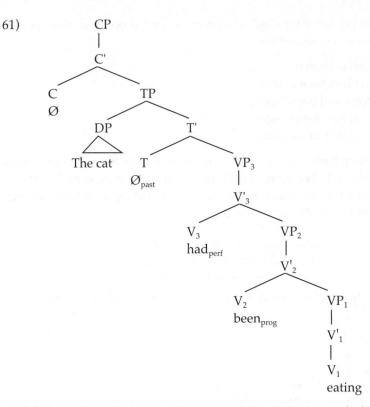

In (60) the main verb *eat* is in the participial form, *eaten*. In (61) the auxiliary verb *been* meets the form requirement of *have*$_{perf}$. The trees in (60) and (61) might surprise you, because they have "stacked VPs" with one VP dominating another. We haven't seen trees like these before, but note that X-bar theory naturally allows such structures, because any category in X-bar theory can serve as a complement to any other category due to the variables in the rules. Such structures are permitted (and even required) if the theta grids of the particular heads specify VPs as their complements.

You now have enough information to try WBE 15.

4.5 Progressive Auxiliaries

Now let's turn to the first of our two possible be auxiliaries: *be*$_{prog}$. Consider the data in (62). The form of the progressive *be* in (62) is the preterite, but the properties we're going to discuss are true of all the forms. *Be*$_{prog}$ can take a main verb as a complement (62a) or a passive as a complement (62b), but it disallows another progressive (62c), a perfect (62d), or a modal (62e). Its syntactic distribution is thus more restricted than the perfect.

62) a) The cat was leaving.
    b) The tuna was being eaten.
    c) *The cat was being eating.
    d) *The cat was having eaten.
    e) *The cat was musting eat.

The analysis of these facts should be obvious now. We use a theta grid to restrict the complements of be_{prog} to Vs (thus excluding modals) that are [−PROGRESSIVE, −PERFECT] (excluding other progressives and perfects). Further, since this is the progressive, this *be* must have a gerund as its complement, encoded via a FORM feature.

63) be_{prog}

The tree for (62b) is given in (64). In this tree, the theme is in the subject position. We return to why this is true in chapter 11.

You now have enough information to try WBE 16 and GPS 7.

---

64)

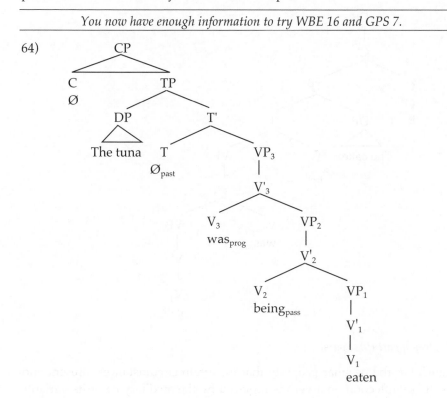

4.6 Passive Auxiliaries

Finally, we have *be*_{pass}. The complements of *be*_{pass} are even more restricted than those of *be*_{prog}. It can only be followed by a main verb (65a), and not by another passive (65b), a progressive (65c), a perfect (65d), or a modal (65e)

65) a) The cake was eaten.   b) *The cake was been eaten.
    c) *The cake was been eating.   d) *The cake was have eaten.
    e) *The cake was musten eat.

So the passive must exclude all verbs except main verbs. Using the features we've already proposed, this means limiting the complement of passives to [–PERFECT, –PROGRESSIVE, –PASSIVE] V, which is in the participle FORM.

66) *be*_{pass}

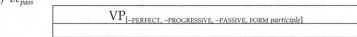

The tree for (65a) is given in (67).

67)

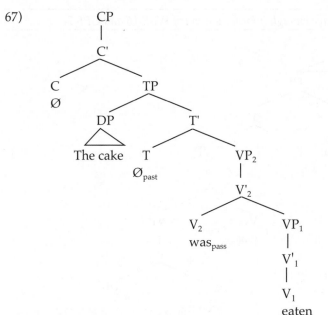

4.7 Do-support (first pass)

English has the peculiar property that in certain circumstances, present and past tense inflection on a verb is replaced by the auxiliary *do* or its variants *does* and *did*. Typically, we find *do* in three situations.

The first is when we negate a verb that has no other auxiliary (in other words when we have only a null T ($\emptyset_{past}$ or $\emptyset_{pres}$) and a main verb in its preterite or past tense form):

68) a)   Reggie chased the ball.
    b)   Reggie did not chase the ball.

When we have negation (*not*), the past tense inflection appears on the auxiliary *did*, not on the verb (which appears in its bare form). This is called **do-support**. We'll refer to this usage as do_{neg} (and of course its inflected forms did_{neg}, $does_{neg}$).

The second case is when we want to emphasize the occurrence of the event described by the verb, when we want to emphasize when the event happened, or when we want to contrast the event with another.

69) a)   Jean: Reggie chased the ball?
         Bob: Oh, he DID chase the ball indeed!
    b)   Jean: I think Reggie is chasing the ball.
         Bob: Not anymore, but he DID chase the ball!
    c)   Jean: Did Reggie catch the mouse?
         Bob: No, but he DID catch a lizard.

We'll refer to this usage as $do/did/does_{emph}$ ("emph" stands for emphatic). Finally, we have the set of forms that are used in questions seen in (70).

70) a)   Did Calvin eat the beef waffles?   b)   What did Calvin eat?

Let's refer to this last case as $do/did/does_Q$ (Q for questions). This last case is quite hard to deal with, because the auxiliary has inverted with the subject. We'll return to this third case in the next chapter. Here, we'll only deal with $do/does/did_{emph}$ and $do/does/did_{neg}$.

Do_{neg} is always followed by the negator *not*, which in turn is always followed by a verb (any verb), which is always in its bare form. It is never preceded by negation and seems to be in complementary distribution with modals.

71) a)   *John must not do have eaten.   b)   *John must do not have eaten.

It's logical to conclude, then, that like modals, do_{neg} is an instance of the T node. To account for the fact that do_{neg} requires a following *not* and *not* requires a bare VP complement, we need a theta grid for do_{neg} (72) and one for *not* (73).

72) do_{neg}

NegP

73) *not*

In other words, negative *do* selects for negation, and negation selects for a bare verb. Negation always occurs with a *do* auxiliary because no other T node selects for negation. All the others select for VPs. The tree for (68b) is given in (74).

74)

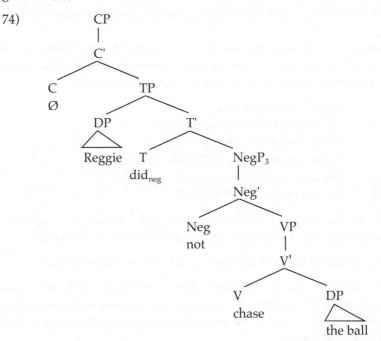

Do_emph is simpler. It behaves in all respects like a modal and requires a bare VP complement (75). The tree for the sentence *Reggie DID chase the ball* is given in (76).

75) *not*

76)

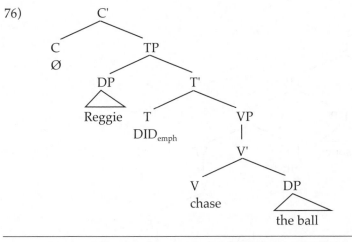

You now have enough information to try CPS 8.

4.8 The Grand Slam

In section 3, we observed that it is possible to have a modal, a perfect, a progressive, and a passive all bundled up into one clause. When this happens, they have to be linearized in precisely this order. The sentence in (77) is a starting point.

77) The prisoner must have been being interrogated when the supervisor walked into the room and saw what was going on and put a stop to it.

Some people have difficulty getting all of these bits into a sentence, and there is no doubt that the kind of structure seen in (77) is very rare and quite hard to process. But with enough context, most native speakers of English find this okay. Admittedly when you Google® auxiliary strings like (77), the top hits are all examples from linguistics papers, but you'll find some real-world examples too. The tree here has a modal that selects for a bare VP, which in this case is headed by perfective *have*. *Have*$_{perf}$ in turn requires that the following VP be in participial form (in this case *been*). This *been* is the progressive *be*$_{prog}$, and requires that the next verb down the chain be in gerund form (the next verb is the auxiliary marking the passive: *being*). *Be*$_{pass}$ requires that the next verb down is a participle (*interrogated* – don't let the *-ed* here fool you. This is a participle not a past tense). Each form is predicted by the theta grid of the auxiliary or modal to its left. The tree for the first clause in (77) is given in (78).

78)

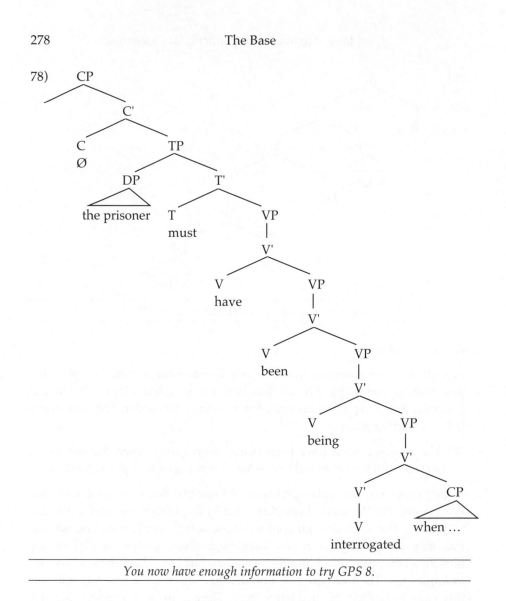

You now have enough information to try GPS 8.

---

5. CONCLUSION

In this chapter, we've extended the use of theta grids to explain other kinds of restrictions on X-bar-theoretic trees. We saw that VPs not only select for specific theta roles, they also select for various features of CPs (such as finiteness). Complementizers themselves select for specific kinds of TPs. For example, *that* can't have a TP headed by *to* as its complement. We also looked at several kinds of determiners, all of which place restrictions on the kinds of nouns they can take as complements. Finally we examined the scary world of English modals and auxiliaries. After breaking down all the parts of a complex verb string in English into its component modal, tense, aspectual, and voice parts, we saw how various auxiliaries select for both the range of possible auxiliary and verbal complements (perfect, progressive, passive, main verbs) and for the form that complement takes (bare, preterite, present, participle, or gerund). This gives us an explanation for the ordering and realization of each of these auxiliaries in sentences like "the grand slam" given in section 4.7 above.

There are a number of issues that remain unaddressed here. The bulk of this chapter has been on English, but other languages function very differently in how they represent this kind of morphology. We also have left unexplained the situations where certain modals and *tensed* auxiliaries behave as a class. Both modals and tensed auxiliaries precede negation, as in the examples (79a and b), and both tensed auxiliaries and modals can undergo subject/auxiliary inversion to form *yes/no* questions as in (79c and d).

79) a)   Fiona must not eat the sautéed candy canes.
    b)   Fiona has not eaten the sautéed candy canes.
    c)   Can Fiona eat sautéed candy canes?
    d)   Has Fiona eaten sautéed candy canes?

The account of auxiliaries given in this chapter is completely silent on the behaviors in (79). In order to account for these facts as well as for patterns in other languages, we need the additional technology afforded us by movement. This is discussed in the next few chapters.

IDEAS, RULES, AND CONSTRAINTS INTRODUCED IN THIS CHAPTER

i)   ***Theta Grids*** can contain material other than theta roles, such as features.

ii)   *[±FINITE]*: A feature of complementizers that indicates if the clause is finite or not. *That* is [+FINITE].

iii)   *[±Q]*: A feature of complementizers that indicates if the clause is a question or not. *If* and *whether* are [+Q].

iv)   *[±INFINITIVE]*: Not to be confused with [±FINITE], this is a feature of T nodes. *To* is [+INFINITIVE].

v)   *[±PLURAL]*: A feature of N heads indicating number.

vi)   *[±PROPER]*: The feature associated with proper names.

vii)   *[±PRONOUN]*: The feature associated with pronouns.

viii)   *[±COUNT]*: This feature distinguishes count nouns from mass nouns.

ix)   ***Tense*** refers to the time of an event relative to the time at which the sentence is either spoken or written.

x)   *The Event Time*: The time at which the event described by the predicate occurs.

xi)   *The Assertion Time*: The time at which the sentence is said.

xii)   *Past Tense*: The event time happened before the assertion time.

xiii)   *Present Tense*: The event time is the same as the assertion time.

xiv)   *Future Tense*: The event time happens after the assertion time.

xv)   *Preterite*: the special form of verbs in the past tense.

xvi)   *Futurates*: the future tense usage of a present tense verb.

xvii)   *Aspect*: a temporal relation that makes reference to some point other than the speech time, then looking at when the event happens relative to that reference point.

xviii) *Perfect*: the aspect when the time of the event occurs before some reference point. $Have_{perf}$ + participle.

xix)   *Participle*: A particular form of the verb used in perfects and passives. It is often formed by suffixing *–en* or *–ed*, although other irregular methods are found too. Same thing as *past participle*.

xx)   *Gerund*: A particular form of the verb used in progressives. It is normally formed by suffixing *–ing*. Traditionally called the *present participle*.

xxi)   *Progressive*: An aspect where the event time and the reference time overlap and the event is ongoing. be_{prog} + gerund.

xxii)   *Voice*: An inflection that indicates the number of arguments and position of arguments that a verb uses.

xxiii) *Active:* A type of voice where the agent or experiencer of the sentence is in subject position and the theme is in the object position. Actives in English are unmarked morphologically.

xxiv)   *Passive*: A type of voice where the theme of the sentence is in subject position. Passives are always marked in English by the combination of a *be* auxiliary and a participle.

xxv)   *Mood*: An inflectional category that refers to the speaker's perspective on the event, indicating possibility, probability, necessity, or obligation.

xxvi)   *Possessive* **Have**: A main verb use of *have*, which indicates possession.

xxvii) *Copular* **Be**: A main verb use of *be*, where the subject is attributed a certain property or is identified with a particular role.

xxviii) *Main Verb* **Do**: The use of the verb *do* to indicate accomplishments.

xxix)   *Modals*: Verbs that can only appear before negation and never take tense inflection. *Auxiliaries*, by contrast, can follow negation and can bear tense inflection.

xxx)   *[FORM] Features* indicate the form of complements. Possible values include bare, participle, gerund, preterite, and present.

xxxi)   **Do-***support*: The use of the auxiliary *do* to bear tense features in the context of negation. This *do* is of category T.

xxxii) *Affix Hopping*: An alternative analysis of multiple auxiliary constructions, where affixes associated with particular tenses, aspects, and voice are generated as part of the same word as the relevant auxiliary, but then "hop" one verbal element to the right.

FURTHER READING: Aarts (2008), Huddleston and Pullum (2005), Lobeck (2000), Sag, Wasow, and Bender (2003), van Gelderen (2010)

GENERAL PROBLEM SETS

GPS1. CATEGORIZING VERBS
[Data Analysis; Intermediate/Advanced]
Part 1: Assign acceptability judgments to the following sentences. If you aren't a native speaker, ask a native speaker friend to help you.

1) a) I wanted that he should leave.   b) I wanted he should leave.
    c) I wanted if he should leave.   d) I wanted him to leave.
    e) I wanted to leave.

2) a) Heidi investigated that Art ate the cauliflower.
    b) Heidi investigated Art ate the cauliflower.
    c) Heidi investigated if/whether Art ate the cauliflower
    d) Heidi investigated Art to eat the cauliflower.
    e) Heidi investigated to eat the cauliflower.

3) a) Art said that Heidi was obsessed with broccoli.
    b) Art said Heidi was obsessed with broccoli.
    c) Art said if Heidi was obsessed with broccoli.
    d) Art said Heidi to eat the broccoli.
    e) Art said to eat the broccoli.

4) a) Andy promised that we would go.
    b) Andy promised we would go.
    c) Andy promised if we would go. (*Note:* don't add an additional clause.)
    d) Andy promised us to go.
    e) Andy promised to go.

Part 2: Based on your judgments above, draw the theta grids for *want, investigate, say,* and *promise.* Use the following principles for deciding whether to use [+Q], use [−Q], or leave [±Q] unspecified:
•   Assign [+Q] if both (a) and (b) are unacceptable, but (c) is acceptable.

- Assign [-Q] if either of (a) or (b) or both are acceptable, but (c) is unacceptable.
- Don't assign any value if either of (a) or (b) is acceptable and (c) is acceptable as well.

Use the following principles for deciding whether to use [+FINITE], use [-FINITE], or leave the verb unspecified for [±FINITE]:

- Assign [-FINITE] if all of (a), (b) and (c) are ungrammatical, but either of (d) or (e) is acceptable.
- Assign [+FINITE] if any of (a), (b) or (c) are grammatical and both (d) and (e) are unacceptable.
- Don't assign any value for [±FINITE] if at least one of (a), (b) and (c) is acceptable, and either (c) or (d) is acceptable.

Some of these verbs can take DPs as well as CPs as complements; ignore that fact in your theta grids (but do put the DP external arguments in).

GPS2. IRISH FINITE COMPLEMENTIZERS
[Data Analysis; Basic]

In English, complementizers are primarily sensitive to whether or not the embedded TP is an infinitive *to*. In Modern Irish, finite complementizers vary along an additional line. Examine the following data and propose theta grids for the complementizers *go* and *gur*. Don't worry about the extra *m* and *h* on either side of the *b* in the embedded verb; that's an effect of the initial consonant mutations in the language and has nothing to do with the answer to the problem. Although the data is limited, assume it is representative of the patterns in the language.

a) Ceapaim   go   mbuaileann sé le   Seán   inniu
    think.1s   that   meets   he with   John   today
    "I think that he meets with John today"

b) Ceapaim   gur   bhuail sé le   Seán   inné
    think.1s   that   met   he with   John   yesterday
    "I think that he met with John yesterday"

GPS3. SUBJUNCTIVE MOOD IN ENGLISH COUNTERFACTUALS
[Data Analysis; Basic]

There are two kinds of *if* in English. One is used for embedded questions and is discussed in the main text above. The other is used for a special kind of conditional clause, called a **counterfactual**. In high-register English this kind of complementizer requires that if you use some form of the verb *to be*, then it must take the form *were*, as seen in the following examples (the judgments given are based on formal academic English; many colloquial varieties allow the asterisked versions).

a) If I were/*was/*am a rich man, I'd buy a diamond ring
b) If he were/*is/*was a rich man, he'd buy a diamond ring

We can call this special usage of the auxiliary *were* here a **subjunctive** and we can represent it with the feature [±SUBJUNCTIVE]. Draw the theta grid for counterfactual *if* in formal English.

GPS4. THESE, THOSE, FEW, AND EVERY
[Application of Knowledge; Basic]
Draw the theta grids for the English determiners *these*, *those, few,* and *every*.

GPS5. SCOTTISH GAELIC COMMON CASE DETERMINERS
[Data Analysis and Application of Knowledge; Basic]
In Scottish Gaelic, the accusative and nominative case forms are identical and are called the common case. In the common case, one finds the following forms of the determiners,[4] varying according to whether the noun is masculine or feminine in gender and singular or plural in number:

a) an càr   "the car" (masculine)   b) a' chaileag "the girl" (feminine)
c) na gillean   "the boys" (plural)

Provide theta grids for *an, a',* and *na* in Scottish Gaelic.

GPS6. TENSE, VOICE, ASPECT, MOOD
[Application of Knowledge; Basic]
For each of the following sentences determine what tense it is in (if it has a modal auxiliary, you don't have to identify the tense), whether or not it has a modal auxiliary, whether it is in the perfect, whether it is progressive or non-progressive, and whether it is in the active or the passive voice.

a) Rory eats.   b) Rory ate muffins.
c) The muffins were eaten.   d) Rory had eaten the muffins.
e) Rory has eaten the muffins.   f)   Rory must have eaten the muffins.
g) Rory may be eating the muffins. h) Rory will eat the muffins.
i)   Rory eats muffins.   j)   Rory is eating muffins.
k) Rory might have been eating the muffins.
l)   The muffins might have been being eaten.

GPS7. THETA GRID OF BE$_{prog}$
[Critical Thinking; Advanced]
In the body of the text in this chapter, we claimed that the theta grid for *be*$_{prog}$ was the following:

be$_{prog}$

---

[4] Note: the forms given here are limited to words beginning with certain letters. The actual pattern is much more complex.

Why is this theta grid specified for [−PERFECT, −PROGRESSIVE]? Wouldn't it be simpler to specify it as [+PASSIVE]? What is the critical piece of data that shows that the specification of the VP here cannot be [+PASSIVE]?

GPS8. ENGLISH TREES
[Application of Skills; Basic to Advanced]
Draw the trees for the following English sentences:

a) The tuna had been eaten.
b) The tuna had been being eaten.
c) Calvin will eat.
d) The tuna will be eaten.
e) Calvin will be eating.
f) Calvin will have eaten.
j) The tuna will be being eaten.
g) The tuna will have been eaten.
h) Calvin will have been eating.
i) Calvin was eating.
j) Calvin had eaten.
k) The tuna had been eaten.
l) Calvin had been eating.
m) The tuna must have been eaten.
n) The tuna will have been being eaten.

CHALLENGE PROBLEM SETS

CHALLENGE PROBLEM SET 1: IRISH COMPLEMENTIZERS REVISITED
[Critical Thinking and Data Analysis; Challenge]
In order to do this problem set you need to complete General Problem Set 2 (Irish complementizers) first. Here's a little more information on *go* and *gur*. *Go* is used in other contexts as well, as in the data in (a). Similarly, *gur* is used in contexts like (b). Taking this data in combination with the data in General Problem Set 2, what would the theta grids for *go* and *gur* look like?

a) Ceapaim   go   mbuailfidh sé le   Seán   inniu
    think.1s   that   meet.FUT   he with   John   today
    "I think that he will meet with John today"

b) Ceapaim   gur   bhuailfeadh   sé le   Seán   inné
    think.1s   that   meet.COND   he with   John   yesterday
    "I think that he would meet with John yesterday"

CHALLENGE PROBLEM SET 2: NORTHERN ITALIAN PROPER NAMES
[Data Analysis and Creative Thinking; Challenge]
In the dialects of Italian spoken in the North of Italy, feminine proper names are often preceded by the feminine article *la* (which is also used with feminine common nouns.) For example, one finds *la Maria* "the Maria". Propose a theta grid for *la* that explains this constellation of facts.

CHALLENGE PROBLEM SET 3: ENGLISH SURNAMES
[Data Analysis and Creative Thinking; Challenge]
English normally disallows determiners with proper names: *the Andrew.* One exception is when one is referring to a family by their last name: *the*

Carnies. Try to come up with an explanation for why this exception might exist.

CHALLENGE PROBLEM SET 4: GERMAN DETERMINERS
[Data Analysis and Creative Thinking; Challenge]
German has four cases (nominative, accusative, dative, and genitive) and three genders (feminine, masculine, and neuter). It also has a plural, which is sensitive to case but not gender. These distinctions are reflected in its determiners. Using the minimum number of features you can, propose a set of features and a set of theta grids that characterize the determiners below. Assume that all these determiners require [+COUNT]. Don't worry about the features [+PROPER] or [+PRONOUN]. *Warning:* you may need to propose more than one theta grid for each determiner.

Indefinite (translates as *a* in English)

	Masculine	Neuter	Feminine
Nominative	ein	ein	eine
Accusative	einen	ein	eine
Dative	einem	einem	einer
Genitive	eines	eines	einer

Definite (translates as *the* in English)

	Masculine	Neuter	Feminine	Plural
Nominative	der	das	die	die
Accusative	den	das	die	die
Dative	dem	dem	der	den
Genitive	des	des	der	der

CHALLENGE PROBLEM SET 5: THE FOUR BOOKS
[Creative Thinking; Challenge]
The determiner *the* normally must be followed by an NP, and can't be followed by another DP. In all the theta grids for *the* that we've seen so far, the article takes an NP as a complement. However, *the* is allowed in front of numerals, which we have previously claimed to be determiners: *the four books*. Posit an explanation for this. (Hint: consider the possibility that numerals are not determiners. If this were true what kind of evidence would you have to find to prove this hypothesis?)

CHALLENGE PROBLEM SET 6: "ALL THE BOOKS" REVISITED
[Creative Thinking; Challenge]
In the text above, I gave you an analysis of the quantifier *all* such that it selects for a DP complement, explaining why you can say *all the books*. There are several problems with this analysis.

- *All* can also take an NP as a complement: *all books*.
- The noun that follows *all* must be plural: **all the book*. However, that NP is separated from the *all* by the determiner in between (i.e., the NP is the

complement of the DP complement of *all*) and theta grids can't make reference to material embedded inside of an argument.

- Not every determiner can follow *all*. The definite determiner *the* and the deictic determiners *these* and *those* are all allowed: *all the books, all these books, all those books*. Numerals can also follow it: *all four books*. But quantifiers like *some, every, many* etc. cannot: **all some books, *all every books, *all many books*.

Discuss possible solutions to these three problems. The third problem, in particular, is very tricky. In fact, I'm not sure I know of a non-stipulative solution to it. But try to provide some discussion of what (a) solution(s) might look like and what kind of data you'd need to find in order to prove or falsify that/those solution(s).

CHALLENGE PROBLEM SET 7: EACH OF THE BOOKS
[Creative Thinking; Challenge]
English has a number of quantifiers that can take prepositional phrases as complements. For example, the quantifier *each* can take a complement PP headed by *of*, giving *each of the men*. We can call these **partitive-taking quantifiers** and use the feature [±PARTITIVE] to characterize the preposition *of* in this context. All of the partitive-taking quantifiers also take DPs as complements (e.g., *each book*). What problem does this create for making the theta grid of these quantifiers? How can the quantifier *each* take either a PP or an NP complement?

CHALLENGE PROBLEM SET 8: NOT
[Creative Thinking; Challenge]
The *not* that follows *did/does/do$_{neg}$* requires that the following verb be in its bare form. What are we to make of the *not* words in the following?

a) is not eating   b) has not eaten   c) was not eaten

How can we account for the fact that *not* is followed by a participial form in (b) and (c) and by the gerund in (a)?

Part 3

Movement

chapter 10

Head-to-Head Movement

Learning Objectives

After reading chapter 10 you should walk away having mastered the following ideas and skills:

1. Understand the distinction between D-structure and S-structure.
2. Determine whether a language is verb-raising or not.
3. Discuss the interaction between V → T and T → C.
4. Explain the evidence for V → T movement in French and Irish.
5. Discuss the position of tensed English auxiliaries as compared to main verbs.
6. Explain how the VP-internal subject hypothesis accounts for VSO languages.
7. Discuss the whens, wheres, and whys of *do*-support.

0. INTRODUCTION

Consider the relation between a verb and its object: According to X-bar theory, an object is the complement to V (sister to V, daughter of V'). This means that *no* specifier or adjunct can intervene between the complement and the head (if it did, the object would no longer be a complement).

Syntax: A Generative Introduction, Third Edition. Andrew Carnie.
© 2013 Andrew Carnie. Published 2013 by John Wiley & Sons, Inc.

The following sentence is from Modern Irish, which is a verb-subject-object (VSO) word order language:

1) Phóg   Máire   an lucharachán.
    Kissed   Mary   the leprechaun
    "Mary kissed the leprechaun."

In this sentence, the subject (a specifier) intervenes between the verb and the object; this sentence cannot be generated by X-bar theory. (Try to draw a tree where the specifier intervenes between the head and the complement – it's impossible.)

Now consider the following sentence from French:

2) Je mange souvent des   pommes.
    I eat   often   of.the apples
    "I often eat apples."

Souvent "often" intervenes between the verb and the object. If *souvent* is an adjunct it is appearing between a head and its complement. X-bar theory can't draw the tree for this one either.

Finally think about the relationship between the auxiliary verb *have* and its complement main verb in (3). In the last chapter, we claimed that the participle is a complement to the auxiliary, yet here it is appearing separated from that complement by the negative word *not*.

3) He has not eaten yet today.

This is surprising. X-bar theory requires that complements be adjacent to the head that introduces them, but here we see three cases where that isn't true. In sum, X-bar theory *under-generates* because it does not produce all the possible grammatical sentences in a language.

Although his concerns were based on very different problems than the ones in (1–3), Chomsky (1957) observed that a phrase structure grammar (such as X-bar theory) cannot generate all the sentences of a language. He proposed that what was needed was a set of rules that change the structure generated by phrase structure rules. These rules are called **transformational rules**. Transformations take the output of X-bar rules (and other transformations) and change them into different trees.

The model of grammar that we are suggesting here takes the form in (4). You should read this like a flow chart. The derivation of a sentence starts at the top, and what comes out at the bottom is your judgment about the acceptability of that sentence.

4)

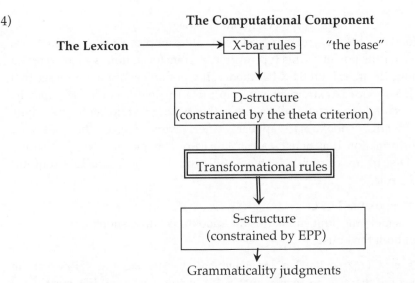

The Computational Component

X-bar theory and the lexicon conspire together to generate trees. This conspiracy is called *the base*. The result of this tree generation is a level we call *D-structure* (this used to be called Deep Structure, but for reasons that need not concern us here, the name has changed to D-structure). You will never pronounce or hear a D-structure. D-structure is also sometimes called the *underlying form* or *underlying representation* (and is similar in many ways to the underlying form found in phonology). The theta criterion filters out ungrammatical sentences at D-structure.

D-structure is then subject to the *transformational rules*. These transformational rules can move words around in the sentence. We've actually already seen one of these transformational rules. In Chapter 7, we looked briefly at T to C movement in subject-aux inversion constructions. (In this chapter, we're going to look in more detail at this rule.) The output of a transformational rule is called the *S-structure* of a sentence. The S-structure is filtered by the EPP, which ensures that the sentence has a subject. What are left are grammatical sentences.

In the version of Chomskyan grammar we are considering here, we will look at two different kinds of transformations: movement rules and insertion rules. Movement rules move things around in the sentence. Insertion rules put something new into the sentence. This chapter is about one kind of movement rule: the rules that move one head into another, called *head-to-head movement*. These transformational rules will allow us to generate sentences like (1–3) above. X-bar theory by itself cannot produce these structures.

Generative Power

Before we go any further and look at examples of transformations, consider the power of this type of rule. A transformation is a rule that can change the trees built by X-bar theory. If you think about it, you'll see that such a device is extremely powerful; in principle it could do *anything*. For example, we could allow X-bar theory to generate sentences where the word "snookums" appears after every word, then have a transformation that deletes all instances of "snookums" (iv). (v) shows the D-structure of such a sentence. (vi) would be the S-structure (output) of the rule.

iv) "snookums" ⇒ Ø
v) I snookums built snookums the snookums house snookums.
vi) I built the house.

This is a crazy rule. No language has a rule like this. However, in principle, there is no reason that rules of this kind couldn't exist if we allow transformations. We need to restrict the power of transformational rules. We do this two ways:

vii)   *Rules must have a motivation.*
viii) *You cannot write a rule that will create a violation of an output constraint.*

As we go along we will consider specific ways to constrain transformational rules so that they don't over-generate.

1. VERB MOVEMENT (V → T)

1.1 French

Let's return now to the problems we raised in the introduction to this chapter. Let's start with the sentence from French:

5) Je mange souvent des   pommes.
     I eat   often   of.the apples
     "I often eat apples."

In this sentence, an adjunct surprisingly appears between the head of VP and its complement. Compare this sentence to the English sentence in (6):

6) I often eat apples.

In the English sentence, the adjunct does not intervene between the verb and the complement. The tree for (6) would look like (7).

7)

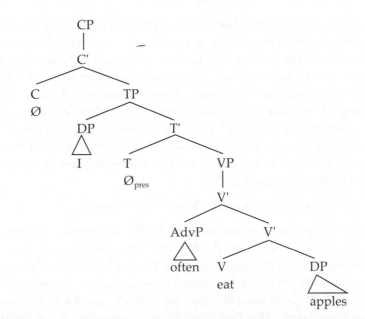

Notice the following thing about this structure. There is a head position that intervenes between the subject DP and the adverb *often*: this is the T position. T, you will recall, selects for the inflection of the verb or surfaces as an auxiliary. Notice that in French (5), the thing that appears between the subject and the adverb is not T, but the tensed main verb.

Keeping this idea in the back of your mind now consider the following chart, which shows the relative placement of the major constituents of a French sentence with a tensed main verb (b), an English sentence with a tensed verb (a), both languages with auxiliary constructions (c and d), and a modal in English (e):

8)

a)	I	$\emptyset_{pres}$	often	eat	apples
b)	Je	mange	souvent		des pommes
c)	I	have	often	eaten	apples
d)	J'	ai	souvent	mangé	des pommes
e)	I	can	often	eat	apples

There are several things to observe about this chart. Recall from chapter 2 that modals are instances of the category T; this being so, V' adjuncts are predicted to invariably follow them. This seems to be the case (e). What is striking about the above chart is that tensed auxiliaries in both languages and tensed main verbs in French also seem to occupy this slot, whereas, in English, main verbs follow the adverb.

Let's start with the differences in the placement of the main verb in the two languages. In French, the position of the main verb alternates in position relative to the adverb. In (8b), the adverb follows the main verb, and in (8d) it precedes it. How can we account for this alternation? Assume that the form has a structure that meets X-bar theory, and the same basic tree is generated for both English and French. The difference between the two is that French has a special *extra* rule that moves verbs out of the VP around the adverb and into the slot associated with T. This is the transformational rule we will call **V → T**; it is also known as *verb movement* or *verb raising*. This rule is informally stated in (9):

9)   *V → T movement:* Move the head V to the head T.

Before looking at an example, consider for a moment why this rule might apply. There is a logic to why this rule would apply. The verb bearing the tense inflection in (8b) ends up in the T (tense) node. By contrast in (8d), the main verb doesn't bear tense inflection, so it doesn't raise into the T node.

Let's do a derivation for the French sentence *Je mange souvent des pommes* (8b). The first step in the derivation is to build an X-bar structure and insert all the words. This gives us the D-structure of the sentence:

10)

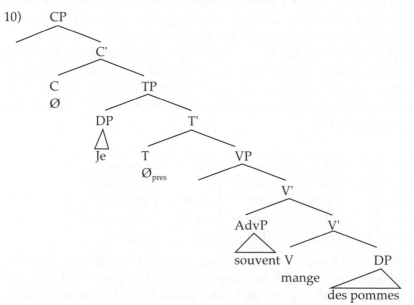

Notice that this D-structure is not a grammatical sentence of French (yet). In fact it has exactly the same word order as the English sentence in (6).

The next step in the derivation is to apply the transformation of verb movement. One typical way of representing a movement transformation is to draw an arrow starting in the D-structure position of the moved element and ending in the S-structure position.

11)

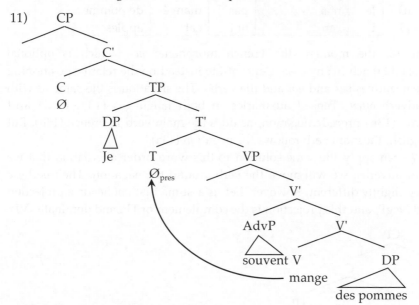

This results in the correct S-structure string:

12) Je mange$_i$ souvent t_i des pommes.

The t_i in (12) stands for "trace" and sits at the D-structure position of the verb. By doing this movement transformation we end up with the order that was not predicted by X-bar theory, and at the same time can maintain the strong hypothesis that X-bar theory is an important part of how sentences are put together. What is critical for this strong claim to be true, is the fact that *mange/mangé* alternates in position between (8b) and (8d). The participle form in (8d) is in exactly the same position as all main verbs in English. The fact that the verb appears in the pre-adverb T node position precisely and *only* when it is tensed has the air of an explanation.

What we have seen so far is a rather technical solution to a relatively small problem. Now I'm going to show you that this solution can be extended. Recall our chart with adverb above in (8). Consider now the same chart, but with negatives:

13)

a)	I	do	not	eat	apples
b)	Je	ne-mange	pas		de pommes
c)	I	have	not	eaten	apples
d)	Je	n'ai	pas	mangé	de pommes
e)	I	can	not	eat	apples

Ignore for the moment the French morpheme *ne-*, which is optional in spoken French in any case. Concentrate instead on the relative positioning of the negatives *pas* and *not* and the verbs. The situation is the same as with the adverb *often*. Tensed auxiliaries in both languages (13a, c, d) and modals (13e) precede negation, as does the main verb in French (13b). But in English, the main verb follows the negation (13a).[1]

We can apply the same solution to this word order alternation that we did for adverbs: we will move the verb around the negation. The tree here will be slightly different, however. Let us assume that *not* heads a projection called NegP, and this projection is the complement of TP, and dominates VP.

14)

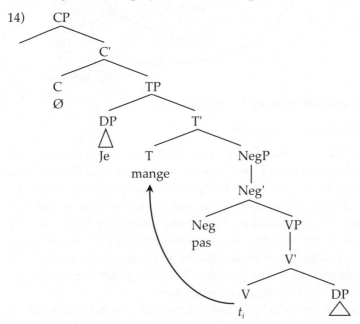

The transformation of verb movement then raises the verb around *pas* as represented by the arrow in (14).[2] Again this derives the correct word order.

---

[1] For the moment, ignore the *do* verb. We will return to this below.

[2] An alternative to this is often found in the literature. In this alternative *ne-* heads the NegP and *pas* is in the specifier of NegP. The verb raises and stops off at the Neg

With a little tweaking, V → T movement also explains tensed auxiliary movement in English and French. Tensed French auxiliaries appear in the same position as tensed main verbs, before negation and before adverbs (8d and 13d). So it appears as if there is verb movement in English too, but only with tensed auxiliaries.

15)

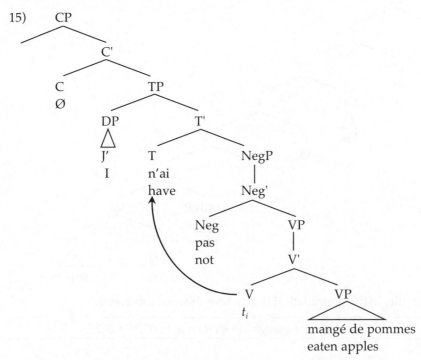

The critical question then becomes why don't tensed main verbs in English move? Tensed auxiliaries do. Tensed main verbs in French do. V → T movement takes tensed Vs and moves them into the T node. Why would tensed English main verbs be different? One solution is to appeal to parameters. Let's claim that all languages have some version of this rule, but they differ in how they implement it. Some set the parameter so that all Vs move to T, while others set it such that only auxiliaries raise.

16) *Verb movement parameter:* All verbs raise (French) *or* only auxiliaries raise (English)

This provides a simple account of the difference between English and French adverbial and negation placement.

---

head (picking up *ne-* on the way) and then moves up to T. This alternative was presented in Pollock (1989).

Consider now the related derivation for the English sentence *He often eats apples*. The D-structure is the same as the French example, except there is the null tense node $\emptyset_{pres}$ that requires that the embedded VP be headed by a verb that is preterite in form. There is no verb raising because of (16).

17)

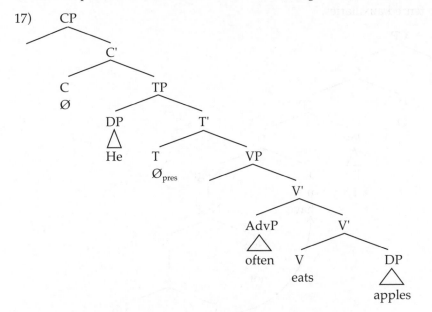

This results in the grammatical S-structure: *He often eats apples*.

You now have enough information to try GPS 1 & 2.

1.2 Vata

Observe that the alternation in position between an auxiliary and a tensed verb is not limited to French. Many (if not most) languages show this same alternation. Take for example the language Vata, a Kru language of West Africa. The underlying word order of Vata is SOV (data from Koopman 1984).

18) a)   A   la   saka li.
         we   have   rice eaten
         "We have eaten rice."

   b)   A   li   saka.
        we   eat   rice
        "We eat rice."

In the sentence with the overt auxiliary, the verb appears to the far right. When there is no auxiliary, the verb appears in the structural slot otherwise occupied by the auxiliary. This alternation can be attributed to V → T movement. When there is an auxiliary (*la*), the verb is untensed so it remains in its base generated position (19).

19)

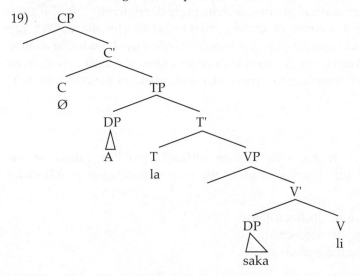

When there is no auxiliary, the verb is tensed and it raises around the object to T:

20)

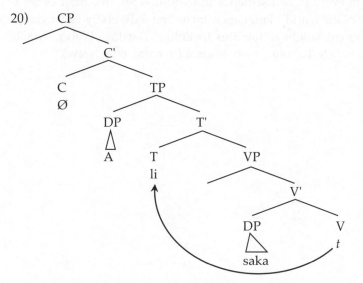

This, of course, is the correct word order (*A li saka*).

The transformational rule of V → T movement thus provides a simple, elegant and motivated account of cases where the verb shows up in the "wrong" position. The motivation for the verb to move is intuitive: the need for the verb to get its inflection. This seems to correlate with the fact that in many languages there are positional alternations where auxiliaries (T) and tensed verbs alternate and are in complementary distribution. This also gives a straightforward account of certain cross-linguistic differences. We can account for the fact that English and French consistently differ in the relative placement of adverbs and negation with respect to tensed verbs. We derived this difference by appealing to a parameter that either has the verb raise to T, or not.

1.3 Irish

Now we'll turn to the other (more difficult) problem raised in the introduction to this chapter. This is the verb-subject-object (VSO) order of Irish.

21) Phóg   Máire an lucharachán.
    Kissed Mary the leprechaun
    "Mary kissed the leprechaun."

As we observed above, there is no way that X-bar theory can generate a sentence of this type. This is true of every basic sentence in Irish. VSO order is found in every tensed sentence in Irish. It is also the basic order of about 9 percent of the world's languages, including a diversity of languages from many different language families including Tagalog, Welsh, Arabic, Mixtec, Mayan, Salish, Turkana, and Maasai (to name only a few).

Digression on Flat Structure

Up until the early 1980s, most linguists considered VSO languages to simply be exceptions to X-bar theory. They proposed that these languages had a **flat structure**:

i)

This structure is called "flat" because there are no hierarchical differences between the subject, the object, and the verb. In other words, there are no structural distinctions between complements, adjuncts, and specifiers. These sentences don't have a VP constituent. In (i) there is no single node dominating both the V and the second DP, but excluding the subject DP.

There is a delicate balance between a theory that is empirically adequate (one that accounts for all the data), like a theory that has *both* flat structure languages and X-bar languages, and one that is explanatorily adequate and elegant (like pure X-bar theory). By claiming that these languages were exceptions, linguists were left with a considerably less elegant theory. Thus the race was on to see if there was some way to incorporate these languages into X-bar theory. Notice, however, that pure elegance alone is not sufficient cause to abandon an empirically adequate but inelegant theory like flat structure – we must also have empirical evidence (data) in favor of the elegant theory.

Flat structure makes the following predications:

a) There is no VP constituent.
b) There is no evidence for a hierarchical distinction between subjects and objects – they both have the same mother and mutually c-command one another.

It turns out that both these predications are wrong. First, if VSO languages have no VP in simple tensed clauses, they should have no VPs in other clause types either. McCloskey (1983) observed for Irish, and Sproat (1985) for Welsh, that this is false.

ii) Tá Máire [ag-pógail an lucharachán].
    Is Mary   ing-kiss the leprechaun
    "Mary is kissing the leprechaun."

In auxiliary sentences in Irish, there is a plausible candidate for a VP: the words bracketed in (ii). If this V + O sequence is a constituent, it should obey constituency tests. Two typical constituency tests from chapter 3, coordination and movement (clefting), show this:

iii) Tá Máire [ag-pógail an lucharachán] agus [ag-goidú a ór].
    Is Mary [ing-kiss the leprechaun] and   [ing-steal his gold]
    "Mary is kissing the leprechaun and stealing his gold."

iv) Is [ag-pógáil an lucharachán] atá Máire.
    It-is [ing-kiss the leprechaun] that.be Mary
    "It's kissing the leprechaun that Mary is."

These sentences show that the bracketed [V + O] sequence in (ii) is indeed a constituent, and a plausible VP.

Now, turn to the second prediction made by flat structure, where all the DPs are on a par hierarchically. This too we can show is false. Recall from chapter 5 that there is at least one phenomenon sensitive to hierarchical position: the distribution of anaphors. Recall that the antecedent of an anaphor must c-command it. If flat structure is correct, then you should be able to have either DP be the antecedent and either DP be the anaphor, since they mutually c-command one another (they are sisters):

v)

The data in (vi) and (vii) show that this is false. Only the object DP can be an anaphor. This means that the object must be c-commanded by the subject. Further, it shows that the subject cannot be c-commanded by the object. Flat structure simply can't account for this.

vi) Chonaic Síle$_i$ í-fein$_i$.
    Saw   Sheila her-self
    "Sheila saw herself."

vii) *Chonaic   í-fein$_i$ Síle$_i$.
     Saw   her-self Sheila
     "Sheila saw herself."

The flat structure approach, if you'll pardon the pun, comes up flat. It makes the wrong predictions. The verb-raising approach proposed in the main text doesn't suffer from these problems. It maintains X-bar theory so has both a VP and a hierarchical distinction between subjects and objects.

You now have enough information to try GPS 3.

The failure of X-bar theory to account for 9 percent of the world's languages is a significant one! However, the theory of transformations gives us an easy out to this problem. If we assume that VSO languages are underlyingly SVO (at D-structure), then a transformational rule applies that derives the initial order.

22) SVO ⇒ VSO

How might we actually structurally implement this rule? Given the discussion in section 1.1 above, the answer should be obvious: we can use verb movement.

There is some straightforward evidence in favor of a verb movement approach to Irish word order: First, we see the same type of positional auxiliary/tensed verb word order alternations that we saw in French.

23) Tá Máire ag-pógáil an lúcharachán.
   Is Mary ing-kiss   the leprechaun
   "Mary is kissing the leprechaun."

24) Phóg Máire an lúcharachán.
   kissed Mary the leprechaun
   "Mary kissed the leprechaun."

As in the French and Vata cases, with respect to a certain position (in Irish the initial position), auxiliaries and main verbs are in complementary distribution. This is evidence for V → T movement.

   Unfortunately the situation here is not as straightforward as the French and Vata cases. If we try to draw the tree for (24) we immediately run into a problem. While moving the verb to T certainly accounts for the alternation between verbs and auxiliaries, it does not derive the correct VSO word order. Instead we still get incorrect SVO order (25). In all the sentences of Irish we've looked at, T (in the form of either an auxiliary or a raised tensed verb) seems to precede its specifier (the subject). One possibility to resolve this might be in exercising the parameters we looked at in chapter 6. So we might try putting the specifier of TP to the right in Irish (26). But this doesn't work – if you look carefully at the order of elements in (26) you'll see this results in VOS order, which is completely ungrammatical in Irish (27)

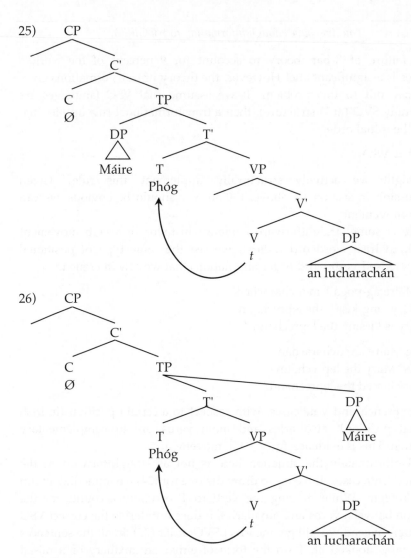

25)

26)

27) *Phóg an lucharachán Máire.
    kissed the leprechaun Mary
    (ungrammatical with the reading "Mary kissed the leprechaun.")

So X-bar parameters clearly aren't the solution. The only alternative is to claim that we've been generating external arguments in the wrong position. That is, external arguments are not generated in the specifier of TP, like we have been assuming. Instead, they are *underlyingly* generated lower in the tree.

Consider the English auxiliary V be_{pass} we introduced in the last chapter. As we'll discuss at length in chapter 11, passive verbs lack external arguments. The presence or absence of arguments that typically become subjects is directly correlated with the presence or absence of be_{pass}, a category that is very low in the tree. Recall that passive is a kind of voice. Perhaps it's the case that all sentences have a voice head in them. It is just that in English active forms are null. In other languages (such as many Austronesian languages like Tagalog) active voice can be morphologically expressed. To put some teeth to this claim then, we might propose that external arguments in actives are in fact generated in the specifier of a null active V head low in the tree:

28)

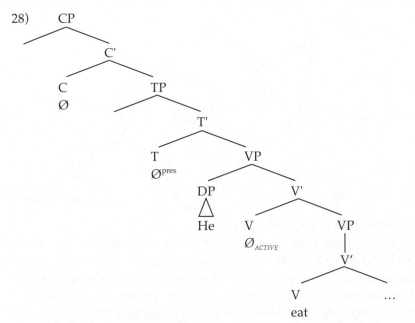

When there is a passive, nothing is generated in the specifier of this VP. We'll argue more carefully that subjects are generated in this position in chapter 14. For the moment, just note that this is not an unreasonable interpretation of what the VP headed by voice might do. It either introduces or suppresses the external theta role. The idea that subjects are generated in the specifier of a VP is called the **VP-internal subject hypothesis**, and was first proposed by Hilda Koopman and Dominique Sportiche (1991).[3]

---

[3] To be entirely accurate, Koopman and Sportiche's claim was that the subject was introduced as the specifier of the main VP. The reinterpretation of this claim where

If we assume the VP-internal subject hypothesis, the derivation of VSO order is trivial: It involves a straightforward instance of V → T movement (29):

29)

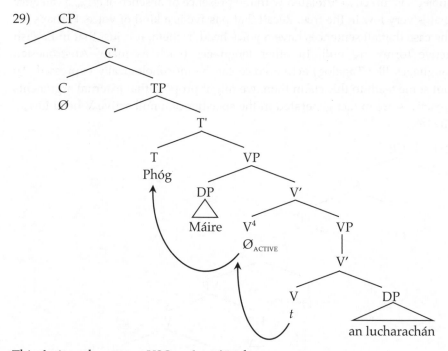

This derives the correct VSO order of Irish.

Now at this point your head is probably spinning and you are saying to yourself "Hold on, what about English, French, and Vata! In all those languages the subject precedes T." Alas, this is true. The solution to the conundrum lies easily within our grasp, however. Perhaps it is the case that in English, French, and Vata (but not the VSO languages) subject DPs *move* from the specifier of the VP to the specifier of TP. A simple French sentence then would have two movements: one for the verb, one for the subject.

---

the external argument is the specifier of the voice-headed VP came in the mid 1990s, especially in the work of Angelika Kratzer.

[4] We haven't yet discussed the extra little hop of the verb into the V_{ACTIVE} head here. This is motivated by a constraint we'll learn about in chapter 13 called the Minimal Link Condition (MLC). Although we haven't discussed it yet, I'm going to include it in the trees in this chapter and the next so that you get used to seeing the extra arrow.

30)

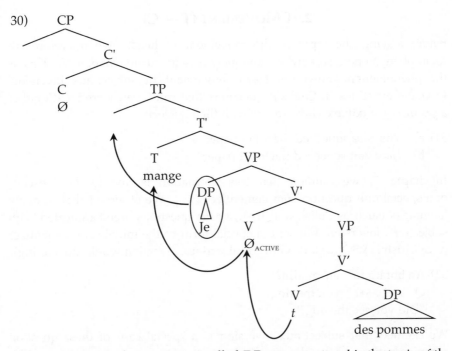

This second kind of movement is called ***DP movement*** and is the topic of the next chapter, where we'll discuss further evidence for VP-internal subjects. The correct formulation and motivations for DP movement are set out there.

You now have enough information to try GPS 4 & 5 and CPS 1.

Let us summarize the (quite complicated) discussion up to now. In section 0, we saw that there are instances where X-bar rules fail to generate the correct orders of sentences. To solve this problem, we looked at a new rule type: the transformation. Transformations take a structure generated by X-bar theory and change it in restricted ways. We've looked at one such transformation: V → T. This rule has the function of moving a verb to the T head. It does so in order that the verb can support inflection. A language is parameterized as to whether it takes the raising or not. The difference in word order between French and English negatives and sentences with adverbials can be boiled down to this parameter. The rule of verb movement itself can explain the fact that an adjunct (the adverb) appears between a head and its complement. Taken together with the VP-internal subject hypothesis, verb movement can also explain the very problematic basic VSO word order. This simple straightforward tool thus allows us to account for a very wide range of complicated facts.

2. T MOVEMENT (T → C)

Before leaving the topic of the movement of heads, we briefly return to a phenomenon somewhat obliquely discussed in chapter 7. This is the phenomenon known as *T → C* movement or subject-aux inversion. In *yes/no* questions in English (questions that can be answered with either a *yes* or *no*), auxiliary verbs invert with their subject:

31) a)   You *have* squeezed the toilet paper.
    b)   *Have* you squeezed the toilet paper?

In chapter 7, we claimed that this alternation is due to the presence of a special null question complementizer $\emptyset_{[+Q]}$. We observed that in many languages (such as Polish and Irish) *yes/no* questions aren't indicated with subject-aux inversion, but with a special form of the initial complementizer (recall Irish is VSO to start with, so subject-aux inversion would do nothing):

32) An bhfaca tú   an madra?
    Q see.PAST   you the dog
    "Did you see the dog?"

We claimed that subject-aux inversion is a special case of these question complementizers. English doesn't have an overt (pronounced) question complementizer like the Irish *an*. Instead, English has a null $\emptyset_{[+Q]}$ complementizer. Being phonologically null, however, is a bit of a problem, since the difference in meaning between a statement and a question is encoded in something you can't hear. English employs a mechanism (which we now know is a transformation) that gives phonological content to that $\emptyset_{[+Q]}$ by moving T to it, *around the subject*:

33)

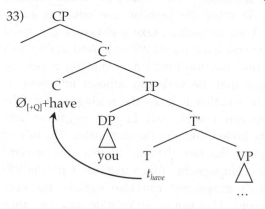

VSO as Raising to C?

In the previous section we claimed that Irish VSO order involves raising the verb to T. We were also forced to claim that subjects were generated VP-internally. Notice that in English, we also have a VS order, found in yes/no questions. These VS orders we analyze as T → C movement, with the subject remaining in its more typical place in the specifier of TP. Why don't we analyze Irish VSO order the same way? Instead of having VP-internal subjects, why don't we simply have verbs raise to T, then do T → C in *all* Irish clauses? This too would derive VSO order. There is a very good reason for this. Recall that in English T → C movement is blocked when there is an overt complementizer. (You don't move T into the C, because it already has phonological content.) If Irish VSO really involves raising to C, then it should be the case that you do *not* get VSO order when there is an overt complementizer. This is false. You get VSO order even when there is a complementizer.

i)   Duirt mé gur *phóg* **Máire** an lucharachán.
     Said I that kissed Mary the leprechaun
     "I said that Mary kissed the leprechaun."

This means that VSO must result from movement of the verb to some position lower than the complementizer. This is the analysis we argued for above, where V raises to T, and the subject is in the specifier of VP.

This kind of analysis is supported by the fact subject-aux inversion (T → C) is in strict complementary distribution with overt question complementizers as seen in the following embedded clauses:

34) a)   I asked *have* you squeezed the toilet paper.[5]
    b)   I asked whether you *have* squeezed the toilet paper.
    c)   *I asked whether *have* you squeezed the toilet paper.

So the process of subject-aux inversion must be a property triggered by complementizers. This rule is very similar to the rule of V → T movement. It is triggered by morphophonological requirements (such as the fact that something contentful must be pronounced, or that an affix needs a host).

---

[5] For many people this sentence is not grammatical unless the embedded clause is a direct quote. (That is, it would properly be written with " " around it.) This fact muddies the waters somewhat in this argument, as it may not be the case that T → C movement is allowed at all in embedded clauses in English. However, the same facts do hold true in other languages, where subject-aux inversion in embedded clauses is more clearly instantiated.

Both movements are instances of moving one head into another, so are considered instances of the same basic operation: ***head-to-head movement.*** This is a cover term for both V → T and T → C.

It appears as if V → T and T → C interact. In English, only auxiliaries ever occupy the T head as free-standing entities. Main verbs do not raise to T in English. So only auxiliaries undergo T → C movement. Main verbs never do:

35) a)   Have you squeezed the toilet paper?
    b)   *Squeezed you the toilet paper?

Contrast this to French. In French, main verbs undergo V → T movement. This means that when French does T → C movement, main verbs are predicted to also invert (because they are in T). This can be seen in the following tree:

36)

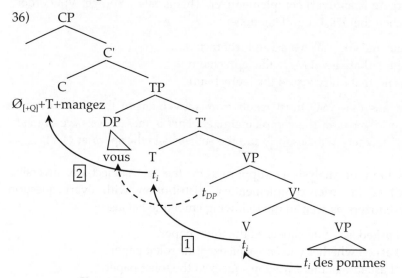

Movement ⊡ is V → T movement. Movement ⊡ is subsequent movement of the verb (in T) to C as part of T → C movement.

This prediction is borne out. Main verbs in French do invert in questions, but English main verbs do not.

37) a)   Mangez-vous des pommes?
    b)   *Eat you the apples?

To summarize, we have looked (again) at the transformation of T → C movement in more detail. We saw that it has a phonological motivation, and is similar in some ways to V → T movement. We also noticed that in a language (such as French) where V → T movement applies, main verbs as well as auxiliary verbs undergo T → C.

You now have enough information to try WBE 1–4, GPS 6–8, and CPS 2–5.

3. *DO*-SUPPORT

In English, an interesting effect emerges when we try to question a sentence with no auxiliary:

38) a)   You eat apples.
    b)   Do you eat apples?

In sentences with no auxiliary, we insert a dummy (= meaningless) auxiliary in *yes/no* questions. There must be a reason for this. We have argued that in English, main verbs do not raise to T. At the same time in questions, the transformation of T → C movement forces the same T to raise. This is a contradiction: T has to raise to C, but there is nothing in it, because unlike sentences with auxiliaries, nothing has raised to this position. The phenomenon of *do*-support appears to be an escape hatch for T. If we insert a dummy (contentless) auxiliary to fill T, then this dummy can undergo T → C movement. This is **do-*support*:**

39) Do-*support*: When there is no other option for supporting inflectional affixes, insert the dummy verb *do* into T.

This rule applies only in the case that there is nothing else you can do. They are, in essence, operations of **last resort**. You only apply them when you absolutely have to and when no movement transformation can apply.

As we discussed in the last chapter, *do*-support doesn't apply only in questions; it also shows up in negative sentences.

40) a)   I ate the apple.
    b)   I didn't eat the apple.

The analysis we gave in the last chapter explains this fact. $\emptyset_{past}$ and $\emptyset_{pres}$ don't select for NegP. The T category in English that selects for NegP is the do_{neg} form.

You now have enough information to do WBE 5 & 6 and GPS 9.

Why Don't Negative Auxiliary Constructions Use *Do*-support?

There is a problem with the claim that do_{neg} is the T category that selects for NegP. In sentences like *Otto is not eating*, we've claimed that the underlying structure is something along the lines of *Otto $\emptyset_{pres}$ not is eating*. This structure then has the rule of V → T raising, which applies to tensed auxiliaries like *is*. If the analysis we've given is correct, then we actually predict – incorrectly – that the negative form of an auxiliary construction would be **Otto did not be eating*. Clearly something extra is going on in sentences with tensed auxiliaries such that they don't allow *do*-support. Can you think of a solution to this problem?

APPENDIX: TESTS FOR DETERMINING IF A LANGUAGE HAS MAIN VERB V → T OR NOT

The following are tests that you can use to determine if a particular language shows main verb V → T or not. These tests work well on SVO languages, but don't work with SOV languages (such as Japanese).

A)   If the language shows Subj V *often* O order then it has main verb V → T.

         If the language shows Subj *often* V O order then it does not.

B)   If the language shows Subj V *not* O order then it has V → T.

         If the language shows Subj *not* V O order then it does not.

C)   If main verbs undergo T → C movement, then the language has V → T.

IDEAS, RULES, AND CONSTRAINTS INTRODUCED IN THIS CHAPTER

i)   *Transformation*: A rule that takes an X-bar-generated structure and changes it in restricted ways.

ii)   *D-structure*: The level of the derivation created by the base. No transformations have yet applied.

iii)   *S-structure*: The output of transformations. The form you perform judgments on.

iv)   *V → T Movement*: Move the head V to the head T (motivated by morphology).

v)   *Verb Movement Parameter*: All verbs raise (French) *or* only auxiliaries raise (English).

vi)   *The VP-internal Subject Hypothesis*: Subjects are generated in the specifier of the voice-headed VP.

vii)   *T → C Movement*: Move T to C when there is a phonologically empty $\emptyset_{[+Q]}$ complementizer.

viii)   **Do-*support***: When there is no other option for supporting inflectional affixes, insert the dummy verb *do* into T.

FURTHER READING: Carnie and Guilfoyle (2000), Emonds (1980), Koopman (1984), Koopman and Sportiche (1991), Lightfoot and Hornstein (1994), McCloskey (1983, 1991), Ritter (1988)

GENERAL PROBLEM SETS

GPS1. ITALIAN
[Data Analysis; Basic]
Consider the following data from Italian. Assume *non* is like French *ne*- and is irrelevant to the discussion. Concentrate instead on the positioning of the word *più*, "anymore". (Data from Belletti 1994.)

a) Gianni non ha più parlato.
    Gianni *non* has anymore spoken
    "Gianni does not speak anymore."

b) Gianni non parla più.
    Gianni *non* speaks anymore
    "Gianni speaks no more."

On the basis of this very limited data, is Italian a verb-raising language or not?

GPS2. HAITIAN CREOLE VERB PLACEMENT
[Data Analysis; Basic]
Consider the following sentences from Haitian Creole. Is Creole a verb-raising language or not? Explain your answer. (Data from DeGraff 2005.)

a) Bouki deja   konnen Boukinèt
    Bouki already knows   Boukinèt   *no*
    "Bouki already knows Boukinèt."

b) Bouki pa   konnen Boukinèt
    Bouki NEG knows Boukinèt   *yes*
    "Bouki doesn't know Boukinèt."

GPS3. FLAT VS. HIERARCHICAL STRUCTURE: BERBER

[Data Analysis; Advanced]
Part 1: Consider the data in (a) from Berber. (Data from Choe 1987.)

a) Yutut   wrba$_k$ *ixfnns$_k$*
    hit   boy-NOM$_k$ himself$_k$
    "The boy$_k$ hit himself$_k$."

Look carefully at this sentence then consider two different analyses:

    (i)   *Flat structure:*

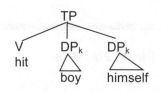

    (ii)   *An analysis that has a VP, a VP-internal subject, and V movement into T:*

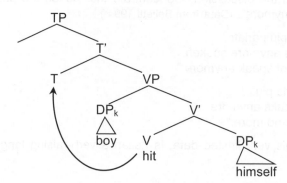

Now, keeping in mind that binding conditions hold under c-command, answer the following five questions:

1) Is Binding Condition A satisfied under hypothesis (i)?
2) Is Condition A satisfied under hypothesis (ii)?
3) Is Condition C satisfied under hypothesis (i)?
4) Is Condition C satisfied under hypothesis (ii)?
5) Given your answers to questions 1–4, does this example provide evidence for a flat structure analysis of Berber (i.e., (i)) or a VP with V movement analysis (i.e., (ii))?

Part 2 (more advanced): Now consider the ungrammatical sentence of Berber in (b). Is this ungrammaticality expected, under (i)? Under (ii)? (Be sure to consider Condition C as well as Condition A.) Does this example help us choose an analysis? Explain why or why not.

b) *Yutut   *ixfnns$_k$*   arba$_k$
   hit   himself$_k$ boy$_k$
   "Himself$_k$ hit the boy$_k$."

GPS4. WELSH
[Data Analysis; Basic]
Using the very limited data from Welsh below, construct an argument that Welsh has V to T movement. Do not worry about the alternation in the form of the word for "dragon"; it is irrelevant to the answer to the question. (Data from Kroeger 1993.)

a) Gwelodd   Siôn   ddraig.
   saw.PAST   John   dragon
   "John saw a dragon."

b) Gwnaeth   Siôn   weld   draig.
   do.PAST   John   seen   dragon.GEN
   "John saw a dragon."

GPS5. VP INTERNAL SUBJECTS: PRACTICE
[Application of Skills; Basic]
Using VP internal subjects, with movement to the specifier of TP where appropriate, and verb movement where appropriate, draw the trees for the following sentences:

a) Tiffany is not taking her syntax class until next year.
b) Christine likes wood furniture with a dark finish.

c) Les enfants n'ont pas travaillé.   (French)
   the children have not worked
   "The children haven't worked."

d) Les enfants (ne)-travaillent pas.   (French)
   the children work   not
   "The children don't work."

GPS6. AMERICAN VS. BRITISH ENGLISH VERB *HAVE*
[Critical Thinking; Basic/Intermediate]
English has two verbs *to have*. One is an auxiliary seen in sentences like (a):

a) I *have* never seen this movie.

The other indicates possession:

b) I never *have* a pen when I need it.

You will note from the position of the adverb *never* that the possessive verb *have* is a main verb, whereas the auxiliary *have* is raised to T.

Part 1: Consider the following data from American English. How does it support the idea that auxiliary *have* ends up in T, but possessive *have* is a main verb and stays downstairs (because of the verb movement parameter)?

c)   I have had a horrible day.
d)   I have never had a pencil case like that!
e)   Have you seen my backpack?
f)   *Have you a pencil?

Part 2: Consider now the following sentence, which is grammatical in some varieties of British English:

g)   Have you a pencil?

Does the possessive verb *have* in these dialects undergo V → T movement? How can you tell?

GPS7. HEBREW CONSTRUCT STATE (N → D)
[Data Analysis; Intermediate]
Background: In the text above we considered two variations on head movement: V → T and T → C. In an influential article in 1988, Ritter proposed that head movement might also apply inside DPs. More particularly she proposed that in many Semitic languages there is a rule of N → D movement. This applies in a possessive construction called the construct state. (Based on the analysis of Ritter 1988, data from Borer 1999.)

a)   beit   ha-more
     house the-teacher
     "the teacher's house"

In the construct state, the noun takes on a special form (the construct):

b)   *Free form*   bayit   "house"
     Construct   beit   "house"

Ritter proposes that the construct arises when the noun moves into the determiner. The construct morphology indicates that this noun is attached to the determiner. A tree for sentence (a) is given below. The possessor noun sits in the specifier of the NP. The possessed N head undergoes head movement to D, where it takes on the construct morphology:

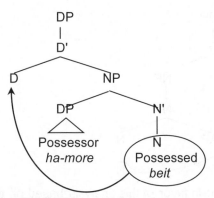

This results in the surface DP *[beit ha-more]*.

Part 1: Consider now the following evidence. How does this support Ritter's N → D analysis?

c)   *ha-beit ha-more
     the house the teacher
     "the house of the teacher"

Part 2: Now look at the positioning of adjectives. How does this support Ritter's analysis? Note in particular what noun the adjective modifies. (If you are having trouble with this question, try drawing the tree of what the whole DP would look like before N → D movement applied.) M stands for "masculine", and F stands for feminine:

d)   more   kita   xadaš
     teacher-M   class-F   new-M
     "a class's new teacher" or "a new teacher of a class"
          but: "*a new class's teacher" or "*a teacher of a new class"

GPS8. ENGLISH[6]
[Data Analysis; Intermediate]
Consider the italicized noun phrases in the following sentences:

a)   I ate *something spicy*.
b)   *Someone tall* was looking for you.
c)   I don't like *anyone smart*.
d)   I will read *anything interesting*.

One analysis that has been proposed for noun phrases like the ones above involves generating elements like *some* and *any* as determiners, and generating elements *one* and *thing* as nouns (under N), and then doing head-to-head movement of the Ns up to D. The tree below illustrates this analysis:

---

[6] Thanks to Jila Ghomeshi for contributing this problem set.

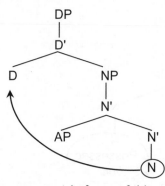

Give an argument in favor of this analysis based on the order of elements within the noun phrase in general, and the order of elements in the noun phrases above.

GPS9. ENGLISH TREES
[Application of Skills; Basic to Advanced]
Draw trees for the following English sentences; be sure to indicate all transformations with arrows.

a) I have always loved peanut butter.
b) I do not love peanut butter.
c) Martha often thinks Kim hates phonology.
d) Do you like peanut butter?
e) Have you always hated peanut butter?
f) Are you always thinking dirty thoughts?
g) Will you bring your spouse?

CHALLENGE PROBLEM SETS

CHALLENGE PROBLEM SET 1: FLOATING QUANTIFIERS
[Critical Thinking; Challenge]
In English, quantifiers normally appear before a DP. Up to this point in the book, we've been treating them as determiners. However, certain quantifiers can appear before determiners. One example is the quantifier *all*: *all the men*. In section 4 above, we argued that we can have stacked VPs. Let's extend that analysis and claim that we can have stacked DPs in certain circumstances (limited by the particular determiners involved). The structure of *all the men* is given below:

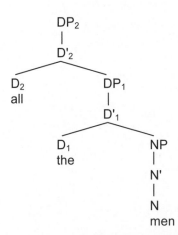

There are two DPs here (DP$_1$ and DP$_2$). In principle either of them could be moved to the specifier of TP. With this in mind provide an argument using the following data to argue that subjects in English start in the specifier of VP:

a)   All the men have gone.
b)   The men have all gone.

CHALLENGE PROBLEM SET 2: VERB MOVEMENT[7]
[Data Analysis; Challenge]

Based on the following data, do German and Persian exhibit V → T movement? Explain how you came to your answer.

German
a)   Sprechen Sie Deutsch?
     speak   you German
     "Do you speak German?"

b)   Ist er nach Hause gegangen?
     is he to   home gone
     "Has he gone home?"

c)   Er sitzt nicht auf diesem Tisch.
     he sits not on   this   table
     "He does not sit on this table."

d)   Sie soll nicht auf diesem Tisch sitzen.
     she must not on this   table sit
     "She must not sit on this table."

---

[7] Thanks to Simin Karimi for contributing this data.

Persian
a) Rafti to madrese?
    went you school
    "Did you go to school?"

b) Bâyad un biyâd?
    must   he come
    "Must he come?"

c) Man keyk na-poxtam.
    I   cake not-cooked
    "I did not bake cakes."

d) Un na-xâhad âmad.
    he not-will   come
    "He will not come."

CHALLENGE PROBLEM SET 3: GERMANIC VERB SECOND
[Data Analysis and Critical Thinking; Challenge]
Background: Many of the languages of the Germanic language family exhibit what is known as **verb second** order (also known as V2). With V2, the main restriction on word order is that, in main clauses, the constituents may appear in essentially any order, as long as the verb is in the second position in the sentence. This is seen in the following data from German:

German (Vikner 1995)
a) Die Kinder haben diesen Film gesehen.
    the children have this   film seen
    "The children have seen this film."

b) Diesen Film haben die Kinder gesehen.

One analysis of this phenomenon uses the specifier of CP as a "topic" position. The most topical constituent (the bit under discussion) is put in the specifier of CP (i.e., is moved there – we'll discuss this kind of movement in chapter 12). Whatever is in T then moves to the C head by T → C movement:

c)

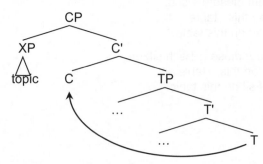

This puts T in second position. For the tree above and this problem set, assume that the VP and the TP have their heads on the right, but CP is left headed.

Part 1: Now consider the following data from embedded clauses in German.

d) Er sagt, [daß die Kinder diesen Film gesehen haben].
    He said that the children this film seen   have
    "He said that the children saw this film."

e) *Er sagt, [daß die Kinder haben diesen Film gesehen].

How does this data support the T → C analysis of V2? (Having trouble? Think about embedded *yes/no* questions in English.)

Part 2: Consider now the following sentence of German and compare it to the embedded clauses in part 1 above.

f) Gestern sahen die Kinder den Film.
    Yesterday saw the children the film
    "The children saw the film yesterday."

Given what you now know about V2 and T → C movement in these languages, is German a V → T raising language or not?

Bonus: Is the data in part 1 above consistent with your answer? If not, how might you make it consistent?

CHALLENGE PROBLEM SET 4: PROPER NAMES AND PRONOUNS
[Data Analysis; Challenge]
Consider the following data from English:

a) Lucy
b) *The Lucy
c) *Smiths
d) The Smiths
e) Him
f) *The him
g) We linguists love a good debate over grammar.

Part 1: One possible analysis of proper names in English is that they involve head movement from an N position into a D position. How does the data in (a–d) above support this idea?

Part 2: Consider now the pronouns in (e–g). What category are they? N or D? Is there any evidence for movement?

CHALLENGE PROBLEM SET 5: ITALIAN N → D[8]
[Data Analysis and Critical Thinking; Challenge]
(You may want to do Challenge Problem Set 4 before attempting this problem.)
In English, proper names cannot co-occur with determiners (e.g. *the John*). However, in Italian, proper names of human beings *can* occur with determiners, as the following example shows. (The presence or absence of the determiner seems to be free or perhaps stylistically governed.)

a) i)   Gianni   mi   ha   telefonato.
         Gianni   me   has   telephoned
         "Gianni called me up."

    ii) Il   Gianni   mi   ha   telefonato.
         the Gianni   me   has   telephoned
         "Gianni called me up."

Now, it has been argued that in the cases where the determiner does *not* occur, the proper name has moved from N to D. Provide an argument to support this view, based on the following examples. (Note: for the purposes of this question treat possessive pronouns such as *my* as adjectives.)

b) i)   Il   mio   Gianni ha   finalmente   telefonato.
         the   my   Gianni has   finally   telephoned

    ii) *Mio   Gianni   ha   finalmente   telefonato.
         my   Gianni   has   finally   telephoned

    iii) Gianni mio   ha   finalmente   telefonato.
         Gianni my   has   finally   telephoned

c) i)   E' venuto   il   vecchio   Cameresi.
         came   the   older   Cameresi

    ii) *E' venuto   vecchio   Cameresi.
         came   older   Cameresi

    iii) E' venuto   Cameresi   vecchio.
         came   Cameresi   older

d) i)   L'   antica   Roma
         the ancient   Rome
         "Ancient Rome"

    ii) *Antica   Roma
         ancient   Rome

    iii) Roma   antica
         Rome   ancient

---

[8] Jila Ghomeshi contributed this problem set based on data from Longobardi (1994).

DP Movement

Learning Objectives

After reading chapter 11 you should walk away having mastered the following ideas and skills:

1. Draw the theta grids of raising predicates like *is likely* and *seem*.
2. Draw trees indicating DP movement of embedded subjects.
3. Explain how the Case filter motivates the movement of NPs out of infinitival clauses into main clauses.
4. Describe how the passive voice head affects the introduction of external arguments and Case assignment by verbs.
5. Show passive DP movement in a tree.

0. INTRODUCTION

In the last chapter, we looked at how certain basic word order facts could not be generated by X-bar theory alone. Instead, we saw that we need another rule type: the transformation. Transformations take X-bar trees and move elements around in them. The kind of transformation we looked at in chapter 10 moved heads into other heads. In this chapter, we are going to look at transformations that move DPs.

Unlike head-to-head movement, where movement is motivated by word orders that cannot be generated using X-bar theory, the movement described here frequently takes X-bar-generated trees and turns them into other acceptable X-bar-generated trees. What motivates the movement is not a failure of X-bar theory, but instead the fact that certain DPs can appear in positions we don't expect given our theory of theta roles.

1. A PUZZLE FOR THE THEORY OF THETA ROLES

Try to sketch out the theta grid for the verb *to leave*. *Leave* requires one obligatory argument: an agent:

1) *leave*

Agent
DP
i

This can be seen from the following paradigm.

2) a) Bradley$_i$ left.
   b) Stacy$_i$ left Tucson.
   c) Slavko$_i$ left his wife.
   d) *It left. (where *it* is a dummy pronoun, not a thing)

The only obligatory argument for the verb *leave* is the agent, which is an external (subject) argument. Other arguments are possible (as in 2b and c) but not required. Now, note the following thing about the obligatory agent theta role. The agent role must be assigned to an argument *within the clause* that contains *leave*:

3) a) *[I want Bradley$_i$ [that left]].
   b) *John$_i$ thinks [that left].

When you try to assign the theta role to a DP that is outside the clause (such as the object *Bradley* or *John* in (3)) you get a stunningly ungrammatical sentence. Let's posit the following constraint:

4) *The Locality Constraint on Theta Role Assignment*
   Theta roles are assigned within the clause containing the predicate that introduces them (i.e., the VP or other predicate).

This constraint requires that the DP getting the theta role be local to the predicate that assigns it. In the sentences in (3) the DP is actually in a different clause than the predicate that assigns it, so (4) correctly predicts them to be ungrammatical.

Now, look at the following sentence:

5)   [John$_i$ is likely [to leave]].

John here is the agent of *leaving*, but the DP *John* appears in the main clause, far away from its predicate. Even more surprising is the fact that there seems to be no subject of the embedded clause. This is in direct violation of (4). The solution to this problem is simple: there is a transformation that takes the DP *John* and moves it from the lower clause to the higher clause.

Let's spell this out in more detail. The theta grid for *is likely* includes only one argument: the embedded clause. This is seen in the fact that it can appear as the sole theta-marked argument:

6)   a)   [[That John will leave]$_j$ is likely].
     b)   It is likely [that John will leave]$_j$.

     c)   *is likely*

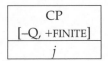

CP
[$-$Q, +FINITE]
j

If this is the case, then in sentence (5), *John* is not receiving its theta role from *is likely*. This should be obvious from the meaning of the sentence as well. There is nothing about *John* that *is likely*. Instead, it is what *John* is doing (his leaving) that *is likely*. The sentence is a clear violation of the locality condition on theta role assignment in its surface form. In chapter 8, we argued that the theta criterion applies before the transformation of expletive insertion occurs. Translated into our new terminology, this means that the theta criterion holds of D-structure. This means that theta role assignment must also happen before all transformations. We can arrange for *John*'s theta role to be assigned clause internally, at D-structure. The D-structure of the sentence would then look like (7) (theta marking is indicated with a dotted large arrow):

7)

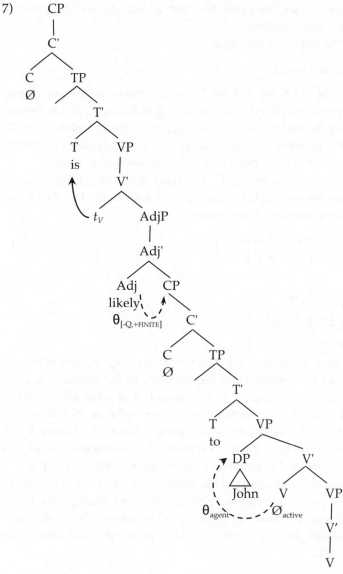

The subject DP is generated in the specifier of the embedded voice VP, where it is assigned the agent theta role.

How do we derive the surface order? We need a transformation that moves this DP to the specifier of the main clause TP. This transformation is called **DP movement**:

8) *DP Movement*
    Move a DP to a specifier position.

Notice that in the D-structure tree in (7) the specifier of the higher clause's
TP is unoccupied. We can thus move the DP *John* into that position, which
results in the tree in (9). (Note: the movement stops off in the specifier
of the embedded TP and then moves on to the higher TP; we'll discuss why
this happens in two hops shortly.)

Predicates Like *Is Likely*
In this chapter we're going to look at a number of predicates that consist
of the auxiliary *be* and an adjective such as *likely* or *obvious*, as in *It is likely
that Daphne likes crème fraîche*. A few words are in order on how to tree
this structure. In the last chapter, we argued that auxiliaries like *is* are
generated in a V and then raise to the T node. The adjective *likely* (this is
an adjective even though it ends in *-ly*, as only other adjectives, like
obvious, *eager*, *easy*, etc., can appear in this position) is the complement of
this verb. These adjectival predicates typically take a CP as a complement.
We can tree these forms as below. We'll revise this slightly in chapter 15.

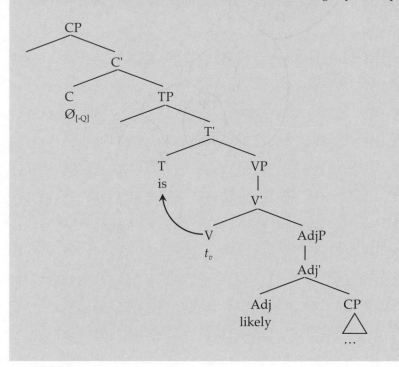

9)

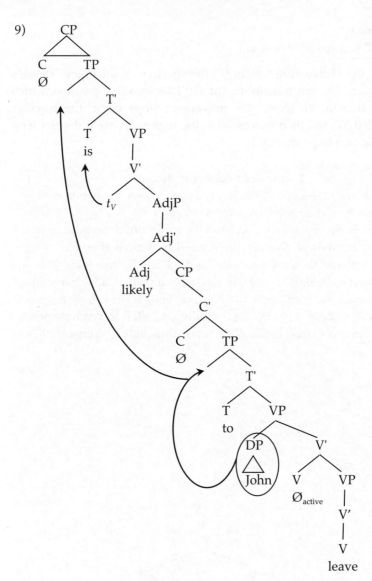

This particular instance of DP movement is frequently called *raising*, because you are raising the DP from the lower clause to the higher. The surface structure of this tree looks like (10), where there is a trace (marked *t*) left in each position that the DP has occupied.

10)

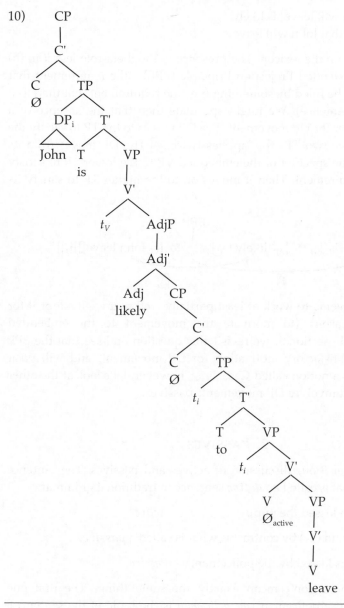

You now have enough information to try WBE 1 & 2 and GPS 1.

As we stated in the last chapter, transformations are very powerful tools, and we want to limit their use. In particular we want to ensure that they only apply when required. Transformations thus need motivations or triggers. Look at the sentences in (11).

11) a)   [That John will leave] is likely.
    b)   It is likely that John will leave.

Recall the chapter on the lexicon. The presence of the theta-role-less *it* in (b) is forced by the Extended Projection Principle (EPP) – the requirement that the specifier of TP be filled by something (i.e., the requirement that there is a subject in every sentence). We might speculate then that the absence of a subject is the trigger for DP movement. The DP moves to the TP to satisfy the EPP. Since we have two TPs this applies twice. ⒶThe DP moves from its theta position in the specifier of the embedded VP to the lower TP to satisfy this TP's EPP requirement. Then it moves on to the higher TP to satisfy its requirements Ⓑ.

12)   EPP   EPP
             \   \
       [CP [TP   T+is [VP *t*V [AP likely [CP [TP   to [VP John leave]]]]]]]
             ‿‿‿‿‿‿‿‿‿‿   ↰‿‿‿‿‿‿‿
                 Ⓑ   Ⓐ

This explanation seems to work at least partially well and we'll adopt it for theory-internal reasons (to motivate the movement to the embedded specifier) at least. In section 3, we revisit this question and see that the EPP is only a partly satisfactory motivation for DP movement, and will posit an approach using a notion called Case. First, however, let's look at the other main situation that involves DP movement: passives.

2. PASSIVES

Recall from chapter 9 our discussion of actives and passives. The sentence given in (13) is what is called an ***active*** sentence in traditional grammar:

13) The policeman kissed the puppy.   *Active*

The sentence given in (14) by contrast is what is called a ***passive***:

14) The puppy was kissed by the policeman.   *Passive*

These two sentences don't mean exactly the same thing. The first one is a sentence about a policeman (*the policeman* is the topic of the sentence); by contrast, (14) is a sentence about a puppy (*the puppy* is the topic).

However, they do describe the same basic event in the world with the same basic participants: there is some kissing going on, and the kisser (agent) is *the policeman* and the kissee (theme) is *the puppy*. At least on the surface then, these two sentences seem to involve the same thematic information. On closer examination however, things change. Notice that in the passive sentence, the agent is represented by an optional prepositional phrase headed by *by*. This is an adjunct; as discussed in the chapter on the lexicon, adjuncts are not included in the basic theta grid and are not subject to the theta criterion. If the agent here is an adjunct and not subject to the theta criterion, it should be optional. This is indeed the case:

15) The puppy was kissed.

It thus seems that passives and actives have different thematic properties. Actives have an agent and a theme, whereas passives lack the agentive theta role in their theta grids.

In chapters 9 and 10, we attributed this behavior to an auxiliary, which serves to introduce the external theta role. Up until this point, I've been a little vague as to how that exactly works. We'll break it down into a detailed account now. Consider the possibility, as extensively argued by the linguists Alec Marantz and Angelika Kratzer, that external theta roles aren't really part of the meaning of the main verb at all. The evidence for this separation of agents from the main verb comes from the behavior of phrasal idioms. Marantz noticed that while there are sentential idioms (the verb plus all the arguments as in *The pot called the kettle black*[1]) and verb+object idioms (such as *kick the bucket*[2]), there are no subject+verb idioms. Similarly, we find that while the meaning of the object can change the interpretation of the verb, as in (16), the subject never does so (17).

16) a) kill a bug   = end the life of the bug
    b) kill a conversation   = cause the conversation to end
    c) kill an evening   = while away the time span of the evening
    d) kill a bottle   = empty the bottle
    e) kill an audience   = entertain the audience

17) a) John laughed
    b) The audience laughed
    c) The manager laughed
    d) The bug laughed

---

[1] For the information of non-native English speakers: this means "to speak hypocritically".

[2] For the information of non-native English speakers: this means "to die".

Where in (17) the verb *laugh* means "laugh" no matter what the agent is, the verb kill doesn't always mean "cause death". Its meaning varies depending upon the theme. This suggests that there is a tight link between the verb and its theme that it doesn't share with its agent. If we adopt an approach where agents are introduced by the voice head, these facts follow directly: the main verb has the theme in its theta grid (18a), so it can combine in unique idiomatic ways with the theme. However the agent is never in the theta grid of the verb root. It comes from the voice element so idiomatic meanings cannot form around it.

18) a) *kiss*

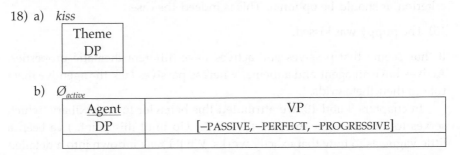

b) $\emptyset_{active}$

The passive form of the voice auxiliary, be_{pass}, has a different theta grid. It lacks the agent role, and requires that the following verb be a participle.

19) be_{pass} *(to be revised)*

VP
[−PASSIVE, −PERFECT, −PROGRESSIVE, FORM *participle*]

Now let's turn to word order in the passive and active. In the active, the theme argument appears in object position; in the passive it appears in the subject position. Let's claim that the theme is generated in the main verb's complement position in both actives and passives, but then is moved to subject position (specifier of TP) in passives. Here is a sample derivation. The D-structure of the passive sentence looks like (20). The dotted arrows in this tree represent theta (θ) assignment, not movement. Because -*en* absorbs the agent role, there is only one DP in this sentence (*the puppy*), the one that gets the theme role. Even if there is a *by* phrase (e.g., *by the policeman*), it does not get its theta role from the verb. It is an adjunct, and adjuncts are never included in theta grids. The theme is the internal argument (i.e., it is not underlined in the theta grid), so it does not appear in the specifier of the VP. It must appear as the complement, like other internal theta roles.

20)

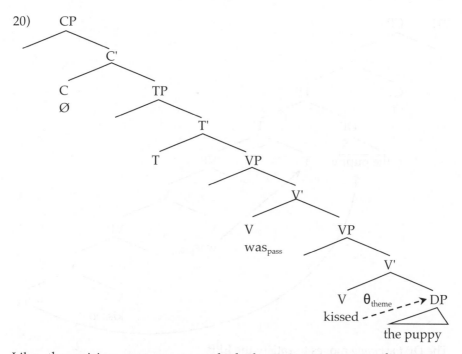

Like the raising sentences we looked at in section 1, the EPP is not satisfied here. There is nothing in the specifier of TP. The surface order of the passive is then derived by DP movement.

Transparency of Ø$_{active}$

We have one important piece of housekeeping to take care of. Consider the structure of an active perfect or progressive sentence as in (i) and (ii)

i)   She has eaten the ice cream.
ii) She is eating the ice cream.

We have just argued that there is a null V head (Ø$_{active}$) between the *have*$_{perf}$ and the main verb in (i), and another between *be*$_{prog}$ and the main verb in (ii). But note that the form of the main verb that follows *have* and *be* is what we would predict if there were no Ø$_{active}$ head in between them (a participle and a gerund, respectively). To explain this we'll just have to stipulate that the [FORM] feature requirements of verbs like *have* and *be* can see through Ø$_{active}$ as if it wasn't there. Can you come up with a better explanation? I'll provide one for you in chapter 14, when we look at AgrO, but in the short term try to think carefully about the stipulation I've made in this box.

21)

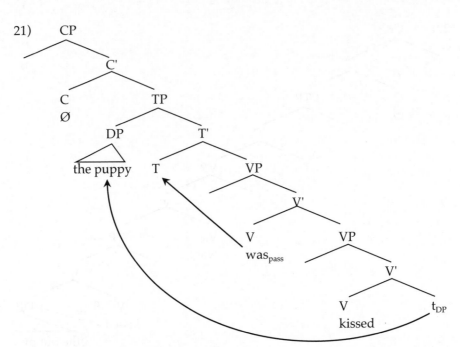

The DP *the puppy* moves to satisfy the EPP.

As mentioned above, passives often also occur with what appears to be the original external argument in a prepositional phrase marked with *by*.

22) The puppy was kissed by the policeman.

We treat these *by*-phrases as optional adjuncts. We draw these *by*-phrases in by adjoining them to V':

23)

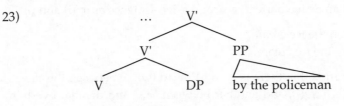

You now have enough information to try WBE 3 & 4 and GPS 2. You can also try CPS 1–3.

Movement or Underlying External Theme?

One might ask why it isn't simpler to say that the passive morpheme just deletes the agent and makes the theme an external argument in the theta grid.

i)

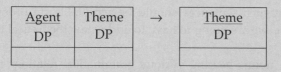

Then the D-structure of the sentence will put the theme into the subject position right from the start with no movement. This is impossible, however, if you look at passives of sentences that take clausal complements. Take the active sentence in (ii):

ii)   Wilma considers [Fredrick to be foolish].

In this sentence, *Wilma* is the experiencer of *consider*, and *Fredrick* is the external theta role of the predicate *is foolish*. When *consider* is made into a passive, the subject of the lower clause raises to become the subject of the main clause:

iii)   Fredrick$_i$ is considered t_i to be foolish.

Notice that *Fredrick* is never theta-marked by the verb *consider*. As such there is no way to make it the external argument like in (i). Because of cases like (iii), the movement account is preferred.

3. CASE

Up until this point we've motivated the movement of DPs using the EPP. In this section, we look at some data that shows that we might need an additional mechanism to account for movement.

Let's start with raising. As we saw in the last chapter, one way to satisfy the EPP is by inserting an expletive. For some reason, this option isn't available in raising environments. All other things being equal, we should be able to satisfy the EPP this way.

24) *It is likely John to leave.   (cf. *It is likely that John left*)

Nor does it explain why *only* the subject DP of an embedded clause can satisfy the EPP; an object DP may not move to satisfy this requirement:

25) *Bill$_i$ is likely John to hit t_i.

The same kind of mystery appears in passives. It isn't clear why it isn't simply permissible to satisfy the EPP by inserting an expletive:

26) *It was kissed the puppy.[3]

Our theory predicts that such sentences should be acceptable. In order to explain why they are not, we are going to have to add a new theoretical tool: *Case*.

In many languages, nouns bearing various grammatical relations take special forms. For example, in Japanese, subjects are marked with the suffix *-ga*, objects are marked with *-o* and indirect objects and certain adjuncts with *-ni*:

27) Asako-ga   ronbun-o   kai-ta.
    Asako-NOM   article-ACC wrote-PAST
    "Asako wrote the article."

28) Etsuko-ga   heya-ni   haitte-kita.
    Etsuko-NOM   room-DAT   in-came
    "Etsuko came into the room."

These suffixes represent **grammatical relations** (see chapter 4). The three most important grammatical relations are **subject**, **object**, and **indirect object**. Notice that these are *not* the same as thematic relations. Thematic relations represent meaning. Grammatical relations represent how a DP is functioning in the sentence syntactically. The morphology associated with grammatical relations is called **case**. The two cases we will be primarily concerned with here are the **nominative case**, which is found with subjects, and the **accusative case**, found with objects.

English is a morphologically poor language. In sentences with full DPs, there is no obvious case marking. Grammatical relations are represented by the position of the noun in the sentence:

29) a)   Jennifer swatted Steve.
    b)   Steve swatted Jennifer.

There is no difference in form between *Jennifer* in (29a), where the DP is functioning as a subject, and (29b), where it is functioning as an object. With pronouns, by contrast, there is a clear morphological difference, as we observed in chapter 1.

---

[3] This sentence becomes grammatical if you put a big pause after *kissed*, but notice that in this circumstance, the *it* is not a dummy, but refers to the *puppy*.

30) a) She swatted him.
    b) He swatted her.

Most pronouns in English have different forms depending upon what case they are in:

31) *Nominative*   I   you   he   she   it   we   you   they
    Accusative   me   you   him   her   it   us   you   them

Can this be extended to full DPs? Well, consider the general poverty of English morphology. The first and second persons in the present tense form of verbs don't take any overt suffix:

32) a) I walk.
    b) You walk.   (cf. He/She/It walk<u>s</u>. You walk<u>ed</u>.)

But one wouldn't want to claim that (32a and b) aren't inflected for tense. Semantically they are. These forms can only refer to the present; they can't refer to the past or the future. We are thus forced to claim that there is an unpronounced or null present tense morpheme in English. It seems reasonable to claim that if there are null tense suffixes, there are also null case suffixes in English. Indeed, in the system we are proposing here all nouns get case – we just don't see it overtly in the pronounced morphology. This is called **abstract Case**. (Abstract Case normally has a capital C to distinguish it from morphological case.)

Case, then, is a general property of language. Furthermore, it seems to be associated with a syntactic phenomenon – the grammatical functions (relations) of DPs. If it is indeed a syntactic property, then it should have a structural trigger. In the Case theory of Chomsky (1981), DPs are given Case if and only if they appear in specific positions in the sentence. In particular, nominative Case is assigned in the specifier of finite T, and accusative Case is assigned as a sister to the verb (prepositions also assign what is often called "prepositional Case" to their complement DP):[4]

33)   NOMinative Case   Specifier of finite T
       ACCusative Case   Sister to transitive V
       PREPositional Case   Assigned by a preposition

Case serves as our motivation for DP movement. You can think of Case as being like a driver's license. You can't drive without a license, and you can only get a license at the Department of Motor Vehicles. So you have to

---

[4] This is an almost ridiculous oversimplification. There are many prepositional cases (datives, locatives, ablatives, jussives, etc.). We abstract away from this here. We are also ignoring the genitive case normally associated with possessive constructions.

go there to get the license. A DP needs a license to surface in the sentence, and it can only get a license (Case) in specific positions. If it isn't in one of those positions, it must move to get Case. A DP without Case can't drive. This is called the **Case filter**:

34) *The Case Filter*
   All DPs must be marked with a Case.
   If a DP doesn't get Case the derivation will crash.

One standard way of implementing the Case filter is by using a mechanism known as **feature checking**. This is based on a notion taken from phonology. The idea is that words are composed of atomic features. A word like *he* is composed of features representing its person, its number, its gender, etc. We can represent these features in a matrix:

35) *he*
$$\begin{bmatrix} \text{masculine} \\ \text{3rd person} \\ \text{singular} \\ \text{nominative} \end{bmatrix}$$

Similarly, we will claim that Case assigners like T have a feature matrix:

36) T ($\emptyset_{pres}$)
$$\begin{bmatrix} \text{present} \\ \text{nominative} \end{bmatrix}$$

You'll notice that both of these feature matrices have a feature [nominative]. The Case filter becomes a requirement that a noun like *he* be close enough to a Case assigner like *is* to check that the noun has the right features. The noun must be close to its Case assigner:

37)   ...

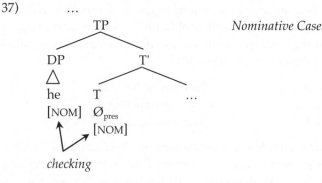

Nominative Case

checking

38)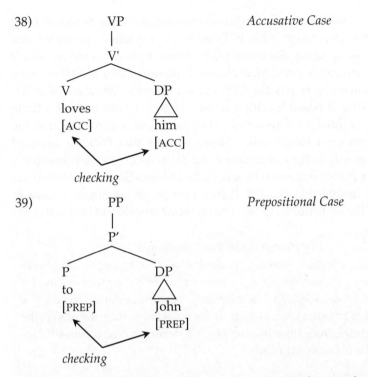

If the noun and the Case assigner are not local (that is, the noun is not in the specifier or complement of the Case assigner), then the feature won't be checked and the Case filter is violated. We'll use this notion of locality in feature checking again in chapter 12, when we look at *wh*-movement.

You now have enough information to try WBE 5 and GPS 3.

---

4. RAISING: REPRISE

Let's now return to the raising sentences we were looking at in section 1, and we'll expand the paradigm to include the following:

40) a)   It is likely that Patrick left.
    b)   That Patrick left is likely.
    c)   *Patrick is likely that t_i left.
    d)   *It is likely Patrick to leave.
    e)   *Patrick to leave is likely.
    f)   Patrick is likely t_i to leave.

Sentences (40a–c) involve a tensed (finite) embedded clause. Sentence (40a) shows that one can satisfy the EPP with an expletive, provided the embedded clause is finite. Sentence (40d) shows that an expletive won't suffice with a non-finite embedded clause. Sentences (40b) and (40e) show that a tensed clause can satisfy the EPP, but a non-finite one cannot. Finally, we see that raising is possible with a non-finite clause (40f) but not a finite one (40c). This is quite a complicated set of facts, but it turns out that the distribution turns on a single issue. Above we saw that DPs are assigned nominative Case only in the specifier of finite T. (In other words, non-finite T does not have a [NOM] feature, whereas finite T does.) Sentences (40d–f) are *non-finite*. This means that the DP *Patrick* cannot get nominative Case in the specifier of the embedded clause. The ungrammaticality of (40d and e) are

---

Ergative/Absolutive Languages

In this book, we are looking exclusively at languages that take nominative and accusative cases. These are a fairly common kind of language in the western hemisphere. In nominative/accusative languages, the same case is assigned to the subjects of transitives and the subjects of intransitives (nominative case); a different case (accusative) is assigned to the objects of transitives.

i)   *Nom/Acc languages*

	Nom	*Acc*
Trans	Subject	Object
Intrans	Subject	

However, there is a huge class of languages that do not use this case pattern, including many Polynesian, Australian, and Central American languages. These languages, called "ergative/absolutive" languages, mark the object of transitives and the subject of intransitives using the same case (absolutive); subjects of transitives are marked with a different case: ergative.

ii)   *Erg/Abs languages*

	Erg	*Abs*
Trans	Subject	Object
Intrans		Subject

From the perspective of structural Case theory, these languages are a mystery and the subject of great debate. They don't fit the theory presented here. Even more mysterious are those languages that use *both* Nom/Acc and Erg/Abs case systems (under different circumstances). This is a topic of a lot of current research in syntax now.

now explained: *Patrick* is not getting Case, so the sentence violates the Case filter. In sentence (40f) by contrast, the DP has moved to the specifier of the *finite* main clause T; it can receive Case here, so the sentence is grammatical:

41)

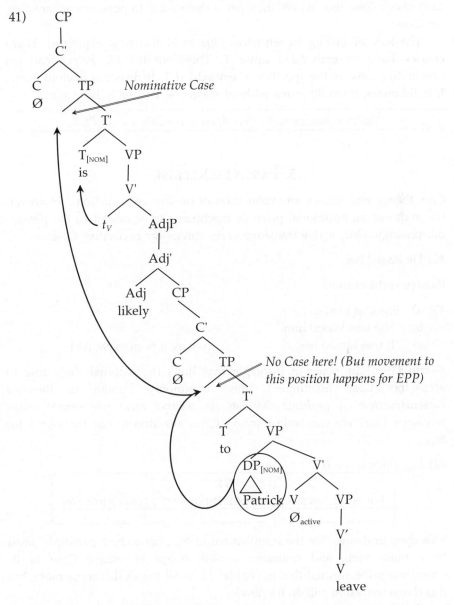

Patrick starts out where it gets its theta role (the specifier of VP), then it moves to the specifier of the embedded TP, where it satisfies the EPP for that TP. But this is not a Case position. The T *to* shows that the clause is non-finite. So the DP moves from this position to the specifier of the higher TP, where it can check its nominative Case. This is a pattern that is repeated over and over again. DPs always move from positions where they can't check Case (but where they get a theta role) to positions where they get Case.

The lack of raising in sentences (40a–c) is also now explained. These clauses have an embedded finite T. Therefore the DP *Patrick* can get nominative Case in the specifier of embedded T. It does not have to move. If it did move, it would move without reason, as it already has Case.

You now have enough information to try GPS 4 and CPS 4.

---

5. PASSIVES: REPRISE

Case theory also allows an explanation of passive constructions. However, this requires an additional piece of machinery to be added to the passive morphology. Only active transitive verbs can assign accusative Case:

42) He kissed her.

Passive verbs cannot:

43) a) She was kissed.
    b) *She was kissed him.[5]
    c) *It was kissed her.   (where *it* is an expletive)

Burzio (1986) proposed a principle that links the external theta role to accusative Case assignment (now commonly known as **Burzio's Generalization**: *A predicate that has no external theta role cannot assign accusative Case.* We can code Burzio's Generalization in our theta grid for be_{pass}.

44) be_{pass} *(to be revised)*

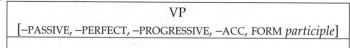

VP
[–PASSIVE, –PERFECT, –PROGRESSIVE, –ACC, FORM *participle*]

This theta grid says that the complement to be_{pass} has to be a participle, must be a main verb, and critically, cannot assign accusative Case to its complement (be warned that in chapter 15, we'll tweak this some more, but this characterization will do for now).

---

[5] This sentence is also a violation of the theta criterion.

45)   ...

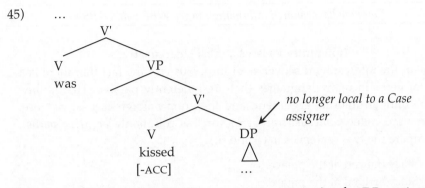

Since the participle is [–ACC], there is now no Case for the DP, so it must move to satisfy the Case filter. With this in mind, reconsider the passive sentence we looked at in section 2:

46)

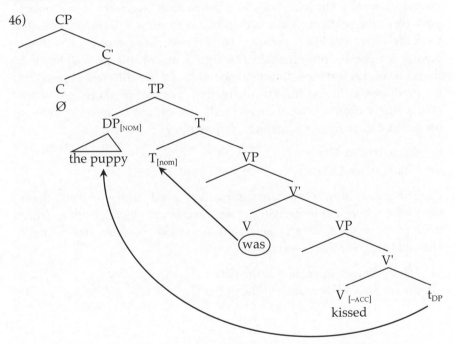

The passive morphology has conspired to absorb both the accusative Case and the external theta role. This means that there is no DP in the specifier of the finite T. There is a Case position open so the theme DP can move to the specifier of TP. Now we have the trigger for DP movement in passives: A DP moves to get Case from its Caseless theta position to the nominative Case-assigning specifier of TP. Notice that this DP now moves for two reasons. First it moves to satisfy the EPP, but it also must move to get Case.

You now have enough information to try WBE 6 and GPS 5.

Inherently Passive Verbs: Unaccusatives

One of the interesting discoveries of the 1980s was the fact that there is a set of verbs in many languages that are inherently passive. That is they have only an internal argument, and they don't assign accusative Case. These are called **unaccusative verbs** (or less commonly *ergative verbs*). Compare the two sentences in (i) and (ii)

i)   Stacy danced at the palace.
ii) Stacy arrived at the palace.

The first sentence is a regular intransitive (often called **unergative**) where *Stacy* bears an external agent theta role. The sentence in (ii) by contrast has no external theta role. *Stacy* is a theme that originates in the object position of the sentence. *Stacy* is then raised to subject position to satisfy the Case filter, just like a passive. These predicates are passive without having any passive morphology. The arguments for this are well beyond the scope of this textbook. But note the following two differences between the predicates in (i) and (ii). The unergative predicate in (i) can optionally take a direct object. Unaccusative predicates cannot (something that is predicted if their subject is underlyingly an object):

iii) Stacy danced a jig.
iv) *Stacy arrived a letter.

Unaccusatives also allow an alternative word order (called **there inversion**) where the underlying object remains in object position. Since unergative subjects aren't generated in object position, they aren't allowed to appear there with *there* inversion.

v)   *There danced three men at the palace.
vi) ?There arrived three men at the palace.

6. TYING UP A LOOSE END

In the last chapter, we were forced to argue (on the basis of evidence from the VSO language Irish) that subject DPs were generated in the specifier of the voice VP and not TP.

47) 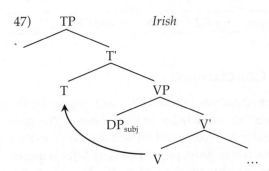 *Irish*

The problem, then, was why subject DPs appear before T in languages like English. The solution should now be clear: All subject DPs move to the specifier of finite T to get Case. In actives and intransitives, this is from the specifier of VP. In passives, the movement is from the underlying object position.

48) 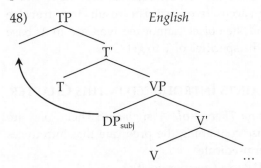 *English*

The difference between SVO languages like English and VSO languages is in where nominative Case is assigned. In SVO languages, nominative Case is assigned in the specifier of finite T. In VSO languages, nominative Case is assigned when the DP is immediately c-commanded by finite T (which allows it to remain inside VP).

49)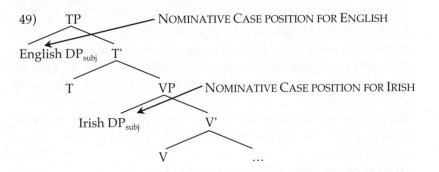

You now have enough information to try WBE 7, GPS 6–9, and CPS 5 & 6.

7. CONCLUSION

In this chapter, we've looked at situations where DPs don't appear in the positions we expect them to (given our knowledge of theta theory). We have argued that these sentences involve movement of DPs to various specifier positions. The motivation for this comes from Case. The Case filter requires all DPs to check a Case in a specific structural position. We looked at two situations where DPs don't get Case in their D-structure position. In raising structures, a DP is in the specifier of an embedded clause with non-finite T. In this position, it can't receive Case so it raises to the specifier of the finite T in the higher clause. We also looked at passive structures. The passive morpheme does two things: it takes the role of external argument and it absorbs the verb's ability to assign accusative Case. This results in a structure where there is no subject DP, and the object cannot receive Case in its base position. The DP must move to the specifier of T to get Case.

IDEAS, RULES, AND CONSTRAINTS INTRODUCED IN THIS CHAPTER

i)   *The Locality Constraint on Theta Role Assignment*: Theta roles are assigned within the clause containing the predicate that introduces them (i.e., the VP or other predicate).

ii)   *DP Movement*: Move a DP to a specifier position.

iii)   *Raising*: A specific instance of DP movement. The DP moves from the specifier of an embedded non-finite T to the specifier of a finite T in the main clause where it can get Case.

iv)   *case (lower-case c)*: The special form DPs get depending upon their place in the sentence.

v)   *Case (capital C)*: Licensing for DPs: NOM is found on the specifier of finite T. ACC is found on the complement of transitive V.

vi)   *The Case Filter*: All DPs must be marked with Case.

vii)   *Passives*: A particular verb form where the external argument (often the agent or experiencer) is suppressed and the theme appears in subject position. The movement of the theme is also an instance of DP movement.

viii)   *Burzio's Generalization*: If a verb does not have an external argument (i.e., is passive or unaccusative), then it can't assign accusative Case.

ix)   *Unaccusatives*: Inherently passive verbs like *arrive*.

Further Reading: Baker, Johnson, and Roberts (1989), Burzio (1986), Chomsky (1995), Jaeggli (1986), Perlmutter and Postal (1984), Sportiche (1988)

General Problem Sets

GPS1. Haitian Creole
[Data Analysis and Critical Thinking; Intermediate]
In the text, we suggested that DP movement leaves what is called a trace (*t*) at the D-structure position of the DP. In English, you can't hear this trace. Now consider the following data from Haitian Creole. (Data from Déprez 1992.)

a) Sanble   Jan   pati.
    seems   John   left
    "It seems that John left."

b) Jan sanble li pati.
    John seems he leave
    "John seems he to have left."

c) *Jan sanble pati.

Questions:
1) How does this data support the idea that raising constructions involve movement from the lower clause to the higher clause, and the movement leaves a trace?
2) Is sentence (b) a violation of the theta criterion? How might we make sure that it isn't?

GPS2. Arizona Tewa
[Data Analysis; Basic]
The following data is from Arizona Tewa. (Data from Kroskrity 1985.)

a) hẹ'i sen nɛ́'i 'enú mánk^{hw}ɛ́di.
    that man this boy 3.3.hit
    "That man hit this boy."

b) nɛ́'i 'enú hẹ'i sen-di   'ók^{hw}ɛ́di.
    This boy that man-DAT 3.PASS.hit
    "This boy was hit by that man."

c) na:bí k^{w}iyó hẹ'i p'o mánsunt'ó.
    my woman that water 3.3.drink
    "My wife will drink that water."

d) hẹ'i p'o   nasunti.
    that water 3.PASS.drunk
    "That water was drunk."

1) Determine the X-bar parameter settings for Tewa.
2) Draw tree for (a). Assume Tewa is does not have V ⟶ T.
3) Describe in your own words the differences between (a) and (b) and between (c) and (d).
4) Draw the tree of (d), showing all the movements.

GPS3. PERSIAN ACCUSATIVE CASE[6]
[Data Analysis and Critical Thinking; Intermediate]
In the text above, we claimed that some verbs have an accusative feature [ACC] that must get checked by a complement DP. In English, we only see the realization of this feature on pronouns. This question focuses on the [ACC] feature in Persian.

Background: Persian is an SOV language. There is no Case distinction among Persian pronouns. For example, the pronoun *man* "I, me" doesn't change whether it is a subject, object of a preposition, or possessor (see (a) below). (iii) shows that possessors are linked to head nouns with a vowel glossed as EZ (for *Ezâfe*).

a) i) *Man*   ruznâme   xarid-am.
        I   newspaper bought-1SG
        "I bought a newspaper."

   ii) *Simâ*   az   *man*   ruznâme   xâst.
        Sima   from   me   newspaper wanted.3SG
        "Sima wanted a newspaper from me."

   iii) Ruznâme-ye   *man*   injâ-st.
        newspaper-EZ me   here-is
        "My newspaper is here."

Hypothesis: It looks like the clitic *-râ* (which is pronounced as *-o* or *-ro*, depending on whether the preceding word ends in a vowel or not) is the realization of the [ACC] feature based on examples like the following:

b) i) Man   jiân-o   didam.
        I   Jian-RÂ   saw.1SG
        "I saw Jian."

   ii) *Man   jiân   did-am.
        I   Jian   saw-1SG

c) i) Jiân   man-o   did.
        Jian   I-RÂ   saw.3SG
        "Jian saw me."

   ii) *Jiân   man   did.
        Jian   I   saw.3SG

---

[6] Thanks to Jila Ghomeshi for contributing this problem set.

d) i) Jiân   in   ketâb-o   xarid.
      Jian   this   book-RÂ   bought.3SG
      "Jian bought this book."

   ii) *Jiân   in   ketâb   xarid.
       Jian   this   book   bought.3SG

One possible analysis is that Persian verbs have an [ACC] feature that gets checked by -râ. That is, -râ contributes the [ACC] feature to the DP that can be used to check the feature of the verb.

The problem: Not all direct objects show up with -râ. Yet we don't want to say that the ones without -râ don't check the [ACC] feature of the verb.

e) i) Jiân   ye ketâb   xund.
      Jian   a book   read.3SG
      "Jian read a book."

   ii) Jiân   ketâb-o   xund.
       Jian   book-RÂ   read.3SG
       "Jian read the book."

f) i) Man   se-tâ   qalam   xarid-am.
      I   three   pen   bought-1SG
      "I bought three pens."

   ii) Man   se-tâ   qalam-o   xarid-am.
       I   three   pen-RÂ   bought-1SG
       "I bought the three pens."

g) i) Jiân   pirhan   xarid.
      Jian   shirt   bought.3SG
      "Jian bought a shirt."

   ii) Jiân   pirhan-o   xarid.
       Jian   shirt-RÂ   bought.3SG
       "Jian bought the shirt."

Suggest a solution to this problem.

GPS4. TURKISH
[Data Analysis and Critical Thinking; Advanced]
In this chapter, we argued that the reason DPs raise from embedded clauses to main clauses is that they cannot get Case in the embedded clause. Consider the following data from Turkish. What problems does this cause for our theory? Is there a simple way to explain why Turkish nouns raise? (Data from Moore 1998.)

a) Biz süt   içiyoruz.
   we milk   drink
   "We are drinking milk."

b)   Biz$_i$ sana [$_{CP}$ t$_i$ süt içtik] gibi göründük.
     We you-DAT   milk drank like appear
     "We appear to you [$_{CP}$ drunk milk]."

GPS5. IMPERSONALS IN UKRAINIAN AND KANNADA
[Data Analysis; Intermediate]
(The Ukrainian and Kannada data are taken from Goodall 1993. The Ukrainian data originally comes from Sobin 1985. The Kannada data is originally from Cole and Sridhar 1976.)
Many languages contain a construction similar to the passive called *the impersonal passive*. Consider the following data from Ukrainian and Kannada. Pay careful attention to the Case marking on the various nouns.

a)   Cerkvu   bulo zbudovano v 1640 roc'i.   *Ukrainian*
     Church-ACC   was built   in 1640 year
     "The church was built in the year 1640."

b)   Rama-nannu   kollalayitu.   *Kannada*
     Rama-ACC   kill.PASS
     "Rama was killed."

What is the difference between these impersonal passive constructions and the more traditional passives of English? Suggest a parameter that will account for the difference between languages like Ukrainian and Kannada on one hand and languages like English on the other. (Hint: the parameter will have to do with the way the passive morphology works.)

GPS6. ENGLISH
[Application of Skills; Basic to Advanced]
Draw the D-structure trees for the following sentences. Be explicit about what transformations derived the S-structure tree (if any). Recall that we have the following transformations: Expletive insertion, DP movement (both raising and passive), verb movement, T → C movement, and *do*-support/insertion. Annotate the D-structure tree with arrows to show the derivation of the S-structure.

a)   Marie is likely to leave the store.
b)   The money was hidden in the drawer.
c)   Donny is likely to have been kissed by the puppy.
d)   It seems that Sonny loves Cher.
e)   Has the rice been eaten?

GPS7. ENGLISH UNGRAMMATICAL SENTENCES
[Application of Skills; Basic to Intermediate]
Explain why the following sentences are ungrammatical. Some sentences may have more than one problem with them.

a)   *It seems Sonny to love Cher.
b)   *Bill was bitten the dog.
c)   *Donny is likely that left.

GPS8. UNACCUSATIVES AND PASSIVES
[Critical Thinking; Advanced]
In a textbox above, we mentioned the existence of a class of verbs that are essentially inherently passive. These are called unaccusatives. A surprising property of unaccusative verbs is that they don't allow passivization.[7] (Data from Perlmutter and Postal 1984.)

a)   The Shah slept in a bed.
b)   The bed was slept in by the Shah.
c)   Dust fell on the bed.   *unaccusative*
d)   *The bed was fallen on by the dust. *unaccusative*

Similar effects are seen in the following Dutch sentences. Sentence (e) is not unaccusative (we call these "unergatives"), while sentence (f) is. Both these sentences are impersonal passives. English doesn't have this construction, so they are difficult to translate into English.

e)   In de zomer wordt er hier vaak gezwommen.
     "In the summer, there is swimming here."

f)   *In de zomer wordt er hier vaak verdronken.
     "In the summer, there is drowning here."

Your task is to figure out why passives of unaccusatives (like c, d, and f) are not allowed. The following data might help you:

g)   Bill was hit by the baseball.
h)   *Was been hit by Bill by the baseball. (passive of a passive)
i)   Bill gave Sue the book.
j)   Sue was given the book by Bill.
k)   *The book was been given by Bill by Sue. (passive of a passive)

GPS9. ICELANDIC QUIRKY CASE
[Data Analysis and Critical Thinking; Advanced]
In Icelandic, some verbs assign irregular case marking to particular arguments. For example, the verb *hjálpað* "help" assigns dative case to its theme argument. (Data from Zaenen, Maling, and Thráinsson 1985.)

---

[7] Strictly speaking, the data in (a–d) do not involve passivization, since the NP that is moved comes from inside a PP. The technical term for these constructions is pseudo-passivization. The differences between pseudo-passivization and passivization are not relevant to this problem set.

a) Ég hjálpaði honum.
   I helped him-DAT
   "I helped him."

This kind of irregular case marking is called **quirky Case** and it seems to be linked to the theta grid of the particular predicate. The dative case is obligatorily linked with whatever noun takes the theme role:

hjálpað "help"

Agent	Theme
DP	DP
i	K

Dative Case

Now consider the following data from Icelandic DP movement constructions.

b) Honum$_k$ var hjálpað t_K.
   him-DAT was helped
   "He was helped."

c) Ég tel honum$_k$ [t_k hafa verið hjálpað t_k í prófinu].
   I believe him-DAT have been helped in the-exam
   "I believe him [to have been helped in the exam]."

What problem does this cause for the theory of DP movement we have proposed above? Can you think of a solution? (A number of possibilities exist – be creative.)

CHALLENGE PROBLEM SETS

CHALLENGE PROBLEM SET 1: THAT DOG DOESN'T HUNT
[Critical Thinking; Challenge]
Consider the idiom: *That dog doesn't hunt* (meaning "that solution doesn't work"). Is this a counterexample to the claim that there are no subject–verb idioms in English? (As a matter of contrast: notice that in verb + object idioms the subject can be any possible DP: *John kicked the bucket, The clown kicked the bucket.*)

CHALLENGE PROBLEM SET 2: MIDDLES AND PASSIVES
[Critical Thinking; Challenge]
Middles are English constructions that are little bit like passives. An example of an active/middle pair is seen below:

a) I cut the soft bread.
b) The soft bread cuts easily.

In (b), the theme appears in the subject position. One analysis of this order has the theme undergoing DP movement to subject position.

Consider now the following triplet of sentences. The first sentence is called a middle, the second an active, and the third a causative.

c) The boat sank. *middle*
d) The torpedo sank the boat. *active*
e) The captain sank the boat (with a torpedo). *causative*

Part 1: Describe the relationship between the active, middle, and causative in terms of their theta grids.

Part 2: Now consider the passives of sentences (c–e). Why should sentence (f) be ungrammatical, but (g) and (h) grammatical?

f) *Was sunk (by the boat).
(also * It was sunk by the boat, where *it* is an expletive)
g) The boat was sunk by the torpedo.
h) The boat was sunk by the captain (with a torpedo).

CHALLENGE PROBLEM SET 3: PASSIVES AND DOUBLE OBJECTS
[Critical Thinking; Challenge]
(For more information on the phenomenon discussed in this problem set, see Larson 1988.) English has two constructions that surface with ditranstive verbs. One is called the prepositional construction, the other the double object construction:[8]

a) I sent a book to Louis. *prepositional*
b) I sent Louis a book. *double object*

It is possible to make passives out of these constructions, but some additional restrictions on how passives work are needed. Consider the following data and posit a restriction on DP movement in passives to account for the ill-formedness of the ungrammatical sentences. Pay careful attention to sentence (g).

c) A book was sent to Louis.
d) *Louis was sent a book to.
e) *To Louis was sent a book.[9]
f) Louis was sent a book.
g) *A book was sent Louis.

---

[8] There is a great deal of literature that tries to derive the double object construction from the prepositional construction using NP movement (see for example Larson 1988). The relationship between the two constructions is not relevant to the question in this problem set, but is an interesting puzzle in and of itself.
[9] This may be marginally acceptable in poetic or flowery speech. Assume for the purposes of this problem set that this is ungrammatical.

CHALLENGE PROBLEM SET 4: TWO KINDS OF RAISING
[Critical Thinking; Challenge]
In the text, we proposed that subjects of non-finite clauses can raise to the subject position of finite clauses in sentences like (a):

a)   John$_i$ seems [t_i to have left].

This kind of raising is sometimes called **subject-to-subject raising**. Now consider the following sentence:

b)   Bill wants John to leave.

This sentence should be ungrammatical, because *to* is a non-finite T, so can't assign Case to *John*. One hypothesis that has been proposed to account for this says there is also a process of **subject-to-object raising**:

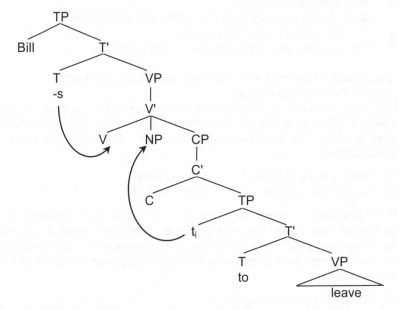

How does the following data support this analysis?

c)   John wants Bill to leave.
d)   John wants him to leave.
e)   John believes him to have been at the game.
f)   ?John$_i$ believes himself$_i$ to have been at the game.
g)   *John$_i$ believes him$_i$ to have been at the game.
h)   He is believed (by John) to have been at the game.

CHALLENGE PROBLEM SET 5: THETA ROLES AND CASE[10]

[Critical Thinking; Challenge]
Consider the following sentences, and then answer the questions in parts 1 and 2 below:

a) Daniel laughed.
b) *Daniel laughed himself.
c) Daniel laughed himself out of the room.
d) We shouted.
e) *We shouted the actors.
f) We shouted the actors off the stage.

Part 1: Why are sentences (a), (c), (d), and (f) grammatical, while sentences (b) and (e) are ungrammatical? Propose an analysis of the construction illustrated in (c) and (f) which accounts for this, using trees to illustrate your analysis. Assume that the DPs in (c) and (f) get their theta-roles in the specifier of the PP, but that the only position available for accusative Case is the complement position to the V.[11]

Part 2: Recall that the theta criterion enforces a one-to-one relationship between θ-roles and referential (i.e., non-expletive) DPs:

> *Every referential DP must have a (distinct) θ-role, and every θ-role must be assigned to a (distinct) referential DP.*

The Case filter is similar to the theta criterion, inasmuch as both conditions talk about the distribution of DPs. However, the Case filter was not stated as a one-to-one condition; it merely requires that every overt DP be assigned abstract Case. It does not require that every case be assigned.

QUESTION: Should we leave the Case filter as it is, or should we rephrase it as a condition like the theta criterion – something like: "Every overt DP must receive abstract Case, and every abstract Case must be assigned to an overt DP"? Refer to the sentences in (a–f) above in arguing for your answer. Ask yourself if the verb *laugh* must always (or never) assign accusative case in every situation.

CHALLENGE PROBLEM SET 6: CHEPANG ANTIPASSIVE[12]

[Data Analysis and Critical Thinking; Challenge]
Consider the following data from Chepang, a Sino-Tibetan language spoken in Nepal. The alternation seen between sentences (a) and (b) is called the antipassive. In sentence (a) the theme is a normal argument (presumably

---

[10] Thanks to Matt Pearson for contributing this problem set.

[11] Treat *out* and *off* as prepositions that can select either a DP complement or a PP complement.

[12] The data for this problem set comes from Chaughley, R. C. (1982), *The Syntax and Morphology of the Verb in Chepang*. Research School of Pacific Studies, Australian National University. p. 68.

with accusative Case, although the case marking is null). In sentence (b), the theme is marked with an oblique goal marking. Can this type of alternation be accounted for using a voice head like our account of passive in English? If not, why not? If so, draw the theta grids for all the relevant V heads.

a) puʔ-nis-ʔi   həw   sat-ʔaka-c-u
    older.bro-DUAL-AGENT   younger.brother   kill-PAST-DUAL-AG
    "The two older brothers killed the younger brothers accidentally."

b) həw-kay   puʔ-nis-ʔi   sat-ʔa-thəy
    younger.bro-GOAL   older.bro-DUAL-AGENT   kill-PAST-GOAL
    "The two older brothers killed the younger brother."

Wh-movement and Locality Constraints

Learning Objectives

After reading chapter 12 you should walk away having mastered the following ideas and skills:

1. Explain the motivation for *wh*-movement.
2. Draw the tree indicating *wh*-movement.
3. Identify various complementizer types.
4. Draw a tree for a relative clause.
5. Identify various island types.
6. Explain why *wh*-island sentences are ungrammatical according to the Minimal Link Condition.
7. Explain, using the MLC, why certain instances of DP movement and head-to-head movement are ungrammatical.

0. INTRODUCTION

In chapter 11, we looked at DPs that were appearing in positions where they didn't get theta roles. Instead, the DPs surfaced in derived positions. That is, they were moved from the position where they got a theta role to a position

Syntax: A Generative Introduction, Third Edition. Andrew Carnie.
© 2013 Andrew Carnie. Published 2013 by John Wiley & Sons, Inc.

where they could get Case. The trigger for this movement was the requirement that DPs check their Case feature, as Case can only be assigned in specific structural positions. In this chapter, we turn to another kind of phrasal movement, one where DPs already have Case. DPs (and other phrases) can move for a different reason, to form what are called **wh-*questions.***

There are several different kinds of questions, only two of which we are concerned with in this book. The first kind is the familiar ***yes/no question*** that we looked at in the chapter on head movement:

1) a)   Are you going to eat that bagel?
   b)   Do you drink whisky?
   c)   Have you seen the spectrograph for that phoneme?

The answers to these questions cannot be anything other than *yes, no, maybe,* or *I don't know.* Any other response sounds strange:

1') a') #Pizza/ ✓yes
     b') #Scotch/ ✓no
     c') #Syntactic tree/ ✓no

The other kind of question is called a *wh*-question. These questions take their name from the fact that the words that introduce them (mostly) begin with the letters <wh> in English: *who/whom, what, when, where, why, which,* and *how.* The responses to these kind of questions cannot be *yes* or *no.* Instead they must be informative phrases.

2) a)   When did you do your syntax homework?   #yes / ✓yesterday
   b)   What are you eating?   #no/ ✓a bagel
   c)   How is Louise feeling?   #yes/✓much better

How these questions and constructions related to them are formed is the focus of this chapter.

Who and *Whom*

In traditional prescriptive grammar, there are two *wh*-phrases that refer to people: *who* and *whom.* *Who* is used when the *wh*-phrase originates in subject position and gets nominative Case. *Whom* is the accusative version. In most spoken dialects of Canadian and American English this distinction no longer exists, and *who* is used in all environments. For the sake of clarity, I use *who(m)* to indicate that the *wh*-phrase originated in object position, but you should note that from a descriptive point of view *who* is perfectly acceptable in object position for most speakers today.

1. MOVEMENT IN *WH*-QUESTIONS

If you look closely at a statement and a related *wh*-question, you'll see that the *wh*-phrase appears in a position far away from the position where its theta role is assigned. Take for example:

3) a) Becky bought the syntax book.
   b) What did Becky buy?

The verb *buy* in English takes two theta roles, an external agent and an internal theme. In sentence (3a), *Becky* is the agent, and *the syntax book* is the theme. In sentence (3b) *Becky* is the agent and *what* is the theme. In the first sentence, the theme is the object of the verb, in the second the theme is at the beginning of the clause. The situation becomes even more mysterious when we look at sentences like (4):

4) What did Stacy say Becky bought?

In this sentence *what* is still the theme of *bought*, yet it appears way up at the beginning of the main clause. This would appear to be a violation of the locality constraint on theta role assignment introduced in chapter 9.

The situation becomes murkier still when we look at Case. Recall that accusative Case is assigned when a DP is the sister to a V:

5) Matt [$_{VP}$ kissed her$_{ACC}$].

But in *wh*-questions the accusative form (like *whom*) is not a sister to V:

6) Whom$_{ACC}$ did Matt kiss?

So it appears as if not only are these *wh*-phrases not in their theta positions, but they aren't in their Case positions either.

Given what we've seen in the previous two chapters, this looks like another case of movement – this one with different triggers. Let's start with the issue of where *wh*-phrases move to. One position that we've had for a while, but have not yet used, is the specifier of CP. This is the place *wh*-phrases move to:

7)

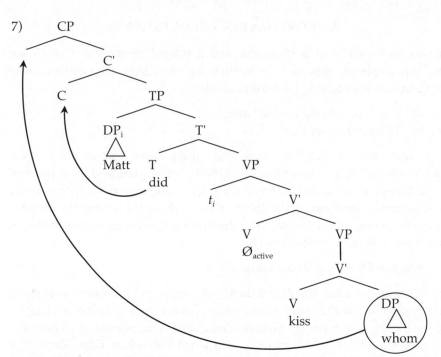

Notice that what moves here is an entire phrase. You can see this if you look at slightly more complex *wh*-questions:

8) a) [To whom] did Michael give the book?
   b) [Which book] did Michael give to Millie?

When you move an entire phrase, it cannot be an instance of head-to-head movement (by definition), so this must be movement to a position other than a head, in this case the empty specifier of CP. The element that is moved can be a DP, a PP, an AdjP, or an AdvP.

The movement to the specifier of CP accounts for another fact about the word order of *wh*-questions: they also involve T → C movement (in main clauses):

9) a) Who(m) are you meeting?
   b) *Who(m) you are meeting?

The *wh*-phrase appears to the left of the auxiliary in C. This means that the *wh*-phrase must raise to a position higher than C. The only position available to us is the specifier of CP:

10)

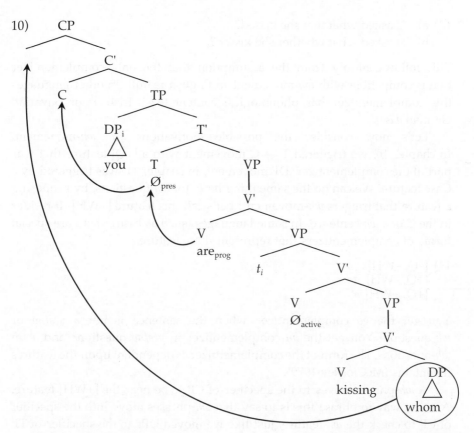

The fact that *wh*-movement is to the CP specifier position can also be seen in languages that allow both a *wh*-phrase and an overt complementizer, such as Irish:

11) Cad a^L tá   sa   seomra?
    What C-*wh*   is   in.the   room
    "What is in the room?"

In Irish, the *wh*-phrase *cad* "what" appears to the left of the complementizer a^L, supporting the idea that the *wh*-phrase is in the specifier of CP, the only position available to it. A similar fact is seen in Bavarian German (Bayer 1984):

12) I woass ned wann dass da Xavea kummt.
    I know not when that the Xavea comes
    "I don't know when Xavea is coming."

In English the only thing allowed to appear in C is an inverted auxiliary; other complementizers are not allowed:

13) a) *I asked what that she kissed?
    b) *I asked what whether she kissed?

This follows simply from the assumption that the only complementizer that is compatible with *wh*-movement in English is null. In other languages this complementizer has phonological content (e.g., Irish a^L or Bavarian German *dass*).

Let's now consider the possible motivations for *wh*-movement. In chapter 10, we triggered T → C movement with a [+Q] feature that was part of the complementizer. DP movement, in chapter 11, was triggered by a Case feature. We can do the same thing here, for *wh*-questions, by proposing a feature that triggers *wh*-movement. Let's call this feature [+WH]. It resides in the C of a *wh*-sentence. In some languages (such as Irish), there are special forms of complementizers that represent these features:

14) [–Q, –WH] *go*
    [+Q, –WH] *an*
    [+Q, +WH] a^L

You get the *go* complementizer when the sentence is not a *yes/no* or *wh*-question. You get the *an* complementizer in *yes/no* questions and a^L in *wh*-questions. The form of the complementizer is dependent upon the features it contains (McCloskey 1979).

A *wh*-phrase moves to the specifier of CP to be near the [+WH] feature. Another way to phrase this is to say that *wh*-phrases move into the specifier of CP to check the *wh*-feature, just like we moved DPs to the specifier of TP to check a [NOM] Case feature in chapter 10. We can formalize *wh*-movement the following way:

15) *Wh-movement*
    Move a *wh*-phrase to the specifier of CP to check a [+WH] feature in C.

Let's do a derivation for the following sentence:

16) Who(m) did Matt kiss?

The D-structure of this sentence will look like (17). *Matt* and *whom* both get their theta roles in these D-structure positions. *Whom* also gets its Case in this base position. Three other operations apply: There is DP movement of *Matt* to the specifier of TP to check the [NOM] feature, there is insertion of *do* to support the past tense and we get T → C movement to fill the null [+Q] complementizer. *Wh*-movement applies to check the [+WH] feature (18).

17)

18)

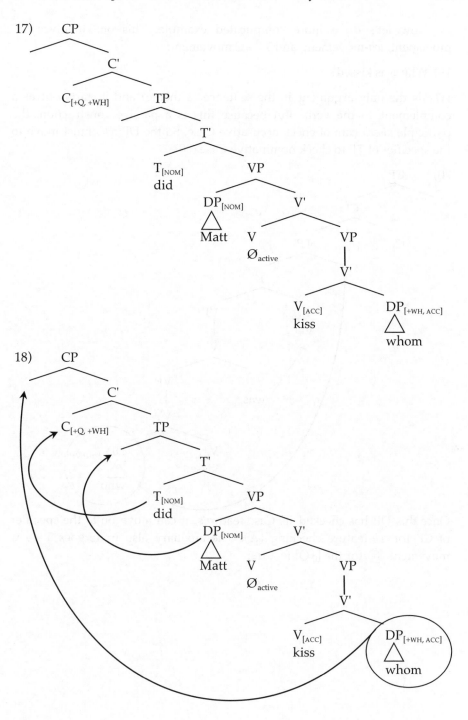

Now let's do a more complicated example. This one involves DP movement, *wh*-movement, and T → C movement:

19) Who was kissed?

Who is the only argument in the sentence (a theme) and it starts out as a complement to the verb. But because this is a passive construction, the participle *kissed* cannot check accusative Case. So the DP *who* must move to the specifier of TP to check nominative Case (20).

20)

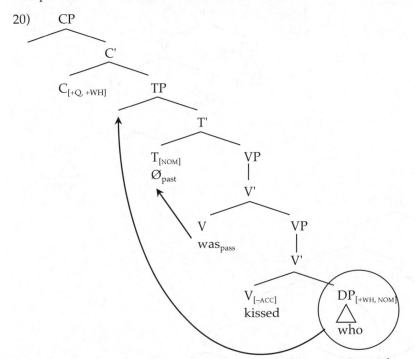

Once this DP has checked its Case features, it can move on to the specifier of CP for *wh*-feature checking (Ⓐ). The auxiliary also undergoes T → C movement (Ⓑ) for the [+Q] feature:

21)

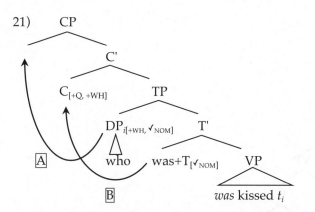

These two movements are "vacuous" in that *who* and *was* are in the order *who was* … both before movements Ⓐ and Ⓑ and after them. However, the feature-checking requirements force us to claim that both movements occur anyway.

You now have enough information to try CPS 1.

Wh-movement can also apply across clauses. Next we'll do a derivation of a sentence where the *wh*-phrase moves from an embedded clause to the specifier of a main clause CP.

22) Who(m) do you think Jim kissed?

In (22), *who(m)* is theta marked by the verb *kiss*, and gets its internal theme theta role in the object position of that verb. The present tense feature on the higher T requires *do*-support. The [+Q] feature on the C triggers T → C movement. The DP *Jim* moves from the specifier of the embedded VP to the specifier of the embedded TP for EPP and Case reasons. The DP *you* does the same in the higher clause. Finally, we have *wh*-movement. For reasons that will become clear later, we do this movement in two hops, moving first to the specifier of the embedded CP, then on to the higher CP to check that C's [+WH] feature (23).

23)

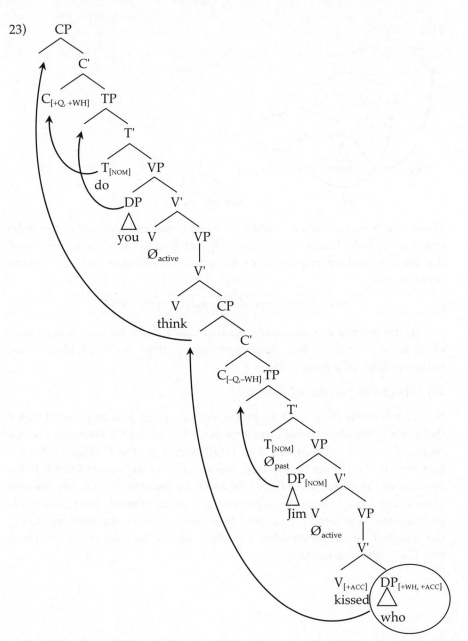

Let's do one more derivation, this time doing a sentence like the one above, but where the *wh*-phrase stops in the specifier position of the embedded CP rather than moving all the way up:

24) I wonder who Jim kissed.

The main difference between this sentence and (23) lies in the nature of the main verb. In (23) the verb was *think*, that subcategorizes for a CP headed by $C_{[-Q, -WH]}$ (25a). The verb *wonder*[1] differs in that it subcategorizes for a CP headed by $C_{[-Q, +WH]}$; that is, the embedded clause has *wh*-movement in it (25b):

25) a) *think*

Agent	Proposition
DP	$CP_{[-Q, -WH]}$

   b) *wonder*

Agent	Proposition
DP	$CP_{[-Q, +WH]}$

The tree for (24) is given in (26); it differs minimally from (24) only in the main verb and the feature structures of the two complementizers. The DPs all get their theta roles in these D-structure positions. Just as in the previous example, *who* gets its Case in its base position; the two agent DPs (*I* and *Jim*) move to their respective specifiers of TP to get Case. Finally we have movement of the *wh*-phrase. Notice that it only goes to the specifier of the embedded CP. This is because of the featural content of the Cs. The embedded CP is [+WH], the main clause CP is [–WH].

No T → C Movement in Embedded Clauses

We've noted that *wh*-movement and T → C movement often go hand in hand. One surprising fact about English is that this is not true of embedded *wh*-questions. When a *wh*-question is embedded, the subject does not invert with the auxiliary (i.e., no T → C movement):

i)   I wonder what he has done?
ii) *I wonder what has he done?

In other words, in embedded clauses there is no $C_{[+Q, +WH]}$. One simple explanation for this is that theta grids simply can't contain $C_{[+Q]}$.

---

[1] We have to assume that there is another verb *wonder*, found in sentences such as *I wonder if Bill left*, that selects for a CP headed by $C_{[+Q,-WH]}$.

26)

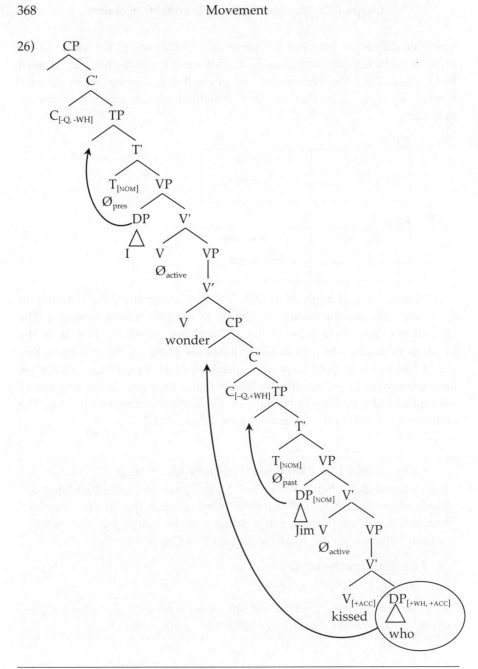

You now have enough information to try WBE 1–3.

Traces and *Wanna*-contraction

You may have noticed that I have been marking the position that movement occurs from with a *t* (coindexed with the word it replaces). The *t* here stands for "trace". Later in this chapter we'll see that traces are required to block certain kinds of illicit movement. But an important question is whether there is any reality behind the notion "trace". This is especially important in a theory like generative grammar, which claims psychological underpinnings. Finding evidence for something that is not pronounced is remarkably difficult. However, there is some straightforward evidence for traces. First a little background: In spoken varieties of English (both standard and non-standard), function words often contract with nearby words. One such contraction takes non-finite T (*to*) and contracts it with a preceding verb like *want*:

i)   I want to leave → I wanna leave.

This phenomenon is called **wanna-*contraction***. Now consider what happens when you have *wh*-movement and *wanna*-contraction going on at the same time. *Wanna*-contraction is permitted when the *wh*-movement applies to an object:

ii)   Who(m)$_i$ do you wanna kiss t_i?

But look what happens when you try to do *wanna*-contraction, when *wh*-movement targets the subject:

iii)   Who$_i$ do you want t_i to kiss the puppy?
iv)   *Who do you wanna kiss the puppy?

English speakers have very strong judgments that *wanna*-contraction is impossible when the subject is *wh*-questioned. Why should this be the case? If we have traces, the explanation is simple: the trace intervenes between the *to* and the verb. It blocks the strict adjacency between the verb and the *to*, thus blocking contraction:

v)   Who$_i$ do you want t$_i$ to kiss the puppy?

The theory of traces provides a nice explanation for this fact. For an alternate view see Pullum (1997).

2. RELATIVE CLAUSES

In this section we'll look at a construction closely related to *wh*-questions. *Relative clauses* involve a special kind of *wh*-movement, where a CP with a *wh*-element in it modifies a noun.

Not all clauses that modify nouns are relative clauses. There is a small set of nouns known as **factives** (e.g., *fact, claim, thought, knowledge, saying, realization, determination*) that take CPs as complements rather than adjuncts. These nouns often correspond to verbs that take complement clauses (although not always). Some examples of factive clauses modifying a noun are seen in (27):

27) a)   [_DP_ The fact [_CP_ that I like begonia-flavored milk shakes]] is none of your business.
    b)   She made [_DP_ the outrageous claim [_CP_ that tuna-flavored milkshakes are good for you.]]

Factive complement clauses always have all of their arguments contained within them and there are no *wh*-phrases. Critically, factive clauses don't have missing elements in the TP. All the arguments and adjuncts are precisely where we expect them to be. Because they lack these gaps, they are not *wh*-constructions.

Relative clauses, by contrast, share with *wh*-questions the property of having an argument or adjunct missing within the clause. Take (28a) as a typical example of an embedded *wh*-question. The *where* word corresponds to a DP or a PP adjunct at the end of clause, indicating a location of the finding action. In (28b), we have a head noun (*place*) that is modified by a relative clause CP. That CP has a gap in the same location as (28a) and there is a *wh*-word at the beginning of that embedded relative clause. A similar pair is seen in (29). The *who wh*-phrase is fronted to the beginning of the clause in (28a), leaving a gap where we expect the argument to be. In (28b), there is a similar *wh*-phrase at the beginning of the relative clause that's associated with the missing theme argument of *kiss*.

28) a)   I [_VP_ asked [_CP_ where [_TP_ you found it _____]]].
    b)   I won't reveal [_DP_ the place_i [_CP_ where_i [_TP_ we found it _____]]].

29) a)   I [_VP_ asked [_CP_ who [_TP_ she kissed _____]]].
    b)   I know [_DP_ several people [_CP_ who [_TP_ she kissed _____]]].

The relative clauses in the (b) examples are formed by moving the *wh*-phrases to the specifiers of the embedded CPs, completely in parallel to the *wh*-movement in the (a) examples. The primary difference between the (b) cases and embedded *wh*-questions is in what category the CPs are attached to. In the (a) examples, the embedded clauses modify a verb; in the (b) examples, they are part of the VP. A tree for the DP in (29b) is given below in (30). In this tree you'll see the *who* phrase is generated as the complement to the verb *kissed*. The embedded CP is adjoined to the N and there is movement of the *wh*-word into the specifier of the CP. Like in all other embedded clauses in English, there is no subject-auxiliary (T → C) movement.

30)

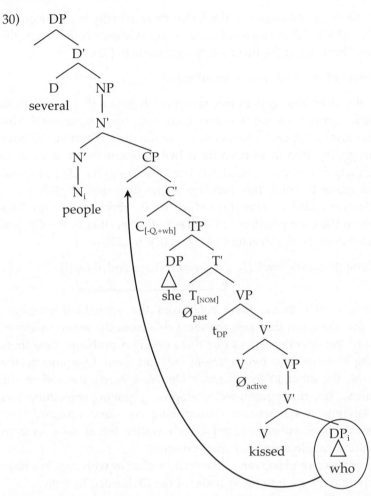

The *wh*-phrase here doesn't serve to mark a question, but instead it links the head noun to the gap. This is indicated by the coindexation between the head noun and the *wh*-element.

The one spanner in the works for this analysis is the fact that not all relative clauses have obvious *wh*-elements in them. For example, take the sentences in (31). Sentence (31a) apparently has nothing in the complementizer zone of the sentence, and sentence (31b) has a *that* complementizer – which is never allowed in other *wh*-contexts.

31) a)   I know [$_{DP}$ several people [$_{CP}$ [$_{TP}$ she kissed ____]]].
    b)   I know [$_{DP}$ several people [$_{CP}$ that [$_{TP}$ she kissed ____]]].[2]

Nevertheless, there's good reason to think that there actually is a *wh*-element in the specifier of the CP in these sentences – the evidence comes from the theta criterion. Think about the theta role assignments in (32):

32) I know I bought the book you recommended _____.

What theta roles does *book* gets in this sentence? It gets a theme role from *buy*. But it also appears to get a theme theta role from *recommend*! This would, on the surface, appear to be a violation of the theta criterion. We have a single noun getting two theta roles from two different verbs. If we're to maintain the theta criterion, we need an alternative analysis. One proposal that has been made to solve this problem is the idea that English has a special DP element called an **operator** (which we'll abbreviate as **Op**). This operator starts in the Case position and moves to the specifier of the CP, just like a *wh*-phrase does. So the structure of (32) is that in (33).

33) I know I bought [$_{NP}$ the book [$_{CP}$ [$_{TP}$ you recommended *Op*]]].

The operator gets the theme theta role from the embedded predicate *recommended* and the noun *book* gets the theta role from the main predicate. The presence of the operator solves our theta criterion problem: Two theta roles are being assigned and two different DPs get them. One goes to the head noun *book*, the other to the operator *Op*. Now here's the kicker: the operator is silent. Yes, that's right, we're proposing moving something you can't hear. Anytime a syntactician claims there's a silent category, you should of course check your pockets for your wallet, but it does seem to solve our technical problem with the theta criterion.

A similar analysis can be given to the relative clauses with *that*. We have a null *wh*-word that moves into the specifier of the CP headed by *that*.

34) I know I bought [$_{NP}$ the book [$_{CP}$ that [$_{TP}$ you recommended *Op*]]].

There is evidence that such a movement occurs. In older varieties of English one finds examples like that in (35) (data from the Helsinki Corpus via

---

[2] Prescriptivists might be unhappy with this use of *that* in this sentence, but this sentence is completely grammatical in my variety of English. The prescriptive objection has to do with the use of a *that* in a non-restrictive relative clause. We'll return to the restrictive/non-restrictive distinction below.

Santorini and Kroch's online syntax textbook[3]). In this example you have both a *wh*-word and the *that* complementizer. A similar example from Bavarian German is seen in (36) (Bayer 1984: 213).

35) thy freend *which that* thou has lorn
    "your friend that you have lost" (cmctmeli.m3, 218.C1.31)

36) der Hund *der   wo* gestern   d' Katz bissn hod
    the dog   who that yesterday the cat   bitten has
    "the dog that bit the cat yesterday"

So cross-linguistically, the movement we've proposed for English does seem to occur, except that the *wh*-element in English is silent but is overt in other languages.

Restrictive vs. Non-restrictive Relative Clauses

Restrictive relative clauses are modifiers of nouns that limit the meaning of a noun the same way an AdjP or a PP might restrict it. So for example, the reference of the noun *skis* includes all the skis in the world. But if we add the adjective *flimsy* in front, then we have a much smaller set of possible objects. Restrictive relative clauses work the same way. [DP *Skis that are flimsy]* is restricted in the same way *flimsy skis* is. **Non-restrictive relative clauses** just provide supplementary information about the NP. Compare the sentences in (i):

i)   a)   The guy who is wearing the red hat just hit me!
     b)   That guy, who I think might be drunk, just hit me!

Sentence (ia) has a subject DP with a restrictive relative clause. I'm telling you that you should look specifically for the guy with the red hat, not some other guy. The non-restrictive relative in (ib) is just giving you some additional parenthetical commentary rather than restricting which guy you're talking about. In English, non-restrictive relatives are set off by pauses in speech and commas in writing. There is an ordering restriction on restrictive and non-restrictive clauses. Restrictive clauses must be closer to the head noun than the non-restrictive ones (ii).

ii) a)   The man that is escaping, who I think might be drunk, hit me.
     b)   *The man, who I think might be drunk, that is escaping hit me.

Demirdache (1991) suggests that restrictive relatives are adjoined to the N', and non-restrictive relatives are right-adjoined higher up to the D'.

---

[3] http://www.ling.upenn.edu/~beatrice/syntax-textbook/

We've now seen two instances where *wh*-movement seems to play a significant role. It shows up both in *wh*-questions and in relative clauses (and in a few other constructions that we haven't discussed here). It's a pretty flexible rule that moves items into the specifier of CP.

You now have enough information to try WBE 4 & 5, GPS 1–3, and CPS 2.

The *That*-trace Effect

In English, *wh*-movement of objects seems to be free – you can do it either when there is a complementizer or when there is no complementizer:

i)   What$_i$ do you think Matt kissed t_i?
ii) What$_i$ do you think that Matt kissed t_i?

This is not the case with subjects. *Wh*-movement from subject position is only possible when there is no overt *that* complementizer:

iii) Who$_i$ do you think t$_i$ kissed Matt?
iv) *Who$_i$ do you think that t_i kissed Matt?

This phenomenon is called the **that-*trace* effect**, from the constraint that is used to rule out sentences like (iv), the **that-*trace* filter**:

v)   * [$_{CP}$ that t...]

The *that*-trace effect is not universal. Many languages (such as Italian), don't have it:

vi) Chi   credi   che t_i venga?
    Who you.think that t$_i$ come
    "Who do you think is coming?" (Rizzi 1982)

The explanation for the *that*-trace effect in English is still a bit of a mystery and is widely debated among syntacticians.

3. ISLANDS

Wh-movement isn't entirely free. There are constraints on what categories you can move *out* of (the categories that contain the *wh*-phrase). Compare the following two sentences, one of which has *wh*-movement out of a simple complement CP (37a). The other (37b) moves a *wh*-phrase out of a factive clause that is contained *inside a DP*:

37) a)   What$_i$ did Bill claim [$_{CP}$ that he read t_i in the syntax book]?

b) *What_i did Bill make [_DP the claim [_CP that he read t_i in the syntax book]]?

In sentence (37a) we see that *wh*-movement *out* of a complement clause is grammatical, but movement out of a CP that is dominated by a DP is horrible (37b). This phenomenon, first observed by Ross (1967), has come to be known as the **complex DP island** phenomenon. The word **island** here is meant to be iconic. Islands are places you can't get off of (without special means like a plane). They are surrounded by water, so you are limited in where you can move: You can only move about within the confines of the island. Islands in syntax are the same. You cannot move *out* of an island, but you can move around within it. DPs are islands.

38) *What_i did Bill make $\boxed{\text{[_DP the claim [_CP that he read } t_i \text{ in the syntax book]]}}$?

Complex DP Island

The example in (41) involves a CP that is a complement to the N head. The same effect is found when the CP is a relative clause (i.e., an adjunct to the N):

39) *[Which cake]_i did you see $\boxed{\text{[_DP the man [_CP who baked } t_i\text{]]}}$?

We can characterize this phenomenon with the following descriptive statement:

40) *The Complex DP Constraint*: *wh_i [... [_DP ... t_i ...] ...]

You now have enough information to try GPS 4.

There are many other kinds of islands. One of the most important is called a **wh-*island***. First, observe that it is possible to move a *wh*-phrase to the specifier of an embedded CP, when the C is [+WH]:

41) I wonder [_CP what_i C_[-Q, +WH] [_TP John bought t_i with the $20 bill]].

It is also possible to move *wh*-phrase to the specifier of the main CP:

42) [_CP How_k do [_TP you think [John bought the sweater t_k]]]?

However, look at what happens when you try to do both (move one *wh*-phrase to the embedded specifier, and the other to the main CP specifier):

43) *[_CP How_k do [_TP you wonder [_CP what_i [_TP John bought t_i t_k]]]]?

This sentence is wildly ungrammatical – even though we have only done two otherwise legitimate transformations. Now, this isn't a constraint on having two *wh*-phrases in a sentence. Two *wh*-phrases are perfectly acceptable in other contexts:[4]

44) a)   How do you think John bought what?
     b)   I wonder what John bought how.

It seems, then, to be a constraint on *moving* both of them. The same kind of example is seen in (45a) and (45b):

45) a)   I wonder [$_{CP}$ what$_i$ [$_{TP}$ John kissed t_i]].
     b)   [$_{CP}$ Who$_k$ did [$_{TP}$ you think [$_{TP}$ t_k kissed the gorilla]]]?

Movement of either the subject (45b) or the object (45a) to the specifiers of the CPs is acceptable. However, movement of both results in terrible ungrammaticality:

46) *[$_{CP1}$ Who$_k$ did [$_{TP}$ you wonder [$_{CP2}$ what$_i$ [$_{TP}$ t_k kissed t_i]]]]?

The central intuition underlying an account of these facts is that once you move a *wh*-phrase into the specifier of a CP, then that CP becomes an island for further extraction:

47) I asked [$_{CP}$ what$_i$ John kissed t_i]   *wh*-island

Movement out of this *wh*-island results in ungrammaticality. We can express this with the following descriptive statement:

48) *Wh-island Constraint*:   *wh$_i$ [... [$_{CP}$ wh$_k$ [... t_i ...] ...] ...]

This constraint simply says that you cannot do *wh*-movement (in the schematic in (48) this is represented by the wh$_i$ and the coindexed t_i) and skip around a CP that has another *wh*-phrase (wh$_k$) in its specifier. We're going to discuss this particular island in much greater detail in the next section.

   Subjects are another kind of island. Consider (49a); it has a CP in its subject position. When you try to *wh*-move the *wh*-equivalent to *several rioters* (*who* in 49b), the sentence becomes ungrammatical.

49) a)   [$_{TP}$ [$_{CP}$ That the police would arrest several rioters] was a certainty].
     b)   *Who$_i$ was [$_{TP}$ [$_{CP}$ that the police would arrest t_i] t_{was} a certainty]?

This is called the **subject condition**:

---

[4] If you have trouble with this judgment, try stressing the word *what* in (44a) and *how* in (44b).

50) *The Subject Condition:*   *wh$_i$ ... [$_{TP}$ [$_{CP}$ ... t$_i$ ...] T ...]

We have one final island to consider. Consider a conjunction like that in (51a). Here we have two DPs conjoined with each other. *Wh*-moving either of these DPs results in ungrammaticality (51b and c).

51) a)   I liked Mary and John.
    b)   *Who$_i$ did you like Mary and t$_i$?
    c)   *Who$_i$ did you like t$_i$ and John?

The same is true if you try to do *wh*-movement from within another structure that is conjoined, such as a conjoined VP in (52):

52) a)   I [$_{VP}$ ate some popcorn] and [$_{VP}$ drank some soda].
    b)   *What$_i$ did you eat t$_i$ and drink some soda?
    c)   *What$_i$ did you eat some popcorn and drink t$_i$?

The island condition that governs these situations is called the **Coordinate Structure Constraint**:

53) *Coordinate Structure Constraint*:
    *wh$_i$ ... [$_{XP}$ [$_{XP}$ ... t$_i$ ...] conj [$_{XP}$ ...]] ...
    or *wh$_i$ ... [$_{XP}$ [$_{XP}$ ...] conj [$_{XP}$ ... t$_i$ ...]] ...
    or *wh$_i$ ... [$_{XP}$ [$_{XP}$ ...] conj t$_i$] ...
    or *wh$_i$ ... [$_{XP}$ t$_i$ conj [$_{XP}$ ...]] ...

We thus have four environments out of which *wh*-movement cannot occur: Complex DPs, subjects, CPs with a *wh*-word in their specifier, and conjuncts in coordination structures. These environments are the subject of much research in syntactic theory right now. In the next section, we will look at one possible explanation for some of these island effects (although it does not account for all of them by any means). This account refers to a constraint known as the Minimal Link Condition.

You now have enough information to try WBE 7.

---

4. THE MINIMAL LINK CONDITION

4.1 Wh-islands and the Minimal Link Condition

Island phenomena beg for explanation. Let's consider *wh*-islands in some detail. As we noticed above, in questions with multiple *wh*-phrases, the movement of each *wh*-phrase is allowed independently of the other:

54) a)   I wonder [$_{CP}$ what$_i$ [$_{TP}$ John kissed t$_i$]].
    b)   [$_{CP}$ Who$_k$ did [$_{TP}$ you think [$_{TP}$ t$_k$ kissed the gorilla]]]?

However, when you combine the movements the sentence becomes nearly incomprehensible:

55) *[$_{CP1}$ Who$_k$ did [$_{TP}$ you wonder [$_{CP2}$ what$_i$ [$_{TP}$ t_k kissed t_i]]]]?

Recall from earlier discussion that syntactic operations like to either be local (for example, anaphors must be bound within their clause – a local relation; similarly theta roles are assigned within their VP – another local relation) or create localities (for example, DPs move to get close or local to their Case assigner; affixes move to get close or adjacent to their host; and *wh*-phrases move to get near a [+WH]). In the next chapter, we will consider a unified approach to movement that tries to capture at least the last set of cases. What is important here is that our grammars seem to like relations that are close. With this intuition in mind, think about *wh*-islands. *Wh*-phrases move to get in the specifier of a C$_{[+WH]}$ so let's hypothesize that there is a further restriction: movement must always target the nearest *potential* position. This is another locality condition: the Minimal Link Condition (MLC).

56) *Minimal Link Condition (MLC) (intuitive version)*
    Move to the closest potential landing site.

In (55) there are two CPs, but both the *wh*-phrases start in the embedded clause. This means that for both *wh*-phrases the embedded CP (CP$_2$) is the closest potential landing site. Here's an abbreviated D-structure of (55); the potential landing sites for the *wh*-phrase are underlined:

57) [$_{CP1}$ ___ C$_{[+WH]}$ [$_{TP}$ you Ø$_{[PRES]}$ wonder [$_{CP2}$ ___ C$_{[+wh]}$ [$_{TP}$ who kissed what]]]]?

If we start by moving *what* to this position, we can check off *what's* *wh*-feature, and this move meets the Minimal Link Condition because the movement has targeted the closest potential landing site:

58) [$_{CP1}$ ___ C$_{[+WH]}$ [$_{TP}$ you Ø$_{[PRES]}$ wonder [$_{CP2}$ what$_k$ C$_{[\checkmark wh]}$ [$_{TP}$ who kissed t_k]]]]?

Now the other *wh*-phrase in this sentence has to check[5] its *wh*-features, but the closest potential position is filled by *what*. While movement to the specifier of CP$_1$ would allow it to check its [+WH] feature, this would be a violation of the MLC, as the movement skips the first potential position:

---

[5] We return to sentences like *I wonder who loves what* where there appears to be no movement in section 5.

59) [$_{CP1}$ __ C$_{[+WH]}$ [$_{TP}$ you Ø$_{[PRES]}$ wonder [$_{CP2}$ what$_k$ C$_{[√wh]}$ [$_{TP}$ who kissed t_k]]]]?

first potential position

Even though the specifier of CP2 is filled with *what*, it still counts as the closest position. But since it is occupied, *who* can't move there, so there is no way for the [+WH] feature to be checked. Notice that it doesn't matter what order we apply the operations in. If we move *who* first, stopping off in the specifier of CP2 (thus meeting the MLC), then that specifier is occupied by the trace, so there is no place for the *what* to move to:

60) [$_{CP1}$ who$_i$ C$_{[+WH]}$ [$_{TP}$ you Ø$_{[PRES]}$ wonder [$_{CP2}$ t_i C$_{[√wh]}$ [$_{TP}$ t_i kissed what]]]]?

?

The MLC thus explains the ungrammaticality of *wh*-islands: When you have multiple *wh*-phrases that require movement, movement of at least one of them will be blocked by the MLC because the closest potential landing site will be occupied by the other.

Before moving on to look at the utility of the MLC in other domains, it's worth noting how a grammatical sentence like (61) is derived when we have a constraint like the MLC. This sentence looks like we have non-local movement. The word *who* gets its theta role in the embedded clause yet ends up in the specifier of the higher CP:

61) [$_{CP}$ Who$_i$ do you think [$_{CP2}$ [$_{TP}$ t_i kissed the gorilla]]]?

This should be a violation of the MLC, since the *wh*-phrase ends up in the specifier of a CP that is higher up in the tree. You will recall we said that *wh*-movement that crosses clause boundaries does so in two hops: first to the specifier of the lower CP, then on to the higher CP.

62) [$_{CP}$ Who$_i$ do you think [$_{CP2}$ t_i [$_{TP}$ t_i kissed the gorilla]]]?

We now have an explanation for why this is the case: The MLC requires that all movement be local. In order to maintain this locality the movement happens in two hops. This phenomenon is called *successive cyclic movement*. In the problem sets section of this chapter there is a question on Irish (General Problem Set 6) that shows a morphological correspondence to successive cyclic movement.

You now have enough information to try GPS 5 & 6 and CPS 3.

It should be noted before we go on that the MLC does not explain all island effects, only the *wh*-islands. Accounting for other island types is a hot topic of research in syntax today.

4.2 The MLC in DP Movement and Head Movement

The MLC has usage above and beyond that of *wh*-islands. We can use it to account for a variety of other locality effects with DP and head movement too.

The predicates *is likely* and *seem* both have empty subject positions and allow the subject-to-subject raising variant of DP movement.

63) a)   Mark$_i$ is likely [t$_i$ to have left].
    b)   Mark$_i$ seems [t$_i$ to have left].

Consider now what happens when you embed one of these in the other. It is only possible for DP movement to occur to the *lower* of the two Case positions. (64a) shows the D-structure. (64b) shows the grammatical S-structure where the DP shifts to the lower position and expletive insertion applies at the higher position. (64c and d) show ungrammatical forms, where the DP has shifted to the higher of the two positions. This kind of movement is ungrammatical, whether or not (64d vs. 64c) expletive insertion applies in the lower specifier of TP.

64) a)   __ seems [that __ is likely [Mark to have left]].
    b)   It seems [that Mark$_i$ is likely [t$_i$ to have left]].
    c)   *Mark$_i$ seems that is likely [t$_i$ to have left].
    d)   *Mark$_i$ seems that it is likely [t$_i$ to have left].

When two Case positions are available movement has to target the closer (lower) one. The MLC explains these facts as well.

65) *[$_{TP}$ Mark$_i$ seems that   [$_{TP}$ it is likely [t$_i$ to have left]]].

first potential nominative position

Sentences (64c and d) are ungrammatical because the movement goes beyond the closest potential position, which is occupied by an expletive into a higher position. It is as if the expletive creates a "Case-island" for the purposes of DP movement.

A similar effect is seen in head movement. Recall from chapter 10 that in French we have both T → C movement and V → T movement. These two operations had to happen in tandem if we had a *yes/no* question with a main verb and no auxiliary:

66) a) [$_{CP}$ C$_{[+Q]}$ [$_{TP}$ vous T$_{[pres]}$ [$_{VP}$ t_{vous} mangez des pommes]]]
                 you   eat   of.the apples

    b) [$_{CP}$ C$_{[+Q]}$ [$_{TP}$ vous T$_{[pres]}$ [$_{VP}$ t_{vous} mangez des pommes]]]

                T → C   V → T

    c) Mangez vous des pommes?
       "Do you eat apples?"

(66a) is roughly the D-structure of the sentence (with the subject DP moved to the specifier of TP for Case). We have two instances of head movement (66b). First V → T applies, then T → C to give the C content. This results in the surface string in (66c). Consider what would happen if the intermediate T position were occupied by an auxiliary (67a) and we tried to do head movement of the verb around it (67b). This would give us the ungrammatical string in (67c):[6]

67) a) [$_{CP}$ C$_{[+Q]}$ [$_{TP}$ vous avez [$_{VP}$ t_{vous} mangé des pommes]]]
                 you   have   eaten   of.the apples

    b) [$_{CP}$ C$_{[+Q]}$ [$_{TP}$ vous avez [$_{VP}$ t_{vous} mangé des pommes]]]

                  first potential position

    c) *Mangé vous avez des pommes
      eaten   you have

The ungrammaticality of (67c) follows easily: the V → C movement has skipped the intermediate T (occupied by *avez*). This T position is the first potential landing site for the verb. This is thus a violation of the Minimal Link Condition.[7]

You now have enough information to try WBE 8 and CPS 4.

     The MLC, then, doesn't only explain *wh*-islands. It also extends to other locality restrictions on movement, such as the requirement that DP movement always target the closest Case position and the requirement that head movement not skip intervening heads. Notice that in each of these

---

[6] For ease of reading these diagrams I'm leaving out the stacked verb analysis of auxiliary constructions and just generating auxiliaries in T; this does not change the MLC effect.

[7] This instance of the MLC is sometimes known by an older name: the Head Movement Constraint (HMC), which was proposed by Travis (1984); the HMC was the inspiration behind the MLC.

cases what counts as a "potential landing site" is different. The same basic constraint holds, but the conditions for each type of movement are different. This discovery was made by Luigi Rizzi in his famous book *Relativized Minimality* (1990). Two things are vague about our preliminary definition of the MLC above: the precise definition of "closest" and the precise definition of "potential landing site". Nevertheless for most people our preliminary definition should be intuitive and sufficient.

5. ECHO QUESTIONS (*WH*-IN-SITU) IN ENGLISH

You may have noticed in the previous section that the MLC, when applied to *wh*-movement, in essence prevents any clause from having two moved *wh*-phrases. Does this mean that a clause can't have two *wh*-phrases at all? Obviously not:

68) Who loves who(m)?

This sentence is grammatical, even though the second *wh*-phrase does not move. This is a phenomenon called **wh-*in-situ*** (from the Latin *in situ* "in place"). We also see *wh*-in-situ in sentences with only one *wh*-phrase:

69) Shelly loves who?   (If this is not grammatical for you, stress *who*.)

We might ask why the *wh*-phrase in (69) and the second *who* in (68) don't move to check their [+WH] features. The answer is simple: these are not *wh*-questions and these apparent *wh*-phrases are [–WH]. These are *echo questions*. Echo questions are not requests for new information; instead they are requests for confirmation of something someone has heard. Consider sentence (69) in a conversational context:

70) *Daniel*:   Hey, I just heard that Shelly loves Ferdinand.
    Andrew: Shelly loves who?
    Daniel: You heard me, Shelly loves Ferdinand.

It's clear from this snippet of discussion that Andrew is incredulous about Shelly loving Ferdinand and is asking for confirmation of what he heard. This is very different from a request for information. There are two relevant properties of echo questions: (i) they don't involve movement, and (ii) they do involve a special intonation, where the in situ *wh*-phrase is stressed. Since echo questions don't involve movement, they aren't going to be subject to the MLC (explaining the grammaticality of (68) and other examples like it). While *yes/no* questions and *wh*-questions have some kind of syntactic licensing, echo questions seem to be licensed by intonation and stress. In this regard they are similar to intonational questions that don't have subject-aux inversion, such as (71) (where the rising curve is meant to indicate raised intonation and the italics represent stress on the words):

71)

Fred saw a spaceship in *the linguistics lounge*?

Note that this question again has a subtly different meaning from the one with subject-aux inversion and *do*-support (*Did Fred see a spaceship in the linguistics lounge?*). The sentence with subject-aux inversion is a request for information. (71) is an expression of doubt and a request for confirmation. How such phonological licensing is encoded into the syntactic tree is very controversial. One solution is that, like *wh*-questions and *yes/no* questions, echo questions and intonational questions involve a special complementizer. We can indicate this as $C_{[+INT]}$. The [+INT] feature doesn't trigger any movements, but it instructs the phonology to put a rising intonation curve on the clause that follows the C. The stress has to do with contrastive focus. In English, contrastively focused material is stressed. *Wh*-in-situ in English (and in closely related languages) seems to be largely limited to echo-question contexts. However, *wh*-in-situ is the norm for real *wh*-questions in languages such as Chinese and Japanese. These languages appear to have no *wh*-movement at all. This will be a major topic of the next chapter.

6. CONCLUSION

In this chapter, we looked at a third kind of movement transformation: *Wh*-movement. This process targets *wh*-phrases and moves them to the specifier of CPs. This movement is triggered by the presence of a [+WH] feature in C. *Wh*-movement of a DP is always from a Case position to the specifier of CP. *Wh*-movement is not totally unrestricted; there is a locality constraint on the movement: the MLC. Movement must be local, where local is defined in terms of closest potential landing site. We saw further that the MLC might be extended to other types of movement.

In the next chapter, we're going to continue this trend and look at movement processes in general and the similarities between them, as well as briefly delve into the interaction between the syntax and the formal interpretation (semantics) of the sentence.

IDEAS, RULES, AND CONSTRAINTS INTRODUCED IN THIS CHAPTER

i)   **Wh-*movement***: Move a *wh*-phrase to the specifier of CP to check a [+WH] feature in C.

ii)   **Wanna-*contraction***: The contraction of *want* and *to*, which does not apply across a *wh*-trace.

iii)   **That-*trace Effect***: Movement of a *wh*-phrase from subject position in English is disallowed when that trace is preceded by the complementizer *that*.

iv)   **That-*trace Filter***: *[$_{CP}$ that *t* ...]

v)   **Relative Clause**: A CP that modifies a noun. These always have a "missing" element in them that corresponds to some kind of *wh*-element.

vi)   **Factive Clause**: A clause that is the complement to a factive verb (*know, claim, recall*, etc.), or to a factive noun (*knowledge, claim, fact, recollection*, etc.).

vii)   **Operator (Op)**: The *wh*-element in relative clauses without an overt *wh*-phrase.

viii)   **Restrictive Relative Clause**: A relative clause that restricts the meaning of a noun as a modifier. Adjoined to N'.

ix)   **Non-restrictive Relative Clause**: A relative clause that adds additional parenthetical commentary about a noun. Adjoined to D'.

x)   **Island**: A phrase that contains (dominates) the *wh*-phrase, and that you may not move out of.

xi)   **The Complex DP Constraint**: *wh$_i$ [... [$_{DP}$ ... t_i ...] ...]

xii)   **Wh-island Constraint**: *wh$_i$ [... [$_{CP}$ wh$_k$ [... t_i ...] ...] ...]

xiii)   **The Subject Condition**: *wh$_i$ ... [$_{TP}$ [$_{CP}$ ... t_i ...] T ...]

xiv)   **Coordinate Structure Constraint**:
        *wh$_i$ ... [$_{XP}$ [$_{XP}$ ... t_i ...] conj [$_{XP}$ ...]] ...
        or *wh$_i$ ... [$_{XP}$ [$_{XP}$ ...] conj [$_{XP}$ ... t_i ...]] ...
        or *wh$_i$ ... [$_{XP}$ [$_{XP}$ ...] conj t_i] ...
        or *wh$_i$ ... [$_{XP}$ t_i conj [$_{XP}$ ...]] ...

xv)   **Minimal Link Condition (MLC)***(intuitive version)*: Move to the closest potential landing site.

xvi)   **Wh-*in-situ***: When a *wh*-phrase does not move.

xvii)   **Echo Questions and Intonational Questions**: Question forms that are licensed by the phonology (intonation and stress) and not by the syntax, although they may involve a special C.

FURTHER READING: Baltin (1981), Bianchi (2002), Cheng (1997), Chomsky (1977, 1986a), Cinque (1981), Koopman (1984), Lasnik and Saito (1984), Lightfoot (1976), Manzini (1992), Richards (1997), Rizzi (1990), Ross (1967)

GENERAL PROBLEM SETS

GPS1. ENGLISH MOVEMENT SENTENCES
[Application of Skills; Basic to Advanced]
For each of the following sentences, give the D-structure tree and annotate it with arrows indicating what transformations have applied. The sentences may have head-to-head movement, *do*-support, expletive insertion, DP movement, and *wh*-movement.

a) What is bothering you?
b) Who has seen my snorkel?
c) How was the plot discovered by the authorities?
d) Which animals appear to have lost their collars?
e) What did Jean think was likely to have been stolen?
f) Car sales have surprised the stockbrokers.
g) Have you seen my model airplane collection?
h) Can you find the lightbulb store?
i) John was bitten by an advertising executive.
j) It is likely that Tami will leave New York.
k) Tami is likely to leave New York.
l) It seems that Susy was mugged.
m) Susy seems to have been mugged.
n) What did you buy at the supermarket?
o) I asked what Beth bought at the supermarket.
p) What is it likely for Beth to have bought at the supermarket?
    (Treat the PP *for Beth* as appearing the specifier of the embedded TP.)
q) What is likely to have been bought at the supermarket?
r) I ate a salad that was filled with lima beans.
s) The trail we walked today was built by slave labor.
t) Bill is always complaining about the guys who work near him.
u) The cost of bagels that are imported from Iceland surprised the teacher who(m) Mike hired last week.

GPS2. BINDING THEORY

[Critical Thinking; Basic]

In chapter 5, you were asked why the sentence below causes a problem for the binding theory. Remind yourself of your answer, and then explain how the model of grammar we have proposed in this chapter accounts for this fact.

Which pictures of himself does John despise?

GPS3. BINDING AND SCRAMBLING

[Critical Thinking; Intermediate/Advanced]
You should complete GPS 2 before attempting this problem set.

Modern Persian has a kind of movement often called **scrambling**. Your task in this problem set is to figure out whether scrambling is DP movement, head-to-head movement or *wh*-movement. The Persian word *hamdiga* means "each other" and is an anaphor. Assume that anaphors are subject to the binding theory of chapter 4, and that they must be in argument positions to be bound. Sentence (a) shows the basic order. Sentences (b) and (c) show the surface word order after scrambling has applied. The scrambled sentences mean almost exactly the same thing as (a). HAB stands for "habitual". Recall that $_{i/*k}$ means that the sentence is okay with the DP having the index $_i$ but not with the index $_k$. (Data from Simin Karimi.)

a) Mo'allem-â$_k$ fekr   mi-kon-an   [$_{CP}$ ke [$_{T'}$ [$_{vP}$ bachche-hâ$_i$
   teacher-PL   thought HAB-do-3PL   that   child-PL

   [$_{vP}$ aks - â -ye hamdiga$_{i/*k}$ - ro be modir   neshun dâd-an]]]].
   picture-PL-EZ each other - RÂ to principal sign   gave-3PL
   "The teachers$_k$ think that the children$_i$ showed [each other's]$_{i/*k}$ pictures to the principal."

b) Mo'allem-â$_k$ [aks-â-ye hamdiga$_{i/*k}$-ro]$_m$ fekr mi-kon-an [$_{CP}$ ke [$_{T'}$ [$_{vP}$ [bachche-hâ$_i$] [$_{vP}$ t$_m$ be modir neshun dâd-an]]]].

c) [Aks-â-ye hamdiga$_{i/*k}$-ro]$_m$ mo'allem-â$_j$ fekr mi-kon-an [$_{CP}$ ke   [$_{T'}$ [$_{vP}$ bachche-hâ$_i$ [$_{vP}$ t$_m$ be modir neshun dâd-an]]]].

GPS4. PICTURE DPs

[Critical Thinking; Intermediate/Advanced]

Why is the grammaticality of the following sentence surprising? Does the theory we have presented in this chapter predict this to be acceptable? What constraint should this sentence violate?

Who(m) did you see a picture of?

GPS5. LOCALITY
[Data Analysis; Basic]
Why is the following sentence ungrammatical?

*Who$_i$ did [$_{TP}$ George try to find out [$_{CP}$ what$_i$ [$_{TP}$ t$_j$ wanted t$_i$]]]?

Draw a tree showing the exact problem with this sentence. Be precise about what constraints rule it out.

GPS6. IRISH
[Data Analysis; Advanced]
Irish has a number of different complementizer forms. In declarative clauses (statements), it uses the complementizer *go/gur*. As discussed in the text above, when there is a question, this complementizer switches to the *wh*-form a^L. (The idea behind this problem set is taken from McCloskey 1979.)

a) Ceapann tú   go   bhuailfidh an píobaire an t-amhrán
     think   you that play.FUT   the piper   the song
     "You think that the piper will play the song."

b) Caidé a^L cheapann tú   a^L bhuailfidh an píobaire?
     What WH think   you WH play.FUT   the piper
     "What do you think the piper will play?"

Note carefully the number of a^L complementizers in sentence (b). (b) provides evidence that *wh*-phrases stop off in intermediate specifiers of CP (for MLC reasons). Explain why. You need to make the assumption that the complementizer a^L only shows up when a *wh*-phrase has at one point shown up in its specifier.

CHALLENGE PROBLEM SETS

CHALLENGE PROBLEM SET 1: WHO ATE THE PIZZA?
[Critical Thinking; Challenge]
In the text we suggested that subject questions involving an auxiliary have vacuous movement of both the *wh*-phrase (to the specifier of CP) and the auxiliary (to C$_{[+Q, +WH]}$), even though that leaves the subject *wh*-phrase and auxiliary in the same order they'd be in if they'd stayed in the TP:

a)

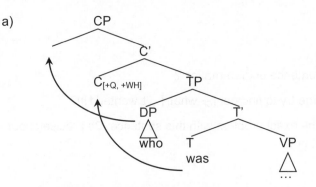

We suggested this was the case so that we could maintain that the feature-checking requirements hold here too.

Consider however the following sentence. Notice that the tense morphology is not realized as *did*, but on the main verb *ate*.

b)   Who ate the pizza?

Question 1: Explain why this is an argument against the vacuous movement shown in (a).

Question 2: If there is no vacuous movement, what then are we to make of the complementizer in subject questions? Is it [+Q, +WH]? Is there some way to explain why the complementizers with subject *wh*-questions are different than complementizers with object and adjunct *wh*-questions (which do show both *wh*-movement and T → C movement)?

CHALLENGE PROBLEM SET 2: MOVEMENT AND BINDING THEORY
[Creative and Critical Thinking; Challenge]
Consider the sentence in (a):

(a) Noah wonders which picture of himself Carlos likes best.

Many speakers report that (a) is ambiguous, with *himself* taking either *Carlos* or *Noah* as its antecedent. Why is the interpretation of *himself* being bound by *Noah* surprising? Can you come up with a creative explanation for why this is possible? Explain your answer thoroughly, illustrating your analysis by drawing a tree for sentence (a).

CHALLENGE PROBLEM SET 3: IRISH
[Data Analysis; Challenge]
Some dialects of English allow a kind of *wh*-construction, where the base position of the *wh*-phrase is filled by a **resumptive pronoun**. (The idea behind this problem set is taken from McCloskey 1991.)

This is the book$_i$ that the police are arresting everyone who reads it$_i$.

In Modern Irish, this kind of construction is very common. Modern Irish has two different *wh*-complementizers (notice that these are *not* wh-phrases, which go in the specifier of CP; these are complementizers): a^L, a^N. The complementizer a^L is found in sentences like (a). Sentence (i) shows a simple sentence without *wh*-movement using the non-*wh*-complementizer *go*. Sentences (ii) and (iii) show two possible forms of the question. (ii) has the question moved only to an intermediate CP specifier. (iii) has the *wh*-phrase moved to the topmost specifier.

a) i)   Bíonn fios   agat   i gconaí [_CP **go** bhuailfidh an píobaire an t-amhrán].
        be.HAB know at.2.S always   that play.FUT the piper   the song
        "You always know that the bagpiper will play the song."

   ii) Bíonn fios   agat   i gconaí [_CP caidé_i **a^L**   bhuailfidh an píobaire t_i].
        be.HAB know at.2.S always   what_i COMP   play.FUT the piper t_i
        "You always know what the bagpiper will play."

   iii) [_CP Cáidé_i **a^L** [_TP bhíonn fios   agat   i gconaí [_CP t_i **a^L** bhuailfidh an píobaire t_i]]]?
        What COMP be.HAB know at.2.S always t_j COMP play.FUT the piper t_i
        "What do you always know the piper will play?"

Now the distribution of the complementizer a^N seems to be linked to the presence of a resumptive pronoun. Consider the (ii) sentences in (b) and (c). Both show resumptive pronouns and the complementizer a^N:

b) i)   Bíonn fios   agat   i gconaí [_CP caidé_i **a^L**   bhuailfidh an píobaire t_i].
        be.HAB know at.2.S always   what_i COMP   play.FUT the piper t_i
        "You always know what the bagpiper will play."

   ii) [_CP Cén Píobaire_j **a^N** [_TP mbíonn fios agat i gconaí [_CP caidé_i **a^L** bhuailfidh **sé_j** t_i]]]?
        Which piper COMP be.HAB know at.2.S always what_i COMP play.FUT he
        "Which bagpiper do you always know what he will play?"

c) i)   Tá   máthair an fhir   san   otharlann.
        Be.PRES mother the man.GEN in.the hospital
        "The man's mother is in the hospital."

   ii) Cé_i **a^N**   bhfuil   **a_i** mháthair san   otharlann?
        who COMP be.PRES his mother   in.the hospital
        "Who is (his) mother in the hospital?"

The a^N complementizer and the resumptive pronouns are boldfaced in the above examples. Where precisely does the a^N-resumptive strategy appear? In what syntactic environment do you get this construction?

CHALLENGE PROBLEM SET 4: FRENCH NEGATION

[Critical Thinking; Challenge]
We've argued that in French the verb raises to T, and T raises to C in *yes/no* questions. Further in this chapter, we've argued that head movement is subject to the Minimal Link Condition. In previous chapters we've treated the French word *pas* as the head of NegP as in (a). Consider an alternative where *pas* isn't the head of NegP but is an adjunct to the VP as in (b):

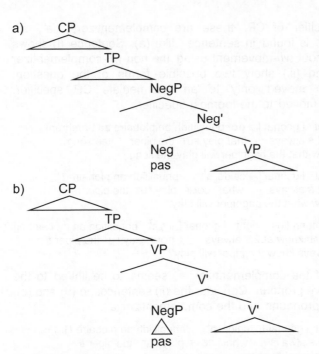

a) CP
   TP
      NegP
         Neg'
            Neg   VP
            pas

b) CP
   TP
      VP
         V'
            NegP   V'
            pas

Keep in mind the restriction in the MLC that the moving element can't skip potential landing sites that c-command it. Recall that V → T movement jumps over the word *pas*:

c) Je n'aime pas t_V des   pommes.
   I like   not   of.the apples.
   "I don't like apples"

Does this support the analysis in (a) or the analysis in (b)? Explain your answer.

chapter 13

A Unified Theory of Movement

0. INTRODUCTION

In the first few chapters of this book, we looked at rules that generate the basic phrase structure of human syntax. These rules generated trees that represent hierarchical structure and constituency. These trees have particular mathematical properties that we investigated in chapters 4 and 5. In chapter 6, we saw that stipulated phrase structure rules missed some very basic generalizations, and refined them into X-bar phrase structure rules. The X-

Syntax: A Generative Introduction, Third Edition. Andrew Carnie.
© 2013 Andrew Carnie. Published 2013 by John Wiley & Sons, Inc.

bar rules, being very general, allow us (informed by parameter settings) to generate a wide variety of trees and capture structural differences between heads, complements, adjuncts, and specifiers. In chapter 7, we extended the rules to various clause types, complementizers, and DPs. In chapters 8 and 9, we saw that, in fact, the X-bar rules actually generated too many structures, and that we had to constrain their power. The devices we used to limit them are semantic ones: the thematic properties of predicates (stored in the lexicon) and the theta criterion. What results from the output of the X-bar schema and the lexicon is called D-structure. The theta criterion holds of D-structures, as do the binding conditions. In chapters 10, 11, and 12, we saw a variety of cases where lexical items either could not be generated by X-bar theory where they surfaced (e.g., head-adjunct-complement ordering in French), or appeared in positions other than the ones predicted by theta theory. We developed a new kind of rule: the movement rule or transformation, which moves items around from their base positions in the D-structure to the actual positions they appear in on the surface. There are three movement transformations: Head-to-head movement (T → C and V → T), DP movement, and *wh*-movement. In each of these cases movement occurs because it *has* to. Each movement has a trigger or motivation. Heads move to fill empty [Q] features or to take an inflectional suffix. DPs move to check Case features. *Wh*-phrases move to be near the [WH] feature. We also posited two insertion transformations: *Do*-support and expletive insertion. The output of the transformations is called S-structure, which is itself subject to several constraints: the Case filter, the EPP and the Minimal Link Condition. The model (i.e., flowchart) of the grammar looks like (1). This straightforward model can generate a large number of sentence types. It is also a system with explanatory adequacy, which makes specific predictions about how a child goes about acquiring a language (via parameters).

The Minimalist Program

The system of grammar described in this chapter provides a very cursory look at some of the principles underlying the most recent version of generative grammar: the Minimalist Program (Chomsky 1993, 1995). The Minimalist Program is motivated by the search not only for explanatory adequacy but also for a certain level of formal simplicity and elegance. What is outlined here is by no means a complete picture, but is meant to give you a taste of what current work is aiming at.

1)

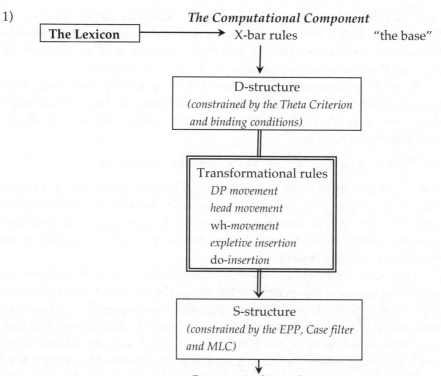

The Computational Component

| The Lexicon | ———————→ X-bar rules   "the base"

D-structure
*(constrained by the Theta Criterion
and binding conditions)*

Transformational rules
*DP movement
head movement
wh-movement
expletive insertion
do-insertion*

S-structure
*(constrained by the EPP, Case filter
and MLC)*

Grammaticality judgments

This is a fairly complete and simple system, but we might ask if the system can be made even simpler. Are we missing any generalizations here? Recent work in syntactic theory that answers this question suggests we might unify the different types of movement into a single rule type with a slight reorganization of the architecture of the grammar.

1. MOVE

In this book we've proposed the following motivations for transformations:

2) a) Head movement   *to get a suffix or fill null [+Q]*
    b) DP movement   *to check Case features [NOM] or [ACC]*
    c) *Wh*-movement   *to check a [+WH] feature*

Notice that while there are significant differences between the motivations for the various types of movement, there is one overwhelming similarity. The movements all occur so that one item can appear near another. In the case of head movement the V or T head needs to appear as part of the same word as the place it moves to. With *wh*-movement, the *wh*-phrase needs to be near the [WH] feature, just as DP movement occurs so the DP can check its Case feature with T or V. All the motivations for movement, then, seem to be **locality constraints**. That is, two items must be near or **local** to one another. This is a trend that we've seen in previous chapters.

If all the movement types are motivated by locality, then there isn't really a significant difference between the rule types. Perhaps we can unify them into a single rule: **Move**. Move says simply "move something" (but only if you have to):

3)   *Move (very informal version):* Move something somewhere.

Now of course, this is a bit vague and we'll have to sharpen it up in some way. In particular, we will want to constrain the rule so there isn't just random movement all over the sentence. So the next step is to formulate a constraint that motivates and forces this transformation to apply (in all the different circumstances).

Let's take *wh*-movement as our paradigm case. In *wh*-movement the *wh*-phrase moves to the specifier of CP so as to be local with a [WH] feature. Another way to think of this, as we suggested in chapter 12, is to say that both the *wh*-phrase and the complementizer have a [+WH] feature, and they need to compare them, or **check** them. Checking of features can only occur in a local configuration. In this case we have what is called a *specifier–head configuration,* for reasons that should be obvious from the following partial tree.

4)

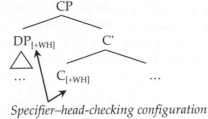

Specifier–head-checking configuration

The constraint that forces this movement to occur is called the **Principle of Full Interpretation** (Chomsky 1993, 1995).

5)   *Full Interpretation (FI):* Features must be checked in a local configuration.

6)   *Local Configuration (preliminary)*
     [WH] features: Specifier–head configuration.

We can extend this to the other cases of movement, too. As we suggested in chapter 11, imagine that Case is not simply an ending, but also a feature. A subject DP bears a [NOM] Case feature. Imagine also that the heads of the phrases that assign Case (T and V) also bear this feature (although they don't show it morphologically). We can thus reduce the Case filter to Full Interpretation: Nominative Case is feature-checking like that in (7) and accusative Case is like that in (8):

7)

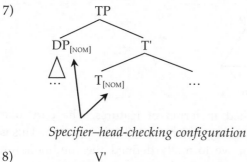

Specifier–head-checking configuration

8)

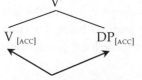

Head–complement-checking configuration

Finally, we can extend this to the head movement cases. Instead of claiming that verbs move to pick up inflectional suffixes in V → T movement, let's claim that both the V and the T head bear some kind of abstract inflectional features (e.g., [±past]). This allows us to capture the behavior of verbs with null T morphology as well as that of ones with affixes. When the verb and T check these features against one another then the suffix representing that tense feature (or agreement feature) is allowed to surface on the verb. The local configuration in this setting is within the head itself (a relationship which is called a head–head configuration):

9)

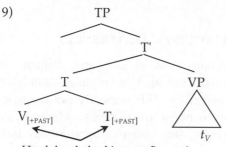

Head–head-checking configuration

Similarly, both T and C bear a [+Q] feature, and they must be in a head–head-checking relationship:

10)

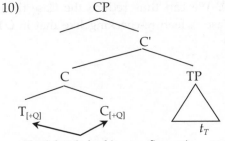

Head–head-checking configuration

Local configuration is thus defined in terms of features. The particular configuration required is determined by which feature is being used. This is very similar to the way in which we formally defined the conditions on the Minimal Link Condition in the previous chapter, where the intervening categories were relativized to the kind of feature being checked by the element that is moving. (11) is a summary of these local configurations.

11) *Local Configuration*:
   [WH], [NOM] features: specifier–head configuration.
   [ACC] features: head–complement configuration.[1]
   [PAST], etc., [Q] features: head–head configuration.

With this in place we actually have a very elegant transformational system. We have combined our three movement rules into one rule: Move; and two constraints: Full Interpretation and the Minimal Link Condition. In previous chapters, we've already argued that constituent structure is created by a few very limited phrase structure rules, which are constrained by the theta criterion and the lexical entries of categories. Computationally speaking, this is a surprisingly simple system of grammar.

2. EXPLAINING CROSS-LINGUISTIC DIFFERENCES

The system outlined above in section 1 is simple and elegant. It does however, make the unfortunate prediction that all languages will have exactly the same set of transformational rules. This is clearly not the case. English does not have V → T movement of main verbs. Many other languages lack passive and raising. Still others appear to lack

---

[1] In the next chapter we will claim that [ACC] is actually checked in a specifier–head configuration like [NOM]. This will allow us to create a phrase structure system that accounts for double object verbs and dative constructions.

wh-movement. Take the case of Mandarin Chinese (data from Huang 1982; tone is omitted).

12) a)   Ni xiang chi shenme?
         you want eat what
         "What do you want to eat?"

   b)   *Shenme ni xiang chi?
         what you want eat
         "What do you want to eat?"

   c)   Ni kanjian-le shui?
         you see-ASP who
         "Who did you see?"

   d)   *Shui ni kanjian-le?
         who you see-ASP
         "Who did you see?"

Chinese appears to have no *wh*-movement. As we discussed in the last chapter this is called **wh-*in-situ***. The Chinese case differs from English, however, in that these are not echo questions. These are real *wh*-questions, but the *wh*-phrase remains in situ. As such they should have [+WH] features on their Cs and on the *wh*-phrases – but no movement occurs. Why, then, is it the case that the unchecked [+WH] features on the *wh*-phrases don't violate Full Interpretation? They have not moved, so they are not in a local configuration with their C. Full Interpretation predicts that (12a) should be ungrammatical and (12b) should be grammatical – the opposite of the facts.

Our solution to this problem is going to surprise you. We're going to claim that in Chinese the *wh*-phrase does move, you just don't hear it! This requires a refinement of our grammar model.

Ferdinand de Saussure (a linguist from the early twentieth century) observed that every linguistic expression consists of two parts: the signifier and the signified. For our purposes, this roughly corresponds to the phonological or *phonetic form* of the sentence (abbreviated as PF) and its semantic or *logical form* (LF). We call these "forms" the *interface levels*, because they represent the interface with the phonological system and with the interpretive system, respectively. This means that when we're computing the grammaticality of a sentence we're really computing two distinct things: its sound (for the purposes of a syntactician this means the sequence of the words) and its meaning. To a certain degree these interface levels are computed together, but they also diverge from one another. When we look at the question cross-linguistically, we see that any particular PF order of elements does not directly correspond to some specific meaning. For example, the English sentence *I saw the man* and the Irish sentence *Chonaic mé an fear* (literally *Saw I the man*) *mean* the same thing, but they have different word orders. One way to represent this conundrum is by having two separate levels in our model of grammar that correspond to these interface levels. These levels represent the final products of our computation, so they should appear at the end of the derivation. This gives us a more refined model of the grammar than the one we saw in (1):

13)   **The Lexicon** ⟶ X-bar rules   The Base

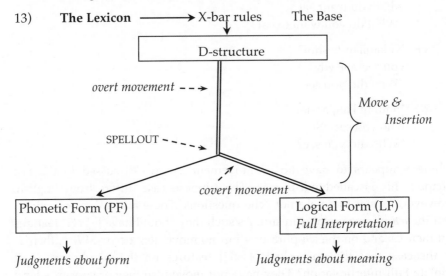

Let me draw your attention to some of the important differences between this model[2] and the model we had in (1). First of all you'll note that there is no S-structure. In the old model, S-structure was the level from which we drew grammaticality judgments. In this new model it is the interface levels PF and LF that give us well-formedness judgments (judgments about form) and semantic judgments respectively. Some of the derivation applies in tandem generating both the PF and the LF; these operations apply on the "stem" of the upside down Y. Then there is a point at which the derivation

---

[2] This model isn't entirely an accurate representation of Chomsky's Minimalist model. I have retained the notion of D-structure here. In Chomsky's version, the X-bar rules are replaced by an operation called Merge and there is no D-structure. In Chomsky's model the constraints we've claimed to be D-structure constraints (the Theta Criterion and the binding conditions) are handled differently. Getting rid of D-structure involves some tricky argumentation that lies beyond the scope of this textbook. Once you are finished reading this book have a look at some of the suggested readings at the end that will take you on to this more advanced material. This aside, the diagram in (13) is a fair representation of the Minimalist Program as understood by most linguists.

branches into operations that are purely about form and sound and operations that are purely about meaning. This branching point is called *SPELLOUT* (usually in all capital letters). After SPELLOUT, the derivation proceeds along two distinct paths, one generating the PF, the other the LF. Chomsky (1993) makes two important claims. First he claims that Full Interpretation is a constraint that holds of sentences at LF. Second, he claims that exactly the same operations that happen between D-structure and SPELLOUT can also happen between SPELLOUT and LF (in (13) this is indicated by means of the double line that extends from D-structure to SPELLOUT and from SPELLOUT to LF). Move can apply anywhere along this double line.

At first this may seem counterintuitive, but there are kinds of movement that can happen *after* SPELLOUT; that is, after the pronounced order has been created, and the "form" portion of the sentence is sent off to PF. This is a mind-bending notion, but actually allows us to make the following remarkable claim about cross-linguistic variation: *Every instance of feature-checking-motivated movement happens in every single language.* Why would we want to do such a thing? Let us assume, not uncontroversially, that the kinds of meaning determined by the syntax are universally held by all humans. This is *not* to say that all humans have identical world-views or identical perceptions of events, etc.; we are not making such a strong claim here. This is not a claim about cultural or personal interpretations. This is simply a *limited* statement that all humans have a notion of what it means to express a declaration, a *yes/no* question, a *wh*-question, a passive, a sentence with raising, etc. These kinds of constructions, and relationships such as constituency and the binding conditions *do* seem to be universal in interpretation even if they do have different forms cross-linguistically. Let us call such basic interpretations **universal semantics**. If, as we have hypothesized throughout this book, this basic semantic content is determined by our X-bar phrase structure system (which creates constituents) and the movement operations (which check to make sure that there is a featural correspondence among the words in the constituent structure), then universal semantics should be generated the same way in every language. Yet it goes without saying that every language has different (yet narrowly limited) ways of expressing that universal semantics. The Y model gives us a straightforward way of accounting for this. The differences between languages are in when that movement occurs: before SPELLOUT or after. Essentially there are two kinds of movement: movement that happens between D-structure and SPELLOUT (called *overt* movement) and movement that happens between SPELLOUT and LF (called *covert* movement). Since covert movement happens after the branching off to the PF (phonology) component, you simply can't hear it happen! The differences between languages, then, are in when they time specific instances of the general operation Move. English times those instances involving [WH] features overtly before SPELLOUT. Chinese times those same movements covertly, after SPELLOUT. This can be simply encoded in a parameter:

14) Wh-*parameter*: Overt/Covert (English: "Overt", Chinese: "Covert")

This parameter determines whether movement applies before S-structure or after:

15)

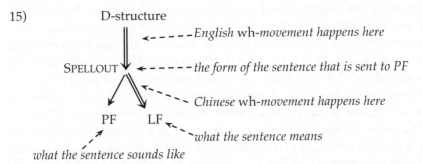

To make this clearer let us abstractly show each step of the derivation for Mandarin Chinese and English (I'm abstracting away from *do*-insertion, etc.):

16)

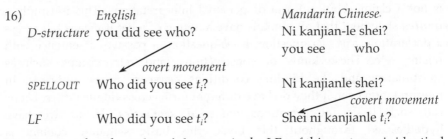

You'll notice that the order of elements in the LFs of this sentence is identical in both languages, but the SPELLOUT form is different. You never hear the LFs. You only hear the SPELLOUT forms. The LFs are identical because the two sentences (in the two languages) mean the same thing.

This kind of analysis has a nice side effect. It also allows us to explain the head movement parameter in a more explanatory way. In chapter 10, it is just a stipulation. Here we can explain it as part of the general architecture of the model. With the system described above English has V → T movement like French, only in English it is timed covertly, so you don't hear it.

17)   *French*   *English*
   D-structure Je souvent mange des pommes.   I often eat apples.
                  I   often ⁄ eat   of.the apples
                           overt movement
   SPELLOUT   Je mange₍ᵢ₎ souvent tᵢ des pommes.   I often eat apples.
                                                         ⁄ *covert movement*
   LF   Je mange₍ᵢ₎ souvent tᵢ des pommes.   I eatᵢ often tᵢ apples.

Again, these sentences mean the same thing, so they have identical LFs. The word order in the two sentences is different, so the SPELLOUTs are different. Again this is encoded in a parameter:

18) *Verb movement parameter*: Overt/Covert
    (French sets at Overt; English sets at Covert)

In this view of things, differences in the word order of the world's languages reduce to a matter of timing in the derivation.

You now have enough information to try WBE 1–3, GPS 1 & 2, and CPS 2.

---

3. Scope, Covert Movement, and the MLC

At first blush the whole notion of a movement you cannot hear seems pretty suspicious (just like empty words that you can't hear seems suspicious). There is some evidence it does exist, however. This evidence comes from the behavior of *wh*-questions in Japanese and from English sentences with quantifiers.

3.1 MLC Effects in Wh-*in-situ Languages*

Let's compare two hypotheses. One is the covert movement hypothesis proposed above in section 1. That is, in languages like Mandarin Chinese and Japanese, *wh*-phrases move just as in English but they move covertly, so that you don't hear the movement. The other hypothesis (on the surface less suspicious) is simply that *wh*-phrases don't move in Mandarin and Japanese. Consider the predictions made by these two hypotheses with respect to island conditions and the MLC. Island effects are seen in English precisely because there is movement. Too long a movement (violating the MLC) causes the sentence to be ill-formed. When there is no movement, obviously, no violations of the MLC will occur. Now compare our two hypotheses about Japanese. The first hypothesis, according to which there is (covert) movement, predicts that Japanese will show MLC violations. The other hypothesis predicts that no violations will appear since there is no *wh*-

movement. The following sentence is only ungrammatical with the meaning indicated (it is grammatical with other meanings, such as an echo-question interpretation).

19) *[Nani-o   doko-de   katta   to]   oboete-iru   no?
       what-ACC   where-at   bought Q   remember   Q
    "What do you remember where we bought?"

If this data can be explained by the MLC, then we know that movement occurs – even if we can't hear it – because this constraint is sensitive to movement.

You now have enough information to try GPS 3 and CPS 2.

3.2 English Quantifiers and Scope

If LF is truly a semantic construct, we expect to find some semantic correlations to covert movement. One typical assumption about semantics is that there are some similarities between it and the semantics expressed by formal logic. With this in mind consider the following discussion of English quantifier scope.

We call words like *every* and *all* **universal quantifiers.** In formal logic these are represented by the symbol ∀. Words like *some* are **existential quantifiers** and are represented by the symbol ∃. In logic, quantifiers are said to hold **scope** over constituents containing variables. Variables are items that stand for arguments in the meaning of the sentence. The logical representation of an expression like *Everyone dances* is given in (20).

20) ∀x [x dances]

This means that for every (∀) person you choose (represented by x), then that person (x) dances. The quantifier ∀ has scope over the variable x. This is indicated by the brackets that surround [x dances]. One popular interpretation of the logical relation of scope is that it corresponds directly to the syntactic relation of c-command. So at LF the structure of (20) is (21):

21)

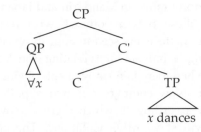

The quantifier phrase (QP) c-commands the TP, thus it holds scope over it. The quantifier is said to bind the variable it holds scope over. (In logic, this is represented as having the first x next to the $\forall$, and then the other x inside the brackets.)

An interesting phenomenon arises when we look at sentences with more than one quantifier. The following sentence is ambiguous in English:

22) Everyone loves someone.

This can have two meanings. The first meaning is that for every person in the world there is some other person who they love: Mary loves John, Bill loves Susy, Rose loves Kim, ..., etc. The other meaning is that there is one person in the world that everyone else in the world loves: Mary loves John, Bill loves John, Rose loves John, ..., etc. Using a pseudo-logical paraphrase we can represent these two meanings as (23). The actual logical representations are given in (24):

23) a)   For every person x, there is some person y, where x loves y.
    b)   For some person y, every person x loves y.

24) a) $\forall x(\exists y[x \text{ loves } y])$ b) $\exists y(\forall x[x \text{ loves } y])$

In logical notation, you'll notice that the difference between the two meanings lies in the order of the quantifiers, which reflects the embedding of the structure. The universal quantifier in (24a) is said to have *wide scope*, whereas in (24b) it has *narrow scope*.

In chapter 3, we claimed that if a sentence is ambiguous, then there are two tree structures for the sentence. It would be nice if we could draw two different trees that represent the two meanings of these sentences. As mentioned above, one hypothesis about scope phenomena is that they reflect c-command. That is, a quantifier has scope over everything it c-commands.[3] Consider the meaning in (23a). We can easily see this scope when we draw the simplified tree (QP stands for quantifier phrase). *Everyone* here c-commands *someone*, so the wide scope reading for the universal quantifier is derived (25). The narrow scope reading is more difficult. If this hypothesis is correct, then in the tree for (23b) *someone* must c-command *everyone*. The only way to get this fact is to move the quantifier. This kind of movement is called *quantifier raising* or *QR* (26). In this QR sentence, *someone* c-commands *everyone*, and so has scope over it. This derives the narrow scope reading for the universal quantifier. Obviously, this quantifier-raising analysis cannot be

---

[3] A full discussion of the semantics and structure of scope lies well beyond the purview of this book. See Heim and Kratzer (1998) for more on this complicated topic.

overt. The surface string for this ambiguous sentence is *everyone loves someone* (not **someone everyone loves*). In order to get the second meaning for this sentence we need to propose movement you can't hear, in other words, covert movement. Covert movement thus has independent justification.

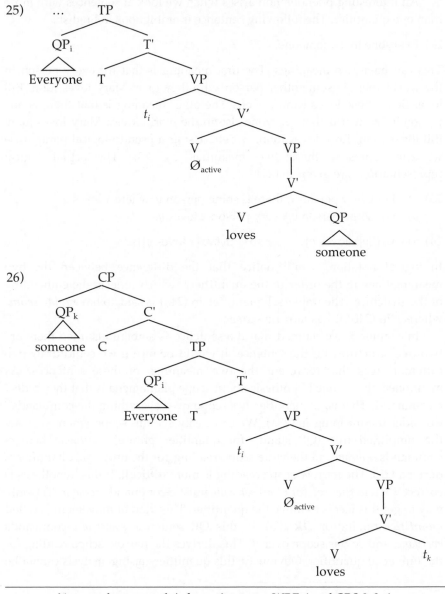

25)

26)

You now have enough information to try WBE 4 and CPS 3 & 4.

---

4. CONCLUSION

In this chapter we made the big jump from three movement rules with different but similar motivations to a single rule with a single motivation (Full Interpretation). We also claimed that cross-linguistic variation in movement, when we assume a universal semantics, requires that movement can both be overt (before SPELLOUT) and covert (after SPELLOUT). The Y model with Saussurean interface levels (LF and PF) allows this to occur. We also looked very briefly at an example from quantifier scope that provides independent support for the notion of covert movement.

IDEAS, RULES, AND CONSTRAINTS INTRODUCED IN THIS CHAPTER

i)   *Move (very informal version)*: Move something somewhere.

ii)   **Full Interpretation**: Features must be checked in a local configuration.

iii)   **Local Configuration**:
    [WH], [NOM] features: specifier–head configuration.
    [ACC] features: head–complement configuration.
    [PAST] etc., [Q] features: head–head configuration.

iv)   *Logical Form (LF)*: The semantic/interpretive system.

v)   *Phonetic Form (PF)*: The overt component of grammar.

vi)   *SPELLOUT*: The point at which the derivation divides into form (PF) and meaning structures (LF).

vii)   *Overt Movement*: Movement between D-structure and SPELLOUT.

viii)   *Covert Movement*: Movement between SPELLOUT and LF.

ix)   **Universal Quantifier (∀)**: A word such as *every, each, all, any*. Identifies all the members of a set.

x)   **Existential Quantifier (∃)**: A word like *some*, or *a*. Identifies at least one member of a set.

xi)   *Scope*: A quantifier's scope is the range of material it c-commands.

xii)   **Wide vs. Narrow Scope**: Wide scope is when one particular quantifier c-commands another quantifier. Narrow scope is the opposite.

xiii)   **Quantifier Raising (QR)**: A covert instance of Move that moves quantifiers.

FURTHER READING: Cheng (1997), Chomsky (1991, 1993, 1995), Heim and Kratzer (1998), Huang (1982), May (1985), Saito and Lasnik (1994)

GENERAL PROBLEM SETS

GPS1. FRENCH
[Data Analysis; Basic]
Go back and look at all the French data in chapter 10 and determine if French has overt or covert DP movement. Explain your answer.

GPS2. IRISH
[Data Analysis; Basic]
Go back and look at all the Irish data in chapters 10, 11, and 12 and determine whether Irish has overt or covert *wh*-movement, overt or covert DP movement, and overt or covert head movement.

GPS3. PF MOVEMENT
[Creative and Critical Thinking; Advanced]
In the text above, we proposed that some movement was covert. That is, it happened between SPELLOUT and LF. This movement affects meaning, but it doesn't affect how the sentence is pronounced. Can you think of any kind of movement that might occur just on the PF branch of the model? That is, are there any phenomena that affect only how the sentence is pronounced, but not its meaning?

CHALLENGE PROBLEM SETS

CHALLENGE PROBLEM SET 1: NEPALI AND MONGOLIAN
[Data Analysis; Challenge]
Consider the following data from Nepali and Mongolian (data from Erin Good and Amy LaCross respectively). Do these languages have overt or covert *wh*-movement? How can you tell?

Nepali:
a) Timilai uu   kahile aunche   jasto-lagcha?
   you   she when coming   think
   "When do you think she is coming?"

b) Timi kahile   aaunchau?
   you when   coming
   "When are you going to come?"

c) Ramle Sitale kun   manche ayecha bhaneko sochecha?
    Ram   Sita which man   came   said   think?
    "Which man did Ram think that Sita said came?"

Mongolian:
d) Ekč   jamar   hɔl hix   ve?
    older-sister which-one food make C$_{[+Q]}$
    "Which food will the older sister make?"

CHALLENGE PROBLEM SET 2: ECHO QUESTIONS IN ENGLISH
[Critical Thinking; Challenge]
Give an argument that echo questions in English involve no movement at all (neither overt nor covert), and thus are very different from the covert movement found in languages like Chinese and Japanese. Hint: The evidence will come from the MLC (which is a condition on **movement**). The following sentences might help you:

a) Who does John think loves *what*?
b) John wonders who loves what.
c) The claim that John ate *what* bothers Sue.

CHALLENGE PROBLEM SET 3: SCOPE OF NEGATION
[Data Analysis, Creative and Critical Thinking; Challenge]
The following sentence is ambiguous:

a) The editor did not find many mistakes in the paper.

This can either mean

i) The editor isn't very good, and although there were many mistakes he didn't find them.
ii) The editor searched thoroughly for mistakes, but the paper didn't have many mistakes in it.

We can express these variations in meaning using scope. With meaning (i), we have a situation where *many* has scope over negation (i.e. *many* c-commands *not* ($\neg$) or in logic: MANYx [$\neg$ find (editor, x)]). (That is, *many* has wide scope.) By contrast, in the narrow scope reading (ii), *not* c-commands *many* ($\neg$ find (editor, MANYx)).

Part 1: Draw the LF tree for each of the meanings. Keep in mind that the word order for (i) will not be the same as the SPELLOUT order, so you are drawing the tree for the LF, which includes movement that is covert. Also assume that only quantifiers move; negation does not move.

Part 2: Consider now the passive form of this sentence:

b) Many mistakes were not found in the paper by the editor.

This sentence is not ambiguous. It only has one meaning: wide scope for many (that is, the meaning in (i) above). This sentence can never have the meaning in (ii) above. Why should this be the case? (Hint: ask yourself if it is possible to create an LF with negation c-commanding *many* for (b). Remember, negation does not move.)

CHALLENGE PROBLEM SET 4: STRONG CROSSOVER[4]
[Data Analysis, Creative and Critical Thinking; Challenge]
Strong crossover is a phenomenon illustrated in (1). The effect of crossover is that *wh*-words can't be moved over a coindexed pronoun. Such movement creates a binding condition violation.

1) a) *Who$_i$ does he$_i$ see t_i?
   b) ?*Who$_i$ does his$_i$ mother love t$_i$?

Consider now the data in (2). Given what you know about the source of the ungrammaticality in the sentences in (1), how does the ungrammaticality of the sentence in (2) serve as an argument for quantifier raising as covert movement of quantifier phrases?

2) *He$_i$ saw me visit nobody$_i$.

---

[4] Thanks to Yosuke Sato for this problem set.

Part 4

Advanced Topics

Expanded VPs

0. INTRODUCTION

In chapters 1–13, we sketched out the major theoretical tools assumed by a large number of syntacticians operating in the generative framework. The next few chapters take us away from these agreed-upon areas, and focus on important material that is both more controversial and more advanced. The discussion in these chapters is going to be more open-ended. Do not expect a perfect answer or even an answer that can be considered "right". Instead, our discussion will consider some major lines of thought about these more difficult topics.

Syntax: A Generative Introduction, Third Edition. Andrew Carnie.
© 2013 Andrew Carnie. Published 2013 by John Wiley & Sons, Inc.

1. THE PROBLEM OF DITRANSITIVE VERBS[1]

In chapters 2 and 8, we discussed a number of ditransitive verbs, such as *put* of subcategory $V_{[DP \_ DP \ PP]}$, *give* of subcategory $V_{[DP \_ DP \ \{DP/PP\}]}$, and *tell* of subcategory $V_{[DP \_ DP \ \{CP/DP\}]}$. In many cases the third argument of these verbs seems to function like a complement, aside from the fact that it is not immediately adjacent to the verb. For example, no adjunct may intervene between the two post-verbal DP arguments of the verb *give*:

1) a) *Josh gave Clay carefully a book.
    b) Josh gave Clay a book carefully.

However, we know from our study of X-bar theory in chapters 6 and 7 that (i) we are only ever allowed one complement and (ii) complements of verbs must be adjacent to their verbs. This follows from the fact that X-bar theory requires trees to be strictly binary-branching. So the place to attach these "second" complements is a mystery (2):

2)

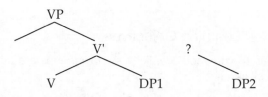

Even if we were to allow ternary branching as in (3), a different problem emerges. In (3) the two DPs c-command one another; thus we might expect a symmetry between them in terms of binding relationships.

3)

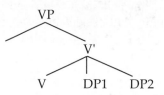

Barss and Lasnik (1986) showed that there is actually a clear asymmetry between these two DPs, as if the first one c-commanded the second, but not vice versa. This can be seen in examples (4a and b) where we have a typical anaphor–antecedent relationship (Principle A). As you can see, the indirect object *Justin* can bind a direct object anaphor; but the reverse is not possible. If the structure of the sentence were (3), then the anaphor should be able

---

[1] Many thanks to Heidi Harley for allowing me access to her teaching materials for the preparation of this chapter.

to appear in either position because the two DPs symmetrically c-command one another.

4) a) Briana showed Justin$_i$ himself$_i$ in the mirror.
    b) *Briana showed himself$_i$ Justin$_i$ in the mirror.

These facts show that in terms of c-command relationships, the two DPs must be in a configuration like that in (5):

5)

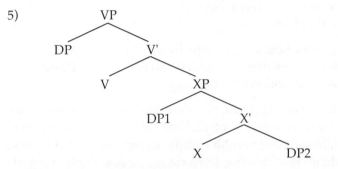

It's only in a configuration like (5) that DP1 c-commands DP2 and DP2 does not c-command DP1. Of course the obvious question that arises then lies in the nature of the category labeled X in (5). We address this question in the next section.

You now have enough information to try GPS 1.

2. THE ACTIVE VOICE HEAD AND OTHER LIGHT VERBS

Back in chapters 9 and 10, we proposed, largely on the basis of the subject position in VSO languages, that subject arguments were introduced into sentences by a silent voice head $\emptyset_{active}$, which sits right atop the lexical verb and alternates with the passive be_{pass}. As I've hinted before, you should be suspicious when a theoretician starts proposing null categories, even in the light of strong evidence such as the need for a subject position in VSO languages. In this section, let's flesh this claim out a bit by looking at a pattern of morphology found in a lot of the world's languages.

In Japanese (6a), Hiaki (6b), and Malagasy (6c), we see that certain simple verbs in English correspond to morphologically complex structures in these languages. These each consist of (at least) a verb root and some other morpheme that speakers report as either marking agentivity, or making the root into a full verb. I have abbreviated this light verb element, following Chomsky (1995), as "v". This is usually called *little v* and it roughly corresponds to $\emptyset_{active}$. From this point forward in the book, I'll replace $\emptyset_{active}$ with one of these little vs.

6) a) Keiko-wa   pizza-o   ag-**e**-ta.
        Keiko-TOP   pizza-ACC   rise-**v**-PAST
        "Keiko raised the pizza."

    b) Huan   u'usit-ta   ee-**tua**-k.
        Juan   child-ACC   feel-**v**-PAST
        "Juan teased the child."

    c) M-**an**-sasa   ny lamba   amin ny savony   Rasoa.
        PAST-**v**-wash   the clothes   with the soap   Rasoa
        "Rasoa washes the clothes with the soap."

A number of scholars have suggested that even in English, agentive verbs are bimorphemic. There is a verb root that indicates the lexical meaning of the word and a light verb that roughly means "cause". So a verb like *clean* really means something like "to cause to be clean". Kratzer (1996) suggests that agentive theta roles are not assigned by the verb, but by the light verb[2] contained within it. So if we take a verb like *clean*, this is really composed of the little v meaning "cause" (CAUSE), which assigns the agent role and takes a VP as a complement (we will refer to the theta role assigned to this VP as "predicate"), and the lexical root √CLEAN, which takes the theme as a complement:

7) CAUSE *(to be revised)*   √CLEAN

Agent	Predicate
DP	VP
i	j

Theme
DP
k

So the tree for the sentence *Ryan cleaned the window* contains a vP dominating a VP. The subject DP moves for the usual Case and EPP reasons. In order to create the verb *clean* out of CAUSE and √CLEAN there is overt head movement of the V into the v category. This verb movement is sometimes called "short" verb movement or V → v movement. There is also covert movement of the v+V to T indicated by a dotted curved line in the tree below. The tree in (8) should be relatively familiar: we've simply replaced $\emptyset_{active}$ with the semantically richer head CAUSE. However, the short verb movement is new.

You now have enough information to try GPS 2.

---

[2] Kratzer actually calls the category *voice*, and suggests that it is of the same category as the auxiliary verb that introduces the passive discussed in chapter 10.

8)

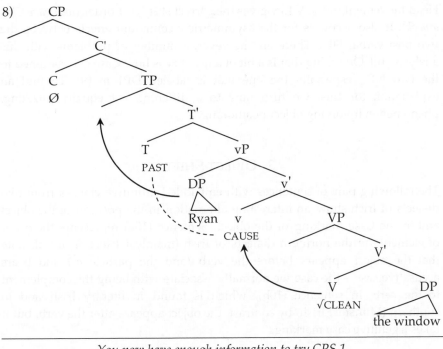

You now have enough information to try CPS 1.

Let's consider how this might extend to ditransitives. It is a simple matter to substitute little v and big V in for the verb and X in (5), giving (9):

9)

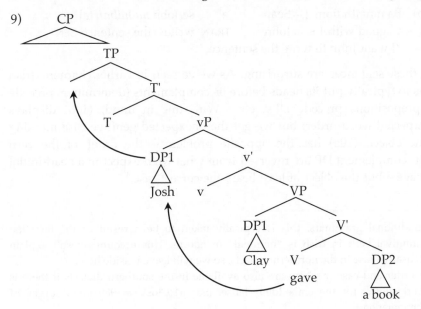

Head movement of the V to v gives the correct SPELLOUT order (*Josh gave Clay a book*). It also accounts for the asymmetric c-command effects between the two post-verbal DPs. There are, however, a number of problems with this analysis still. One thing that is a bit of a mystery is how Case gets assigned to the two NPs, especially the one that is labeled DP1 in (9). To find an explanation for this, we turn now to a different, yet equally puzzling, phenomenon involving object positioning.

3. OBJECT SHIFT

The following pair of sentences with embedded infinitive clauses from two dialects of Irish show an interesting alternation in the position of the object and in the Case marking of the object. Sentence (10a) represents the order of elements in the northern dialects of Irish (mainly Ulster). You will note that the object appears before the verb (and the particle a^L) and bears accusative case – the case we normally associate with being the complement to the verb. In sentence (10b), which is found in literary Irish and in southern (Munster) Irish, by contrast, the object appears after the verb, but it takes a genitive case marking.[3]

10) a)   Ba mhaith liom   [$_{CP}$ Seán   ***an abairt***   a^L scríobh].
        C   good with.1.S   John   the sentence.ACC TRAN write
        "I want John to write the sentence."

    b)   Ba mhaith liom [$_{CP}$ Seán   a^L scríobh ***na habairte***].
        C   good with.1.S   John   TRAN   write   the sentence.GEN
        "I want John to write the sentence."

Both these sentences are surprising. As we've seen in earlier chapters, Irish seems to typically put its heads before its complements (determiners precede Ns, prepositions precede DPs, etc.). With this in mind, (10b) displays the expected word order; but we get the unexpected genitive case marking on the object. (10a) has the opposite problem – the order of the verb and its complement DP are reversed from what we'd expect in a head-initial language – but the object at least bears the correct case.[4]

---

[3] In traditional grammars, this is typically taken to be a result of the fact that the infinitival verb in Irish is "nominal" in nature. This account doesn't explain the accusative case in the northern dialects, so we will leave it aside here.

[4] This order and case marking are also available in the southern dialects if there is no overt subject for the embedded clause. (See McCloskey 1980 for a survey of the phenomenon.)

We find a similar variation in literary Irish when we look at main clauses in different aspects. In the progressive aspect (11b), objects follow the main verb and take the genitive case. In the recent perfect (11a), objects precede the main verb (and the particle a^L), and take the accusative case:

11) a)   Tá   Seán tar eis ***an abairt*** a^L scríobh.
         be.PRES John PERF   the sentence TRAN write
         "John has just written the sentence."

   b)   Tá   Seán ag   scríobh ***na habairte***.
         be.PRES John PROG write the sentence
         "John is writing the sentence."

This kind of alternation, known as ***object shift***, is not an esoteric property of Irish; it is found in a wide variety of languages. Take the embedded clauses below taken from German (data from Diesing 1992); in particular focus on the order of negation and the DP referring to "the cat":

12) a)   ... weil ich *nicht* [DP eine einzige Katze] gestreichelt habe
              since I   not   a   single cat   petted   have
         "... since I have not petted a single cat"

   b)   ... weil ich [DP die Katze] *nicht* streichle
              since I   the cat   not   pet
         "... since I do not pet the cat"

The conditions for object shift here are different from the Irish example (the alternation is around negation instead of around the verb; and the alternation seems to be linked to definiteness/specificity rather than case), but this also appears to be a case of object alternation.

We can even find a related alternation in English. Consider complex verbs like *blow up*. With full NPs, the direct object can either precede or follow the particle *up* (13a and b), but pronouns – the only nouns in English to morphologically express case – must appear in the middle of the complex verb (13c and d):

13) a)   I blew up the building.
   b)   I blew the building up.
   c)   *I blew up it.
   d)   I blew it up.

These alternations in object position all differ in their specifics, but clearly we have some kind of movement operation that affects the position of objects.

The Irish case is particularly illustrative, as it shows an alternation in case marking. Accusative case is only available in the shifted position.

Building upon a proposal of Pollock (1989) and Chomsky (1991) we can propose that there is a special functional category whose sole purpose is accusative Case assignment. The name of this category is *AgrO* (standing for object agreement, the basic idea behind this name being that the Case assigner is usually the constituent that agrees with the object). The head of AgrO in Irish is the particle a^L,[5] which follows the shifted object. For Irish object shift, then, we have a structure where the object moves from the position where it gets its theta role to this shifted position where it gets accusative Case:

14)

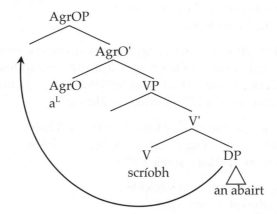

AgrOP seems to be located between VP and vP. This can be seen in the following sentence from Scots Gaelic (a language closely related to Irish), where the shifted object appears before the a^L AgrO morpheme but after the auxiliary light verb *bhith*:

15) Bu toigh leam [$_{CP}$ sibh a^L bhith air ***an dorus*** a^L dhùnadh].
     be like with me   you AGR v   PERF the door AGR close
     "I'd like you to have shut the door." (Adger 1996)

You now have enough information to try GPS 3 & 4 and CPS 2.

Leaving aside the upper portion of the tree, the structure of the expanded VP then is at least as follows, with CAUSE.

---

[5] This is a different a^L from the one seen in the problem sets in chapter 12. It is simply homophonous in the same way that the English infinitive marker *to* is homophonous with the preposition *to*.

16)

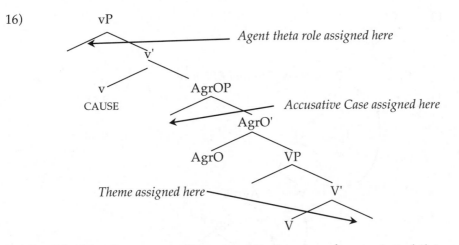

AgrOP also gives us an elegant explanation for why passives fail to assign accusative Case. Be_{pass} doesn't select for AgrO in its theta grid. Instead, it selects directly for VP. We can contrast CAUSE with be_{pass} in terms of what category they select as in (17):

17) a) CAUSE *(final)*

| Agent | AgrOP |
DP	
i	j

   b) Be_{pass}

VP[FORM *participle*]
j

Since be_{pass} doesn't have an AgrO complement, and selects directly for the VP, there's no place for the theme argument of the VP to get Case, so it has to raise to subject position. This contrasts with the active CAUSE v, which does select for an AgrO, so there is a Case position. I've illustrated these two options in the following trees for the active sentence *I struck the ball* and the passive *the ball was struck*. First in (18) we have an active sentence, where there is a CAUSE light verb that selects for AgrOP. This, in turn, selects for the VP with a theme. The V raises to CAUSE (through AgrO because of the MLC), which puts it in front of the specifier of AgrO. The object raises to the specifier of AgrOP where it gets accusative Case. The subject argument moves to the specifier of TP for nominative Case and the EPP.

18)

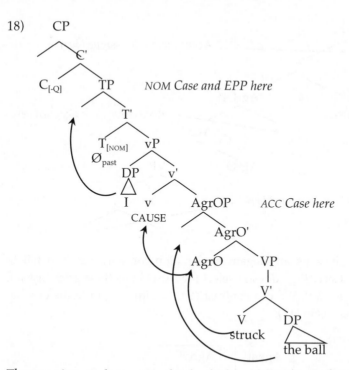

The passive v be_{pass} completely lacks AgrO (and the agent role). So simultaneously there is no agent to move into the subject position and no AgrO to assign accusative Case. So the object moves to the specifier of TP instead – the closest position for Case given the MLC (19). The main verb is in its participle form and doesn't move into the little v. Splitting the VP into two bits and putting AgrOP (in some cases) between the vP and VP has a fair amount of explanatory force. It allows an explanation of the phenomenon of object shift, but also allows us to explain the differences in Case assignment in actives and passives, without stipulation beyond the selectional requirements of the two types of light verbs. If you do the exercises at the end of this chapter you'll have an opportunity to come up with a couple of additional arguments in favor of splitting the VP this way, using some other kinds of data.

19)

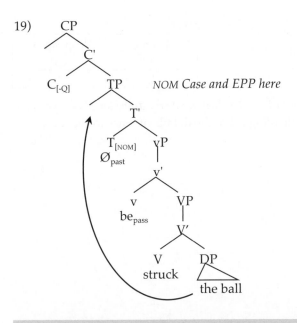

NOM Case and EPP here

The Form of the Main Verb

There's an interesting side effect of the short V to v movement here. Recall, way back in chapter 11, we were forced to stipulate that the $\varnothing_{active}$ was transparent to the FORM feature requirements of the verb above it. We needed to do this to make sure that the $\varnothing_{past}$ T node could see through $\varnothing_{active}$ to the verb and force the verb to be in a preterite form. But here, you'll see that the V raises to the *cause* head. Now it is in the head of the phrase selected by $\varnothing_{past}$, so it's going to take the preterite form. No stipulation that $\varnothing_{active}$ or CAUSE is transparent for the purpose of the form feature is necessary. The V is inside CAUSE, which is the head of the complement of $\varnothing_{past}$, so it naturally takes the preterite form

4. DITRANSITIVES: REPRISE

Let's now return to ditransitive verbs. For verbs where the final argument is a PP and CP we have a straightforward account of where all the arguments get theta roles and Case. First let's look at a verb like *tell* which can take both a DP and a CP complement. First we have the theta grids for the little v and the root √TELL.

20) CAUSE

Agent	AgrOP
DP	
i	j

√TELL

Theme	Proposition
DP	CP
k	l

Given a sentence like *Nate told Brandon that Kimberly drove an SUV*, we have a D-structure tree as in (21) (leaving aside the details of tense inflection).

21)

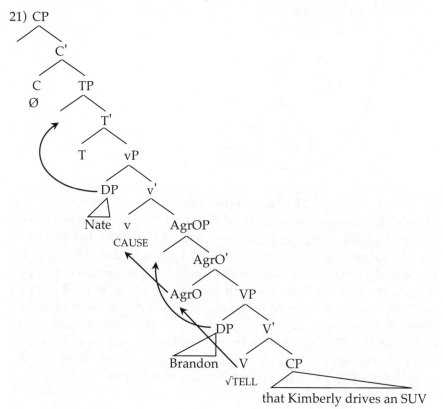

that Kimberly drives an SUV

The root moves through AgrO and into CAUSE; it must stop in AgrO on its way up to the little v in order to meet the MLC. The DP *Brandon* shifts to the specifier of AgrOP to get Case.

A similar analysis can be applied to verbs like *put*, which take a PP second complement, as in the sentence *Briana put the mug on the counter*:

22) CP

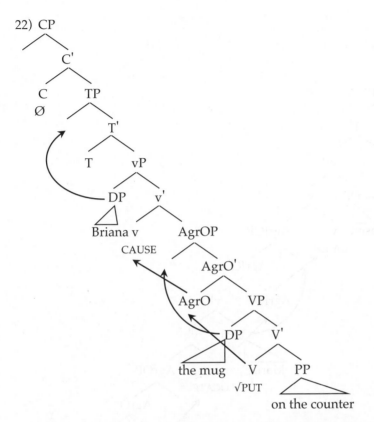

The last kind of ditransitive is more difficult. This is the case of *give*. *Give* allows two possible argument structures. One has a DP theme and a PP goal (as in *Jason gave the tape recorder to Maria*). This version of *give* presumably has a structure like that in (28). The other version of *give* takes two DP complements (*Jason gave Maria the tape recorder*). There are two puzzles with this kind of construction. First we have the issue of the source of accusative Case for the goal DP. Second and more curious is the fact that the indirect object goal precedes the direct object theme. If the theme moves to the specifier of AgrOP for Case, then the goal must be moving to a higher position than that. One possibility that has been proposed is that goals can be introduced by two distinct mechanisms. One is via a preposition like *to*. The other is using another light verb, this one meaning LOCATE or POSSESS instead of CAUSE. This second mechanism could be paired with another Case-assigning functional category, this time for indirect objects (AgrIOP). Under such a story the architecture of the complex VP for a verb like *give* looks like (23).

23) CP

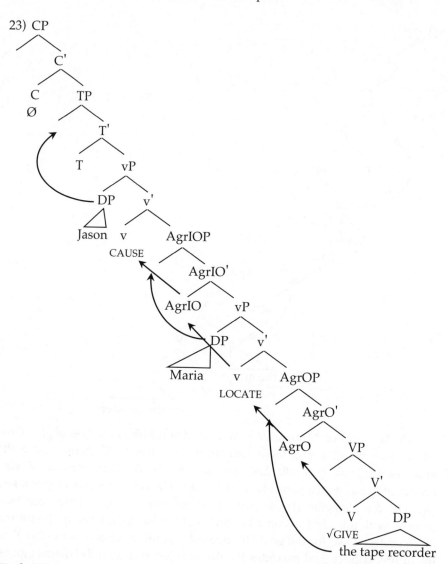

Each DP moves to its Case position, and the root √GIVE moves through AgrO, Locate, AgrIO, into CAUSE. This gives the correct surface order.

There are, of course, a number of open issues here, not least of which is the relationship between the two structures for the verb *give*. However, these complex split VP structures seem to provide a mechanism for explaining the hierarchical properties of ditransitive verbs and the Case marking of their arguments and provide an explanation for such diverse facts as double object constructions and object shift. In the next few chapters, we see that the AgrO category also helps us in providing a landing site for a new kind of DP movement (subject to object raising) and explains a number of surprising facts about ellipsis or deletion structures.

You now have enough information to try WBE 1 & 2 and GPS 5 & 6.

IDEAS, RULES, AND CONSTRAINTS INTRODUCED IN THIS CHAPTER

i) *Light Verbs (Little v)*: the higher part of a complex verb, usually meaning CAUSE (or LOCATE, in the case of ditransitive double object verbs).

ii) *Object Shift*: the phenomenon where accusatively marked objects shift leftwards.

iii) *AgrO*: the head that checks accusative Case in the split VP system.

FURTHER READING: Adger (1996), Barss and Lasnik (1986), Beck and Johnson (2004), Chomsky (1991), Chung (1976), Collins and Thráinsson (1996), den Dikken (1995), Diesing (1992), Harley (2002), Iatridou (1990), Johnson (1991), Koizumi (1993), Kratzer (1996), Larson (1988), Marantz (1984), McCloskey (1980), Pesetsky (1994), Pollock (1989), von Stechow (1996)

GENERAL PROBLEM SETS

GPS1. NPIS AND DOUBLE OBJECT VERBS
[Data Analysis and Critical Thinking; Intermediate]
The words *anything* and *anyone* are negative polarity items, and must be licensed by a negative word like *no one* or *nothing*. Explain how the following data supports the structure given above in the main text in (5). (Hint: think structural relations.) (Data from Barss and Lasnik 1986.)

a) Amanda gave no one anything.
b) *Amanda gave anyone nothing.

GPS2. COMPLEX VERBS
[Data Analysis and Critical Thinking; Intermediate]
Sentence (a) is from Persian and sentence (b) is from Chicheŵa. Explain how these data support the idea that verbs are really composed of a v and a V.

a) Kimea az ra'ise edâre   da'vat **kard**
   Kimea of boss   office   invitation **v**
   "Kimea invited the office boss."

b) Mtsikana   anagw-**ets**-a   kuti   mtsuko
    Girl   fall-**v**   that   waterpot
    "The girl knocked over that waterpot."

GPS3. PARTICLES
[Data Analysis and Critical Thinking; Advanced]
Using the split vP-AgrOP-VP system, explain the verb-particle facts of
English given in example (13). Assume that a verb like *blow up* is structured
as in (i) and that the *blow* portion of this complex verb can move
independently of the preposition/particle *up*. You do *not* have to explain
why the shifted order is obligatory with pronouns and not with DPs.

i)

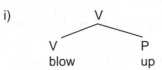

GPS4. THETA GRIDS
[Application of Skills; Intermediate]
The theory involving AgrOP requires that we modify the lexical entries given
in the text above in (7). Provide new theta grids for little v meaning CAUSE
and the root √CLEAN that take into account AgrOP.

GPS5. TREES
[Application of Skills; Intermediate to Advanced]
Using split VP structures and AgrOP draw the trees for the following
sentences:

a) Susan sent the package to Heidi.
b) Carolyn sent Heidi a package.
c) Peter placed the letter in the envelope.
d) I asked Mike if he had seen the Yeti.
e) I bought some flowers for Manuel.
f) I bought Manuel some flowers.

GPS6. APPLICATIVES IN BAHASA INDONESIA
[Data Analysis; Advanced]
Consider the following data from Bahasa Indonesia (Chung 1976).
This language has two orders that are similar to the prepositional order and
the double object orders of English *give* type verbs. What is interesting is the
presence in the construction with two DPs of a morpheme in the verb that is
typically called the applicative (APPL). Explain how this data is evidence
for the split VP approach proposed in this chapter.

a) Saja mem-bawa surat itu kepada Ali.
    I   CAUSE-bring letter the to   Ali
    "I brought the letter to Ali."

b) Saja mem bawa-kan   Ali surat itu.
    I   CAUSE-bring-APPL   Ali letter the
    "I brought Ali the letter."

CHALLENGE PROBLEM SETS

CHALLENGE PROBLEM SET 1: AGAIN
[Critical Thinking; Challenge]
As discussed in von Stechow (1996) and Beck and Johnson (2004) the following sentence is ambiguous:

> John opened the door again.

It can have either of the following meanings:

i) The door was open before (perhaps opened by Susan) and now it's open again due to John's action.
ii) John opened the door before, and he did it again.

Keeping in mind the Principle of Modification, explain how this data is evidence for a little v meaning CAUSE and the split VP hypothesis.

CHALLENGE PROBLEM SET 2: AGRS
[Creative Thinking; Challenge]
In the chapter above we proposed AgrO and AgrIO. There may well be evidence that Case is not assigned by TP, but by an AgrSP. In particular it has been proposed that the EPP is a property of TP, but Case is assigned lower in the structure, in an AgrSP:

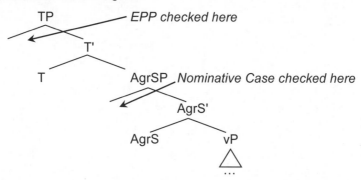

Part 1: Using the following data from English argue for an AgrS in the position suggested above. Assume *there* is an expletive (without a theta role). Note what the auxiliary agrees with.

a) There was a man arriving at the station when I pulled up.
b) There were four men arriving at the station when I pulled up.

Part 2: The following data from Scots Gaelic was given above as evidence for the position of AgrO between v and V. This data also contains evidence for AgrS. Explain what it is. (Scots Gaelic data from Adger 1996.)

c) Bu toigh leam   [$_{CP}$ sibh a^L bhith air   an doras a^L dhúnadh.]
    be like with me   you AGR v   PERF the door AGR close
    "I'd like you to have shut the door."

chapter 15

Raising, Control, and Empty Categories

Learning Objectives

After reading chapter 15 you should walk away having mastered the following ideas and skills:

1. Distinguish between raising and control predicates.
2. Distinguish between subject-to-subject raising (SSR) and subject control constructions.
3. Distinguish between subject-to-object raising (SOR) and object control constructions.
4. Apply the idiom, clausal subject, and expletive tests.
5. Draw theta grids and trees of SSR, SOR, OC, and SC sentences.
6. Describe the restrictions on control of PRO.
7. Explain why PRO is null.
8. Distinguish between PRO and *pro*.
9. Determine how a language has set the null subject parameter.

Syntax: A Generative Introduction, Third Edition. Andrew Carnie.
© 2013 Andrew Carnie. Published 2013 by John Wiley & Sons, Inc.

0. INTRODUCTION

The following two sentences look remarkably alike:

1) a) Jean is likely to leave.
    b) Jean is reluctant to leave.

But these sentences are structurally very different. Sentence (1a) is a raising sentence like those we saw in chapter 11. Sentence (1b), however, is a different matter. This is what we call a ***control sentence***; it does not involve any DP movement. We will claim there is a special kind of null DP in the subject position of the embedded clause. Syntacticians call this special DP ***PRO***, which stands for "null pronoun". The differences between these two constructions are schematized below.

2) Jean$_i$ is likely [t_i to leave].   *subject-to-subject raising*

3) Jean is reluctant [PRO to leave].   *(subject) control*

The bracketed diagram in (3) shows the DP raising construction we looked at in chapter 10. The structure in (4), which has no movement, is the control construction. The evidence for this kind of proposal will come from the thematic properties of the various predicates involved. In addition to contrasting the sentences in (1a and b), we'll also look at the differences between sentences like (4a and b):

4) a) Jean wants Brian to leave.
    b) Jean persuaded Brian to leave.

Again, on the surface these two sentences look very similar. But, again, once we look at these in more detail we'll see that they have quite different structures. We will claim that *Brian* in (4a) raises to the object position of the verb *wants*. This is called ***subject-to-object raising***, and was discussed in an exercise in the last chapter. The structure of the sentence in (4b) parallels the structure of the control sentence in (1b). Both *Jean* and *Brian* are arguments of the verb *persuade*. There is no raising, but there is a PRO in the subject position of the embedded clause.

5) Jean wants Brian$_i$ [t_i to leave].   *subject-to-object raising*

6) Jean persuaded Brian [PRO to leave].   *object control*

The construction in (6) is called ***object control*** (because the object "controls" what the PRO refers to).

This chapter ends with a short discussion of the various kinds of empty elements we've looked at so far (null heads, PRO, traces, etc.), and introduces a new one, which is found in languages like Spanish and Italian.

1. RAISING VS. CONTROL

1.1 Two Kinds of Theta Grids for Main Predicates

If you look at the following two sentences, you will see that the predicate *is likely* only takes one argument: a proposition.

7) a) [That Jean left] is likely.   *clausal subject*
    b) It is likely [that Jean left].   *extraposition*

Sentence (7a) shows the proposition *that Jean left* functioning as the predicate's subject. Sentence (7b) has this embedded clause as a complement, and has an expletive in subject position. For reasons having to do with the history of generative grammar, but that need not concern us here, the first construction (7a) is often called a ***clausal subject*** construction, and the second (7b) an ***extraposition*** construction. The theta grid for the predicate is given in (8). As is standard (see chapter 8), expletives are not marked in the theta grid, as they don't get a theta role.

8) *is likely*

We assume that the D-structures of the sentences given in (7) are identical. These sentences have the embedded clause as a complement to the predicate, and nothing in the subject position (9). In the clausal subject construction, the embedded CP moves to the specifier of TP, presumably to satisfy the EPP requirement that every clause have a subject. (10) shows the SPELLOUT for sentence (7a). Sentence (7b) has a slightly different derivation. Instead of moving the clause to satisfy the EPP, an expletive *it* is inserted into the specifier of TP, as seen in the SPELLOUT in (11).

9) ... TP

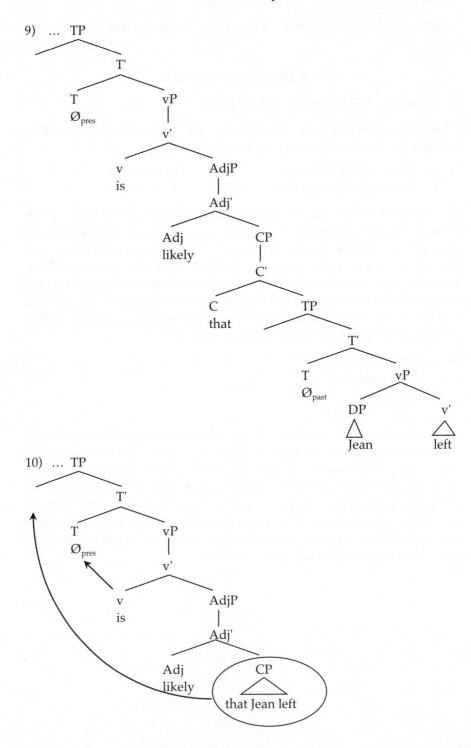

10) ... TP

11)

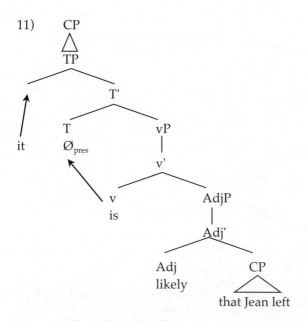

Observe that the embedded clause is finite in both these sentences. This means that its subject gets nominative Case. As we saw in chapter 10, if the embedded clause is non-finite (as in 12), then the subject must move to get Case. Fortunately, *is likely* does not have an external (subject) theta role, but does have a nominative Case feature to check. This means that the specifier of the higher TP is available for Case feature checking. This is a typical raising construction.

12) _____ is likely [Jean to leave].

13)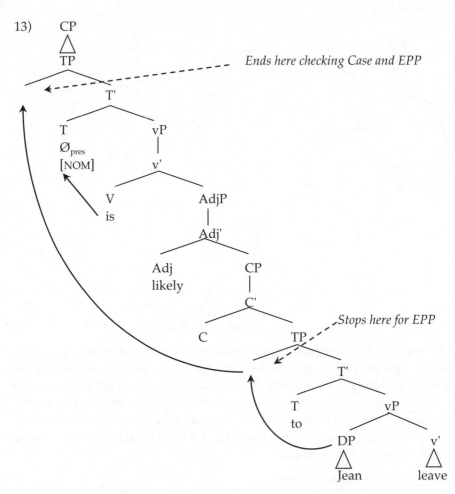

As we noted in chapter 10, the *Jean* in this sentence gets its theta role from *leave*. *Jean* is going *to leave*, she isn't *likely*. What *is likely* is the whole proposition of Jean leaving. With *is likely*, then, there is only one theta role assigned (to the embedded clause). Three possible sentences emerge with this structure: clausal subject, extraposition, and raising.

Let's contrast this with the predicate *is reluctant*. If you think carefully about it, you'll notice that this predicate takes two arguments: the person who is reluctant (the experiencer) and what they are reluctant about (the proposition):

14) *is reluctant*

Experiencer	Proposition
DP	CP

This means that, unlike *is likely*, *is reluctant* assigns a theta role to its subject. Because of this, both clausal subject and extraposition (expletive) constructions are impossible. The specifier of the TP of the main clause is already occupied by the experiencer (it moves there to get Case), so there is no need to insert an expletive or move the CP for EPP reasons. This explains why the following two sentences (an extraposition and a clausal subject example) are ill-formed with the predicate *is reluctant*:

15) a)   *It is reluctant [that Jean left].   (where *it* is an expletive)
    b)   *[that Jean left] is reluctant.

Both of these sentences seem to be "missing" something. More precisely they are both missing the external experiencer role: the person who is reluctant. Consider now the control sentence we mentioned above in the introduction:

16) Jean is reluctant to leave.

Jean here is the experiencer, and the embedded clause is the proposition:

17) a)   *is reluctant*

Experiencer	Proposition
DP	CP
i	k

    b)   Jean$_i$ is reluctant [to leave]$_k$.

So *Jean* is theta-marked by *is reluctant*. Note, however, that this isn't the only predicate in this sentence. We also have the predicate *leave*, with the following theta grid:

18) *leave*

Agent
DP
m

Who is this theta role assigned to? It also appears to be assigned to the DP *Jean*:

19) Jean$_{i/m}$ is reluctant [to leave]$_k$.

As we saw in chapter 8, the theta criterion only allows one theta role per DP. This sentence seems to be a violation of the theta criterion, as its subject DP gets two theta roles. How do we resolve this problem? The theta criterion says that there must be a one-to-one mapping between the number of theta roles and the number of arguments in a sentence. This sentence has three theta roles (agent, experiencer, and proposition), but only two arguments. The logical conclusion, if the theta criterion is right – and we have every reason to believe it is, since it makes good predictions otherwise – is that there is actually a third DP here (getting the surplus agent theta role); you just can't hear it. This DP argument is called PRO (written in capital letters). PRO only appears in the subject positions of non-finite clauses. The structure of a control construction like (19) is given below. Indices mark the theta roles from the theta grids in (17) and (18). You'll notice that PRO is appearing in a position where no Case can be assigned. We return to this below, as well as to the question of why PRO must obligatorily refer to *Jean*.

20)

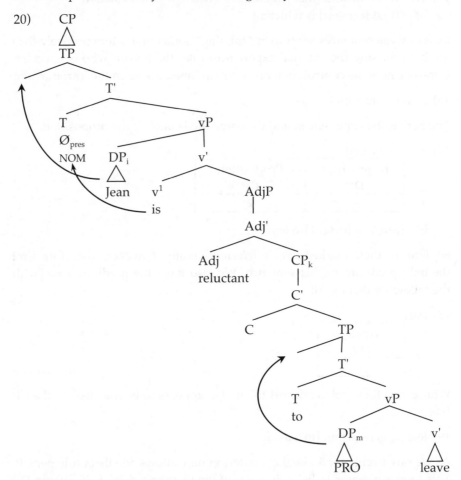

Before looking at any more data it might be helpful to summarize the differences between control constructions and raising constructions. The main predicate in a raising construction does not assign an external

---

[1] Again this is not CAUSE. This little v probably means something like "perceive".

theta role (it has an empty specifier of vP at D-structure). The subject of the embedded clause is Caseless, and raises to the empty specifier of the higher TP for Case checking (and to satisfy the EPP). In control constructions, the main clause predicate *does* assign an external argument. There is no raising; the external theta role of the embedded predicate is assigned to a null Caseless PRO. This is summarized in the following bracketed diagrams:

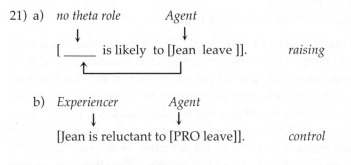

21) a)   *no theta role*   *Agent*

    [_____ is likely to [Jean leave]].   *raising*

    b)   *Experiencer*   *Agent*

    [Jean is reluctant to [PRO leave]].   *control*

1.2 Distinguishing Raising from Control

One of the trials of being a syntactician is learning to distinguish among constructions that are superficially similar, but actually quite different once we dig a little deeper. Control and raising constructions are a perfect example. There are, however, some clear tests we can use to distinguish them. First, note that whether you have a raising or control construction is entirely dependent upon the main clause predicate. Some main clause predicates require raising, others require control (and a few rare ones can require both). The tests for raising and control, then, mostly have to do with the thematic properties of the main clause's predicate.

To see this we'll contrast our two predicates *is likely*, which is a raising predicate, and *is reluctant*, which takes a control construction.

The most reliable way to distinguish raising constructions from control constructions is to work out the theta grids associated with the matrix predicates. If the matrix predicate assigns an external theta role (the one that is underlined, the one that appears in subject position), then it is not a raising construction. Take for example:

22) a)   Jean is likely to dance.
    b)   Jean is reluctant to dance.

Contrast the role of *Jean* in these two sentences (as we did above in section 1.1). In the second sentence *is reluctant* is a property we are attributing to *Jean*. In (22a), however, there is nothing about *Jean* that *is likely*. Instead, what *is likely* is Jean's dancing.

One nice test that works well to show this is the behavior of idioms. Let's take the idiom *the cat is out of the bag*. This construction only gets its idiomatic meaning ("the secret is widely known") when the expression is a whole. When it's broken up, it can only get a literal interpretation ("the feline is out of the sack"). You can see this by contrasting the meanings of the sentences in (23):

23) a)   The cat is out of the bag.
    b)   The cat thinks that he is out of the bag.

Sentence (23b) does not have the meaning "the secret is widely known". Instead our first reading of this sentence produces a meaning where there is actual cat-releasing going on. The subject of an idiom must at some point be local to the rest of the idiom for the sentence to retain its idiosyncratic meaning. We can use this as a diagnostic for distinguishing raising from control. Recall that in the D-structure of a raising construction the surface subject of the main clause starts out in the specifier of the embedded VP, moving to the specifier of TP for EPP reasons. Therefore in raising constructions, at D-structure, the subject of an embedded sentence is local to its predicate:

24) [_____ is likely [to [Jean dance]]].

If D-structure is the level at which we interpret idiomatic meaning, then we should get idiomatic meanings with raising constructions.[2] With control constructions, on the other hand, the subject of the main clause is never in the embedded clause, so we don't expect to get idiomatic readings. This is borne out by the data.

25) a)   The cat is likely to be out of the bag.   *(idiomatic meaning)*
    b)   The cat is reluctant to be out of the bag.   *(non-idiomatic meaning)*

We can thus use idiom chunks like *the cat* in (25) to test for raising versus control. If you get an idiomatic reading with a predicate, then you know raising is involved.

Another test you can use to distinguish between raising and control constructions is to see if they allow the extraposition construction. Extraposition involves an expletive *it*. Expletives are only allowed in non-thematic positions, which are the hallmark of raising:

---

[2] This is not an implausible hypothesis. Idioms have the feel of lexical items (that is, their meaning must be idiosyncratically memorized, just like the meanings of words). Remember that the lexicon is the source of the material at D-structure, so it makes sense that D-structure is where idiomatic meanings are inserted.

26) a)   It is likely that Jean will dance.
    b)   *It is reluctant that Jean will dance.

At the end of this chapter, there is a problem set (General Problem Set 4) where you are asked to determine for a list of predicates whether or not they involve raising or control. You'll need to apply the tests discussed in this section to do that exercise.

You now have enough information to try WBE 1–7.

1.3 What is PRO?

You may have noticed a fairly major contradiction in the story we've been presenting. In chapter 11, we claimed that DPs always need Case. However, in this section we've proposed that PRO can appear in the specifier of non-finite TP. This is not a Case position, so why are we allowed to have PRO here? Shouldn't PRO get Case too? It is, after all, a DP. Chomsky (1981) claims that the reason PRO is null and silent is precisely *because* it appears in a Caseless position. In other words, PRO is a very special kind of DP. It is a Caseless DP, which explains why it can show up in Caseless positions like the specifier of non-finite TP.

Why do we need PRO? If we didn't have PRO, then we would have violations of the theta criterion. Notice that what we are doing here is proposing a null element to account for an apparent hole in our theory (a violation of either the theta criterion or the Case filter). There is good reason to be suspicious of this: It seems like a technical solution to a technical problem that is raised only by our particular formulation of the constraints. Nonetheless, it does have a good deal of descriptive power. It can account for most of the data having to do with embedded infinitival clauses. Until a better theory comes along, the PRO hypothesis wins because it can explain so much data.

You now have enough information to try GPS 1.

2. Two Kinds of Raising, Two Kinds of Control

2.1 Two Kinds of Raising

Up to this point we have been primarily looking at raising from the subject of an infinitive complement clause to the specifier of a main clause TP. This raising happens so the DP can get Case. However, raising doesn't have to target the specifier of TP; there are other instances of DP raising where the DP ends up in other positions. Consider the verb *want*. *Want* can take an accusatively marked DP:

27) a) I want cookies.
    b) Jean wants Robert.
    c) Jean wants him.

Want can also take an infinitive CP complement (sentence (28) is an instance of a control construction).

28) I_i want [PRO_i to leave].

This flexible verb can also show up with both an accusatively marked DP and an infinitive complement:

29) I_i want [$Jean_j$ to dance]$_k$.

Think carefully about the theta grids of the verbs here. *Jean* is the agent of *dance*, *I* is the experiencer of *want*, and the proposition *Jean to dance* takes up the second theta role of *want*.

30) a) *dance*

Agent
DP
j

    b) *want*

Experiencer	Proposition
DP	CP
i	k

Notice that *Jean* does not get a theta role from *want*; it only gets one from *dance*. This means that this is not a control construction. You can see this if we apply our idiom test to the sentence:[3]

31) I want the cat to be let out of the bag.

Although the judgment isn't as clear here, it is possible to get the idiomatic reading of *the cat to be let out of the bag*.

Since this isn't a control construction, then how does the DP *Jean* get Case? The embedded TP is non-finite, so its specifier is not a Case position. The answer to this puzzle is that the DP raises to the object position of *want*, where it can get accusative Case. The verb root raises through AgrO

---

[3] The expletive subject test will not work here. Remember, expletives are usually only found in subject position (because of the EPP). *Jean* here is found in object position, so testing using an expletive won't work.

into v. The DP *Jean* moves first to the specifier of the embedded TP for EPP reasons, then moves on to the specifier of AgrOP where it gets accusative case.

32)

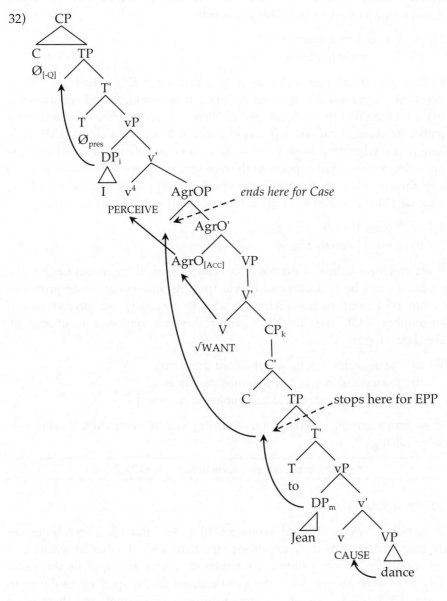

---

[4] This v is not CAUSE, as there is no agent role here. This v probably means something like "perceive".

We can see that this is the right analysis of these facts by looking at the Case marking a pronoun would get in these constructions. Since the DP shows up as the specifier of AgrOP with an [ACC] Case feature, we predict it will take accusative Case. This is correct:

33) a)   I want *her* to dance.
    b)   *I want *she* to dance.

Binding theory also provides us with a test for seeing where the DP is. Recall the fundamental difference between a pronoun and an anaphor. In the binding theory we developed in chapter 5, an anaphor must be bound within its clause, whereas a pronoun must be free. What clause a DP is in determines whether it is an anaphor or a pronoun. We can use this as a test for seeing where a DP appears in the tree structure. We are considering two hypotheses: (34a) has the DP in the object position of *want* (just as in (32)), whereas (34b) has the DP in the subject position of the non-finite TP.

34) a)   I want Jean$_i$ [t$_i$ to dance].
    b)   I want [Jean to dance].

If we can have a bound pronoun, instead of *Jean*, then we know that the pronoun must be in a different clause from its antecedent, since pronouns cannot be bound within their own clause. Similarly we predict that if an anaphor is OK, then the DP is within the same clause as its antecedent. The data supports (34a).

35) a)   *Jean$_i$ wants her$_i$ to be appointed president.
    b)   Jean$_i$ wants her$_j$ to be appointed president.
    c)   ?Jean$_i$ wants herself$_i$ to be appointed president.

These forms exhibit a second kind of raising, which we might call subject-to-object raising.

You now have enough information to try GPS 2 & 3.

2.2 Two Kinds of Control

In section 1, we contrasted sentences like (36a and b). These sentences differed in terms of their argument structure and in what movement, if any, applies. (36a) is a raising construction, where *Jean* gets its theta role only from *to leave*, and raises for Case reasons to the specifier of the main clause TP. In (36b), *Jean* gets a theta role from *is reluctant*, and there is no movement from the embedded to the matrix clause. Instead there is a null Caseless PRO in the specifier of the tenseless clause.

36) a) Jean$_i$ is likely [t$_i$ to leave].
    b) Jean$_i$ is reluctant [PRO$_i$ to leave].

In this subsection, we'll make a similar claim about the structures in (37).

37) a) Jean wants Robert$_i$ [t$_i$ to leave].
    b) Jean persuaded Robert$_i$ [PRO$_i$ to leave].

Sentence (37a) is an instance of subject-to-object raising. Sentence (37b), while on the surface very similar to (37a), is actually also a control construction. There are two major kinds of control constructions. To see this I'll put the two (b) sentences side by side in (38). (38a) is what we call **subject control**, because the subject DP of the main clause is coreferential with PRO. (38b) is **object control**, where the main clause object is coreferential with PRO.

38) a) (=36b) Jean$_i$ is reluctant [PRO$_i$ to leave].   *subject control*
    b) (=37b) Jean persuaded Robert$_i$ [PRO$_i$ to leave].   *object control*

Consider first the thematic properties of the raising construction:

39) Jean$_i$ wants Robert$_j$ [t$_j$ to leave]$_k$.

We are now well familiar with the theta grid for *to leave*, which takes a single agent argument. The theta grid for the subject-to-object raising verb *want* is repeated below:

40) a) *leave*

Agent
DP
i

   b) *want*

Experiencer	Proposition
DP	CP
i	k

Robert is the agent of *leave*, but is not an argument of *want*. In section 2.1 above, we used the idiom test to show that this is the case. Now, contrast this situation with the object control verb *persuade*:

41) Jean$_i$ persuaded Robert$_m$ [PRO$_j$ to leave]$_k$.[5]

---

[5] The indices on this sentence mark theta roles (as marked in the grid in (42)). They do not mark coindexing. In this sentence, the index $_m =$ $_j$ (m and j are the same index).

The DP *Robert* in this sentence *is* theta-marked by *persuade*. So in order not to violate the theta criterion we have to propose a null PRO to take the agent theta role of *leave*.

42) a) *leave*

Agent
DP
j

  b) *persuade*

Agent	Theme	Proposition
DP	DP	CP
i	m	k

We can see this again by comparing the idiomatic readings of subject-to-object raising vs. object control.

43) a) Jean wants the cat to get his/Bill's tongue.
  b) #Jean persuaded the cat to get his/Bill's tongue.

Sentence (43a) is slightly odd but it does allow the idiomatic reading, but (43b) only takes the literal (non-idiomatic) meaning.

2.3 Summary of Predicate Types

In this section we've argued for four distinct types of embedded non-finite constructions: subject-to-subject raising, subject-to-object raising, subject control, and object control. Which construction you get seems to be dependent upon what the main clause predicate is. For example, *is likely* requires a subject-to-subject raising construction whereas *is reluctant* requires a subject control construction. It should be noted that some verbs allow more than one type of construction. For example, the verb *want* allows either subject control or subject-to-object raising:

44) a) Jean$_i$ wants [PRO$_i$ to leave].   *subject control*
  b) Jean wants Bill$_i$ [t$_i$ to leave].   *subject-to-object raising*

An example of these types is given in (45) and a summary of their properties in (46):

45) a) Jean is likely to leave.   *subject-to-subject raising*
  b) Jean wants Robert to leave.   *subject-to-object raising*
  c) Jean is reluctant to leave.   *subject control*
  d) Jean persuaded Robert to leave.   *object control*

46) a) *subject-to-subject raising*
- Main clause predicate assigns one theta role (to the proposition) and no external (subject) theta role.
- DP movement of embedded subject to the specifier of TP for EPP and Case.
- Allows idiomatic readings.
- Allows extraposition.

b) *subject-to-object raising*
- Main clause predicate assigns two theta roles (an external agent or experiencer and a proposition).
- Main clause predicate has an [ACC] Case feature.
- DP movement of the embedded clause subject to the specifier of AgrOP for Case reasons.
- Allows idiomatic readings.

c) *subject control*
- Main clause predicate assigns two theta roles (external agent or experiencer and proposition).
- Caseless PRO in embedded clause.
- No DP movement for Case, but DP movement of PRO to the specifier of TP for EPP.
- Does not allow idiomatic readings or extraposition

d) *object control*
- Main clause predicate assigns three theta roles (external agent or experiencer, an internal theme, and a proposition).
- Caseless PRO in embedded clause.
- No DP movement for Case, but DP movement of PRO to the specifier of TP for EPP.
- Does not allow idiomatic readings or extraposition.

You now have enough information to try WBE 8–10, GPS 4 & 5, and CPS 1.

---

3. CONTROL THEORY

In chapter 5, we developed a set of noun types (anaphors, pronouns, R-expressions) that have different properties with respect to how they get their meanings. R-expressions get their meaning from the discourse or context and can never be bound; anaphors are bound by antecedents within their clauses; and pronouns can either be bound by antecedents outside their clause or be free. In this section, we consider the troubling question of what kind of DP PRO is. Unfortunately, we are going to get a bit of a mixed answer.

Let us start by defining some terminology. This terminology is subtly similar to that of the binding theory, but it is different. If PRO gets its meaning from another DP, then PRO is said to be **controlled**. This is identical to the notion **coreferent** and very similar to the notion **bound** (we will make this distinction clearer below). The DP that serves as PRO's antecedent is called its **controller**.

We are going to contrast two different kinds of PRO. The first kind is called **arbitrary PRO** (or PRO_{arb}). The meaning of this pronoun is essentially "someone":

47) [PRO_{arb} to find a new mate], go to a dating service.

Arbitrary PRO is not controlled by anything. Arbitrary PRO is a bit like an R-expression or a pronoun, in that it can get its meaning from outside the sentence.

Non-arbitrary PRO (henceforth simply PRO) also comes in two varieties. On one hand we have what is called **obligatory control**. Consider the sentence in (48). Here, PRO must refer to *Jean*. It can't refer to anyone else:

48) Jean$_i$ tried $PRO_{i/*j}$ to behave.

There are other circumstances where PRO does not have to be (but can be) controlled. This is called **optional control**, and is seen in (49):

49) Robert$_i$ knows that it is essential [$PRO_{i/j}$ to be well-behaved].

PRO here can mean two different things. It can either refer to Robert or it can have an arbitrary PRO_{arb} reading (indicated in (49) with the subscript $_j$). You can see this by looking at the binding of the following two extensions of this sentence:

50) a)   Robert$_i$ knows that it is essential [PRO_i to be good on his$_i$ birthday].
    b)   Robert$_i$ knows that it is essential [PRO_j to be good on one's$_j$ birthday].

(50a) has the controlled meaning (as seen by the binding of *his*); (50b) has the arbitrary reading (as seen by the presence of *one's*).

With this in mind let's return to the central question of this section. Is PRO an anaphor, a pronoun, or an R-expression? We can dismiss the R-expression option right out of hand. R-expressions must always be free. PRO is only sometimes free (= not controlled). This makes it seem more like a pronoun; pronouns can be either free or bound. The data in (49) seems to support this – PRO is behaving very much like a pronoun. Compare (49) to the pronoun in (51).

51) Robert$_i$ knows it is essential [that he$_{i/j}$ is well-behaved].

You'll notice that the indexing on (51), which has a pronoun, is identical to the indexing on PRO in (49). We might hypothesize then that PRO is a pronoun. This can't be right, however. Recall that we also have situations where PRO must be bound (= controlled) as in the obligatory control sentence *Jean$_i$ tried PRO$_{i/*j}$ to behave.* This makes PRO look like an anaphor, since anaphors are obligatorily bound. Williams (1980) suggests that in obligatory control constructions PRO must be c-commanded by its controller, just as an anaphor must be c-commanded by its antecedent. However, as should be obvious, this can't be right either. First, as noted above, we have situations where PRO is free (as in 47); anaphors can never be free. Second, if we take the binding theory we developed in chapter 5 literally, PRO and its controller *Jean* are in different binding domains, violating Principle A.[6] We thus have a conundrum: PRO doesn't seem to be an R-expression, a pronoun, or an anaphor. It seems to be a beast of an altogether different color.

Since the distribution of PRO does not lend itself to the binding theory, an entirely different module of the grammar has been proposed to account for PRO. This is called **control theory**. Control theory is the bane of professional theoreticians and students alike. It is, quite simply, the least elegant part of syntactic theory. We'll have a brief look at it here, but will come to no satisfying conclusions.

First let's observe that some parts of control are sensitive to syntactic structure. Consider what can control PRO in (52):

52) [Jean$_i$'s father]$_j$ is reluctant PRO$_{j/*i}$ to leave.

If you draw the tree for (52), you'll see that while the whole DP *Jean's father* c-commands PRO, *Jean* by itself does not. The fact that *Jean* cannot control PRO strongly suggests that there is a c-command requirement on obligatory control, as argued by Williams (1980). This said, the structure of the sentence doesn't seem to be the only thing that comes into play with control. Compare now a subject control sentence to an object control one:

53) a)   Robert$_i$ is reluctant [PRO$_i$ to behave].   *subject control*
    b)   Susan$_j$ ordered Robert$_i$ [PRO$_{i/*j}$ to behave].   *object control*

In both these sentences PRO must be controlled by *Robert*. PRO in (53b) cannot refer to *Susan*. This would seem to suggest that the closest DP

---

[6] Recall from chapter 5 that our definition of binding domain as a clause is probably wrong. One might even hypothesize on the basis of data like *Jean is likely to behave herself* that the definition of binding domain requires some kind of tensed clause, rather than just any kind of clause. I leave as an exercise the implications of such a move.

that c-commands PRO must control it. In (53a), *Robert* is the only possible controller, so it controls PRO. In (53b), there are two possible controllers: *Susan* and *Robert*. But only *Robert*, which is structurally closer to PRO, can control it. This hypothesis works well in most cases, but the following example shows it must be wrong:

54) Jean$_i$ promised Susan$_j$ [PRO$_{i/*j}$ to behave].   *subject control*

In this sentence it is *Jean* doing the behaving, not *Susan*. PRO must be controlled by *Jean*, even though *Susan* is structurally closer. So structure doesn't seem to be the only thing determining which DP does the controlling.

   One hypothesis is that the particular main clause predicate determines which DP does the controlling. That is, the theta grid specifies what kind of control is involved. There are various ways we could encode this. One is to mark a particular theta role as the controller:

55) a)   *is reluctant*

Experiencer	Proposition
DP *controller*	CP

   b)   *persuade*

Agent	Theme	Proposition
DP	DP *controller*	CP

   c)   *promise*

Agent	Theme	Proposition
DP *controller*	DP	CP

In this view of things, control is a thematic property. But a very careful look at the data shows that this can't be the whole story either. The sentences in (56) all use the verb *beg*, which is traditionally viewed as an object control verb, as seen by the pair of sentences in (56a and b), where the (b) sentence shows an embedded tense clause paraphrase:

56) a)   Louis begged Kate$_i$ [PRO$_i$ to leave her job].
    b)   Louis begged Kate that she leave her job.
    c)   Louis$_i$ begged Kate [PRO$_i$ to be allowed [PRO$_i$ to shave himself]].
    d)   Louis$_i$ begged Kate that he be allowed to shave himself.

Sentences (56c and d), however, show subject control. The PROs in (c) must be controlled by the subject *Louis*. The difference between the (a) and the (b) sentences seems to be in the nature of the *embedded* clause. This is mysterious at best. Examples like these might be used to argue that control is not entirely syntactic or thematic, but may also rely on our knowledge of the way the world works. This kind of knowledge, often referred to as *pragmatic* knowledge,[7] lies outside the syntactic system we're developing. The study of the interaction between pragmatics, semantics, and syntax is one that is being vigorously pursued right now, but lies beyond the scope of this book. See the further reading section below for some places you can go to examine questions like this in more detail.

You now have enough information to try WBE 11 & 12 and CPS 2–4.

---

4. ANOTHER KIND OF NULL SUBJECT: "LITTLE" *pro*

In chapter 8, we made the claim that all sentences require subjects, and encoded this into the EPP. However, many languages appear to violate this constraint. Take, for example, these perfectly acceptable sentences of Italian:

57) a)   Parlo.   b)   Parli.
       speak.1SG   speak.2SG
       "I speak."   "You speak."

The subject DP in these sentences seems to be missing. But there is no ambiguity here. We know exactly who is doing the talking. This is because the verbs are inflected with endings that tell us who the subject is. This phenomenon is called either *pro-drop* or *null subjects*. Ideally, we would like to claim that a strong constraint like the EPP is universal, but Italian (and many other languages) seem to be exceptions. One technical solution to this issue is to posit that sentences in (57) actually do have DPs which satisfy the EPP. Notice again that this is merely a technical solution to a formal problem.

   You might think that the obvious candidate for this empty DP would be PRO. But in fact, PRO could not appear in this position. Remember PRO only appears in Caseless positions. We know that Italian subject position is a Case position, because you can have an overt DP like *io* in (58).

58) Io parlo.
     I speak.1SG
     "I speak."

---

[7] See for example Landau's (1999) dissertation.

So linguists have proposed the category *pro* (written in lower-case letters). *pro* (called **little pro** or **baby pro**) appears in Case positions; PRO (called **big PRO**) is Caseless.

English doesn't have *pro*. This presumably is due to the fact that English doesn't have a rich agreement system in its verbal morphology:

59) a) I speak.   b) You speak.   c) He/she/it speak<u>s</u>.
    d) We speak.   e) They speak.

In English, only third person forms of verbs take any special endings. One of the conditions on *pro* seems to be that it often appears in languages with rich agreement morphology.[8] The means we use to encode variation among languages should now be familiar: parameters. We use this device here again in the **null subject parameter**, which governs whether or not a language allows *pro*. Italian has this switch turned on. English has it set in the off position.

You now have enough information to try GPS 6.

---

5. Conclusion

We started this chapter with the observation that certain sentences, even though they look alike on the surface, can actually have very different syntactic trees. We compared subject-to-subject raising constructions to subject control constructions, and subject-to-object raising constructions to object control constructions. You can test for these various construction types by working out their argument structure, and using the idiom test. Next under consideration was the issue of what kind of DP PRO is. We claimed that it only showed up in Caseless positions. We also saw that it didn't meet any of the binding conditions, and suggested it is subject, instead, to control theory. Control theory is a bit of a mystery, but may involve syntactic, thematic, and pragmatic features. We closed the chapter by comparing two different kinds of null subject categories: PRO and *pro*. PRO is Caseless and is subject to the theory of control. On the other hand, *pro* takes Case and is often "licensed" by rich agreement morphology on the verb.

---

[8] This is not a universally true statement. Many Asian languages allow *pro*-drop even though they don't have rich agreement systems. For discussion, see Huang (1989).

IDEAS, RULES, AND CONSTRAINTS INTRODUCED IN THIS CHAPTER

i)   ***PRO (Big PRO)***: A null (silent) DP found in Caseless positions.

ii)   **pro** (***Little* pro *or Baby* pro**): A null (silent) DP often found in languages with "rich" agreement. *pro* does get Case.

iii)   ***Clausal Subject Construction***: A sentence where a clause appears in the specifier of TP.

iv)   ***Extraposition (Expletive Subject)***: A sentence where there is an expletive in the subject position and a clausal complement.

v)   ***Subject-to-subject Raising***: A kind of DP movement where the subject of an embedded non-finite clause moves to the specifier of TP of the main clause to get nominative Case.

vi)   ***Subject-to-object Raising*** (*also called **Exceptional Case Marking** or **ECM***): A kind of DP movement where the subject of an embedded non-finite clause moves to the specifier of AgrO in the main clause to get accusative Case.

vii)   ***Control Theory***: The theory that governs how PRO gets its meaning.

viii)   ***Pragmatics***: The science that looks at how language and knowledge of the world interact.

ix)   ***Subject Control*** (*also called **Equi***): A sentence where there is a PRO in the embedded non-finite clause that is controlled by the subject argument of the main clause.

x)   ***Object Control***: A sentence where there is a PRO in the embedded non-finite clause that is controlled by the object argument of the main clause.

xi)   ***Obligatory vs. Optional Control***: Obligatory control is when the PRO must be controlled. Optional control is when the DP can be controlled or not.

xii)   ***PRO_{arb}***: Uncontrolled PRO takes an "arbitrary" reference.

xiii)   ***Null Subject Parameter***: The parameter switch that distinguishes languages like English, which require an overt subject, from languages like Italian that don't, and allow *pro*.

FURTHER READING: Brame (1976), Bresnan (1972), Chomsky (1965, 1981), Hornstein (1999), Hyams (1986), Jaeggli and Safir (1989), Landau (1999), Manzini (1983), Petter (1998), Postal (1974), Rizzi (1982), Rosenbaum (1967), Williams (1980)

GENERAL PROBLEM SETS

GPS1. THE EXISTENCE OF PRO
[Critical Thinking; Intermediate]
Explain how the following sentences provide evidence for PRO.

a)   [To behave oneself in public] is expected.
b)   Robert$_i$ knew [$_{CP}$ that it was necessary [$_{CP}$ PRO$_i$ to behave himself$_i$]].

GPS2. RAISING TO OBJECT
[Critical Thinking; Intermediate]
We claimed that subject-to-object raising targets the specifier of AgrOP as the landing site of the movement for Case. Consider the following sentences, keeping in mind that *out* and *incorrectly* modify the main verb. How do these sentences support the idea that subject-to-object raising lands in AgrOP? Draw the tree for sentence (b).

a)   She made Jerry out to be famous.
b)   Mike expected Greg incorrectly to take out the trash.

GPS3. ICELANDIC PRO AND QUIRKY CASE
[Data Analysis and Critical Thinking; Intermediate/Advanced]
Background. In order to do this question it will be helpful to have reviewed the discussion of floating quantifiers in chapter 10, and to have done the question on Icelandic quirky Case in chapter 10.

As discussed in chapter 10, in English it is possible to "float" quantifiers (words like *all*) that modify subject arguments:

a)   The boys don't all want to leave.

Icelandic also allows floating quantifiers, but with a twist. The quantifier takes endings indicating that it has the same Case as the DP it modifies. Recall from the last chapter that certain verbs in Icelandic assign irregular or "quirky" Cases to their subjects. The verb *leiddist* "bored" is one of these. In sentence (b), the subject is marked with its quirky dative Case. The floating quantifier *öllum* "all" is also marked with dative. (Data from Sigurðsson 1991.)

b)   Strákunum leiddist öllum   í skóla.
     boys.DAT   bored all.DAT   in school
     "The boys were all bored in school."

We might hypothesize, then, that floated quantifiers must agree with the noun they modify in terms of Case.

The question. Now consider the following control sentence. What problems does it make for our claim that PRO does not get Case? Can you relate your solution to the problem of Icelandic passives discussed in the problem sets of chapter 11? Note that the noun in the main clause here is marked with nominative rather than dative Case.

c)   Strákarnir vonast til að PRO leiðast ekki öllum í skóla.
     boys.NOM hope for to   bore not all.DAT in school
     "The boys hope not to be bored in school."

GPS4. ENGLISH PREDICATES
[Application of Skills; Intermediate]
Using your knowledge of theta theory and the tests of extraposition and idioms determine if the predicates listed below are subject-to-subject raising (SSR), subject-to-object raising (SOR), subject control (SC), or object control (OC). **Some predicates fit into more than one category**. (The idea for this problem set comes from a similar question in Soames and Perlmutter 1979.)

     is eager   is believed seems persuaded expect force   ask
     promise   want   is likely imagine

GPS5. TREES AND DERIVATIONS
[Application of Skills; Intermediate/Advanced]
Draw trees for the following sentences. Annotate your trees with arrows so that they show all the movements, and write in all PROs with appropriate coindexing indicating control. You may wish to do this problem set *after* you have completed General Problem Set 4.

a)   Jean wants Bill to do the Macarena.
b)   Robert is eager to do his homework.
c)   Jean seems to be in a good mood.
d)   Rosemary tried to get a new car.
e)   Susan begged Bill to let her sing in the concert.
f)   Susan begged to be allowed to sing in the concert.
g)   Christina is ready to leave.
h)   Fred was believed to have wanted to try to dance.
i)   Susan consented to try to seem to have been kissed.
j)   Alan told me who wanted to seem to be invincible.
k)   What did John want to eat?

GPS6. IRISH *pro*
[Data Analysis; Advanced]
Irish is a null subject language. Discuss how Irish *pro*-drop differs from that found in Italian. Can these differences be explained using our theory?

a) Rinceamar.
   Dance.3PL.PAST
   "We danced."

b) Tá mé.   c) Táim.   d) *Táim   mé.
   Am I   Am.1SG   Am.1SG I
   "I am."   "I am."   "I am."

CHALLENGE PROBLEM SETS

CHALLENGE PROBLEM SET 1: IS EASY
[Critical Thinking; Challenge]
Consider the following sentences:

a) This book is easy to read.   b) John is easy to please.

Is *is easy* a raising or a control predicate or both? If it is a raising predicate, which argument is raised? If it is a control predicate, where is the PRO? What kind of PRO is it?

CHALLENGE PROBLEM SET 2: CONTROLLERS
[Critical Thinking; Challenge]
Williams (1980) claimed that obligatorily controlled PRO requires a c-commanding controller. What problem do the following sentences hold for that hypothesis?

a) To improve myself is a goal for next year.
b) To improve yourself would be a good idea.
c) To improve himself, Bruce should consider therapy.
d) To improve herself, Jane went to a health spa.

CHALLENGE PROBLEM SET 3: PSYCH PREDICATES[9]
[Data Analysis and Critical Thinking; Challenge]
A psych predicate is a predicate (typically a verb or an adjective) that denotes a mental or emotional state. Transitive psych predicates assign an

---

[9] Thanks to Matt Pearson for contributing this problem set.

experiencer θ-role to one of their arguments, and a theme θ-role to the other (the theme is the subject matter or focus for the mental or emotional state). There are two main kinds of transitive psych predicates in English, illustrated below.

Part 1: Based on the examples in (a–h) below, discuss how the two types of psych predicates differ in terms of the mapping of θ-roles to argument positions.

Type I
a) Kathleen really **hates** her job.
b) The children **admire** their mother.
c) My brother **likes** collecting jazz records.
d) Martina is deathly **afraid** of spiders.

Type II
e) That kind of behavior **annoys** me.
f) The news **pleased** the students.
g) Horror films **disturb** Milo.
h) The exhibition really **impressed** the critics.

Part 2: Clauses with Type II psych predicates appear to violate Condition A of the binding theory, as well as the requirement that PRO must be c-commanded by its controller (if any). Examples of apparent violations are given in (m–p) below. (Assume these are all grammatical for purposes of this exercise.)

Type I
i) Kathleen$_i$ **hates** those pictures of herself$_i$.
j) The children$_i$ **admired** photos of each other$_i$.
k) He$_i$ would **like** [PRO$_i$ to introduce himself$_i$].
l) Sandra$_i$ **hates** [PRO$_i$ reading about herself$_i$ in the tabloids].

Type II
m) Pictures of himself$_i$ always **disturb** Milo$_i$.
n) ?The exhibitions of each other$_i$'s work **impressed** the artists$_i$.
o) [PRO$_i$ to be able [PRO$_i$ to buy myself$_i$ a car]] would **please** me$_i$ to no end.
p) [PRO$_i$ reading about herself$_i$ in the tabloids] always **annoys** Sandra$_i$.

Propose an analysis which allows us to account for the unusual binding properties of Type II psych predicates without having to alter or abandon Principle A or the c-command condition on controlled PRO. Illustrate your analysis with sample trees.

CHALLENGE PROBLEM SET 4: LOGICAL FORM AND QUANTIFIER RAISING[10]

In (a), the quantifier in the main clause takes scope over the quantifier in the subordinate clause. The universal quantifier in the embedded clause cannot scope over the existential quantifier in the main clause.

a)   Someone believes that everyone will be invited. [∃ > ∀, *∀ > ∃]

The most common explanation for this is that quantifier raising typically is clause-bound. That means that QR only moves as far as the nearest CP. In the case of *someone* in (a) that's the embedded CP, so the universal quantifier is always c-commanded by the existential.

Now contrast (a) with (b).

b)   Someone believes everyone to be invited.   [∃ > ∀, ∀ > ∃]

The interpretation of this sentence is surprising given the possible interpretation of (a). (b) is ambiguous, and either scope is possible. Why is scope ambiguous in (b) but not in (a)? Be sure to explain this in structural terms.

---

[10] Thanks to Yosuke Sato for contributing this problem set.

Ellipsis

Learning Objectives

After reading chapter 16 you should walk away having mastered the following ideas and skills:

1. Identify cases of VP ellipsis (including antecedent-contained deletion and pseudogapping) and sluicing.
2. Explain the licensing conditions on ellipsis and sluicing.
3. Provide arguments for and against the PF-deletion hypothesis and for and against the LF-copying analysis of ellipsis.
4. Explain the difference between strict and sloppy pronoun identity and why it occurs.
5. Demonstrate how movement of a DP through either QR or DP movement explains antecedent-contained deletion.
6. Show how DP movement of objects explains the non-constituent deletion effects in pseudogapping.

0. ELLIPSIS

In many languages, there are phenomena where a string that has already been uttered is omitted in subsequent structures where it would otherwise have to be repeated word for word. For example, we get sentences like (19):

Syntax: A Generative Introduction, Third Edition. Andrew Carnie.
© 2013 Andrew Carnie. Published 2013 by John Wiley & Sons, Inc.

1) Darin will eat a squid sandwich but Raiza won't.

The second CP here *[Raiza won't]* is obviously missing the VP *[eat a squid sandwich]*. Phenomena like this are called *ellipses* [ɛlɪpsiz] (the singular of this noun is *ellipsis* [ɛlɪpsəs]). The ellipsis in (1) appears to be the deletion of the VP under identity with VP in the preceding clause, and is called **VP ellipsis**:

2) Darin will [eat a squid sandwich]ᵢ but Raiza won't [eat a squid sandwich]ᵢ.

In this chapter, we're going to investigate this and related phenomena.

Let's start by doing a quick overview of some of the various types of ellipsis we find in languages. I mainly present data from English, but if you look in the problem sets you'll find some examples in other languages. The most commonly studied type of ellipsis is that shown above in (1) and (2), where a VP is missing when it's identical to one that has appeared earlier in the clause. Simple VP ellipsis always targets an entire VP, and typically does so under coordination of two clauses where there is an equivalent VP in the other clause. A specialized form of VP ellipsis that does not use coordination is called **antecedent-contained deletion** (or ACD). ACD finds a VP elided that corresponds to a VP that dominates it. Take (3) as an example. What is elided out of the clause *that Meagan read every book* is the VP (or more accurately vP) *[vP read every book]* seen in (4). What's puzzling about this is that this VP is dominated by the VP that serves to license the antecedent (i.e. the antecedent for the ellipsis contains the VP that is elided). We return to this phenomenon below in section 2.

3) Brandon [vP read every book that Megan did [vP ...]].

4) [vP ... [DP ... [CP ... [vP ...]ᵢ ...]]]ᵢ

There is another kind of ellipsis that appears not to target whole vPs/VPs, but only parts of them, typically stranding the direct object or other verbal modifiers. This kind of ellipsis is called *pseudogapping*. The most generally acceptable versions of pseudogapping are found in comparative constructions (and are called **comparative subdeletion**). Examples not in comparatives are possible, although sometimes less acceptable to native speakers. An example of a comparative subdeletion case of pseudogapping is in (5a), where the missing item in the second clause is the non-constituent *been reading*, but the DP *short stories* survives the ellipsis. (5b) is a relatively acceptable example of non-comparative pseudogapping taken from Agbayani and Zoerner (2004: 185)

5) a) Brandon has been reading more novels than he has ___ short stories.
   b) Robin will eat rutabagas but she won't ___ ice-cream.

We return to pseudogapping in section 2 below.

The last kind of ellipsis we'll look at in this textbook is called *sluicing* – a name given to the phenomenon by Haj Ross in the late 1960s. Sluicing appears to be the deletion of a TP rather than a VP, because the missing constituent includes any subject DP or auxiliary that might be in the missing string as well: but it does not elide a CP, as it requires that a *wh*-phrase remain. An example is given in (6), where the elided phrase is *[he could bake]*.

6) John could bake something, but I'm not sure what.

Sluicing provides some really interesting insights about how the missing constituents in ellipsis disappear; we'll discuss it in depth in section 2.

Gapping and Other Kinds of Ellipsis

The topic of ellipsis constructions actually forms an entire sub-discipline within the study of syntax. There are a number of other kinds of ellipsis phenomena that we won't have space to cover here.

Similar to pseudogapping is *gapping*, where apparent non-constituents are missing from the structure. See Levin (1979/1986) or Johnson (2009) for a discussion of the difference between the two. Gapping allows, among other things, the omission of modals and auxiliaries as well as the verb: *Jeff can play the piano and Sylvia ___ the mandolin*. Other kinds of ellipsis include:

- *Comparative deletion*: I've read more books than you ___.
- *Stripping*: My mum is coming tomorrow not ___ Friday.
- *N-ellipsis*: I only brought one book, but I see you have two ___.

We don't have space to talk about these and other kinds of ellipsis here, but if you're interested, you should go out and investigate these on your own.

There appear to be two major restrictions on where ellipsis can occur. First, the constituent that is elided must be identical to its antecedent. There are some provisos to what is meant by "identical" here (see for example the extensive discussion in Tancredi 1992), but for the purposes of this textbook we'll rely on an intuitive characterization, where the stuff that gets deleted in the ellipsis must contain all the material in the antecedent. Second, the string that is elided must be the complement of some "licensor". In the case of VP ellipsis (including ACD and pseudogapping) this is a tensed auxiliary or modal. If you look at sentences (1), (3), and (5) above you'll see that they all have a modal or tensed auxiliary overtly expressed right before the place where the missing constituent belongs. With sluicing, the licensor is the *wh-*

phrase (or perhaps more accurately a complementizer that has a [+WH] feature, which triggers *wh*-movement).

In the next section, we investigate precisely how ellipsis works. We consider a couple of hypotheses and look at the evidence that distinguishes them.

You now have enough information to try WBE 1 & 2 and GPS 1.

---

1. LF-COPYING OR PF-DELETION

Ellipsis is unlike any syntactic process we've seen before. It appears, at least at first glance, to be a process that deletes items. We've seen plenty of silent elements (and operations) before. For example, we've posited a number of empty DPs (*pro*, PRO, *Op*), and a number of empty heads, including: the complementizers $\emptyset_{[-Q, -WH]}$ and $\emptyset_{[+Q, -WH]}$; the T nodes $\emptyset_{past}$, $\emptyset_{pres}$; null AgrO; and the v heads CAUSE and PERCEIVE. So it's worth considering if different kinds of ellipsis are really like these phonologically null elements, or if the absence of material in VP ellipsis is actually the consequence of a deletion process. Both of these hypotheses have been vigorously debated in the recent literature on syntax (see the reading list at the end of this chapter for just a few of the many papers and books on the topic).

Let's put some meat on the bones of these proposals and then see how they stand up to the evidence. The analysis where the missing structure is an empty category – the verbal equivalent of a null pronoun – is called the **LF-copying hypothesis**. We haven't talked much about how the interpretation of pronouns and anaphors might work. One hypothesis is that coindexation in the syntax results in a special copying operation that gives a reference to a pronoun or anaphor, but this copying operation happens covertly on the way to LF after SPELLOUT. Take the anaphor in (7). The idea is that at LF, to give the anaphor an appropriate interpretation, there is a rule that copies the content of the antecedent into the anaphor itself. This copying rule is triggered by the coindexation. A similar process applies to coindexed pronouns (8).

7) a) Frank$_i$ loves himself$_i$.   *SPELLOUT and PF*

      ⇓ *covert copying rule*

   b) Frank$_i$ loves Frank$_i$.   *LF*

8) a) Frank$_i$ thinks he$_i$ might have insulted Morgan.   *SPELLOUT and PF*

     ⇓ *covert copying rule*

    b) Frank$_i$ thinks Frank$_i$ might have insulted Morgan.   *LF*

The LF-copying hypothesis holds that something similar happens with VP ellipsis. The elided VP is really a null pronominal that is coindexed with the VP antecedent. On the surface and at PF this pronominal is just a garden-variety null element that isn't pronounced, but at LF, the antecedent is copied over:

9) a) Frank will [eat an apple]$_i$ and Morgan will [$_{VP}$ Ø$_i$] too. *SPELLOUT/ PF*

     ⇓ *covert copying rule*

    b) Frank will [eat an apple]$_i$ and Morgan will [eat an apple] too.   *LF*

Ellipsis under this story then simply reduces to the way that bound pronouns get their reference. The ellipsis site is simply a null pro-verb, and its content is copied in via the same copying rule.

The alternative hypothesis is that the elided VP is fully structured as a syntactic object (in particular at D-structure) and is present through the application of all the syntactic movement rules. It is different from other elements in that its phonological structure is deleted by a rule under identity with a preceding VP. One thing is clear: it is not deleted entirely, because we're able to give it an interpretation at LF. So this isn't a "tree pruning" rule that lops off the entire phonological structure. There must be something present at LF to be interpreted. However, the phonological content of the phrase is absent. Since the VP must be present in the LF to be meaningful, the deletion must happen in the part of the grammatical model where LF is not affected. This is the part of the derivation after SPELLOUT, on the way to LF. Recall our model in (10). We've argued that there is overt movement between D-structure and SPELLOUT, covert movement between SPELLOUT and LF. What we're proposing here is an operation that happens between SPELLOUT and PF. It affects the pronunciation of the sentence, but not its interpretation. This deletion operation is called the *PF-deletion hypothesis*.

10)   D-structure

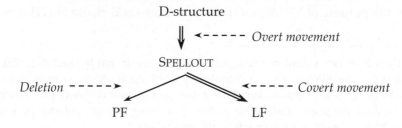

An example of the deletion rule at work is given in (11). The SPELLOUT (SO) and LF contain a fully specified VP in the second clause, but the formation of the PF from the SPELLOUT includes a special rule that deletes the coindexed VP.

11) a)   Frank will [eat an apple]$_i$ and Morgan will [eat an apple] too. ***SO, LF***

⬇ *PF-deletion rule*

   b)   Frank will [eat an apple]$_i$ and Morgan will [eat an apple] too.   ***PF***

The debate around which of these two hypotheses is correct evokes great emotion at linguistics conferences and both hypotheses have their supporters and champions.[1] We'll consider evidence for both of these positions, but I'll leave it up to you to figure out which one does better in the end.

The two hypotheses differ in two critical ways, whether or not the elided VP has its own independent structure, both before SPELLOUT and after it. Under the LF-copying hypothesis, there is no structure to the pro-verb before SPELLOUT, and any structure at LF is provided as a copy from the antecedent VP. Under the PF approach, by contrast, the VP is fully structured throughout the derivation (i.e., before SPELLOUT and on the road to LF) and this structure is not a result of copying the antecedent VP, but just happens to be identical to it.

Let's start with an argument for the copying approach. What we're going to show is that the elided VP has properties it could only have got if it were covertly copied over from the antecedent VP, and not if it was present all along and then its phonological structure deleted. Let's start off by thinking about binding theory. You'll recall that due to Condition A of the binding theory, anaphors must find a c-commanding antecedent (a binder) within their own clause. So in the following sentence, each anaphor has the subject of its own clause as its antecedent. In particular, the second *himself* cannot take *Calvin* as an antecedent, only *Otto*, because *Otto* is its clausemate.

12) [$_{CP}$ Calvin$_i$ will strike himself$_i$ and [$_{CP}$ Otto$_k$ will strike himself$_{k/*i}$ too]].

Now think about the sentence above when it comes to the identity of the VPs for the purpose of VP ellipsis. The VP in the second clause in (12) is present

---

[1] There is in fact a third position, posited by Culicover and Jackendoff (2005). They claim that the ellipsis site isn't occupied by anything at all at any level, not even a null element. The interpretation of the missing constituent is simply provided by our contextual pragmatic knowledge rather than being a real syntactic or semantic structure. We won't pursue this third alternative here.

throughout the derivation, and it can only take *Otto* as antecedent. So the PF-deletion approach predicts that if the phonological form of this VP is simply deleted on the way to PF – an operation that does not affect the interpretation or LF – then this should be the only possible interpretation for a sentence with ellipsis. However, this is not the case. The equivalent sentence to (12) with an elided VP in the second clause, (13), is actually ambiguous with respect to the interpretation of the (missing) anaphor.

13) Calvin will strike himself and Otto will [$_{VP}$ ___] too.

Sentence (13) allows two possible interpretations. One interpretation, which is identical to that in (12), holds that Otto is hitting himself. This interpretation is called *sloppy identity*. The other possible meaning of (13) is that Otto is hitting Calvin.[2] This interpretation, called *strict identity*, is extremely surprising given the interpretation of (12). If the elided VP were present throughout the derivation, as claimed by the PF-deletion hypothesis, then there is no way that the elided anaphor should ever be able to take the subject of the first clause as its antecedent. Not only is the elided anaphor not in the same clause as *Calvin*, it isn't c-commanded by *Calvin* either! The coindexation required by the PF-deletion hypothesis would result in a clear violation of Condition A.

The LF-copying hypothesis, however, gives a simple explanation for the strict/sloppy ambiguity problem shown in (13). The ambiguity results from different orderings of the copying rules for pronouns and pro-verbs. Let's start with the sloppy reading, where Calvin is hitting Calvin and Otto is hitting Otto. For this interpretation, the VP-copying rule applies first (a and b). Then the rule that copies NPs into anaphors applies. This rule is clause-bound, so it will only look for a c-commanding antecedent in the same clause. The *himself* in the first clause will get replaced by *Calvin* and the *himself* in the second clause will get replaced by *Otto*. This results in the sloppy interpretation where Calvin strikes Calvin and Otto strikes Otto.

---

[2] There are some people who have trouble getting this reading for this sentence. It's a clear judgment for many people, including me and my entire immediate family, but other people I have asked have trouble with this strict interpretation. If you can't get this reading of the anaphor, the same argument can be made with the sentence *Calvin will honor his father and Otto will too.* This sentence is ambiguous such that Otto can be honoring either his own father or Calvin's father. If you're one of the people who don't get two readings for (13) you can just substitute the above sentence in the argument below instead of (13). The effect is the same, although the argument isn't as strong, as pronouns in general allow long-distance antecedents.

13) a)   Calvin will strike himself and Otto will [$_{VP}$ Ø] too.   *SPELLOUT*

⇓ *covert VP-copying rule*

   b)   Calvin will [strike himself] and Otto will [strike himself] too.

⇓ *covert anaphor-copying rule*

   c)   [$_{CP}$ Calvin will [strike Calvin]] and [$_{CP}$ Otto will [strike Otto] too. *LF*

The strict interpretation is created by applying the two copying rules in the
other order. First *himself* is replaced with *Calvin* (14b), and then the empty VP
is replaced with the VP *[strike Calvin]* (14c). This gives the reading where
Otto is hitting Calvin.

14) a)   Calvin will strike himself and Otto will [$_{VP}$ Ø] too.   *SPELLOUT*

⇓ *covert anaphor-copying rule*

   b)   [$_{CP}$ Calvin will [strike Calvin]] and Otto will [$_{VP}$ Ø] too.

⇓ *covert VP-copying rule*

   c)   Calvin will [strike Calvin] and Otto will [strike Calvin] too. *LF*

These facts, then, are evidence for an LF-copying analysis, because it's only
under that story that there is a version of the sentence where the reflexive
object in the second clause is not c-commanded by Otto at some point in the
derivation.

   While this is impressive validation of the LF-copying hypothesis, there
are also many arguments in favor of the PF-deletion hypothesis. Recall that
the LF-copying hypothesis holds that during the part of the syntax between
D-structure and SPELLOUT, there is only a pro-verb. This pro-verb VP has no
internal structure in this part of the derivation of the sentence. This means
that operations that affect elements that are inside the VP should not be in
effect in sentences with VP ellipsis. There is significant evidence that this is
false. It appears as if the overt syntax is sensitive to the internal structure of
the elided material.

   Let's start with the least obvious example: antecedent-contained
deletion. When you have a sentence like that in (15a), there is a *wh*-phrase in
the specifier of the CP that had to have moved there from within the VP (as
seen in (15b)). If the VP is a pro-form Ø category, it's unclear where that *wh*-
phrase comes from. Under the PF-deletion hypothesis, the *wh*-phrase
originates within the deleted VP.

15) a)   Calvin has dated every girl who Jeff has.
    b)   Calvin has dated [$_{DP}$ every girl [$_{CP}$ who [$_{TP}$ Jeff has [$_{VP}$ ̶d̶a̶t̶e̶d̶ ̶t̶_i̶]]]].

A similar effect is seen in (16a). A *wh*-phrase originates in the elided VP, which could only have occurred if the VP was fully present and structured at the time of overt *wh*-movement (16b). Under the analysis where the VP is just a single word (the pro-form), the origins of the moved *wh*-phrase are utterly mysterious.

16) a) I know which guys you've dated, but I don't know which guys you haven't.
    b) I know which guys$_i$ you've dated t_i, but I don't know [which guys]$_i$ you haven't [$_{VP}$ ~~dated t_i~~].

We know that the relationship between the *wh*-phrase and its trace is one of movement, because it's subject to island effects, which demonstrate that the MLC (a condition on movement) is at work. (17a) is a fairly standard *wh*-island, moving the *wh*-phrase *which language* over *who* is a violation of the MLC. Example (17b), taken from Merchant (2001), demonstrates that the same condition holds if the movement happens out of an elided VP. If the MLC is a restriction on movement, then the *wh*-word must have started inside of the elided clause, which in turn entails that the clause had structure and isn't just a null pronoun.

17) a) *Which language do you want to hire someone who speaks t_i?
         (cf. I want to hire someone who speaks Bulgarian.)
    b) *They want to hire someone who speaks a Balkan language, but I don't know which language$_i$ they do [$_{VP}$ ~~want to hire someone who speaks t_i~~].

Merchant (2001) presents a series of arguments from the sluicing construction that also show that the elided string must have an internal syntax. Recall that sluicing appears to be the ellipsis of a TP, licensed by a *wh*-phrase.

18) Calvin will fire someone today, but I don't know who [$_{TP}$ ___].

Like the examples in (15) and (16), if there isn't a TP here throughout the derivation but only a pro-form instead, the source of the *wh*-phrase is a bit mysterious.

Some languages allow *wh*-movement to "strand" a prepositional phrase – despite the prescriptive admonitions never to end a sentence with a preposition. English is a prototypical example.

19)   Who$_i$ has Peter talked with t_i?

But in other languages preposition stranding is disallowed. Greek is a good example:

20)   *Pjon   milise   me?   *Greek*
        who   she.spoke   with
        "Who did she speak with?"

The difference between these two types of language carries over to sluiced examples. English allows a preposition to be stranded within the TP that was elided (of course it also allows it to front to the beginning of the clause with the *wh*-phrase).

21)   Peter was talking with someone but I don't know who.

But Greek doesn't allow this, just like it doesn't allow preposition stranding in general.

22) *I   Anna milise   me   kapjon,   alla dhe ksero pjon
     the Anna spoke.3s with   someone, but not know who
     "Anna spoke with someone, but I don't know who."
     (cf. *I Anna milise me kapjon, alla dhe ksero me pjon*, which is grammatical)

Note that in both English and Greek the TP is completely missing. However, the restrictions that Greek can't strand a preposition and English can are retained even though the TP where that restriction is completely missing. An LF-copying theory can't account for this, but a theory like PF deletion, where the TP is present when *wh*-movement (and the restriction on preposition stranding) applies, can.

So we have conflicting evidence about what the right analysis of ellipsis should be. Some evidence points towards a VP pro-form with copying of the antecedent VP at LF. The other evidence points to the VP being fully structured, but having its phonological structure deleted in PF. I'm not going to resolve this for you here. In the problem sets and the workbook I've given you some data that you can use to construct further arguments in favor of one hypothesis or another. I'll leave it up to you to decide which camp you fall into.

You now have enough information to try WBE 3 & 4, GPS 2 & 3, and CPS 1 & 2.

2. ANTECEDENT-CONTAINED DELETION AND PSEUDOGAPPING

Before we leave the topic of ellipsis it's worth spending a few pages looking at two of the trickier subtypes of VP ellipsis: antecedent-contained deletion and pseudogapping.

2.1 Antecedent-Contained Deletion

As discussed above in section 0, **antecedent-contained deletion** (ACD) is a special case of ellipsis, where an elided VP is contained within a DP that is itself contained within the very VP that serves as the antecedent for the ellipsis. This is schematized in (24). An example of ACD is given in (25).

23) [$_{VP}$ … [$_{DP}$ … [$_{CP}$ … [$_{VP}$ ····]$_i$ …]]]$_i$

24) Brandon [$_{VP}$ read every book that Megan did [$_{VP}$ …]].

ACD has the property of infinite regress. The antecedent of the ellipsis contains the ellipsis, so how can the content of the elided VP ever be recovered? The LF copy theory is particularly challenged by these forms. The antecedent of the missing constituent also contains that constituent. Hornstein (1994) overcomes this problem by making use of the shift of objects into AgrO. The DP containing the gap is always an object, so it shifts out of the antecedent VP into the specifier of AgrOP. After this happens the elided VP is no longer contained within its own antecedent, so the problem of infinite regress vanishes, as the actual gap is no longer contained within the VP antecedent.

25)

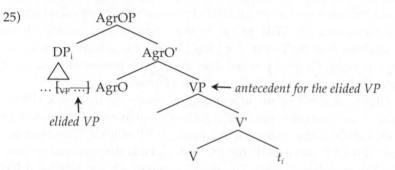

Sag (1976) proposes a different analysis, but with the same effect: the DP raises out of the VP, so the VP can serve as an antecedent for the deletion of the VP inside the DP. For Sag, the movement is covert Quantifier Raising instead of DP movement to the specifier of AgrO. The DP involved in ACD is always headed by a quantifier, so QR is expected of these DPs. When QR occurs, the DP containing the ellipsis is again no longer contained inside the VP that serves as its antecedent. The LF is given in (26).

26) [Every book that Megan did [$_{VP}$══]]$_i$ Brandon [VP read t$_i$]

There are two big differences between these approaches. One is that the QR in (26) is covert, but DP movement in (25) is overt. The other is in the landing site of the movement. In Challenge Problem Set 2 you're asked to think about how you might distinguish these two approaches to ACD.

You now have enough information to try CPS 3.

2.2 Pseudogapping

There is one variant of the ellipsis phenomenon that doesn't delete the entire VP: *pseudogapping*. This is puzzling, since ellipsis phenomena typically target only constituents. In pseudogapping constructions, the accusative DP is left behind and not elided.

27) Darin has eaten more squid than Raiza has *octopus*.

Note that this isn't simply deleting a verb: everything but the accusative-marked DP is deleted from the second VP (28) (example from Agbayani and Zoerner 2004). Both the verb *prove* and the additional adjunct *innocent* are obligatorily absent from the second clause.

28) The lawyer can't prove Paul innocent but he can ~~prove~~ *Della* ~~innocent~~.

There are two common approaches to pseudogapping. One uses VP ellipsis, and the other uses a special kind of movement process called across-the-board movement (or ATB). Just as in our discussion of normal ellipsis and our discussion of ACD, I'm not going to tell you which of these two hypotheses is right. I'll give you the data that's been presented in favor of and against them both and you can decide for yourself.

The ellipsis analysis of pseudogapping is presented in Lasnik (1999a) and requires the complex split vP-AgrOp-VP architecture proposed in chapter 14. Lasnik claims that pseudogapping is VP ellipsis. The object has moved out of the VP into AgrOP, but the verb and all other material remains inside the VP, and gets deleted. The object survives ellipsis because it has shifted outside of the VP.

29)

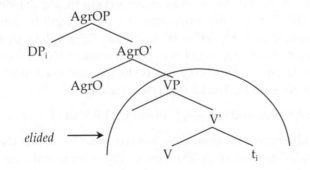

Regular vanilla VP ellipsis is really vP ellipsis, which is why the object disappears in regular VP ellipsis.

The alternative analysis, proposed by Agbayani and Zoerner (2004), which builds on the insights of Johnson (1994) claims that pseudogapping isn't really an ellipsis phenomenon at all. Instead, they claim it's a particular instance of a rather peculiar movement process called **across-the-board movement** (ATB). The most typical kind of ATB movement involves a *wh*-question, where the *wh*-phrase seems to have been moved from two different places, both within a coordinated VP. In (30), for example, the word *what* serves both as the object of the verb *like* and as the object of the verb *hate*.

30) What$_i$ does Calvin like t$_i$ but Rory hate t$_i$?

Agbayani and Zoerner claim that pseudogapping is the same kind of thing. The verb raises to little v, and has two traces – one in each coordinate. Modifying their analysis slightly to fit the assumptions outlined in this book, this involves a CP which is attached to the VP as an adjunct, and the verb moves both from within this CP and from within the VP itself, via ATB movement (leaving two traces). To make the tree in (31) easier I'm omitting any AgrPs and the details of the CP itself.

31)

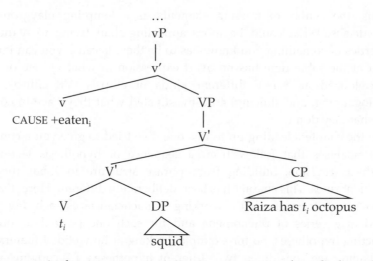

There are both advantages and disadvantages to each of the hypotheses. The ellipsis account reduces the explanation of pseudogapping to two otherwise attested processes (ellipsis and movement of the object to the specifier of AgroP). The ATB account reduces the phenomenon to an otherwise attested but nonetheless mysterious process too. On the downside there are serious counterexamples to both approaches. Lasnik's ellipsis approach elides the VP under AgrO, but there are plenty of examples where auxiliaries higher than AgrO are elided along with it. Sentence (5a) from section 0 above, repeated here as (32), has deleted the auxiliary *been*, which is higher in the tree than the shifted object. At no time has that auxiliary ever been part of the lowest VP, which is the bit that Lasnik proposes has been deleted.

32) a)   Brandon has been reading more novels than he has short stories.

　　b)   … he has [$_{VP}$ ~~been~~ [$_{AgrO}$ short stories [$_{VP}$ ~~read~~]]]

The ATB account runs into problems with discontinuous pseudogapping like that in (28) above, because the ATB movement involves head movement of the missing constituent. The discontinuous phrase *prove … innocent* is not a head, so shouldn't undergo head movement. Agbayani and Zoerner acknowledge this problem and propose a solution where *prove* and *innocent* become "reanalyzed" as a single head. While this solves the immediate problem, it adds the need for additional explanation of what it means to reanalyze a structure into a head.

3. CONCLUSION

Ellipsis, the syntax of missing elements, is a tempting playground for syntacticians. What could be more appealing than trying to deduce the properties of something you know has to be there because you can interpret it, but at the same time has no overt expression in what we see or write? We've looked at a few different kinds of ellipsis (VP ellipsis, ACD, pseudogapping, and sluicing) and investigated what they have in common and what they don't.

In the chapters leading up to this one, I've tried to give you a consistent set of analyses that follow from a sequence of hypothesis testing and hypothesis revision, building from phrase structure to X-bar theory to movement rules. This chapter has been deliberately different. Here, I've tried to give you a taste of what a working syntactician faces each day. We've looked at a series of phenomena and for each one posited a couple of conflicting hypotheses. So for example, looking at how elided material gets its meaning we considered two different hypotheses: LF copying and PF deletion. We looked at conflicting evidence that shows that either of them might be right or wrong. We did the same with ACD and pseudogapping. This kind of investigation is the bread and butter of what syntacticians do each day. They look at a puzzling set of data, consider different hypotheses and the predictions they make and weigh the evidence one way or another.

IDEAS, RULES, AND CONSTRAINTS INTRODUCED IN THIS CHAPTER

i)   *Ellipsis*: A construction that omits a constituent when it is identical to a string that has previously been uttered.

ii)   *VP Ellipsis*: A process that omits a VP (or vP) under identity with a previously uttered identical VP, normally in a conjunction. (E.g., *I will eat a squid sandwich and you will too.*)

iii) *Antecedent-Contained Deletion (ACD)*: A kind of ellipsis where the antecedent of the ellipsis contains the ellipsis site. (E.g., *She read every book that I did.*)

iv)   *Pseudogapping*: A variety of ellipsis where the accusative object is not omitted, but the rest of the VP is. (E.g., *Dan can't prove Paul innocent but he can ~~prove~~ Della ~~innocent~~.*)

v)   *Comparative Deletion*: The deletion in a comparative construction; often more than just a VP is missing. We did not attempt an account of comparative deletion in this chapter. (E.g., *I've read more books than you ~~[have read books]~~.*)

vi)   *Comparative Subdeletion*: A kind of comparative deletion that is effectively equivalent to one kind of pseudogapping. (E.g., *I've eaten more popcorn than you have ~~eaten~~ fries.*)

vii) *Stripping*: An ellipsis process where only one argument remains and the rest of the clause is elided. (E.g., *Frank read the* Times *last night, or maybe the* Post.)

viii) *N-ellipsis*: The deletion of some part of a DP, typically including the N head. (E.g., *I read these three books not those two ____.*)

ix)   *Sluicing*: A kind of ellipsis, where a TP is elided after a *wh*-phrase (E.g., *I saw someone come into the room, but I don't remember who ____.*)

x)   *LF-copying hypothesis:* The idea that VP ellipsis consists of a null pronominal VP that is replaced by a copy of its antecedent after SPELLOUT and before LF.

xi)   *PF-deletion hypothesis:* The idea that VP ellipsis targets a fully structured VP, which is deleted under identity with an antecedent after SPELLOUT and before PF.

xii) *Sloppy Identity:* In an ellipsis structure an elided pronoun or anaphor takes its reference from a local subject (e.g., where *John loves his father and Bill does too* has an interpretation where Bill loves Bill's father).

xiii) *Strict Identity*: In an ellipsis structure an elided pronoun or anaphor takes its reference from the subject in the antecedent clause (e.g., where *John loves his father and Bill does too* has an interpretation where Bill loves John's father).

xiv)   ***Preposition Stranding***: The phenomenon in English and related
         languages where prepositions do not move with the *wh*-phrase.
         (E.g., *Who did you take a picture of?*)

xv)   ***Sag's Analysis of ACD***: To avoid infinite regress, the quantified DP
         undergoes covert QR to the top of the clause, which places it outside
         of the VP that is its antecedent.

xvi)   ***Hornstein's Analysis of ACD***: To avoid infinite regress, the DP
         undergoes DP movement to the specifier of AgrOP, which places it
         outside of the (lowest) VP that is its antecedent.

xvii)   ***Lasnik's Analysis of Pseudogapping (Ellipsis Analysis)***: To explain
         why accusative objects survive ellipsis in pseudogapping structures,
         the accusative object moves to the specifier of AgrOP, which places it
         outside the VP that is elided. Normal VP ellipsis is really vP ellipsis.

xviii)   ***Across-the-Board Movement (ATB)***: The movement, typically of a
         wh-phrase, that appears to originate in two different conjoined VPs
         or clauses (e.g., *Who did [Evan despise t_i] and [Calvin adore t_i?]*)

xix)   ***Agbayani and Zoerner's Analysis of Pseudogapping (ATB Analysis)***:
         Pseudogapping is not VP ellipsis; instead, it is the overt ATB head
         movement of a V head in two different phrases into a single little v
         node. The second trace of this movement corresponds to the
         "ellipsis" site in pseudogapping.

FURTHER READING: Agbayani and Zoerner (2004), Chung, Ladusaw, and
McCloskey (1995), Culicover and Jackendoff (2005), Fiengo and May (1994),
Hankamer (1979), Hornstein (1994), Jackendoff (1971), Johnson (2001, 2009),
Kennedy and Merchant (2000), Kitagawa (1991), Lappin (1996), Lasnik
(1999a, 2010), Levin (1979/1986), Lobeck (1995), Merchant (2001), Ross (1967,
1970), Sag (1976), Tancredi (1992)

GENERAL PROBLEM SETS

GPS1. IRISH VP ELLIPSIS
[Data Analysis and Critical Thinking; Intermediate]
Consider the following data from Irish. Sentence (a) represents a typical VP
ellipsis structure in the language. The sentences in (b) represent a related
phenomenon known as "responsive ellipsis", where a question is replied to
with a bare verb in its positive or negative form (instead of a "yes" or "no").

a)   Dúirt   mé   go   gceannóinn   é   agus cheannaigh.
      said   I   that   buy.COND.1s   it   and   bought.
      "I said that I'd buy it and I did." (literally "I said that I'd buy it and
      bought.") (McCloskey 1991)

b)   Q: Ar cheannaigh tú é?
             Q buy you it
             "Did you buy it?"

      A: Cheannaigh   *or*   Níor   cheannaigh
             buy.PAST   NEG.PAST buy.PAST
             "yes" (literally "bought")   "no" (literally "not bought")

Now recall our analysis of VSO order in Irish. The verb moves V → v → T,
and the subject stays in the specifier of vP. With that in mind, what is the
predicted result of ellipsis if you omit a VP in Irish? What is the predicted
result of ellipsis if you omit a vP instead of a VP in Irish? So is VP ellipsis
really ellipsis of a VP or a vP? How does the data above support your
analysis? Draw a tree for sentence (a) demonstrating what structure gets
elided in a VP ellipsis structure in Irish.

GPS2. SPECIFIC INDEFINITES AND VP ELLIPSIS[3]
[Data Analysis and Critical Thinking; Advanced]
The sentence in (1a) is ambiguous. It can have either of the paraphrases in
(1b) and (1c).

1) a) Alexandra wants to catch a fish.
   b) There is a certain fish that Alexandra wants to catch.
   c) Alexandra hopes her fishing is successful.

One common explanation for the interpretation in (1b) is that the existentially
quantified DP *a fish* undergoes covert QR to the front of the sentence as in
(2). This results in an interpretation where there is some fish that Alexandra
wants to catch.

2) [CP [a fish]I [TP Alexandra wants to catch tI]]

When one combines two clauses like (1a) into a VP ellipsis construction, the
sentence is only two ways ambiguous, not four ways as might be expected.
The second clause must have an interpretation that parallels the
interpretation of the first clause. They cannot be mismatched. So (3a) can
mean either (3b) or (3c) but it can't mean (3d) or (3e).

---

[3] Data and discussion based on Lasnik (2010).

3) a) Alexandra wants to catch a fish and Sylvia does too.
   b) *paraphrase 1:* There is a certain fish that Alexandra wants to catch and there is a certain fish that Sylvia wants to catch.[4]
   c) *paraphrase 2:* Alexandra hopes her fishing is successful and Sylvia hopes her fishing is successful.
   d) *impossible paraphrase 1:* *There is a certain fish that Alexandra wants to catch and Sylvia hopes her fishing is successful.
   e) *impossible paraphrase 2:* *Alexandra hopes that her fishing is successful and there is a certain fish that Sylvia wants to catch.

Explain how the parallelism requirement exemplified in (3), such that either QR of the indefinite has applied in both conjuncts or it applies in neither, is evidence for an LF-copying approach to ellipsis. Also discuss why the PF-deletion account makes the wrong predictions about these data.

GPS3. GERMAN SLUICING AND CASE MATCHING[5]
[Data Analysis and Critical Thinking; Advanced]

In German, certain verbs require that their complement DP show up in a specific case. For example, the verb *loben* "praise" requires that its object DP takes an accusative form. The verb *schmeicheln* "flatter", by contrast, requires that its object DP takes a dative case. This is true both of normal DPs and of *wh*-phrases that are DP objects, as seen in (1):

1) a) Er will   jemanden   loben,   aber   sie   wissen
      He wants   someone.ACC praise   but   they   know

      nicht   wen/*wem   er loben   will.
      not   who.ACC/*who.DAT he praise   want
      "He wants to praise someone but they don't know who he wants to praise."

   b) Er will   jemandem   schmeicheln,   aber   sie   wissen
      He wants   someone.DAT flatter   but   they   know

      nicht   wem/*wen   er schmeicheln   will.
      not   who.DAT/*who.ACC he praise   wants
      "He wants to flatter someone but they don't know who he wants to flatter."

This is true in sluices as well. The *wh*-phrase must match the case of the verb that is elided by sluicing, as seen in (2):

---

[4] Or alternately "There is a certain fish that both Sylvia and Alexandra want to catch." The difference between these two interpretations is irrelevant to the problem set.

[5] Data and discussion based on Merchant (2001).

2) a) Er will jemanden loben, aber sie wissen
      he wants someone.ACC praise but they know

   nicht wen/*wem
   not who.ACC/*who.DAT
   "He wants to praise someone but they don't know who."

   b) Er will jemandem schmeicheln, aber sie wissen
      He wants someone.DAT flatter but they know

   nicht wem/*wen
   not who.DAT/*who.ACC
   "He wants to flatter someone but they don't know who."

Use this data to construct an argument that ellipsis (or sluicing at least) is a PF-deletion phenomenon, not an LF-copying phenomenon. Keep in mind that the PF side of the derivation cannot reference anything that happens on the LF side.

CHALLENGE PROBLEM SETS

CHALLENGE PROBLEM SET 1: CONDITION C
[Critical and Creative Thinking; Challenging]
In this chapter, we proposed that at LF pronouns and anaphors are replaced by the DP that they are coindexed with (and elided VPs might be replaced at LF by the VP they are coindexed with). So for example (1a) becomes (1b) at LF:

1)   a)   Calvin$_i$ admired himself$_i$ in the mirror
      b)   Calvin$_i$ admired Calvin$_i$ in the mirror

Does this operation of copying create violations of Condition C of the binding theory? Explain why or why not. If it does can you think of a creative way of getting around the problem?

CHALLENGE PROBLEM SET 2: DAHL'S PUZZLE[6]
[Critical and Creative Thinking; Very Challenging]
Consider the possible interpretations of the sentence in (1). To make things simple, assume that the first *he* and the first *his* are coindexed with *Morgan*. The second clause allows four possible interpretations, given in (b–e). The first pronoun in the second clause can be interpreted as referring to either *Rory* or *Morgan*, as can the second. When either pronoun refers to Morgan, we'll call it the "strict" reading. When it refers to Rory, we'll call it the "sloppy" reading.

---

[6] Based on observations in Dahl (1974).

1) a) Morgan$_i$ said he$_i$ loves his$_i$ mother and Rory said that he loves his
        mother, too.
    b) Rory said Morgan loves Morgan's mother.   (strict + strict)
    c) Rory said Rory loves Rory's mother.   (sloppy + sloppy)
    d) Rory said Rory loves Morgan's mother.   (sloppy + strict)
    e) Rory said Morgan loves Rory's mother.   (strict + sloppy)

Dahl (1974) observed that when the second clause in (1a) is elided as in
(2a), the reading in (1e) vanishes:

2) a) Morgan$_i$ said he$_i$ loves his$_i$ mother and Rory did, too.
    b) Rory said Morgan loves Morgan's mother.   (strict + strict)
    c) Rory said Rory loves Rory's mother.   (sloppy + sloppy)
    d) Rory said Rory loves Morgan's mother.   (sloppy + strict)
    e) *Rory said Morgan loves Rory's mother.   (strict + sloppy)

Assume as we did in the text that strict readings are achieved by applying
first the pronominal copying rule and then the VP-copying rule, and sloppy
readings are constructed by applying first the VP-copying rule and then the
pronoun-copying rule. Can the LF-copying approach explain the absence of
the reading in (e), but the acceptability of the sentence in (d)? Explain why or
why not.

CHALLENGE PROBLEM SET 3: ACD
[Critical and Creative Thinking; Very Challenging]
What are the different predictions made by the Sag (QR) approach to ACD
and the Hornstein (DP movement to the specifier of AgrOP) explanation of
ACD? Can you test those differences and come up with discussion of which
approach works best?

Advanced Topics in Binding Theory

Learning Objectives

After reading chapter 17 you should walk away having mastered the following ideas and skills:

1. Explain why the binding conditions appear to hold both before and after movement.
2. Describe the copy theory of movement.
3. Explain how the copy theory of movement explains the ordering paradox.
4. Explain the data that shows that pronouns and anaphors seem to have different binding domains.
5. Be able to identify the new binding domains for pronouns and anaphors making reference to "potential antecedents".

0. INTRODUCTION

In chapter 5, we sketched out a brief version of the binding theory that allowed us to see the utility of structural relations and gave us a tool to

Syntax: A Generative Introduction, Third Edition. Andrew Carnie.
© 2013 Andrew Carnie. Published 2013 by John Wiley & Sons, Inc.

probe the c-command structures in a tree. That chapter contained a number of simplifications. For example, it isn't very hard to find counterexamples to the theory proposed there. In this chapter, we give binding relations a slightly more nuanced look. The version of the binding theory presented here is loosely based on the one found in Chomsky's (1986b) *Knowledge of Language*, but with an eye towards more recent developments in the theory.

1. LEVELS OF REPRESENTATION

In chapter 5, we claimed that the binding domain was a clause (CP). This nicely accounts for the ungrammaticality of sentences like (1) below:

1)   *Chris$_i$ said [$_{CP}$ that himself$_i$ was appealing].

However, on the face of it, this runs into trouble with sentences such as:

2)   Chris$_i$ wants himself$_i$ to be appealing.

Assuming that *himself* is the subject of the predicate *to be appealing*, here the binding relation seems to cross clause boundaries. However, the analysis we developed of subject-to-object raising in the chapter 15 solves this particular problem. If the DP *himself* moves to the specifier of the AgrOP for case reasons it moves out of the CP where it gets its theta role. Once it is part of the higher clause structure its new binding domain contains the antecedent *Chris*. In (3) the old binding domain is shown with the rightmost arc. The raising of the DP extends this to the higher CP.

3)   [$_{CP}$ Chris$_i$ wants [$_{AgrOP}$ himself$_i$ [.. [$_{CP}$ ... t$_{himself}$ to be appealing]]]].

            binding domain   *binding domain*

            after movement   *before movement*

This fact, then, suggests that the binding principles must hold **after** movement has applied. Given the model that we sketched in chapter 13, this would be the level of LF. This makes a fair amount of sense, since binding is at least partly a semantic relation and LF is the level that interacts with the conceptual/semantic component of the grammar. Were things so simple, however! If you did General Problem Set 2 in chapter 12, you will have learned that there is at least some evidence that binding principles hold before movement. Take the sentence in (4):

4)   [Which pictures of himself$_i$] did Chris$_i$ like?

The *wh*-moved DP here contains an anaphor (*himself*). This anaphor is only c-commanded by its antecedent **before** the movement:

5)   C$_{[+Q,+WH]}$ Chris$_i$ did like [which pictures of himself$_i$]   (D-structure)

In chapter 12, this was taken to be evidence that the binding principles held at D-structure, before movement.

So we have an apparent contradiction here. Raising sentences such as (2) provide an argument for the claim that the binding principles happen after movement, but *wh*-questions such as (4) suggest that binding principles happen before movement. The theory of movement we have, however, provides a straightforward solution, if we make a minor adjustment to our assumptions. We have up to now been marking the source of movement with a *t* for trace. Let us consider the possibility that these traces have more to them than this. Chomsky (1993) suggested that movement was really an operation of copying, where you don't pronounce the original copy. So for example, when we do *wh*-movement in a sentence like (4), the LF of the sentence is really as in (6) where the DP that is struck through is the trace and isn't pronounced – much like an elided VP from the previous chapter.

6)   [Which pictures of himself$_i$] did Chris$_i$ like [which pictures of himself$_i$]?

In this view, movement consists of two parts, a copying operation that duplicates part of the tree and then puts the copy somewhere in the tree and then an operation that (usually) silences the original. The technical name for the two DPs in (6) is the **chain**. Chains are the combination of the moved copy and any silent originals (traces) they leave behind.

With this technology in hand we have a simple account of the timing dilemma we sketched above. Binding principles all hold at LF. We can claim that at LF at least one link in the chain (one copy or original) is subject to the binding principles. In a sentence like (6), the version of the anaphor in the trace is c-commanded by *Chris*. This version is present at LF, it just isn't pronounced. Binding Principle A is met because one copy of the anaphor is c-commanded by a local antecedent.

In the case of sentences like (2), a different copy of the anaphor is locally c-commanded by its antecedent. This time it is the moved copy that meets the binding Principle A:

7)   Chris$_i$ wants himself$_i$ [... [$_{CP}$ ... himself$_i$ to be appealing]] .

Defining the binding principles over the chains of DPs rather than over DPs themselves solves this timing problem. We can claim that the binding principles hold of LF representations and that, in the case of anaphors, at least one copy must appear in the right binding configuration:

8) *Binding Principle A (revised)*: One copy of an anaphor in a chain must be bound within its binding domain.

An exercise at the end of the chapter asks you to consider if the same property is true of pronouns and Principle B.

You now have enough information to try WBE 1 & 2 and CPS 1.

---

2. THE DEFINITION OF BINDING DOMAIN

2.1 A Miscellany of Domain Violations

There are significant reasons for thinking that our definition of binding domain in terms of clauses is far too simplistic. Consider the sentences in (9). In most major dialects of English, sentence (9b) is ungrammatical with coindexation between *Heidi* and *herself*, despite the fact that sentence (9a), which is very similar in structure to (9b), is entirely grammatical. (There is a dialect of English, spoken mainly in the western US, where (9b) is acceptable. If you are a speaker of that dialect, bear with me and assume that the judgments given here are correct. There is a problem set about this alternate dialect at the end of this chapter.)

9) a) Heidi$_i$ believes any description of herself$_i$.
    b) *Heidi$_i$ believes Martha$_k$'s description of herself$_i$.

In both (9a) and (9b), the anaphor is c-commanded by a coindexed antecedent contained in the same clause as the anaphor. By all of the definitions and constraints we have looked at so far (9b) should be acceptable, but it isn't.

The next set of sentences we need to consider has the reverse problem. Recall from chapter 5 that pronouns must be free within their binding domain. (10) is ungrammatical with the coindexation given because the pronoun and its c-commanding antecedent are in the same clause:

10) *Heidi$_i$ likes her$_i$.

But a pronoun inside an embedded CP is okay with coindexation or without it:

11) Heidi$_i$ thinks that she$_{i/k}$ has won.

We explained this phenomenon in terms of the clause serving as the binding domain. Pronouns must be free within their immediate clause. Consider now the following problem sentence:

12) Heidi likes her violin.

(12) is ambiguous in precisely the same way that (11) is. *Her* can be bound by *Heidi* or not:

13) a)   Heidi$_i$ likes her$_i$ violin.   b)   Heidi$_i$ likes her$_k$ violin.

The interpretation in (13a) is particularly surprising, since *her* and *Heidi* are both dominated by the same CP, so are both in the same binding domain. The indexation in (13a) should be a violation of Principle B, yet the sentence is entirely acceptable.

To round off our survey of binding puzzles, consider the sentence in (14). This sentence is acceptable, contrary to all principles of the binding theory:

14)   Heidi$_i$ thinks that pictures of herself$_i$ should be hung in the Louvre.

The anaphor is not in the same clause as its antecedent at all. This should be a clear Principle A violation, yet the sentence is reasonably acceptable.

2.2 *Anaphors*

The problem in every case that we have looked at has to do with the definition of binding domain. Let us start to probe this question by looking more closely at the differences between (9a and b). The main difference between the two sentences seems to be the presence of the extra DP *Martha* that intervenes between the anaphor and its antecedent in the unacceptable form. However, not just any intervening DP will do:

15)   Heidi$_i$ gave a present to herself$_i$.

In (15) *a present* intervenes between the antecedent and the anaphor (and furthermore it c-commands the antecedent), but it doesn't intervene in the binding possibilities the way the middle DP does in (9b). The DP that causes the problems seems to be the DP in the specifier of another DP (i.e., the possessor DP). Possessor DPs in the specifier position of another DP are a little like the "subject" of those DPs.

16) a)   The army's destruction of the palace
    b)   The army destroyed the palace.

There seems to be a real parallel between (16a) and (16b). So the DP that interferes with binding seems to be the "subject" of the DP. A similar pattern with the subject of a TP is seen in control vs. subject-to-object raising constructions in (17):

17) a)   Heidi wants to kiss herself.
    b)   *Heidi$_i$ wants Fred to kiss herself$_i$.

The ungrammaticality of (17b) seems to be due to the presence of *Fred*. One hypothesis that might work is to claim that the binding domain is either a CP (to account for cases like (9a, 10, and 11) or a DP (as in 9b and 17). But then we are left with the question of determining which one is appropriate in which context. The answer to this seems to make reference to this intermediate "subject". Chomsky (1986b) proposes a revision to the binding theory where the binding domain of an anaphor can change depending upon whether there is a ***potential antecedent*** (= "subject"). What we find when we look at sentences like those in (9) is that the binding domain seems to be a DP, when that DP has a potential antecedent (as in 9b):

9') b)   *Heidi$_i$ believes $[_{DP}$ Martha$_k$'s description of herself$_i$].
                                               ↑
                                     potential antecedent

This sentence is ungrammatical because the DP here is the binding domain – it contains the potential antecedent *Martha* (note, not the actual antecedent, just a potential[1] one). This means that the anaphor is not bound in its binding domain, and is a violation of Principle A.

But now consider (9a) again. Here the anaphor can be bound by *Heidi*. The main difference between this sentence and (9b) is that the object DP contains no potential antecedent for the anaphor. The first potential antecedent is the actual antecedent. So the binding domain for this sentence is the whole clause.

9') a) $[_{CP}$ Heidi$_i$ believes $[_{DP}$ any description of herself$_i$]].
                 ↑
           potential antecedent

The surprising result that binding domains for anaphors seem to be able to shift around depending upon whether there is an antecedent or not is captured in our revised Principle A below:

18) **Binding Principle A** (final): One copy of an anaphor in a chain must be bound within the smallest CP or DP containing it and a potential antecedent.

This version of Principle A makes an interesting prediction about the distribution of anaphors that appear in the subject position of an embedded

---

[1] The notion of "potential" antecedent is very loose. The potential antecedent need not agree with the anaphor, nor must it even be a semantically plausible antecedent.

a)   *Heidi$_i$ believes Art's description of herself$_j$.
b)   *Heidi$_i$ dislikes the TV's depiction of herself$_j$.

The only principle seems to be that it is in the specifier of the DP or TP.

clause. Let us make the reasonable assumption that an anaphor can't serve as its own antecedent, and that a DP dominating the anaphor can't serve as that anaphor's antecedent.[2] If we have an embedded clause where the anaphor is in the subject, the smallest CP containing a subject is the main clause. This means that a DP can bind an anaphor in an embedded clause if that anaphor is inside the subject position. Quite surprisingly, this is true: such sentences are grammatical (19 below and 14 above):

19) $[_{CP}$ Heidi$_i$ said $[_{CP}$ that $[_{DP}$ pictures of herself$_i$] were embarrassing]].

This DP does not count as a potential antecedent because it dominates the anaphor.

This CP does not count as the binding domain for the anaphor because it does not contain a potential antecedent.

This is the first potential antecedent for the anaphor (it is also the actual antecedent).

This is the binding domain for the anaphor as it is the smallest CP or DP containing a potential antecedent.

When we add a possessor within the embedded subject, the binding domain shifts:

20) *$[_{CP}$ Heidi$_i$ said $[_{CP}$ that $[_{DP}$ Martha$_k$'s pictures of herself$_i$] were embarrassing]].

potential antecedent

smallest DP or CP containing the anaphor and a potential antecedent

This is a truly surprising result, but one that follows directly from the binding principle in (18).

Before leaving this topic, it's worth noting that this binding principle does leave one sentence unexplained, and this is a fairly important sentence at that. The ungrammaticality of sentence (1) (repeated here as 21) is now a mystery:

21) *Chris$_i$ said $[_{CP}$ that himself$_i$ was appealing].

According to the principle in (18) this should be acceptable. If *himself* can't count as its own potential antecedent, then the smallest CP or DP containing a potential antecedent for the anaphor is the main clause (with the actual

---

[2] This is known as the *i-within-i* condition, the details of which need not concern us here.

antecedent *Chris* serving as the potential antecedent). This means that *himself* would be bound within its binding domain, so the sentence should be grammatical contrary to fact. In order to account for (21) we are going to have to appeal to something other than the binding principle in (18). Fortunately, there is a relatively simple solution to this problem. The anaphor in (21) is in the specifier of TP. This is the position where nominative case is assigned. Notice that English does not have any nominative anaphors (**heself, *sheself, *Iself* etc.). Perhaps the ungrammaticality of (21) is not due to any binding principle violations but is a simple case conflict instead. *Himself* is accusative in case, but it is in a position that is associated with nominative case.

You can now try GPS 1 and CPS 2 & 3.

2.3 Pronouns

Our definition of binding domain as the smallest CP or DP containing a potential antecedent seems to work well for anaphors, but unfortunately it doesn't fare so well for our examples with pronouns. Take the examples in (13) (repeated here as 22):

22) a) Heidi$_i$ likes her$_i$ violin.   b) Heidi$_i$ likes her$_k$ violin.

Here again we have a case where a DP is acting like a binding domain. Recall that pronouns must be free within their binding domain. In order to explain the grammaticality of (22a), the pronoun must be in a different binding domain than its antecedent. The obvious candidate for this is the DP [*her violin*]. But in the previous section we argued that the binding domain was the smallest DP or CP containing a potential antecedent. Assuming that pronouns can't be their own antecedents, the DP [*her violin*] contains no such potential antecedent, so it can't be a binding domain. By the potential antecedent definition the binding domain is the whole CP, which would mean that in (22a) the pronoun would be bound by *Heidi* within its domain, in violation of Principle B. Yet the sentence is grammatical. Chomsky (1986b) came up with an ingenious solution to this problem. He suggested that binding domains for pronouns and anaphors are defined differently. The difference lies in the inherent nature of the DP types. Anaphors are DPs that need to be bound, so they are going to look for the smallest structure containing a potential antecedent. Pronouns, by contrast, need to be free! Pronouns look for structures where they might *not* find an antecedent. So the DP [*her violin*] is the smallest DP and happens not to contain a potential antecedent.

23) [$_{CP}$ Heidi$_i$ likes ([$_{DP}$ her$_i$ violin]].

                ↑

      (*smallest DP or CP <u>not</u> containing a potential antecedent*

This constraint is encoded in (24):

24) ***Binding Principle B*** (Dialect 1): A pronoun must be free within the smallest CP or DP containing it.

The fact that binding domain is defined differently for pronouns and anaphors not only reflects that they are different animals with different requirements, but more importantly it explains the contrasts outlined in section 2.1.

    The constraint in (24) also explains why the sentence in (25a) is ungrammatical, but the sentence in (25b) is ok.

25) a)   *Heidi$_i$ likes her$_i$.
    b)   Heidi saw Peter's picture of her.

In sentence (25) the smallest DP or CP containing *her* is the root clause CP. So the pronoun in (25a) is bound within its domain, violating Principle B. In (25b), by contrast, the pronoun *her* is contained within another DP, namely *[$_{DP}$ Peter's picture of her]*. This DP, then, is the smallest DP containing the pronoun, and *her* is free within this domain.

    Things of course are never easy. Consider the sentence in (26). There is some dispute about whether or not *her* can be coreferent with *Heidi*.

26) a)   Heidi saw drawings of her.
    b)   *Dialect 1:* Heidi$_i$ saw drawings of her$_i$.
    c)   *Dialect 2:* *Heidi$_i$ saw drawings of her$_i$.

In the dialect that appears to be prevalent in the northeastern US – which I'll call "dialect 1" – coreference is permissible. This is exactly what's predicted by the version of Principle B in (24). The binding domain is the DP *[drawings of her]* and *her* is coreferent with *Heidi* but is free within this domain. For other speakers of English (including me and all my family) – a group of speakers I'll call "dialect 2" – coreference is impossible. This sentence is a Condition B violation and an anaphor is required.

    The version of Principle B given in (24) works perfectly for speakers of dialect 1. The DP *[drawings of her]* is the smallest DP containing *her*, so it defines the binding domain. The pronoun *her* is free within this domain (it's bound by *Heidi*, but free within its domain). This is precisely what the version of Principle B in (24) predicts.

    For speakers of dialect 2, however, (24) makes the wrong predictions. They contrast sentences like (26), where coreference is unacceptable, with sentences like (25b), where coreference is fine. The difference between the DP in (25b) and the one in (26) is that the specifier of the DP in (26) is filled by something. For speakers of dialect 2, we need to make a slight adjustment to Principle B:

24′) *Binding Principle B* (Dialect 2): A pronoun must be free within the smallest DP (with a filled specifier) or CP containing it.

(26a) is ruled out because *[drawings of her]* has no specifier, so the binding domain is the root CP. *Her* is not free in this domain.

This approach sketched in this chapter makes a very interesting prediction. Recall sentence (19) from above, repeated here as (27):

27) [$_{CP}$ Heidi$_i$ said [$_{CP}$ that [$_{DP}$ pictures of herself$_i$] were embarrassing]].

One surprising fact is that for most speakers, anaphors like those in (27) can freely alternate with pronouns:

28) [$_{CP}$ Heidi$_i$ said [$_{CP}$ that [$_{DP}$ pictures of her$_i$] were embarrassing]].

Under our old chapter 5 theory – where the binding domains for pronouns and anaphors were identical – the fact that both (27) and (28) are grammatical would be a real puzzle. Under the older approach, pronouns and anaphors were by definition in complementary distribution (pronouns had to be free in their clause, anaphors had to be bound in their clause). The fact that (27) and (28) can both exist shows that the domains for the binding principles are more nuanced. The definitions have to allow for a situation where the anaphor in (27) is bound by *Heidi* in its binding domain but where the pronoun is free in its binding domain in the structurally identical (28). But if binding domains are defined relative to the type of the DP involved, then (27) and (28) do not form a contradiction. In (27) the smallest DP or CP that contains a potential antecedent for the anaphor is the main clause CP. In (28) the smallest DP or CP is the DP *[pictures of her]*. So the anaphor in (27) can be bound in its domain, while the pronoun in the exact same position in (28) can be free in its domain.

You now have enough information to try WBE 3 and GPS 2–4.

IDEAS, RULES, AND CONSTRAINTS INTRODUCED IN THIS CHAPTER

i)   *The Copy Theory of Movement*: Movement is a two-part operation. First, the moved element is copied and put into the surface position; second, the original is made silent.

ii)   *Chain*: The moved copy and all its traces.

iii)   *Potential Antecedent*: A DP in the specifier of TP or another DP. The potential antecedent cannot be the anaphor or pronoun itself, nor can it be a DP that contains the anaphor or pronoun.

iv)   *Binding Principle A* (final): One copy of an anaphor in a chain must be bound within the smallest CP or DP containing it and a potential antecedent.

v)   *Binding Principle B* (Dialect 1): A pronoun must be free within the smallest CP or DP containing it.

vi)   *Binding Principle B* (Dialect 2): A pronoun must be free within the smallest DP (with a filled specifier) or CP containing it.

FURTHER READING: Büring (2005), Chomsky (1986b)

GENERAL PROBLEM SETS

GPS1. BINDING DOMAIN FOR ANAPHORS
[Application of Skills; Intermediate]
Draw the trees for each of the following sentences, then identify the binding domain of the anaphors. For the ungrammatical forms, explain why the sentence is ungrammatical. In all cases assume that *John* and *himself* are coindexed. Assume the judgments given.

a)   John loves himself.
b)   John loves pictures of himself.
c)   *John loves Mary's pictures of himself.
d)   *John thinks that Mary loves himself.
e)   *John thinks that Mary's depiction of himself is wrong.
f)   John thinks that most depictions of himself are wrong.
g)   Which pictures of himself does John like?
h)   John seems to like pictures of himself.
i)   John believes himself to be the best at baseball.
j)   John wants to congratulate himself.

GPS2. BINDING DOMAIN FOR PRONOUNS
[Application of Skills; Intermediate]
Draw the trees for each of the following sentences, then identify the binding domain of the pronouns. For the ungrammatical forms, explain why the sentence is ungrammatical. In all cases assume that John and the pronoun are coindexed. Assume the judgments given.

a)   *John loves him.
b)   John loves his puppy.
c)   John asked if the unflattering description of his work would be published in the paper.

d)   John asked if his essay would be published in the paper.
e)   *John wants to kiss him.
f)   *John believes him to be fantastic.

GPS3. ZIBUNZISIN
[Data Analysis; Intermediate]
In chapter 5, Challenge Problem Set 4, the following data was presented. Make a proposal about why *zibunzisin* is acceptable in subject position of embedded clauses. Be sure to be clear about case marking and about what the binding domain for the anaphor is.

a)   Johnwa_i [$_{CP}$ [$_{TP}$ Maryga$_k$ zibunzisino$_{k/*i}$ hihansita] [$_C$ to]] itta.
     John   Mary   zibunzisin   criticized   that said
     "John said that Mary$_k$ criticized herself$_k$."
     "*John$_i$ said that Mary criticized himself$_i$."

b)   Johnwa_i [$_{CP}$ [$_{TP}$ zibunzisinga$_i$ Maryo korosita] [$_C$ to]] omotteiru.
     John   zibunzisin   Mary killed   that think
     "John thinks that himself killed Mary." (*note:* grammatical in Japanese!)

GPS4. PERSIAN
[Data Analysis; Advanced]
In chapter 5, Challenge Problem Set 3, the following data was presented. The binding domain for *xodesh* is different from that of either pronouns or anaphors in English. What kind of structure does *xodesh* need to determine a binding domain? (*Râ* means "the" when it follows object NPs. 3SG means "third person singular".)

a)   Jân$_i$ goft [$_{CP}$ ke [$_{TP}$ Mery$_k$ ketâb-â ro be xodesh$_{i/k}$ bargardune]].
     John said that   Mary book-PL râ to himself/herself return
     "John said that Mary (should) return the books to him/herself."

b)   Jân$_i$ goft [$_{CP}$ ke [$_{TP}$ Mery$_j$ ketâb-â ro be xodesh$_{i/j}$ barmigardune]].
     John said that   Mary book-PL râ to himself/herself return3SG.FUT
     "John said that Mary will return the books to him/herself."

Now consider (c) and (d): in these examples, *xod* "self" instead of *xodesh* "himself" is used. How is the binding domain for *xod* determined?

c)   Jân$_i$ goft [$_{CP}$ ke [$_{TP}$ Mery$_k$ ketâb râ   barâye   xod$_{*i/k}$ bexânad]].
     John said that   Mary book râ   for   self   read3SG
     "John said that Mary (should) read the book to *himself/herself."

d)   Jân$_i$ goft [$_{CP}$ ke [$_{TP}$ Mery$_k$ ketâb râ   barâye xod$_{*i/k}$ negahdârad]].
     John said   that Mary book râ   for   self   keep3SG
     "John said that Mary (should) keep the books for *himself/herself."

CHALLENGE PROBLEM SETS

CHALLENGE PROBLEM SET 1: PRONOUNS
[Critical Thinking; Challenge]
We argued above that at least one link of a movement chain containing an anaphor must meet Principle A of the binding theory and be bound within its binding domain. Is this true for pronouns as well? Provide examples to support your answer.

CHALLENGE PROBLEM SET 2: POSSESSIVE PRONOUNS
[Critical Thinking; Challenge]
Up to now we've treated possessive pronouns as being of category D. One alternative is that pronouns like *his* are really bimorphemic and take the form below:

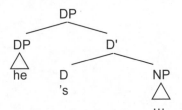

And then there are morphological rules that turn *he's* into *his* (and *she's* into *her*, etc.). Using our definition of "potential antecedent", how does the following sentence argue for the tree above instead of treating *his* as a D? Assume the judgment given.

*Mary doesn't like his pictures of herself.

CHALLENGE PROBLEM SET 3: WESTERN AMERICAN DIALECTS OF ENGLISH
[Critical Thinking; Challenge]
For most speakers of English the sentence *Heidi$_i$ doesn't like Nate's pictures of herself$_i$.* is ungrammatical with the indexation given. However, there is a significant dialect area in the western United States (Andy Barss has found speakers from Arizona, California, and New Mexico that all have this judgment) where this sentence is typically judged as fully acceptable. What minor adjustment must we make to Principle A to explain the grammaticality of this sentence in this dialect?

chapter 18

Polysynthesis, Incorporation, and Non-configurationality

0. INTRODUCTION

The focus of this book has been largely about the nature of constituency and order. We have looked at: how constituents are built; the lexical restrictions on constituents; how they interact with each other through movement; how they interact through structural relations in binding and control theory; and even how there is evidence for empty and null constituents and categories, including empty functional categories, ellipses, PRO, *pro*, and so on. We have also spent a fair amount of time thinking about how those categories get into

Syntax: A Generative Introduction, Third Edition. Andrew Carnie.
© 2013 Andrew Carnie. Published 2013 by John Wiley & Sons, Inc.

their surface orders. Obviously, languages that appear to lack strict constituency, have very free word orders, or pack whole sentences into single words are going to be a real challenge to the approach we have sketched up to this point in the book. Keep in mind that I have made the strong claim that large parts of the grammatical system are universal and innate, so if that's true we'd better have a good explanation for these significant variations away from fixed orders and strong constituency.

In this chapter, we are going to look at a number of interrelated but distinct phenomena that have been presented as challenges to the kind of grammatical system we've presented in the first 17 chapters of the book. Interestingly, we will see that these constructions actually have many properties associated with the more mundane languages we have looked at previously, and the things that make the languages different are systematic and straightforwardly accounted for in a theory with UG and parameters.

The first set of languages that we're going to look at here exhibit *polysynthesis*, where entire sentences are expressed as a single word – typically a very richly inflected verb. We'll investigate the possibility that this phenomenon is simply an extreme form of the pro-drop phenomenon discussed in chapter 15. We'll also look at what might be a variant on polysynthesis, called *incorporation*. This is a phenomenon where an argument of the verb (typically the object) appears to be part of the verb itself. We'll see how one major theory of incorporation holds that it is a kind of head-to-head movement. After this we turn to a range of phenomena that might be called "free word order". We'll see that these phenomena actually fall into two broad categories: those that exhibit a rule process called *scrambling* and those that are typically called *non-configurational*. We're going to examine a couple of different hypotheses about non-configurational languages, including one where the explanation for non-configurationality is the same as the explanation for scrambling, and others where non-configurationality is proposed to be related to a phenomenon found in Romance languages called *clitic left dislocation*. Part of the argument will concern whether there is a relationship between polysynthetic languages and non-configurationality. I'll leave open the question of what the right analysis is, just as I did in the chapter about ellipsis, but we'll explore the kinds of data that can be used to distinguish these analyses from one another.

1. POLYSYNTHESIS

The first major challenge our theory of constituents and movements faces is languages that appear to lack sentences in general, and instead use very complicated multimorphemic words that stand for the predicates and arguments in a sentence. An example from Chukchi is given in (1).

1) Təmeyŋəlevtpəγtərkən.   Chukchi
    1S.SUBJ.great-head-hurt.PRES
    "I have a fierce headache." (Skorik 1961: 102)

Languages that do this are often called *polysynthetic languages* or *extreme head-marking languages*.

There are at least two common proposals about languages like these. The first approach claims that the morphemes representing the arguments in the complex verb are themselves the arguments of the verb. So in an example like (2) from Mohawk, the morpheme *ke* is in fact the agent argument and the null Ø is the actual theme.

2) Wa'-ke-tshári-'-Ø
    FACT-1S-find-PUNC-3S
    "I found it."

In this approach, which we'll call the *syntax-free hypothesis*, the morphology in these languages does all the work done by the syntax in languages like English. The claim is that these languages effectively lack a syntactic grammatical component. They only use morphological rules to realize their predicates and arguments. If the syntax-free hypothesis is correct, it's a serious challenge to the central view of generative grammar that significant parts of the grammatical system are innate and universal.

The alternative view – perhaps expressed most cogently in Mark Baker's (1996) book *The Polysynthesis Parameter* but also available in a less technical and more readable form in his (2002) book *The Atoms of Language* – holds that there is real syntactic structure in (2). He makes extensive use of the empty category *pro*, discussed at the end of chapter 15. Lower-case *pro*, you'll recall, is an empty pronoun that occupies the subject position of clauses in languages like Spanish. It is licensed when the verb has sufficient inflection to indicate the content of the subject.

3) Hablo   italiano   *Spanish*
    speak.1S   Italian
    I speak Italian.

Baker's proposal is that in a Mohawk example like (2), there are *pros* corresponding to the arguments and these *pros* occupy the argument positions. (I'm abstracting away from vP and AgrO, etc., for the purposes of tree drawing since it isn't critical to understanding the point of the tree.)

4)

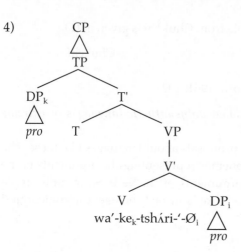

wa'-ke$_k$-tsh$\land$ri-'-$\varnothing$$_i$

Under this view, there really is a syntax, not just morphology, for these languages. The difference between a language like Mohawk and a language like English (or even Spanish) is that the subject and the object arguments must correspond to some morpheme on the verb (possibly a null one). This is encoded in a parameter (5).

5) *Polysynthesis Parameter* (Baker 1996)
    Every argument of a head must be related to a morpheme in the word
    that contains the head.
        Mohawk: On;   English: Off

This proposal, of course, brings polysynthetic languages into the fold of Universal Grammar and generative linguistics. Polysynthetic languages, it is claimed, are actually very similar in structure to languages like English, except in how the arguments are realized by the morphology. Let's call Baker's approach the **radical pro-drop hypothesis**. The polysynthesis parameter has implications for non-configurational languages that we'll return to in section 3.

You now have enough information to try CPS 1.

---

2. INCORPORATION

A phenomenon that – at least at first glance – appears to be related to polysynthesis is *incorporation*. In simple polysynthesis like that discussed in section 1, the morpheme that appears in the verb usually reflects inflectional information like person, number, and maybe case, and is in many ways similar to the kind of information found in pronouns. Incorporation, by contrast, seems to take a fully lexical noun and put it inside of the verb. Compare the two Mohawk sentences in (6).

6) a) Wa'khninu'   ne ka-nàkt-a'   Mohawk[1]
        fact.1S.buy.PUNC   the bed
        "I bought a/the bed"

    b) Wa'ke-*nakt*-ahnìnu'.
        FACT.1s-bed-buy.PUNC
        "I bought a/the bed."

Baker (1988) proposes that the alternation seen in (6) is the result of a special kind of head-to-head movement, shown in (7):

7)   ...
                        VP
                        |
                        V'

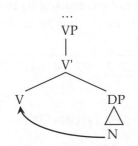

This approach makes two interesting predictions, both of which appear to be correct. First it predicts that if there are additional things in the DP, such as determiners, adjectives, PPs, etc., then those modifiers can be stranded behind, and yet still be semantically connected to the N. This seems to be generally true. Look at the sentence in (8), from Greenlandic Eskimo. Greenlandic is an OV language, so objects are to the left of the verb. You'll note in (8) that although the object *illo* is incorporated into the verb, the remnants of the DP are still to be found in basic object position: The modifying adjective and the case marker *-mik*.

8) Qisum-mik illo-qar-poq
    wood-INST house-have-INDIC.3s
    "He has a wooden house."

The head-to-head movement analysis in (7) also predicts that objects, but not subjects, can incorporate. This is true. Sentence (9), from Mapadungun, can only mean "My father is looking for the cows" and never "The cows are looking for my father". The subject cannot be incorporated.

---

[1] Throughout this chapter, I've simplified irrelevant aspects of the glossing of sentences. Before quoting any data here, you should cross-check it against the original sources. The data in (6) is taken from Baker (1988).

9) Ñi chao   kintu-waka-ley
   my father   seek-cow-INDIC.3s
   "My father is looking for the cows."

The reason for this is straightforward: You may have noticed throughout this book that movement always goes "up" the tree. The reasons for this aren't entirely clear, but probably reduce to a requirement on traces that in a different form used to be called the *Empty Category Principle* (or ECP).[2]

10) *The Empty Category Principle.*

   Traces must be c-commanded by the moved element (their antecedent).

If incorporation is movement, then it must obey the ECP. If one were to lower the subject into the V, the subject would not c-command its trace. By contrast, movement of an object N into V always results in a structure wherein the incorporated N c-commands the trace.

You now have enough information to try WBE 1 & 2, GPS 1–4 and CPS 2.

3. SCRAMBLING AND NON-CONFIGURATIONALITY

The Australian language Warlpiri (along with many other languages of Australia) is perhaps the ultimate "free word order" language. In Warlpiri, the only clear restriction on word order is that the auxiliary must appear in the second position; all other orders are possible (11) (data from Simpson 1983: 140).

11) a) Kurdu-ngku   ka-ju   nya-nyi   ngaju   *Warlpiri*
        child-ERG   pres1sOBJ   see-NONPAST   me-ABS
        "The child sees me."
    b) Kurdu-ngku ka-ju ngaju nya-nyi
    c) Nya-nyi ka-ju Kurdu-ngku ngaju
    d) Nya-nyi ka-ju ngaju Kurdu-ngku
    e) Ngaju ka-ju nya-nyi Kurdu-ngku
    f) Ngaju ka-ju Kurdu-ngku nya-nyi

For generative linguists – who believe that theoretical constructs like case and binding relations are established in specific structural positions correlating to word order – such data are terrifying. But many brave generativists have taken a deeper look at the facts in languages like Warlpiri.

---

[2] This constraint is formulated quite differently from traditional definitions. It is greatly simplified here.

They have come to the surprising conclusion that languages like Warlpiri actually have more in common with more familiar languages than you might think.

We'll start our discussion by looking at languages that impose many restrictions on order, as English does, but allow also just a little more flexibility in order than English. These languages place restrictions on what order elements come in that are based on whether the information is new or old in the discourse between speakers. The term *scrambling* is generally reserved for such languages. After that we'll look at the more radical free word order languages like Warlpiri, which we group (probably inaccurately) under the title *non-configurational*.

3.1 Scrambling

Japanese exhibits some freedom in word ordering. Sentence (12a) is the normal neutral order in Japanese, but sentence (12b) is also acceptable in certain circumstances. Unlike in Warlpiri, not every order is possible (12c–f) (data from Speas 1990).

12) a) Mary-ga   okasi-o   taberu
        Mary-NOM   cakes-ACC   eats
        "Mary eats cakes."
  b) Okasi-o Mary-ga taberu.
  c) *Mary-ga taberu okasi-o.
  d) *Okasi-o taberu Mary-ga.
  e) *Taberu Mary-ga Okasi-o.
  f) *Taberu Okasi-o Mary-ga.

But even the orders in (12a) and (12b) are not completely free. These two sentences mean different things. *Information focus* is the new information in a sentence that hasn't been expressed previously in the discourse. In English, when we utter a simple SVO sentence with no special intonation or stress, the VP provides us with new information that we haven't heard before.

13) A: I just saw Bill outside in the hall.
    B: Oh really? You know that Bill and Julie are having an affair?

In (13), the VP in the first sentence introduces the new information that speaker A just saw Bill in the hall. In the second sentence, the VP is new information about Bill – he and Julie are having an affair. That's something that the speaker presupposes that the listener doesn't already know. This is the information focus. The interpretations of (12a) and (12b) differ precisely along these lines. In (12a) *okasi-o* is the new information, in (12b) *Mary-ga* is.

Persian (Farsi) shows similar ordering effects. In Persian the basic word order is subject + PP + O + V (14a). But the object can appear in a variety of positions when it is specific in reference. It appears before the PP in (14b). This ordering is probably an instance of object shift (discussed in chapter 14) to the specifier of AgrOP. You'll notice that this order correlates with the presence or absence of the *-o* accusative case suffix.[3] The case we are most interested in is (14c), where the object appears before the subject (data from Karimi 2005).

14) a) Parviz barâ   Kimea pirhan xarid.
        Parviz for   Kimea shirt   bought
        "Parviz bought shirts for Kimea."

   b) Parviz pirhan-o   barâ   Kimea xarid.
        Parviz shirt-ACC   for   Kimea bought
        "Parviz bought the shirt for Kimea."

   c) Pirhan-o   Parviz barâ   Kimea xarid.
        shirt-ACC   Parviz for   Kimea bought
        "As for the shirt, Parviz bought it for Kimea." or
        "It was the SHIRT that Parviz bought for Kimea."

When it appears before the subject, it takes on the meaning of a topic or contrastive focus. **Topics** represent given information in the discourse. That is they refer to information that has already been discussed in the discourse somewhere. In English, we often indicate topics by fronting the element, sometimes with a resumptive pronoun (*John, he's a bastard*). **Contrastive focus** is the marking of an expression in contrast to a previously expressed idea. For example, Lloyd might say *Freddie brought tuna salad to the party* and Morag might respond *No, I think he brought SPINACH salad*. In English, we most commonly mark contrastive focus with special emphatic stress, but it's also possible to front the constituent with clefting or similar devices (*I despise lima beans. Now, chocolate beans, I like!*).

Rizzi (1997) proposes that what we've been calling a CP really consists of several categories on the left side of the clause. He actually proposes five different phrases, but we'll only be concerned with two here. He suggests that on the left edge of every clause there is a TopicP and (at least) a FocusP. Scrambling can be viewed as movement (parallel to *wh*-movement) into the

---

[3] I'm calling this suffix the accusative case marker here, but this is a simplification. To learn more about how this marker works, search for the literature on *-râ* (of which *-o* is an allomorph).

specifier of either TopicP or FocusP, depending upon what discourse effect the operation has.

15)

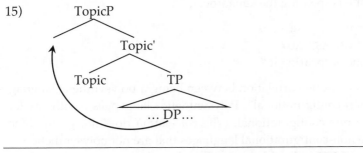

You now have enough information to try CPS 3.

3.2 Non-configurationality

Languages like Warlpiri are a much harder nut to crack, however. In addition to allowing far more orders than scrambling languages do (as in 11), they also have a number of other surprising properties. Not only do they allow constituents to appear in any order, they often (but not always) allow some of the DP constituents to be split up and separated by other material as in (16) (Simpson 1991: 257), where "children" and "small" bracket the rest of the clause, even though they are semantically connected. Example (17) from Passamaquoddy shows a similar discontinuous constituent (data from Bruening 2001), as does the data from Kiowa in (18) (Adger et al. 2011).

16) **Kurdu-jarra-ngku** ka-pala   maliki wajilipi-nyi wita-jarra-rlu
     child-DUAL-ERG   pres-3DS   dog   chase-NONPST small-DUAL-ERG
     "Two small children are chasing the dog."   *Warlpiri*

17) Keq   nikt   itom-uksipsis-ok?
     what   those   say-3P bird-3P
     "What are those birds saying?"   *Passamaquoddy*

18) **Páá**   hón **kɔ́ítɔ̀gya**   yą́– pêide-haigɔɔ
     some   NEG Kiowa words   1/3–straight-know.NEG
     "There are some Kiowa words I don't really understand."   *Kiowa*

Non-configurational languages are also often "radically" pro-drop. For example in Warlpiri (data from Hale 1983), a sentence can omit one (19a and b) or more (19c) of its arguments.

19)   a) Ngarrka-nku   ka   panti-rni
        man-ERG   AUX   spear-NONPAST
       "The man is spearing it."

b) Wawirri   ka   pantri-rni
   kangaroo   AUX   spear-NONPAST
   "He/she is spearing the kangaroo."

c) Panti-rni   ka
   spear-NONPAST AUX
   "He/she is spearing it."

Indeed there is a strong correlation between being a polysynthetic language and being non-configurational. Polysynthetic languages, with a few exceptions, are non-configurational. (The correlation does not go the other way. There are non-configurational languages that are not polysynthetic.)

To explain these kinds of facts, we'll explore three common hypotheses about how these languages work. There are other approaches beyond these (see, for example, Speas 1990 and Adger et al. 2011), but the following three are the most common ways of addressing the problem.

3.2.1   Dual-structure Approaches

Perhaps the oldest approach to non-configurational languages in the generative tradition dates to Hale (1983), although similar approaches have been given in the theory of Lexical-Functional Grammar (see chapter 19, which is available in the online materials that accompany this book). Hale observed that in Warlpiri, while evidence for surface constituency seems not to exist (you can freely order, and constituents can be discontinuous as well as optional), there are also processes that appear to distinguish among arguments. For example, reflexives are limited to object position, just as in English. Similarly, there are distinct subject and object case markings, which typically correspond to thematic relations in a way similar to that found in English – for example, agents are most often subjects and themes are commonly (although by no means always) objects. Hale suggests that syntax is really divided into two different structures. This is an idea very similar to the idea of PF and LF sketched in chapter 13 and to the idea of c-structure and f-structure described in chapter 19 (available on the website). He calls these levels PS, for phrase structure, and LS, for lexical structure. PS is the structure that realizes word order, and LS represents thematic and grammatical relations. We will call this the **dual-structure hypothesis.** Non-configurational languages differ from configurational languages (languages like English) in that they have a phrase structure system very different from X-bar theory. Hale claims that non-configurational languages are parameterized to include a rule like that in (20):

20)[4] TP ⟶ X T Z+

This rule says you can put any element (X) first, before the auxiliary (T), followed by any number of other elements (Z). Order beyond this is essentially free. There is no mention of constituency so discontinuous constituents are predicted. The meaning of an expression is computed at LS (roughly our LF), so arguments can be omitted if their presence can be inferred from the context.

There is a great deal to like about the dual-structure hypothesis. It is a fairly clear explanation of the facts, and the difference between non-configurational and configurational languages reduces to the parameterization of the rule in (20). Nevertheless, later investigators have found good reasons to think that an alternative approach is appropriate.

3.2.2   *The Pronominal Argument Hypothesis/Polysynthesis Parameter*

Note the freedom of ordering that adverbs have in English. Take the temporal adverb *yesterday* as a starting point. It can, with slightly different interpretations, appear in a variety of positions (21).

21) a)   *Yesterday*, I bought a marshmallow and sausage stew from Morgan.
    b)   I bought a marshmallow and sausage stew *yesterday* from Morgan.
    c)   I bought a marshmallow and sausage stew from Morgan *yesterday*.

As we discussed in the chapters on X-bar theory, this freedom of ordering is expected of adjuncts. In another paper on Warlpiri, Jelinek draws upon this intuition and suggests that the freedom of elements in non-configurational languages arises from the fact that the items we're identifying as DP arguments aren't really arguments at all. Instead, she claims, they are actually adjuncts that just contribute additional information to the clause, just like adjuncts in more familiar languages. She claims that the real arguments in the clause are pronouns (which can be null). This is encoded in the parameter in (22).

22) *The Pronominal Argument Parameter*
    Only pronouns can function as the arguments of predicates.
        Non-configurational languages: On.
        Configurational languages: Off.

---

[4] I've adjusted the notation of Hale's rule to be more consistent with the rules we have been using in this book. I have also glossed over some of the details of how this parameterization works. For Hale, it isn't the PS rule itself that's parameterized, but the projection principle. See the original for details.

Baker (1996) extends this analysis by drawing a strong parallel with a construction found in many Romance languages, called *clitic left dislocation* (commonly abbreviated CLLD). In CLLD, a DP, which is typically a topic, is shifted to the left edge of the sentence. The DP is represented in the clause by a pronominal clitic (in 23 this is *le*). An example from Spanish (taken from López 2009: 3) is in (23).

23) A Maria, no le enviaré ningun paquete
    to Maria NEG her send.1S.FUT no package
    "To Maria, I won't send her a package."

The intuition that Baker is trying to express is that speakers of non-configurational language all talk as if instead of saying *The man kissed the cat*, they are saying *The man, he kissed it, the cat*. The actual arguments are the pronouns *he* and *it*. But there are DPs adjoined to the clause in order to give those pronouns additional information. Baker enriches this view by suggesting that the pro arguments in polysynthetic languages also serve this pronominal argument function.

The idea that the DPs one sees in non-configurational languages are just adjuncts and not the actual arguments explains a number of the basic facts about non-configurational languages. Since the DPs are adjuncts they allow freedom of order. Similarly, like adjuncts in general, they are typically optional. Discontinuous constituents require a subtler account. Notice that one can have multiple adjuncts modifying the same basic element in the clause. The time of the eating event described in the sentence *Yesterday, John ate lunch at noon* is modified by two different adjuncts, *yesterday* and *at noon*. If apparently discontinuous constituents are really multiple adjuncts, each adding information to the pronoun, there is no need for them to form actual constituents.

Another consequence of the view that DPs are CLLD adjuncts comes from the binding theory. Recall condition C of the binding theory from chapter 5: R-expressions must be free. This means that an R-expression can c-command and bind a pronoun (as in 24a), but the reverse is not true (24b).

24) a) Bill$_i$ hid his$_i$ book.
    b) *He$_i$ hid Bill$_i$'s book.

Now, consider the following parallel facts from Mohawk, taken from Baker (1996). The Mohawk equivalent to (24b) is completely acceptable with coreference between the pronoun and *Bill*.

25) a) Ro-ya'takéhnh-ʌ [$_{NP}$ ne thíkʌ Sak raó-a'share']
    MSObj-help-STAT PART that Sak MSP-knife
    "That knife of Sak's is helping him." (coreference is ok)

b) Wa'-t-há-ya'k-e'   [NP ne   thíkʌ   Sak raó-a'share']
    FACT-DUP-3SGS-break-PUNC   PART   that   Sak MSP-knife
    "He broke that knife of Sak's." (coreference is ok)

This fact is predicted if DPs are adjoined to the TP or CP. In this position, R-expressions always c-command the pronouns, and the pronouns never c-command the R-expressions. The acceptability of (25a) follows if DPs are adjuncts, as asserted in the pronominal argument hypothesis.

You now have enough information to try WBE 3.

3.2.3   Discourse-driven Movement Rules

There are a few problems with a CLLD/pronominal argument analysis. Adger et al. (2011) present some evidence from another non-configurational language, Kiowa, all of which suggests that DPs in Kiowa can't be adjuncts.

First, they note, there is a very particular semantics associated with CLLD in Romance languages. Elements that are clitic left dislocated in Romance cannot serve as information focus (new information). This is not true for DPs in general in non-configurational languages. A typical context for introducing new information is the answer to a question. But in Kiowa, a full DP can be part of the answer to a question (indeed is the normal answer to a question):

22) Q: Hâatêl   yán– thą́ą́ɔɔmei?
        who.Q   3s:2s:3P[5]–help.PF
        "Who helped you?"

    A: Ɔ́úelmaa   yą́– thą́ą́ɔɔmei
        Carrie   3s:1s:3P–help.PF
        "Carrie helped me."

Of similar concern is the position of DPs in Kiowa. Kiowa has a number of particles that we might associate with functional categories in the tree; we have evidential particles (glossed as MIR for mirative), which we could analyze as a kind of C category, modals (T), negation, and aspect particles. These items appear to be strictly ordered in precisely the order that we might expect given the trees we've drawn earlier in the book: C precedes T, which precedes Neg, which precedes aspectual markers. Deviation from that order is not allowed. Under the CLLD approach, the DPs are adjoined very high in the tree, perhaps inside the CP. But in Kiowa, the arguments can appear

---

[5] The 3S:2S:3P marking in the Kiowa glosses refers to the person and number marking. It isn't crucial to understanding the point of this section.

interleaved between functional categories that we know are much lower in the tree, such as negatives and aspectual nodes.

23) a) Béthɔɔ   T!ą́ík!opę́-   példoudei
       MIR   Laurel   3s:1s–think about.IMPF.EVID
       "I didn't realize Laurel was still thinking about me."

   b) Hɔ́n   an   êlk!yoi   gyát– sém- hɔ́ɔ̨nɔ̂ɔ- de
      NEG   HAB   old men   :1P:3P–longing-give up.NEG-NOM
      "[We] old men don't give up our desires."

   c) Hɔ́n hábé   ɔnk!îi   éįhɔde tɔ́ɥgya bát– guudɔɔ
      NEG sometime PAST   this   word   1IN.D:3p–write.NEG
      "We never wrote this word in the past."

Furthermore, at least some of the ordering seems to be driven by discourse factors. For example, focused items such as the answers to questions must appear before the particles, as must topics.

24) Q: Hâatêl   an   gɔ– gûugu?
        who.q   HAB   3s:2s–hit.IMPF
        "Who hits you?"

    A: Carl ané- gûugu.
        Carl HAB 3s:1s–hit.IMPF
        "Carl hits me."

25) **Á-xɔɔ-de**   béthɔɔ hégóán– dôi-hį- khyakɔnhel
     3- mother-D   MIR   just :3s:3p–too-real-incompetent.EVID
     "I had no idea his mother was totally incompetent."

The fact that discourse sensitivity seems to play a significant role in determining word order in non-configurationality motivated Legate (2001) and Bruening (2001)[6] to propose (for Warlpiri and Passamaquoddy respectively) that non-configurational languages are actually just languages with significant movement operations, similar to scrambling, but simply more extensive. Of course there are issues with scrambling type approaches, too. They are hard-pressed to explain discontinuous constituents as well as the binding facts discussed in the previous subsection. Again, I'll leave the choice of which theory (if any of them) is right up to you.

You now have enough information to try CPS 3.

---

[6] Adger et al. do not propose a movement analysis, at least not for the vast majority of ordering alternations. Their analysis is based in the Mirror Theory of Michael Brody. We don't have the space to discuss this interesting alternative here.

4. CONCLUSIONS

Polysynthesis, incorporation, scrambling, and non-configurationality are certainly serious challenges to innate generative grammar. But they aren't insurmountable ones. A nuanced approach to investigating languages with these phenomena shows that they might have more in common with more familiar languages than we might think at first glance. For each phenomenon, I have given brief sketches of some common analyses within generative grammar. As in the previous few chapters, I've left it open as to whether these analyses are right or not. I encourage you to discuss these phenomena and the hypotheses about them with your fellow students and professors and try to figure out what parts of them are right and what are wrong. We started this book with the observation that syntax was a science. We propose hypotheses, test them, revise them in some cases and discard them in others. As in any other science there are plenty of open questions and unresolved issues. I hope the past few chapters have given you a taste for this.

In part 5 of this book – which is only available on the website for this book, I offer a brief description of two alternative approaches to syntax. Again like any science, we have competing approaches to difficult questions. As you work your way to becoming a syntactician, it's worth taking your time to consider alternatives and test your hypotheses against new and challenging data like that found in this chapter.

IDEAS, RULES, AND CONSTRAINTS INTRODUCED IN THIS CHAPTER

i)   *Polysynthesis*: The phenomenon where all the required arguments of a verb surface as morphemes on that verb.

ii)   *Syntax-free Hypothesis*: A hypothesis where polysynthetic languages are said to lack a syntactic component. All the work of the grammar is done by the morphology instead.

iii)   *Polysynthesis Parameter*: Every argument of a head must be related to a morpheme in the word that contains the head.

iv)   *Radical Pro-drop Hypothesis*: A hypothesis about polysynthetic languages, where the morphemes on a verb are agreement morphemes related to null *pro* arguments.

v)   *Incorporation*: A phenomenon where the direct object appears as part of the inflected verb.

vi)   *The Empty Category Principle*: Traces must be c-commanded by the moved element (their antecedents).

vii)   *Scrambling*: A movement rule that positions DPs in specifier of FocusP or TopicP.

viii)   *Topics*: DPs that represent given (old) information in the discourse.

ix)   *Information Focus*: The new information in a discourse.

x)   *Contrastive Focus*: A phrase that is presented in contrast to a previously expressed idea.

xi)   *Non-configurationality*: Non-configurational languages exhibit very free word order, discontinuous constituents, and missing DP arguments.

xii)   *The Dual-Structure Hypothesis*: The idea that syntax is divided into two structures.

xiii)   *Hale's Phrase Structure Rule for Non-configurational Languages*: TP → X T Z+

xiv)   *The Pronominal Argument Parameter*: Only pronouns can function as the arguments of predicates.

FURTHER READING: Adger, Harbour, and Watkins (2011), Austin and Bresnan (1996), Baker (1988, 1996, 2000, 2001a, 2006, 2009), Bruening (2001), É. Kiss (2008), Erteschik-Shir (2007), Hale (1983), Jelinek (1984, 2006), Jelinek and Demers (1994), Karimi (2003, 2005), Legate (2001), López (2009), Mithun (1984), Pensalfini (2004), Rizzi (1997), Sadock (1991), Simpson (1983, 1991), Speas (1990)

GENERAL PROBLEM SETS

GPS1. MAPADUNGUN INCORPORATION
[Application of Skills; Basic]
Draw the tree for the following sentence of Mapadungun (data from Baker 2006). Assume the *-ley* suffix is in T.

> Ñi chao   kintu-waka-ley
> my father seek-cow-INDIC.3s
>   "My father is looking for the cows."

GPS2. ONODAGA
[Application of Skills; Basic]
The following data from Onodaga is taken from Baker (1996). Using trees to illustrate your answer, explain the alternation between (a) and (b).

a) Pet wa?ha-htu-?t-a?   ne?   hwist
    Pat PAST.3MS-lost-CAUSE-ASP   the   money
    "Pat lost the money."

b) Pet wa?ha-hwist-ahtu-?t-a?
    Pat PAST.3MS-money-lost-CAUSE-ASP
    "Pat lost money."

GPS3. MOHAWK *WH*-MOVEMENT AND INCORPORATION
[Data Analysis and Critical Thinking; Advanced]
Explain how the following data from Mohawk (data from Baker 1996) is
evidence for a movement account of incorporation.

   Ka niáyʌ   t-ʌ-hse-wír-ahkw-e'?
   which   DUP-FUT-2s-baby-Ø-pick.up-PUNC
   "Which baby are you going to pick up?"

GPS4. PONAPEAN
[Data Analysis; Intermediate]
Explain how the placement of the affix *-la* in the following forms is evidence
for the movement of *wini(h)* into the V. COMPL stands for completive aspect.

       a) I   kanga-**la**   wini-o.
           I   eat-COMPL medicine-that
           "I took all that medicine."

       b) I   keng-winih-**la**.
           I   eat-medicine-COMPL
           "I completed my medicine taking."

CHALLENGE PROBLEM SETS

CHALLENGE PROBLEM SET 1: RADICAL PRO-DROP VS. SYNTAX-FREE
[Critical Thinking; Challenge]
What are the different predictions made by the radical pro-drop hypothesis
and the syntax-free hypothesis? How would you go about figuring out which
one is right and which one is wrong? What kind of data would you need to
find?

CHALLENGE PROBLEM SET 2: VSO LANGUAGES AND INCORPORATION
[Critical Thinking; Challenge]
If incorporation is head movement of the head of an argument into a verb, should subjects be allowed to incorporate in VSO languages? Explain your answer with an abstract tree.

CHALLENGE PROBLEM SET 3: JAPANESE SCRAMBLING AND CONDITION C
[Critical Thinking; Challenge]
In the previous chapter we claimed that the fact that some binding effects seemed to be sensitive to the SPELLOUT position of a DP, and others appeared to be sensitive to the LF position, was due to the nature of movement chains, where silent copies of the DP were found in all the trace positions. But one constraint we didn't talk about was Condition C. Condition C says that R-expressions can't be bound (at any level). This explains why the English sentence *He$_i$ loves John$_i$'s mother* is unacceptable with coreference between *he* and *John*. Now consider the Japanese sentences in (a) and (b). Sentence (a) parallels the English ungrammatical Condition C example. But it appears as if scrambling in (b) repairs the Condition C violation.

a) *Soitu-ga   Taroo-no   hono   mituke-ta.
   guy-NOM   Taro-GEN   book-ACC   found-PAST
   "The guy$_i$ found Taro's$_i$ book." (R-expression can't be bound)

b) ?Taroo-no hono   soitu-ga   mituke-ta.
   Taro-GEN   book-ACC   guy-NOM   found-PAST
   ?"Taro's$_i$ book the guy$_i$ found." (coreference is ok)

Why is the amelioration of (b) after scrambling unexpected if the copy theory of movement is correct?

CHALLENGE PROBLEM SET 4: HYPOTHESES ABOUT NON-CONFIGURATIONALITY
[Critical Thinking; Challenge]
Find data from some published source on the syntax of a non-configurational language (try searching for languages from Australia or the Americas), and evaluate our three theories of non-configurationality with respect to that data. Which of the theories works best for the data you found? Is there data that none of the theories can account for?

Conclusions
and Directions
for Further Study

We started this textbook with the question of what a person needs to know about their language in order to understand a simple sentence. We hypothesized that some of language is innate and other parts are parameterized. In the first thirteen chapters of this book, we sketched out some of the major research threads in one approach to syntax: the Principles and Parameters (P&P) view. In part 1, we looked at how rules generate hierarchical tree structures. These structures are geometric objects with mathematical properties. We looked at one set of phenomena (binding) that is sensitive to those properties. In part 2, we looked at a more sophisticated view of tree structures, developing our hypothesis into X-bar theory, and the thematic (lexical) constraints In part 3, we looked extensively at how problematic word orders, such as passives, raising, VSO languages, and *wh*-questions could all be accounted for using movement. In chapter 13, we brought these threads together and started looking at a unified approach to movement. Part 4 addressed three more advanced topics in syntax. We looked at split VP/vPs and the way they account for ditransitives and object shift; we looked at raising and control, and ellipsis constructions; and we revisited binding theory and came up with a more sophisticated version. Finally we looked at a range of language phenomena including polysynthesis, incorporation and non-configurationality that on the surface seem to contradict the theory we've proposed, but when probed more deeply actually support it.

In the web resources[1] for this book you'll find two more chapters on some popular alternatives to P&P/Minimalism: HPSG and LFG. I've provided these for you so that you can read papers and books written in those alternatives, as well as giving you a taste for other, related, ways we can approach topics in syntax.

Congratulations for getting through all this material. I hope this book (and the workbook, if you purchased it) has whetted your appetite for the

---

[1] http://www.wiley.com/go/carnie.

Syntax: A Generative Introduction, Third Edition. Andrew Carnie.
© 2013 Andrew Carnie. Published 2013 by John Wiley & Sons, Inc.

study of syntax and sentence structure, and that you will pursue further studies in syntactic theory. To this end, I've appended a list of books that can take you to the next level.

Older books on Government and Binding Theory (all of which are fairly consistent with chapters 1–12 of this book):

Cowper, Elizabeth (1992) *A Concise Introduction to Syntactic Theory: The Government and Binding Approach*. University of Chicago Press.

Haegeman, Liliane (1994) *Introduction to Government and Binding Theory*. Blackwell.

Ouhalla, Jamal (1999) *Introducing Transformational Grammar: From Principles and Parameters to Minimalism* (2nd ed.). Hodder Education.

More modern volumes (mostly Minimalist, in line with chapters 13–18):

Boeckx, Cedric (2008) *Understanding Minimalist Syntax: Lessons from Locality in Long-distance Dependencies*. Blackwell.

Carnie, Andrew (2011) *Modern Syntax: A Coursebook*. Cambridge University Press.

Cook, V. J. and Mark Newson (2007) *Chomsky's Universal Grammar: An Introduction* (3rd ed.). Blackwell.

Hornstein, Norbert, Jairo Nunes, and Kleanthes Grohmann (2005) *Understanding Minimalism*. Cambridge: Cambridge University Press.

Lasnik, Howard, Juan Uriagereka, and Cedric Boeckx (2005) *A Course in Minimalist Syntax*. Blackwell.

Radford, Andrew (1997a) *Syntactic Theory and the Structure of English: A Minimalist Approach*. Cambridge University Press.

Radford, Andrew (2004) *Minimalist Syntax: Exploring the Structure of English*. Cambridge University Press.

Roberts, Ian (1997) *Comparative Syntax*. Edward Arnold.

Tallerman, Maggie (2011) *Understanding Syntax*. 3rd edition. Hodder Education.

References

Aarts, B. (2008) *English Syntax and Argumentation*. Palgrave Macmillan.

Abney, S. (1987) *The English Noun Phrase in its Sentential Aspect*. Ph.D. dissertation, MIT.

Adger, D. (1996) Aspect, agreement and measure phrases in Scottish Gaelic. In R. Borsley and I. Roberts (eds.) *The Syntax of the Celtic Languages*. Cambridge University Press, pp. 200–22.

Adger, D. (2003) *Core Syntax*. Oxford University Press.

Adger, D., D. Harbour, and L. J. Watkins (2011) *Mirrors and Microparameters: Phrase Structure Beyond Free Word Order*. Cambridge University Press.

Agbayani, B. and E. Zoerner (2004) Gapping, pseudogapping and sideward movement. *Studia Linguistica* 58, 185–211.

Aikawa, T. (1994) Logophoric use of the Japanese reflexive *zibun-zisin* 'self-self'. In M. Koizumi and H. Ura (eds.) *Formal Approaches to Japanese Linguistics: Proceedings of FAJL1 (MIT Working Papers in Linguistics* 24), pp. 1–22.

Aissen, J. (1987) *Tzotzil Clause Structure*. Reidel.

Anderson, S. and P. Kiparsky (eds.) (1973) *A Festschrift for Morris Halle*. Holt, Rinehart and Winston.

Aoun, J. (1985) *A Grammar of Anaphora*. MIT Press.

Austin, P. and J. Bresnan (1996) Non-configurationality in Australian Aboriginal languages. *Natural Language and Linguistic Theory* 14, 251–68.

Baker, C. L. and J. McCarthy (eds.) (1981) *The Logical Problem of Language Acquisition*. MIT Press.

Baker, M. C. (1988) *Incorporation: A Theory of Grammatical Function Changing*. Chicago University Press.

Baker, M. C. (1996) *The Polysynthesis Parameter*. Oxford University Press.

Baker, M. C. (2000) The natures of nonconfigurationality. In M. Baltin and C. Collins (eds.) *The Handbook of Contemporary Syntactic Theory*. Blackwell, pp. 407–38.

Baker, M. C. (2001a) Configurationality and polysynthesis. In M. Haspelmath (ed.) *Language Typology and Language Universals: An International Handbook*. De Gruyter, vol. 2, pp. 1433–41.

Baker, M. C. (2001b) *The Atoms of Language: The Mind's Hidden Rules of Grammar*. Basic Books.

Baker, M. C. (2003) *Lexical Categories*. Cambridge University Press.

Baker, M. C. (2006) On zero agreement and polysynthesis. In P. Ackema, P. Brandt, M. Schoorlemmer, and F. Weerman (eds.) *Arguments and Agreement*. Oxford University Press, pp. 289–320.

Baker, M. C. (2009) Is head movement still needed for noun incorporation? *Lingua* 119, 148–65.

Baker, M. C., K. Johnson, and I. Roberts (1989) Passive arguments raised. *Linguistic Inquiry* 20, 219–51.

Baltin, M. (1981) Strict bounding. In C. L. Baker and John McCarthy (eds.) *The Logical Problem of Language Acquisition*. MIT Press, pp. 257–95.

Baltin, M. and A. Kroch (1989) *Alternative Conceptions of Phrase Structure*. University of Chicago Press.

Bard, E. G., D. Robertson, and A. Sorace (1996) Magnitude estimation of linguistic acceptability. *Language* 72, 32–68.

Barker, C. and G. Pullum (1990) A theory of command relations. *Linguistics and Philosophy* 13, 1–34.

Syntax: A Generative Introduction, Third Edition. Andrew Carnie.
© 2013 Andrew Carnie. Published 2013 by John Wiley & Sons, Inc.

Barsky, R. (1997) *Noam Chomsky: A Life of Dissent.* MIT Press.

Barss, A. and H. Lasnik (1986) A note on anaphora and double objects. *Linguistic Inquiry* 17, 347–54.

Bayer, J. (1984) COMP in Bavarian syntax. *The Linguistic Review* 3, 209–74.

Beck, S. and K. Johnson (2004) Double objects again. *Linguistic Inquiry* 35, 97–124.

Belletti, A. (1994) Verb positions: Evidence from Italian. In D. Lightfoot and N. Hornstein (eds.) *Verb Movement.* Cambridge University Press, pp. 19–40.

Bianchi, V. (2002) Headed relative clauses in generative syntax. *Glot International* 6.7, 197–204 and 6.8, 1–13.

Bickerton, D. (1984) The language bioprogram hypothesis. *Behavioral and Brain Sciences* 7, 173–88.

Bock, K. and C. A. Miller (1991) Broken agreement. *Cognitive Psychology* 23, 45–93.

Boeckx, C. (2008) *Understanding Minimalist Syntax: Lessons from Locality in Long-distance Dependencies.* Blackwell.

Boiko, K. (2000) *Līvõ Kēļ. Līvõd Īt.*

Borer, H (1999) Deconstructing the construct. In K. Johnson and I. Roberts (eds.) *Beyond Principles and Parameters.* Kluwer, pp. 43–89.

Borsley, R. (1996) *Modern Phrase Structure Grammar.* Oxford: Blackwell.

Bošković, Ž. (1997) Superiority and economy of derivation: Multiple *wh*-fronting. Paper presented at the 16th West Coast Conference on Formal Linguistics.

Brame, M. (1976) *Conjectures and Refutations in Syntax and Semantics.* Elsevier.

Bresnan, J. (1972) *Theory of Complementation in English.* Ph.D. dissertation, MIT.

Bruening, B. (2001) *Syntax at the Edge: Cross-Clausal Phenomena and the Syntax of Passamaquoddy.* Ph.D. dissertation, MIT.

Büring, D. (2005) *Binding Theory.* Cambridge University Press.

Burzio, L. (1986) *Italian Syntax.* Reidel.

Carnie, A. (1995) *Head Movement and Non-Verbal Predication.* Ph.D. dissertation, MIT.

Carnie, A. (2010) *Constituent Structure,* 2nd ed. Oxford University Press.

Carnie, A. (2011) *Modern Syntax: A Coursebook.* Cambridge University Press.

Carnie, A. and E. Guilfoyle (eds.) (2000) *The Syntax of Verb Initial Languages.* Oxford University Press.

Chametzky, R. (1996) *A Theory of Phrase Markers and the Extended Base.* SUNY Press.

Cheng, L. (1997) *On the Typology of Wh-Questions.* Garland.

Choe, H.-S. (1987) An SVO analysis of VSO languages and parameterization: A study of Berber. In M. Guerssel and K. L. Hale (eds.) *Studies in Berber Syntax (Lexicon Project Working Paper 14),* 121–58.

Chomsky, N. (1957) *Syntactic Structures.* Janua Linguarum 4. Mouton.

Chomsky, N. (1965) *Aspects of the Theory of Syntax.* MIT Press.

Chomsky, N. (1970) Remarks on nominalization. In R. Jacobs and P. Rosenbaum (eds.) *Readings in English Transformational Grammar.* Ginn, pp. 184–221.

Chomsky, N. (1973) Conditions on transformations. In S. Anderson and P. Kiparsky (eds.) *A Festschrift for Morris Halle.* Holt, Rinehart and Winston, pp. 232–86.

Chomsky, N. (1975) *The Logical Structure of Linguistic Theory.* Plenum.

Chomsky, N. (1977) On *wh*-movement. In P. Culicover, T. Wasow, and A. Akmajian (eds.) *Formal Syntax.* Academic Press, pp. 71–132.

Chomsky, N. (1980) On binding. *Linguistic Inquiry* 11, 1–46.

Chomsky, N. (1981) *Lectures on Government and Binding.* Foris.

Chomsky, N. (1986a) *Barriers.* MIT Press.

Chomsky, N. (1986b) *Knowledge of Language: Its Nature, Origin, and Use*. Praeger.

Chomsky, N. (1991) Some notes on economy of derivation and representation. In R. Friedin (ed.) *Principles and Parameters in Comparative Grammar*. MIT Press, pp. 417–54.

Chomsky, N. (1993) A minimalist program for linguistic theory. In K. L. Hale and S. J. Keyser (eds.) *The View from Building 20: Essays in Honor of Sylvain Bromberger*. MIT Press, pp. 1–52.

Chomsky, N. (1995) *The Minimalist Program*. MIT Press.

Chomsky, N. and H. Lasnik (1978) A remark on contraction. *Linguistic Inquiry* 9, 268–74.

Chung, S. (1976) An object-creating rule in Bahasa Indonesia. *Linguistic Inquiry* 7, 1–37.

Chung, S., W. Ladusaw, and J. McCloskey (1995) Sluicing and Logical Form. *Natural Language Semantics* 3, 239–82.

Cinque, G. (1981) *Types of A'-Dependencies*. MIT Press.

Cole, P. and S. N. Sridhar (1976) Clause union and relational grammar: Evidence from Hebrew and Kannada. *Studies in the Linguistic Sciences* 6, 216–27.

Collins, C. and H. Thráinsson (1996) VP-internal structure and object shift in Icelandic. *Linguistic Inquiry* 27, 391–444.

Cook, V. J. and M. Newson (2007) *Chomsky's Universal Grammar: An Introduction*. 3rd ed. Blackwell.

Cowper, E. (1992) *A Concise Introduction to Syntactic Theory: The Government and Binding Approach*. University of Chicago Press.

Culicover, P. (1997) *Principles and Parameters: An Introduction to Syntactic Theory*. Oxford University Press.

Culicover, P. and R. Jackendoff (2005) *Simpler Syntax*. Oxford University Press.

Culicover, P., T. Wasow, and A. Akmajian (eds.) (1977) *Formal Syntax*. Academic Press.

Dahl, Ö. (1974) How to open a sentence: Abstraction in natural language. *Logical Grammar Reports* 12, University of Göteberg.

Dedrick, J. and E. Casad (1999) *Sonora Yaqui Language Structures*. University of Arizona Press.

DeGraff, M. (2005) Morphology and word order in "creolization" and beyond. In G. Cinque and R. Kayne (eds.) *The Oxford Handbook of Comparative Syntax*. Oxford University Press, pp. 293–372.

Demirdache, H. (1991) *Resumptive Chains in Restrictive Relatives, Appositives and Dislocation Structures*. Ph.D. dissertation, MIT.

den Dikken, M. (1995) *Particles: On the Syntax of Verb-Particle, Triadic, and Causative Constructions*. Oxford University Press.

Déprez, V. (1992) Raising constructions in Haitian Creole. *Natural Language and Linguistic Theory* 10, 191–231.

Derbyshire, D. (1985) *Hixkaryana and Linguistic Typology*. Summer Institute of Linguistics.

Diesing, M. (1992) *Indefinites*. MIT Press.

Doron, E. and G. Khan (2011) PCC and ergative case: Evidence from Neo-Aramaic. Paper presented at the West Coast Conference on Formal Linguistics 29, April 2011, Tucson, Arizona.

É. Kiss, K. (2008) Free word order, (non)configurationality, and phases. *Linguistic Inquiry* 39, 441–75.

Emonds, J. (1980) Word order in generative grammar. *Journal of Linguistic Research* 1, 33–54.

Erteschik-Shir, N. (2007) *Information Structure: The Syntax–Discourse Interface*. Oxford University Press.

Escalante, F. (1990) *Voice and Argument Structure in Yaqui*. Ph.D. dissertation, University of Arizona.

Fiengo, R. and R. May (1994) *Indices and Identity*. MIT Press.

Friedin, R. (ed.) (1991) *Principles and Parameters in Comparative Grammar*. MIT Press.

Gair, J. (1970) *Colloquial Sinhalese Clause Structure*. Mouton.

Garrett, M. (1967) *Syntactic Structures and Judgments of Auditory Events*. Ph.D. dissertation, University of Illinois.

Goodall, G. (1993) On case and the passive morpheme. *Natural Language and Linguistic Theory* 11, 31–44.

Grimshaw, J. (1990) *Argument Structure*. MIT Press.

Gruber, J. (1965) *Studies in Lexical Relations*. Ph.D. dissertation, MIT.

Haegeman, L. (1994) *Introduction to Government and Binding Theory*. Blackwell.

Haegeman, L. and J. Guéron (1999) *English Grammar: A Generative Perspective*. Blackwell.

Hale, K. L. (1983) Warlpiri and the grammar of non-configurational languages. *Natural Language and Linguistic Theory* 1, 5–49

Halle, M. and A. Marantz (1993) Distributed morphology and the pieces of inflection. In K. L. Hale and S. J. Keyser (eds.) *The View from Building 20: Essays in Honor of Sylvain Bromberger*. MIT Press, pp. 111–76.

Hankamer, J. (1979). *Deletion in Coordinate Structures*. Garland.

Harley, H. (2002) Possession and the double object construction. In P. Pica (ed.) *Linguistic Variation Yearbook* 2. John Benjamins, pp. 29–68.

Harley, H. (2006) *English Words: A Linguistic Introduction*. Blackwell.

Haspelmath, M. (1993) *A Grammar of Lezgian*. Mouton de Gruyter.

Heim, I. and A. Kratzer (1998) *Semantics in Generative Grammar*. Blackwell.

Higginbotham, J. (1980) Pronouns and bound variables. *Linguistic Inquiry* 11, 697–708.

Higginbotham, J. (1985) A note on phrase-markers. In D. Archangeli, A. Barss, and R. Sproat (eds.) *Papers in Theoretical and Applied Linguistics* (*MIT Working Papers in Linguistics* 6), pp. 87–101.

Holzman, M. (1997) *The Language of Children*. 2nd ed. Blackwell.

Hornstein, N. (1994) An argument for minimalism: The case of antecedent-contained deletion. *Linguistic Inquiry* 25, 455–80.

Hornstein, N. (1999) Movement and control. *Linguistic Inquiry* 30, 69–96.

Hornstein, N., J. Nunes, and K. Grohmann (2005) *Understanding Minimalism*. Cambridge University Press.

Huang, C.-T. J. (1982) *Logical Relations in Chinese and the Theory of Grammar*. Ph.D. dissertation, MIT.

Huang, C.-T. J. (1989) PRO-drop in Chinese. In Osvaldo Jaeggli and Kenneth Safir (eds.) *The Null Subject Parameter*. Kluwer, pp. 185–214

Huddleston, R. and G. Pullum (2005) *A Student's Introduction to English Grammar*. Cambridge University Press.

Hyams, N. (1986) *Language Acquisition and the Theory of Parameters*. D. Reidel.

Iatridou, S. (1990) About Agr(P). *Linguistic Inquiry* 21, 551–7.

Jackendoff, R. (1971) Gapping and related rules. *Linguistic Inquiry* 2, 21–35.

Jackendoff, R. (1977) *X-bar Syntax: A Theory of Phrase Structure*. MIT Press.

Jackendoff, R. (1993) *Patterns in the Mind*. Harvester-Wheatsheaf.

Jaeggli, O. (1986) Passive. *Linguistic Inquiry* 17, 587–622.

Jaeggli, O. and K. Safir (eds.) (1989) *The Null Subject Parameter*. Kluwer.

Jelinek, E. (1984) Empty categories, case, and configurationality. *Natural Language and Linguistic Theory* 2, 39–76.

Jelinek, E. (2006) The Pronominal Argument parameter. In Peter Ackema, P. Brandt, M. Schoorlemmer, and F. Weerman (eds.) *Arguments and Agreement*. Oxford University Press, pp. 289–320.

Jelinek, E. and R. Demers (1994) Predicates and pronominal arguments in Straits Salish. *Language* 70, 697–736.

Jelinek, E. and F. Escalante (2003) Unergative and unaccusative verbs in Yaqui. In E. H. Casad and T. L. Willett (eds.) *Uto-Aztecan: Structural, Temporal and Geographic Perspectives: Papers in Honor of Wick R. Miller by the Friends of Uto-Aztecan*. Universidad Autonoma de Sonora, pp. 171–82.

Johnson, K. (1991) Object positions. *Natural Language and Linguistic Theory* 9, 577–636.

Johnson, K. (1994) Bridging the gap. Ms. University of Massachusetts, Amherst.

Johnson, K. (2001) What VP ellipsis can do, and what it can't, but not why. In M. Baltin and C. Collins (eds.) *The Handbook of Contemporary Syntactic Theory*. Blackwell, pp. 439–79.

Johnson, K. (2009) Gapping is not (VP) ellipsis. *Linguistic Inquiry* 40, 289–328.

Johnson, K. and I. Roberts (eds.) (1991) *Beyond Principles and Parameters*. Kluwer.

Karimi, S. (2003) *Word Order and Scrambling*. Blackwell.

Karimi, S. (2005) *A Minimalist Approach to Scrambling: Evidence from Persian*. Mouton de Gruyter.

Katamba, F. (2004) *English Words*. Routledge.

Kayne, R. (1994) *The Antisymmetry of Syntax*. MIT Press.

Kennedy, C. and J. Merchant (2000) Attributive comparative deletion. *Natural Language and Linguistic Theory* 18, 89–146.

Kester, E.-P. and P. Sleeman (2002) N-ellipsis in Spanish. In H. Broekhuis and P. Fikkert (eds.) *Linguistics in the Netherlands 2002*. John Benjamins, pp. 107–16.

Kim, J.-B. and P. Sells (2008) *English Syntax: An Introduction*. CSLI.

Kitagawa, Y. (1991) Copying identity. *Natural Language and Linguistic Theory* 9, 497–536.

Koizumi, M. (1993) Object agreement phrases and the split VP hypothesis. In J. D. Bobaljik and C. Phillips (eds.) *Papers on Case and Agreement I (MIT Working Papers in Linguistics* 18), 99–148.

Koopman, H. (1984) *The Syntax of Verbs: From Verb Movement Rules in the Kru Languages to Universal Grammar*. Foris.

Koopman, H. (1992) On the absence of case chains in Bambara. *Natural Language and Linguistic Theory* 10, 555–94.

Koopman, H. and D. Sportiche (1991) The position of subjects. *Lingua* 85, 211–58.

Kratzer, A. (1996) Severing the external argument from its verb. In J. Rooryck and L. Zaring (eds.) *Phrase Structure and the Lexicon*. Kluwer, pp. 109–37.

Kroeger, P. (1993) *Phrase Structure and Grammatical Relations in Tagalog*. CSLI.

Kroskrity, P. (1985) A holistic understanding of Arizona Tewa passives. *Language* 61, 306–28.

Kuno, S. (1973) *The Structure of the Japanese Language*. MIT Press.

Landau, I. (1999) *Elements of Control*. Ph.D. dissertation, MIT.

Lappin, S. (1996) The interpretation of ellipsis. In Shalom Lappin (ed.) *The Handbook of Contemporary Semantic Theory*. Blackwell, pp. 145–75.

Larson, R. (1988) On the double object construction. *Linguistic Inquiry* 19, 335–91.

Lasnik, H. (1989) *Essays on Anaphora*. Kluwer.

Lasnik, H. (1999a) *Minimalist Analyses*. Blackwell.

Lasnik, H. (1999b) On feature strength. *Linguistic Inquiry* 30, 197–219.

Lasnik, H. (2010) On ellipsis: Is material that is phonetically absent but semantically present, present or absent syntactically? In H. Götzsche (ed.) *Memory, Mind and Language*. Cambridge Scholars, pp. 221–42.

Lasnik, H. and M. Saito (1984) On the nature of proper government. *Linguistic Inquiry* 15, 235–89.

Lasnik, H., J. Uriagereka, and C. Boeckx (2005) *A Course in Minimalist Syntax*. Blackwell.

Legate, J. A. (2001) The configurational structure of a nonconfigurational language. In P. Pica (ed.) *Linguistic Variation Yearbook* 1. John Benjamins, pp. 61–104.

Legate, J. A. (2005) Two types of nominal split. Paper presented at the 36th Annual Meeting of the North East Linguistic Society (NELS 36), October 28–30, Amherst, MA.

Lehmann, W. (1978) The great underlying ground-plans. In W. Lehmann (ed.), *Syntactic Typology: Studies in the Phenomenology of Language*. University of Texas Press, pp. 3–56.

Levin, B. (1993) *English Verb Classes and Alternations: A Preliminary Investigation*. University of Chicago Press.

Levin, N. (1979/1986) *Main-verb Ellipsis in Spoken English*. Ph.D. dissertation, Ohio State University (published in 1986 by Garland).

Lightfoot, D. (1976) Trace theory and twice-moved NPs. *Linguistic Inquiry* 7, 559–82.

Lightfoot, D. (1991) *How to Set Parameters: Evidence from Language Change*. MIT Press.

Lightfoot, D. and N. Hornstein (eds.) (1994) *Verb Movement*. Cambridge University Press.

Lobeck, A. (1995) *Ellipsis: Functional Heads, Licensing, and Identification*. Oxford University Press.

Lobeck, A. (2000) *Discovering Grammar*. Oxford University Press.

Longobardi, G. (1994) Reference and proper names: A theory of N-movement in syntax and Logical Form. *Linguistic Inquiry* 25, 609–65.

López, L (2009) *A Derivational Syntax for Information Structure*. Oxford University Press.

Manning, C. and I. Sag (1998) Argument structure, valence and binding. *Nordic Journal of Linguistics* 21, 107–44.

Manzini, M. R. (1983) On control and control theory. *Linguistic Inquiry* 14, 421–46.

Manzini, M. R. (1992) *Locality: A Theory and Some of Its Empirical Consequences*. MIT Press.

Marantz, A. (1984). *On the Nature of Grammatical Relations*. MIT Press.

Marcus, G., S. Pinker, M. Ullman, M. Hollander, T. J. Rosen, and F. Xu (1992) *Overregularization in Language Acquisition*. Monographs of the Society for Research in Child Development 57. University of Chicago Press.

Marler, P. and M. Tamura (1962) Culturally transmitted patterns of vocal behavior in sparrows. *Science* 146.3650, 1483–6.

May, R. (1985) *Logical Form*. MIT Press.

McCloskey, J. (1979) *Transformational Syntax and Model Theoretic Semantics: A Case Study in Modern Irish*. Reidel.

McCloskey, J. (1980) Is there raising in Modern Irish? *Ériu* 31, 59–99.

McCloskey, J. (1983) A VP in a VSO language. In G. Gazdar, G. Pullum, and I. Sag (eds.) *Order Concord and Constituency*. Foris, pp. 9–55.

McCloskey, J. (1991) Clause structure, ellipsis and proper government in Irish. *Lingua* 85, 259–302.

Merchant, J. (2001) *The Syntax of Silence: Sluicing, Islands, and the Theory of Ellipsis*. Oxford University Press.

Mithun, M. (1984) The evolution of noun incorporation. *Language* 60, 847–94.

Moore, J. (1998) Turkish copy raising and A-chain locality. *Natural Language and Linguistic Theory* 16, 149–89.

Norris, M. (2011) Towards an analysis of Concord (in Icelandic). Paper presented at the West Coast Conference on Formal Linguistics 29, April 2011, Tucson, Arizona.

Ouhalla, J. (1999) *Introducing Transformational Grammar: From Principles and Parameters to Minimalism*. 2nd ed. Hodder Education.

Pensalfini, R. (2004) Towards a typology of configurationality. *Natural Language and Linguistic Theory* 22, 359–408.

Perlmutter, D. and P. Postal (1984) The 1-Advancement Exclusiveness Law. In D. Perlmutter and C. Rosen (eds.) *Studies in Relational Grammar*, vol. 2. University of Chicago Press, pp. 81–125.

Perlmutter, D. and C. Rosen (eds.) (1984) *Studies in Relational Grammar*, vol. 2. University of Chicago Press.

Pesetsky, D. (1994) *Zero Syntax: Experiencers and Cascades*. MIT Press.

Petter, Marga (1998) *Getting PRO under Control*. Holland Academic Graphics.

Pinker, Steven (1995) *The Language Instinct*. Harper Perennial.

Pollock, J.-Y. (1989) Verb-movement, Universal Grammar, and the structure of IP. *Linguistic Inquiry* 20, 365–424.

Postal, P. (1974) *On Raising*. MIT Press.

Pullum, G. (1997) The morpholexical nature of English *to*-contraction. *Language* 73, 79–102.

Pullum, G. and G. Scholz (2005) Contrasting applications of logic in natural language syntactic description. In P. Hájek, L. Vladés-Villanueva, and D. Westerståhl (eds.) *Logic, Methodology and Philosophy of Science*. King's College Publications, pp. 481–503.

Radford, A. (1988) *Transformational Grammar: A First Course*. Cambridge University Press.

Radford, A. (1997a) *Syntactic Theory and the Structure of English: A Minimalist Approach*. Cambridge University Press.

Radford, A. (1997b) *Syntax: A Minimalist Introduction*. Cambridge University Press.

Radford, A. (2004) *Minimalist Syntax: Exploring the Structure of English*. Cambridge University Press.

Reinhart, T. (1976) *The Syntactic Domain of Anaphora*. Ph.D. dissertation, MIT.

Reinhart, T. (1983) *Anaphora and Semantic Interpretation*. London: Croom Helm.

Richards, N. (1997) *What Moves Where When in Which Language?* Ph.D. dissertation, MIT.

Ritter, E. (1988) A head-movement approach to construct-state noun phrases. *Linguistics* 26, 909–29.

Rivero, M.-L. (1991) Long head movement and negation: Serbo-Croatian vs. Slovak and Czech. *Linguistic Review* 8, 319–51.

Rizzi, L. (1982) *Issues in Italian Syntax*. Foris.

Rizzi, L. (1990) *Relativized Minimality*. MIT Press.

Rizzi, L. (1997) The fine structure of the left periphery. In L. Haegeman (ed.) *Elements of Grammar*. Kluwer, pp. 281–337.

Roberts, I. (1997) *Comparative Syntax*. Edward Arnold.

Rosenbaum, P. (1967) *The Grammar of English Predicate Complement Constructions*. MIT Press.

Ross, J. R. (1967) *Constraints on Variables in Syntax*. Ph.D. dissertation, MIT.

Ross, J. R. (1969) Guess who? In R. Binnick, A. Davison, G. Green, and J. Morgan (eds.) *Papers from the Fifth Regional Meeting of the Chicago Linguistic Society, April 18–19, 1969*. Dept. of Linguistics, University of Chicago, pp. 252–86.

Ross, J. R. (1970) Gapping and the order of constituents. In M. Bierwisch and K. Heidolph (eds.) *Progress in Linguistics: A Collection of Papers*. Mouton, pp. 249–59.

Sadock, J. (1991) *Autolexical Syntax: A Theory of Parallel Grammatical Representations*. University of Chicago Press.

Sag, I. (1976) *Deletion and Logical Form*. Ph.D. dissertation, MIT.

Sag, I., T. Wasow, and E. Bender (2003) *Syntactic Theory: A Formal Introduction*. 2nd ed. CSLI.

Saito, M. and H. Lasnik (1994) *Move Alpha: Conditions on Its Application and Output*. MIT Press.

Sampson, G. (1997) *Educating Eve: The Language Instinct Debate*. Cassell.

Sapir, E. and M. Swadesh (1939) *Nootka Texts, Tales, and Ethnological Narratives, with Grammatical Notes and Lexical Materials*. Linguistic Society of America.

Saxon, L. (1984) Disjoint anaphora and the binding theory. In M. Cobler, S. MacKaye, and M. T. Wescoat (eds.) *Proceedings of the West Coast Conference on Formal Linguistics* 3. Stanford University Department of Linguistics, pp. 242–51.

Seiler, W. (1978) The modalis case in Iñupiat. In *Work Papers of the Summer Institute of Linguistics* 22. Summer Institute of Linguists, pp. 71–85.

Sells, P. (1985) *Lectures on Contemporary Syntactic Theories*. CSLI.

Sigurðsson, H. Á. (1991) Icelandic case-marked PRO and the licensing of lexical arguments. *Natural Language and Linguistic Theory* 9, 327–65.

Simpson, J. (1983) *Aspects of Warlpiri Morphology and Syntax*. Ph.D. dissertation, MIT.

Simpson, J. (1991) *Warlpiri Morpho-Syntax: A Lexicalist Approach*. Kluwer.

Skorik, P. (1961) *Grammatica čukotskogo jazyka*. Akamadija Nauk.

Soames, S. and D. M. Perlmutter (1979) *Syntactic Argumentation and the Structure of English*. University of California Press.

Sobin, N. (1985) Case and agreement in the Ukrainian morphological passive construction. *Linguistic Inquiry* 16, 649–62.

Speas, M. (1990) *Phrase Structure in Natural Language*. Kluwer.

Sportiche, D. (1988) A theory of floating quantifiers and its corollaries for constituent structure. *Linguistic Inquiry* 19, 425–49.

Sproat, S. (1985) Welsh syntax and VSO structure. *Natural Language and Linguistic Theory* 3, 173–216.

Stenson, N. (1989) Irish autonomous impersonals. *Natural Language and Linguistic Theory* 7, 379–406.

Stowell, T. (1981) *Origins of Phrase Structure*. Ph.D. dissertation, MIT.

Szabolcsi, A. (1994) The noun phrase. In F. Kiefer and K. É. Kiss (eds.) *The Syntactic Structure of Hungarian*. Syntax and Semantics 27. Academic Press, pp. 179–279.

Tallerman, M. (2011) *Understanding Syntax*. 3rd ed. Hodder Education.

Tancredi, C. (1992) *Deletion, Deaccenting, and Presupposition*. Ph.D. dissertation, MIT.

Tomlin, R. S. (1986) *Basic Word Order: Functional Principles*. Croom Helm.

Travis, L. d-M. (1984) *Parameters and Effects of Word Order Derivation*. Ph.D. dissertation, MIT.

Uriagereka, J. (1998) *Rhyme and Reason: An Introduction to Minimalist Syntax*. MIT Press.

van Gelderen, E. (2010) *An Introduction to the Grammar of English*. Rev. ed. John Benjamins.

Vikner, S. (1995) *Verb Movement and Expletive Subjects in the Germanic Languages*. Oxford University Press.

von Stechow, A. (1996) The different readings of *wieder* 'again': A structural account. *Journal of Semantics* 13, 87–138.

Webelhuth, G. (1995) *Government and Binding Theory and the Minimalist Program*. Blackwell.

Weerman, G. (1989) *The V2 Conspiracy*. Foris.

Williams, E. (1980) Predication. *Linguistic Inquiry* 11, 203–38.

Williams, E. (1983) Semantic vs. syntactic categories. *Linguistics and Philosophy* 6, 423–46.

Williams, E. (1994) *Thematic Structure in Syntax*. MIT Press.

Zaenen, A., J. Maling, and H. Thráinsson (1985) Case and grammatical functions: The Icelandic passive. *Natural Language and Linguistic Theory* 3, 441–83.

Index

Syntax: A Generative Introduction, Third Edition. Andrew Carnie.
© 2013 Andrew Carnie. Published 2013 by John Wiley & Sons, Inc.